JOHN

NCCS | New Covenant Commentary Series

The New Covenant Commentary Series (NCCS) is designed for ministers and students who require a commentary that interacts with the text and context of each New Testament book and pays specific attention to the impact of the text upon the faith and praxis of contemporary faith communities.

The NCCS has a number of distinguishing features. First, the contributors come from a diverse array of backgrounds in regards to their Christian denominations and countries of origin. Unlike many commentary series that tout themselves as international the NCCS can truly boast of a genuinely international cast of contributors with authors drawn from every continent of the world (except Antarctica) including countries such as the United States, Puerto Rico, Australia, the United Kingdom, Kenya, India, Singapore, and Korea. We intend the NCCS to engage in the task of biblical interpretation and theological reflection from the perspective of the global church. Second, the volumes in this series are not verse-by-verse commentaries, but they focus on larger units of text in order to explicate and interpret the story in the text as opposed to some often atomistic approaches. Third, a further aim of these volumes is to provide an occasion for authors to reflect on how the New Testament impacts the life, faith, ministry, and witness of the New Covenant Community today. This occurs periodically under the heading of "Fusing the Horizons and Forming the Community." Here authors provide windows into community formation (how the text shapes the mission and character of the believing community) and ministerial formation (how the text shapes the ministry of Christian leaders).

It is our hope that these volumes will represent serious engagements with the New Testament writings, done in the context of faith, in service of the church, and for the glorification of God.

Series Editors:
Michael F. Bird (Crossway College, Queensland, Australia)
Craig Keener (Asbury Theological Seminary, Wilmore, KY, USA)

Titles in this series:
Romans Craig Keener
Ephesians Lynn Cohick
Colossians and Philemon Michael F. Bird
Revelation Gordon Fee

Forthcoming titles:
James Pablo Jimenez
1–3 John Sam Ngewa
Pastoral Epistles Aída Besançon-Spencer
Mark Kim Huat Tan
Acts Youngmo Cho and Hyung Dae Park
Luke Diane Chen
2 Peter and Jude Andrew Mbuvi

Matthew Scot McKnight
1 Peter Eric Greaux
1–2 Thessalonians David Garland
Philippians Linda Belleville
Hebrews Tom Thatcher
Galatians Brian Vickers
1 Corinthians Bruce Winter
2 Corinthians David deSilva

JOHN
A New Covenant Commentary

Jey J. Kanagaraj

CASCADE *Books* • Eugene, Oregon

JOHN
A New Covenant Commentary

New Covenant Commentary Series 4

Copyright © 2013 Jey J. Kanagaraj. All rights reserved. No part of this publication may be reproduced or transmitted in any form, electronic or mechanical, or stored on any information storage and retrieval system without prior permission in writing from the publishers. For permissions write to Wipf and Stock Publishers, 199 W. 8th Avenue, Suite 3, Eugene, OR 97401.

Cascade Books
An Imprint of Wipf and Stock Publishers
199 W. 8th Ave., Suite 3
Eugene, OR 97401

www.wipfandstock.com

ISBN 13: 978-1-60608-906-4

Cataloging-in-Publication data:

Kanagaraj, Jey J.

John : a new covenant commentary / Jey J. Kanagaraj.

xxviii + 264 p. ; 23 cm. Includes bibliographical references and index(es).

New Covenant Commentary Series 4

ISBN 13: 978-1-60608-906-4

1. Bible. N.T. John—Commentaries. I. Title. II. Series.

BS2615.53 K33 2012

Manufactured in the U.S.A.

To
Prof. James D.G. Dunn, my doctor-father,
with profound gratitude and fondness

Contents

Outline of John / ix
Preface / xiii
Abbreviations / xv
Introduction / xix

John 1: The Origin of Jesus and of the New Community / 1
    Excursus: The Understanding of the Logos in the First Century / 9
    Fusing the Horizons / 10
John 2: The Beginning of Jesus' Public Ministry / 20
    Excursus: "Sign" in John / 27
John 3: Testimonies of Jesus and the Baptist / 29
John 4: The Inclusive Nature of Jesus' Community / 39
    Fusing the Horizons / 51
John 5: Self-Defense of Jesus before His Accusers / 53
John 6: Two Signs and a Discourse / 62
John 7: Is Jesus the Christ?: Conflict with "the Jews" / 78
John 8: Intensification of Jesus' Conflict with "the Jews" / 87
John 9: The Holistic Healing of a Man Born Blind / 99
John 10: The Impact of Jesus on His Community and on Others / 106
    Fusing the Horizons / 113
John 11: Lazarus' Resurrection and Its Implications / 114
John 12: The Final Journey of Jesus to Jerusalem / 123
    Fusing the Horizons / 132
John 13: Jesus' Last Supper with His Disciples / 134

Contents

John 14: Jesus' Pastoral Speech I / 144

John 15: Jesus' Pastoral Speech II / 152

John 16: Jesus' Pastoral Speech III / 158

John 17: Pastoral Prayer of Jesus / 165

    Fusing the Horizons / 170

John 18: Arrest and Trials Faced by Jesus / 172

John 19: The Supreme Revelation of God's Glory / 182

    Fusing the Horizons / 193

John 20: Visions of the Risen Jesus / 195

John 21: Epilogue / 205

Bibliography / 215

Author Index / 221

Subject Index / 224

Scripture Index / 230

Ancient Sources Index / 261

Outline of John

Prologue (1:1–18) / 1
    Pre-existence of Christ as the Word (1:1–5) / 1
    Witness of John the Baptist to the Logos (1:6–8, 15) / 3
    New humanity enlightened by the Light (1:9–13) / 4
    Dwelling of the Logos-in-flesh among humans (1:14, 16–18) / 5

Foundation of the Community of Faith (1:19–51) / 11
    Witness of John the Baptist (1:19–28) / 11
    Content of the Baptist's witness to Jesus (1:29–34) / 12
    Emergence of Jesus' new community (1:35–51) / 14

Jesus' Public Ministry (2:1–12:50) / 20
    First sign of Jesus in John (2:1–12) / 20
    Jesus' revolutionary act in the temple (2:13–22) / 23
    Supernatural knowledge of Jesus (2:23–25) / 26

    Jesus' testimony before Nicodemus (3:1–21) / 29
        Jesus' dialogue with Nicodemus (3:1–12) / 29
        Jesus' monologue (3:13–21) / 32
    The Baptist's testimony to Jesus (3:22–30) / 35
    Summary statements (3:31–36) / 37

    Proper setting for the dialogue (4:1–6) / 39
    Jesus' self-revelation to the Samaritan woman (4:7–26) / 40
    Jesus' injunction on his disciples' mission (4:27–38) / 45
    Inclusion of Samaritans into God's new community (4:39–42) / 48
    Entry of a Roman official's family into God's community (4:43–54) / 49

    Holistic healing given to a sick man (5:1–18) / 53
    The Son's authority to give life and to judge (5:19–30) / 56
    Four witnesses to Jesus who judges the "judges" (5:31–47) / 58

Outline of John

Feeding of the multitude (6:1–15) / 62
Jesus walking on the sea (6:16–21) / 65
Jesus' self-revelation as the life-giving bread (6:22–59) / 67
    Arrival of the people to Capernaum (6:22–25a) / 67
    Jesus' encounter with the crowd (6:25b–34) / 67
    Jesus' discourse on the living bread (6:35–59) / 69
        Jesus' heavenly origin (6:35–51) / 69
        The necessity to eat Jesus' flesh and drink his blood (6:52–59) / 73
Jesus' dialogue with his disciples (6:60–71) / 75

Jesus, his brothers, and "the Jews" (7:1–13) / 78
Veiled references to Jesus as the Christ (7:14–36) / 79
The authorities' rejection of Jesus' proclamation (7:37–52) / 82

Reversal of the Law's condemnation (7:53–8:11) / 87
Jesus, the Light of the world (8:12–20) / 89
Jesus' oneness with and submission to the Father (8:21–30) / 91
Jesus' verbal attack on the hostile Jews (8:31–47) / 93
Existence of Jesus before Abraham (8:48–59) / 96

Recovery of sight for a blind man (9:1–12) / 99
The Pharisees' investigation on the healing (9:13–34) / 100
Jesus' self-revelation as the Son of Man (9:35–41) / 104

Jesus, the self-giving shepherd (10:1–21) / 106
Jewish rejection of Jesus intensified (10:22–42) / 110
    Is Jesus the Christ? (10:22–31) / 110
    Is Jesus the Son of God? (10:32–39) / 111
    Others who believed in Jesus (10:40–42) / 112

Raising of Lazarus from the dead (11:1–44) / 114
    The death of Lazarus (11:1–16) / 114
    Martha's confession of Jesus as the Christ (11:17–27) / 116
    Jesus' mourning over Lazarus' death (11:28–37) / 117
    Exit of Lazarus from the tomb (11:38–44) / 119
Decision of the Jewish council to kill Jesus (11:45–57) / 121

Outline of John

Mary's anointing of Jesus (12:1–11) / 123
Revolutionary entry of Jesus into Jerusalem (12:12–19) / 125
Coming of the Greeks to Jesus (12:20–36) / 126
    Dying for oneself (12:20–26) / 126
    The lifting-up of the Son of Man (12:27–36) / 128
Unbelief and judgment (12:37–50) / 130

Jesus' Private Ministry (13:1—17:26) / 134
Washing of the disciples' feet (13:1–20) / 134
Two predictions sandwiched by Jesus' new commandment (13:21–38) / 139
    Judas' betrayal predicted (13:21–30) / 139
    The new commandment (13:31–35) / 141
    Peter's denial foretold (13:36–38) / 142

The Son's revelation of the Father (14:1–14) / 144
Jesus' promise to send the *paraklētos* (14:15–31) / 147

The true vine and the branches (15:1–17) / 152
The world's hatred and Jesus' remedy (15:18–27) / 155

Intensification of the world's hatred (16:1–4) / 158
The Functions of the Spirit (16:5–15) / 159
Joy and peace after tribulation (16:16–33) / 161

Jesus' prayer for his glorification (17:1–5) / 165
Jesus' prayer for his disciples (17:6–19) / 166
Jesus' prayer for his expanding community (17:20–26) / 169

Jesus' Passion and Resurrection (18:1—20:31) / 172
The betrayal of Jesus (18:1–11) / 172
The Jewish trial and Peter's denial (18:12–27) / 174
The Roman trial, part 1 (18:28–40) / 178

The Roman trial, part 2 (19:1–16) / 182
Jesus' reign from the cross (19:17–30) / 185
The aftermath of Jesus' death (19:31–42) / 189
    Jesus, the Passover Lamb (19:31–37) / 189
    Jesus' burial (19:38–42) / 191

Outline of John

        The resurrection of Jesus (20:1–10) / 195
        Mary Magdalene, an apostle to the apostles (20:11–18) / 196
        Jesus' appearances to the male disciples (20:19–29) / 198
            Appearance and empowerment (20:19–23) / 198
            Jesus' encounter with Thomas (20:24–29) / 201
        John's purpose as conclusion (20:30–31) / 203

Epilogue (21:1–25) / 205
        The third revelation of the risen Jesus (21:1–14) / 205
        Final reference to Peter and the beloved disciple (21:15–23) / 209
            Prediction on Peter's ministry and destiny (21:15–19) / 209
            Prediction on the beloved disciple (21:20–23) / 211
        Concluding statements (21:24–25) / 212

Preface

Volumes have been written on various themes, including ecclesiology, in John's Gospel. However, some advanced works on the formation, empowerment, and development of the church, God's new community or the new covenant community, in John are called for in view of the growing threat and persecution to churches today. This would be possible if we study the Gospel with an analytical approach by way of exegesis. This is what I have attempted to do in this commentary, written for the New Covenant Commentary Series. I have argued that the church, God's new community that consists of those who believe in Jesus as the Christ, was founded and expanded by Jesus globally through the working of the Holy Spirit. I have also detected that the progressing new community has its root at the cross of Christ and is empowered by the Holy Spirit to continue Jesus' mission in the world. I develop these ideas by emphasizing the believers' covenant relationship with God in Jesus and by allowing the text to speak for itself through a community to the present community, both social and ecclesiastical. The terms such as "God's new community," "Jesus' community," "the new covenant community," "the believing community," "community of faith," and "the church" point to the same group.

I have given my own translation in English, wherever necessary, based on the 28th edition of Nestle-Aland's Greek text. "The Jews" (in quotation marks) denotes the Jewish leaders or those who reject Jesus because of their unbelief. Otherwise it denotes the Judeans or the Jews in general, whether in dispersion or in Palestine. In this study, though brief, the readers, I believe, will not miss the kernel of John's Gospel in its "new covenant community" perspective. The given outline of the Gospel is based on the proposals of Brown (2010), Lincoln (2006), and Michaels (2010).

I am indeed thankful to Profs. Craig Keener and Michael Bird for entrusting me with the responsibility of writing a commentary on John for the New Covenant Commentary Series and for their useful comments and suggestions to improve all the chapters for better reading. My sincere thanks are due to my doctoral mentor, Prof. James D. G. Dunn, to whom this volume is warmly dedicated, for having given me access to some of his

Preface

fresh writings on John's Gospel. I am indebted to Wycliffe Hall, Oxford, whose acceptance and unreserved support for four months enabled me to complete a few chapters in the preliminary stage. I express my gratitude to Langham Partnership in the UK and Ireland for their kindness to sponsor me as a visiting scholar at Wycliffe Hall. My sincere thanks are due to Cascade Books, an imprint of Wipf and Stock Publishers, for publishing this work as one in the New Covenant Commentary Series.

Jey J. Kanagaraj
Aruppukottai, TN, India
December 2012

Abbreviations

Periodicals, Reference Works, and Serials

AB	Anchor Bible
ABCS	Asia Bible Commentary Series
BDAG	W. Bauer, F. W. Danker, W. F. Arndt, and F. W. Gingrich, *A Greek-English Lexicon of the New Testament and Other Early Christian Literature*, 3rd ed. (Chicago: University of Chicago Press, 2000)
BECNT	Baker Exegetical Commentary on the New Testament
BJRL	*Bulletin of John Rylands Library*
BNTC	Black's New Testament Commentaries
BST	The Bible Speaks Today
BT	*Bible Translator*
ECC	Eerdmans Critical Commentary
ESV	English Standard Version
ExpTim	*Expository Times*
ICC	International Critical Commentary
IVPNTCS	Inter-Varsity Press New Testament Commentary Series
JBL	*Journal of Biblical Literature*
JSNT	*Journal for the Study of the New Testament*
JSNTSS	Journal for the Study of the new Testament Supplement Series
LCL	Loeb Classical Library
LNTS	Library of New Testament Studies
NCB	New Century Bible
NCBC	New Cambridge Bible Commentary
NICNT	New International Commentary on the New Testament
NIV	New International Version

Abbreviations

NJB	The New Jerusalem Bible
NovTSup	Supplements to Novum Testamentum
NRSV	New Revised Standard Version
NT	New Testament
NTS	*New Testament Studies*
OM	Operation Mobilization
OT	Old Testament
RSV	Revised Standard Version
Str-B	Strack, H. L., and P. Billerbeck, *Kommentar zum Neuen Testament aus Talmud und Midrash*, 6 vols. (Munich, 1922–61)
TDNT	*Theological Dictionary of the New Testament*
TNIV	Today's New International Version
TNTC	Tyndale New Testament Commentaries
TynBul	*Tyndale Bulletin*
WBC	Word Biblical Commentary
WUNT	Wissenschaftliche Untersuchungen zum Neuen Testament
ZNW	*Zeitschrift für die neutestamentliche Wissenschaft und die Kunde der* älteren *Kirche*

General

ET	English Translation
LXX	Septuagint
MT	Masoretic Text
par.	parallel

Ancient Sources

Adv. Haer.	*Adversus Haereses (Against Heresies)*
Corp. herm.	*Corpus hermeticum*
Hist. eccl. / Eccl. Hist.	Eusebius, *Historia ecclesiastica*

Apocrypha

Bar	Baruch
1 Esd	1 Esdras
1/2 Macc	1/2 Maccabees
Sir	Sirach
Wis	Wisdom of Solomon

Abbreviations

Dead Sea Scrolls

CD-A	Cairo Genizah copy of the *Damascus Document*^{a}
1QM	*War Scroll*
1QH	*Thanksgiving Hymns*
1QS	*Rule of the Community*
1QSa	*Messianic Rule*
4QFlor	*Florilegium*
4QTest	*Testimonia*

Josephus

Ant.	*Jewish Antiquities*
J.W.	*Jewish War*

Philo of Alexandria

Agr.	*De agricultura* (On Angriculture)
Cher.	*De cherubim* (On the Cherubim)
Det.	*Quod deterius potiori insidari soleat* (The Worse Attacks the Better)
Her.	*Quis rerum divinarum heres* (Who Is the Heir?)
Leg.	*Legum allegoriae* (Allegorical Interpretation)
Opif.	*De opificio mundi* (On the Creation of the World)
Post.	*De posteritate Caini* (On the Posterity of Cain)
QG	*Quaestiones et solutiones in Genesin* (Questions and Answers on Genesis)
QE	*Quaestiones et solutiones in Exodum* (Questions and Answers on Exodus)
Sac.	*De sacrificiis Abelis et Caini* (On the Sacrifices of Abel and Cain)
Somn.	*De somniis* (On Dreams)
Spec.	*De specialibus legibus* (On the Special Laws)
Mos.	*De vita Mosis* (On the Life of Moses)

Pseudepigrapha

Ascen. Isa.	*Ascension of Isaiah*
1 En.	*1 Enoch* (Ethiopic Apocalypse)
Jub.	*Jubilees*

Abbreviations

3/4 Macc	3/4 Maccabees
Pss. Sol.	Psalms of Solomon
T. Abr	Testament of Abraham
T. Dan	Testament of Dan
T. Gad	Testament of Gad
T. Jud.	Testament of Judah
T. Naph.	Testament of Naphtali

Rabbinic Literature

b.	Babylonian Talmud
B. Bat.	Baba Batra
ʿErub	ʿErubin
Mek.	Mekilta
m.	Mishnah
Bek.	Bekorot
Ber.	Berakot
Ketub.	Ketubbot
Mid.	Middot
Ned.	Nedarim
Nid.	Niddah
Pesaḥ	Pesaḥim
Rab.	Rabbah
Roš Haš.	Roš Haššanah
Sanh.	Sanhedrin
Šabb.	Šabbat
t.	Tosefta
Tg. Exod.	Targum on Exodus
Tg. Isa.	Targum on Isaiah
Tg. Onq. Gen.	Targum Onqelos on Genesis
Gen Rab.	Genesis Rabbah
Exod Rab.	Exodus Rabbah

Introduction

There have been many commentaries on the Gospel of John since 125 CE, when the Valentinian gnostic leader Heracleon first wrote one. Commentators, particularly after the Reformation, have usually taken an exegetical and sociohistorical approach. Some scholars have used rhetorical criticism, a social-scientific approach, narrative criticism, and/or a sociorhetorical perspective based on literary/rhetorical and cultural perspectives for interpreting John.[1]

Any writing of the first century needs to be set in its historical, religious, and social contexts for a proper understanding of its complexity. Previous studies have located John's Gospel in a context of purported conflict between Jewish Christians and the unbelieving Jews in the late first century.[2] By observing the literary and rhetorical texture of John's Gospel, Keener attempts to reconstruct the social contexts in which John was written.[3] The events recorded in the Gospel and the writings of the late first century and early second century help us to reconstruct the historical situation in which John's Gospel was probably written.

In this commentary I attempt to set the Fourth Gospel in its historical setting and then to show that the vision of Jesus for the world, according to John, goes beyond his sacrificial death, resurrection, and appearance to the constitution and function of a new humanity, called "God's new community," that is bound to God by the new covenant made in Jesus.[4]

WHO WROTE JOHN'S GOSPEL AND WHERE?

John's Gospel declares that it was written by "the disciple whom Jesus loved," who "has seen" the crucified Jesus and has borne witness (19:35),

---

1. E.g., Culpepper 1989; Stibbe 1993; Malina and Rohrbaugh 1998; and Neyrey 2007.
2. Cf. Brown 1978: 1.lxxii–lxxv; *idem* 1979: 166–67; Martyn 2003: 37–62; Dunn 1983: 318–25.
3. Keener 2005: 1.xxv, 140–70.
4. Pryor calls this community "the covenant community" (Pryor 1992: 157–80).

Introduction

not merely by verbal proclamation, but also by putting the Jesus tradition in writing. What this disciple spoke and wrote is categorically attested by a community as "true" (21:24).

The epithet "The Gospel According to John" appears in the papyri manuscripts P^{66} (second century CE) and P^{72} (ca. third century CE). Who is this John? Is he "the disciple whom Jesus loved," who is traditionally identified as John the Son of Zebedee? Was he one of the Twelve or a disciple outside the Twelve? Was he a historical figure or a symbolic figure created by the writer? Why does he appear only in the later part of the Gospel (13:23; 19:26–27; 20:2–5, 8; 21:7, 20–24)? Some accept "the disciple whom Jesus loved" as both a historical and symbolic figure from Judea and as one of Jesus' disciples, but not as one of the Twelve.[5] There is little doubt about the Beloved Disciple as an eyewitness who wrote the Gospel. But scholars are not sure of the identity of this disciple.

The fact that this unnamed disciple was lying close to the breast of Jesus during the Passover meal (13:23) gives us the clue that he must have been one of the twelve disciples of Jesus. Otherwise, John's use of the phrase "having loved *his own*" in the context of Jesus' supper with them (13:1–2); the presence of Judas Iscariot (13:2, 27), Simon Peter (13:6, 24, 36, 37), Thomas (14:5), Philip (14:8–9), and Judas (not Iscariot; 14:22); Jesus' exemplary act before those who called him "Teacher and Lord" (13:13–15); the whole "farewell discourse" after the Supper (13:31–16:33); and Jesus' subsequent prayer for the men whom God had given to him (17:1–26) would all be inexplicable. The Synoptic tradition shows that the Twelve alone were eating the Passover with Jesus (Matt 26:20; Mark 14:17–18; cf. Luke 22:11, 14). The intimate relationship between the Beloved Disciple and Peter and their complementary roles in the community, as drawn from John (e.g., 13:23; 20:1–10), show that the Beloved Disciple is likely John the Son of Zebedee (cf. Acts 1:13; 3:1, 3, 4, 11; 4:13, 19; 8:14; see also comment on 13:23). The arguments against the view that the Beloved Disciple is John the Son of Zebedee[6] depend mainly on the fact that John's name is plainly mentioned in the Synoptic Gospels but not in John's Gospel. This observation ignores the fact that John uses the Synoptic tradition freely in combination with his own tradition.[7]

---

5. Quast 1989: 16–25; Culpepper 2000: 84; Bauckham 2006: 127–29, 402–16.

6. See Culpepper 2000: 75–76.

7. Both Brown (1979: 33–34) and Schnackenburg (1982: 3.385) changed their view that the beloved disciple was John, the Son of Zebedee, by arguing that the disciple whom

Introduction

The statement "This is the disciple who . . . has written these things" (21:24) does not necessarily imply that he wrote the Gospel as we have it today. The assumption that John the Son of Zebedee, a Galilean Jew, wrote the whole of John ignores the numerous Judean elements that the Gospel contains, including the correct geographical references to the events that took place in Judea.[8] True, John, being a leader in Jerusalem church, would have known well the places and practices in Judea. However, the numerous parallels between John and the Qumran documents, the underlying rabbinic and targumic traditions, John's christological apologetic rooted in the OT, and the reinterpreted Jewish mysticism, etc. presented in John far exceed the possible intellectual knowledge of a Galilean fisherman.

Hengel contends that the author of the Fourth Gospel, John the Elder, being a Jew from Jerusalem, migrated at the verge of the fall of Jerusalem in 66–70 CE to Asia Minor, most probably to Ephesus, where he started a school, normally known as the Johannine School.[9] However, we have evidence for the migration of John the Son of Zebedee to Ephesus. The apocryphal *Acts of John* (ca. 150–60 CE) shows that John was widely involved in evangelistic and pastoral ministry in Asia, including Ephesus.[10] Irenaeus (ca. 130–200 CE) had heard Polycarp (ca. 70 CE–160 CE), who received information about the works and words of the Lord from the eyewitnesses, including John (*Eccl. Hist.* 5.20.4). Irenaeus writes that John the disciple of the Lord ministered in the church in Ephesus, founded by Paul, until the time of Trajan (98–117 CE; *Eccl. Hist.* 3.23.3–4; cf. 5.8.4).

Dionysius of Alexandria (the third century CE) indicates that there are in Ephesus tombs of two Johns (see *Eccl. Hist.* 3.23.6; 7.25.16; cf. 3.31.3; 3.39.6; 5.24.3 for Polycrates' confirmation that the resting place of John was in Ephesus). The *Apostolic Constitutions* (third century CE) mentions that the apostle John installed another John in Ephesus as his successor. Papias refers to two Johns in his writing (125–35 CE), in the context of his enquiry with those who had contacts with some of the disciples of Jesus about "what John and Matthew said" and about "the things which Aristion and John the elder, the disciples of the Lord, say" (*Eccl. Hist.* 3.39.4).

Jesus loved is an anonymous, but historical, figure who was not one of the twelve, but who was probably a man from Jerusalem. However, their arguments for later position are not as convincing as their original arguments for the beloved disciple as the son of Zebedee.

8. Cf. Brown 2010: 200–202.
9. Hengel 1989: 80–83, 109–10.
10. Barrett 1978: 103.

Introduction

The above-mentioned writings enable us to infer that there were two Johns: John the Son of Zebedee, who was the apostle John, and John the Elder. Both of them were Jesus' disciples who were ministering in Ephesus, though John the Elder was not one of the Twelve. Hengel, who finds a close parallel between the order in which Papias gives the names of disciples (*Eccl. Hist.* 3.39.4) and that in John's Gospel, identifies Aristion and John the Elder with the "two others of his disciples" of John 21:2.[11]

John the Son of Zebedee, who may be the "disciple whom Jesus loved," must have moved with a group of his followers, among whom was also the presbyter John, from Palestine to Asia Minor around 66–70 CE and perhaps joined the church in Ephesus founded by Paul.[12] This community eventually accepted the authority and leadership of the Beloved Disciple and hence is known as the "Johannine community." John the Elder (cf. 2 John 1; 3 John 1), who was ordained by the apostle John to be his successor in Ephesus, could have been a Jew, possibly from a priestly family in Jerusalem.[13] He might have founded a learning center in Ephesus on behalf of the Johannine community for studying, learning, teaching, and writing.[14]

By reconstructing the available information, we may say that John the Elder composed the Fourth Gospel in Ephesus by using the sources written and orally communicated by John the Son of Zebedee, an eyewitness of the life and ministry of Jesus, when the apostle had died (ca. 98–117 or 98–101 CE).[15] The experience of John the Elder, who himself was a disciple of Jesus, and the sharing he had in the community of Jesus' life and ministry, would have been an added source to compose the Gospel with his own theology.

We may also see the hand of an editor in the final stage of the writing the Gospel in the glosses, comments, and explanations, including the translations of Hebrew/Aramaic words into Greek. The addition of chapter 21 after a proper conclusion in 20:30–31, with a final conclusion in 21:24–25, confirms the additional work of an editor. While the phrase "I suppose" (21:25) implies the editor as an individual, the phrase "we know" (21:24)

---

11. Hengel 1989: 17–21; Culpepper 2000: 111–12.

12. Cf. Anderson 2011: 135.

13. Hengel 1989: 7, 125, 144 n. 29; Barrett 1978: 101–2. However, Polycrates, the bishop of Ephesus (189–98 CE), identifies John, who leaned back on the Lord's breast, as a priest (*Eccl. Hist.* 3.31.3; 5.24.3). This indicates the confusions prevailing in the "John tradition."

14. Hengel (1989: 22, 159 n. 122) gives evidence of several fragments that show a direct connection existed between Papias and the presbyter John.

15. Köstenberger 2009: 7–8.

Introduction

refers to a community on whose behalf the editor gave final shape to the Gospel.

The authorship of John's Gospel, then, needs to be placed in at least three stages of development: in the Johannine community at Ephesus[16] with the real author (John the Elder of Judea, who actually wrote the Gospel), the implied/ideal author (the Beloved Disciple, who could probably be John the Son of Zebedee) whose writings were used, and finally an editor from Johannine community who added explanatory notes and the epilogue.[17]

WHEN WAS JOHN'S GOSPEL COMPOSED AND PUBLISHED?

Some have argued that John's Gospel must have been written in the mid second century. In fact, the first commentary, at least partly, was written by a gnostic in 125 CE, and by 173 CE it came to be well established and highly regarded by, for example, Tatian, as found in his fourfold Gospel harmony, the *Diatessaron*.[18] The presence of a part of the passion narrative of John in the second-century CE papyri manuscripts (P^{52}, P^{90}, P^{66})[19] speaks in favor of the Gospel as in circulation in the early or mid second century CE. However, the Gospel must have existed some time before it came to be written in papyrus scrolls after being circulated in Asia Minor and then in Palestine and other Christian centers before it came to be known in Egypt. So Barrett argues that a date around 110 CE may be placed as the extreme limit for the *composition* of the Gospel, while 140 CE may be considered as the extreme limit for its *publication*.[20] P^{52}, dated about 130 CE, makes us hesitant to conclude that John was written after 110 CE.[21]

Dodd detected the earliest tradition (the Synoptic tradition) in John's Gospel,[22] while Robinson argued for the procedural priority of John's Gospel.[23] The Fourth Gospel contains precise topography, precise chronology,

16. Alexandria, Antioch, and Transjordan are proposed as other possible places for the composition of John's Gospel; cf. Brown 2010: 202–6.
17. For the three-person theory see Culpepper 1989: 3–49.
18. Perrin 2010: 301–18, esp. 315.
19. See von Wahlde 2010: 1.7 n. 6.
20. Barrett 1978: 110, 128.
21. So Hengel 1989: 81. More recently Czachesz (Czachesz 2010: 69 n. 75) has rejected that P^{52} necessitates a first-century date for John by uncritically following Nongbri's.
22. Dodd 1965.
23. Robinson (1985: 3–5) argues for a "procedural" priority of John rather than for a temporal priority; for him John's Gospel is the nearest to the source because it is believed

Introduction

selectivity of narratives, discourses, and dialogues, narrative asides, and the firsthand testimony of the eyewitnesses—all being distinctive features of Greco-Roman historiography.[24] Dunn detects in John the Jesus tradition (or the "earlier oral tradition") remembered and retold in a different way from the Jesus tradition used by the Synoptic writers.[25] These studies point to a date in reasonable proximity to the eyewitnesses and the Jesus tradition from which the composition of John derives.

The references to Christians being excommunicated from the synagogue (9:22; 12:42; 16:2) bring us close to 85 CE, when the chart of "Eighteen Benedictions" was prepared to curse Christians as heretics in the synagogue services. It is justifiable, then, to suggest that John was written ca. 85–90 CE[26] and published ca. 100 CE.

What Is the Historical Setting in Which John's Gospel Emerged?

(i) If our contention for John as the late-first-century document is correct, then the persecution and threat of death faced by Christians from "the Jews" at that time is the milieu in which John might have been written (9:22; 12:42; 16:2). The Jewish authorities could not accept Jesus as the Christ because Jesus, for them, made himself equal to God (5:18; 10:33, 36) but was eventually crucified as a criminal. This religio-historical situation explains why John emphasizes the present availability of the life of the age to come for those who believe in the crucified Jesus as the Christ.

(ii) After the fall of Jerusalem with its temple in 70 CE, the rabbis attempted intensively to revive Judaism. Rabbis like Yohanan ben Zakkai (1–84 CE) and other religious Jews meditated on the Law with the aim of bringing the presence of God down to earth in the absence of the temple. Belief in angels as mediators between the transcendent God and human beings became common. At this point, interest on "Merkabah mysticism," an experience of ascending to heaven in a trance by means of meditation on the Scripture (e.g., Ezekiel 1, Isaiah

---

to have come from the inner circle of the Twelve; cf. Robinson 1976: 307–8 n. 218.

24. Bauckham 2007: 17–36.
25. Dunn 2011: 157–85.
26. Keener 2005: 1.140–42 suggests a date around 90 CE as a working hypothesis.

Introduction

6, and Daniel 7) to see God's glory as seated on the throne in human form, was developing. John addresses this trend by emphasizing that God's kingly glory is to be seen in Jesus here on earth itself (1:14, 18, 50b–51; 3:13; 12:41; 14:9–11).

(iii) "The Jews" perceived the Christians' worship of Jesus as a threat to Jewish monotheistic faith because of the Christian claim of divine revelation in Jesus Christ. Christians were accused of believing in two divine powers in heaven. In this context, one should understand the monotheistic faith of Christians reflected in John's Gospel (e.g., 5:18; 8:28, 29; 10:15, 30; 12:44–45; 14:8–11).

(iv) The Johannine community at this time faced several problems:

   a. At the end of the first century, the apostolic eyewitnesses, particularly the Beloved Disciple, had died. This situation possibly could have led the Johannine community into confusion, insecurity, and a sharp leadership crisis. John 10:1–18 and 13:1–20 seem to address the problem of leadership.

   b. Because of the delay in Jesus' second coming, the community was losing hope, for some were expecting the return of Jesus within the lifetime of the Beloved Disciple himself (cf. 21:23). This situation may explain why John focuses more on the present experience of eternal life and on the indwelling of Jesus and the Father within the believers (e.g., 5:24; 6:40; 20:31; 15:4; 17:21–23) without diminishing the hope of future possession of eternal life.

   c. The heretical groups, which questioned either the divinity of Jesus or his humanity, were influencing Christians, particularly the members of Johannine community. A group in Ephesus seems to have claimed John the Baptist as the Light from heaven and as the Messiah himself (cf. Acts 19:1–7).

   Some believed that Jesus was the son of Joseph while Christ was a celestial aeon who descended on Jesus at the time of his baptism and left him before he was crucified. They did not accept the *divinity* of Jesus. This belief resembles that of Cerinthus, who possibly lived in the late first century (cf. Irenaeus, *Adv. Haer.* 3.3.4; 3.11.1).

Introduction

The Docetists, on the other hand, claimed that Jesus Christ did not truly come in the flesh, and that his flesh was only an appearance. For them Christ only seemed to be a man. Thus the Docetists refused to accept the *humanity* of Jesus.

In the late first century there seems to have been followers of Gnosticism in its embryonic stage. Gnosticism claimed that people became ignorant by the influence of evil forces and that God sent his messenger to cast away their ignorance and give them salvation in terms of the knowledge (*gnōsis*) that they belong to the other world. Their dualistic thought led the Gnostics to reject Christ who came in flesh, presuming that a holy God cannot take up human flesh, which is evil. John argues against such teachings, saying that eternal life is possible in "knowing" the only true God who was manifested in Jesus (17:3).

d. The influence of these heresies began to threaten the love and unity that existed in the Johannine church and led the members into perplexity about the person Jesus and his teachings, particularly his teaching on end-time events. While John's Gospel foresees a threat to the unity in the church (cf. 17:21–23), 1 John indicates that the split has already taken place (cf. 1 John 2:19).

(v) In the late first century there was an intermingling of religious and philosophical ideas; cults and philosophies influenced one another. It does not seem that John was "influenced" by Hellenistic and Gnostic ideas as such, but he uses language and ideas familiar in the religious and philosophical environment.[27] John thus seems to have been written in a pluralistic context quite similar to our own time.

WHY WAS THE GOSPEL OF JOHN WRITTEN?

We may now pose the question as to why John was written when the other three canonical Gospels were already in circulation.

Some suggest that John was written to supplement the Synoptic Gospels in content, chronology, and interpretation and to produce what Clement of Alexandria (ca. 150–215 CE) called "a spiritual Gospel," as it was believed that the other three Gospels contain only the earthly aspects of

---

27. Kanagaraj 2002: 47–60.

Introduction

Jesus' story.[28] If so, then it is difficult to explain some of the outward differences found between the Synoptic Gospels and the Fourth Gospel.

Another view is that John's primary purpose was to replace the Synoptic Gospels by producing a Gospel *par excellence* that would render the others superfluous and would eventually drive them out of circulation. This idea appears dimly in the Muratorian Canon (ca. 200 CE).[29] However, John widely uses the Gospel tradition, some of which appears in the Synoptic Gospels, in his writing and there is no clue that he wished to supersede the already existing Gospels. If he had planned so, then his omission of such key passages as the birth of Jesus, the Sermon on the Mount/Plain, the Synoptic parables, etc. becomes inexplicable.

Another theory supports the polemical purpose of John. Irenaeus argued that John's Gospel was written to refute the rising heresies of the Nicolaitans and Cerinthians.[30] One can feel the polemical purpose of John when he emphasizes that the pre-existent Word became "flesh," without using the word "man" or "body" (1:14; cf. 6:51–56), and that John the Baptist was neither the Light (1:8) nor the Christ (1:20), but was only a "lamp" (5:35) who came to bear witness to the Light. John's teaching on Jesus' oneness with the Father (5:18; 10:30; 12:44–45; 14:9–11; 17:21–23; 20:28) and equally on his subordination to the Father (5:19–23; 8:16, 28–29; 12:49; 14:28) can better be understood as a polemic against the prevailing heresies about the person Jesus. It seems, however, that John goes beyond this polemic purpose.

John himself categorically states his purpose: "But these things have been written so that you may believe that Jesus is the Christ, the Son of God, and that as you believe, you may have life in his name" (20:31). The primary purpose of John, then, is to proclaim the gospel that in Jesus one can experience divine life and to persuade his readers to believe in Jesus as the Christ.

However, the question is: Was the Gospel written to unbelievers or to those who believed in Jesus? The word "to believe" has two different readings, which have equal support in Greek manuscripts (see comment on 20:31). If *pisteuēte* ("to continue believing") is read, then John could have written the Gospel with a didactic purpose to teach young believers to be steadfast in faith in the wake of increasing heretical teachings and persecution. Actually the polemic and the didactic purposes go together, for the

---

28. *Eccl. Hist.* 6.14.5–7.
29. Santram 1975: 108, 111–12.
30. Cf. Brown 2010: 153–80.

Introduction

believers could withstand the heresies without proper teaching. If *pisteusēte* ("to start believing") is read, then the primary purpose of John would be to proclaim the gospel of Jesus Christ to those who have not yet come to faith, whether they be Jews or proselytes or Gentiles or Samaritans. He persuades them to believe Jesus as the Christ, the Son of God, so that they might receive divine life through him.

John's concern for evangelizing all people becomes very obvious, for example, in his use of the term "world" (*kosmos*)—seventy-eight times in the Gospel, whereas it is used only fourteen times in the Synoptics. In the prologue and in 3:16–21 the author of the Gospel shows great concern for the salvation of the "world" (cf. 1:5, 9–11; 3:19–21). The universal outlook is reflected in the Gospel by oft-repeated words such as "as many as," "everyone," "all people," etc.[31] However, proclamation would be impossible unless God's new community becomes active by being equipped and guided by the Holy Spirit to share its faith (15:26–27; 17:20–21, 23).[32] The purpose of John, then, was mainly twofold: (i) to proclaim Jesus as the Christ, the Son of God, to the world; and (ii) to confirm the faith of the believers who will witness to Jesus in the world.

In course of reading this commentary, readers will understand how a new community was formed around Jesus in a covenantal relationship with God and how it drew into itself a diverse range of people, including those who live in our own day (cf. 17:20). One may perceive that the community envisioned by Jesus is rooted in and shaped by the cross. The new life given by the risen Jesus will lead them eventually to continue his mission in the world in the power of the Holy Spirit (20:21–23). The community motif found in John has led many scholars to read the Gospel as "embodying the history of Johannine community."[33] However, the inclusive nature of the Gospel leads us to look into John's community as a universal and inclusive movement.

---

31. Bauckham (1998: 9–48) argues that the Gospels were written for a wider circulation rather than to a particular audience; cf. Evans 2008: 112.

32. Cf. Brown 2010: 180–83.

33. Bauckham 2007: 21; cf. Pryor 1992: 157–80; Brown 1979.

JOHN 1
The Origin of Jesus and of the New Community

Prologue (1:1–18)

The Gospel of John commences with the prologue (1:1–18), which, by virtue of major themes it covers, is called the "window" through which the whole Gospel may be read.[1] The structure of the prologue betrays a Jewish poem or hymn rather than "rhythmical prose" with at least six strophes (1:1–3, 3–5, 10–11, 12–13, 14–16, 17–18), with the author's insertion of verses 6–8 and 15.[2] The prologue serves as a "poetic preamble" to John's Gospel, composed by the author himself, perhaps by using the hymn on Wisdom.

Pre-Existence of Christ as the Word (1:1–5)

John's opening statement, "In the beginning was the Word," takes us not only to the existence of the Word (*logos* in Greek) before creation, but also sets God's redemptive work in the context of the eternal existence of the Logos. The phrase "in the beginning," unlike that in Genesis 1:1, speaks of the time before the genesis (cf. Prov 8:23). The word *Logos* here is a title used in an absolute sense.

By referring to the Logos, John uses a term that was familiar to all sections of the society in the first century CE (see the excursus below). The Logos was in existence *as a personal being* and the sphere of his existence was God himself, as the assertion "the Logos was with God" (1:1b) shows. The phrase "with God" does not have the sense of "motion towards God" but the sense of "being from God" (6:46) or "living in communion with God." That is, the Logos was living so close to God that he was sharing in

---

1. Dunn 1989: xxviii.
2. Hengel 2008: 268–89.

Prologue

the very life of God. The Logos and God, as two personalities, were living so close with one another that they cannot be separated one from the other. Such union means an active partnership or a reciprocal indwelling between two personalities.³

The Word's mutual indwelling and life in oneness with God are eternal, as the statement "the Word was God" (1:1c) shows. Like Philo, John also identifies the pre-existent Logos with God without the definite article, for in 1:1c the Logos, as God, is differentiated from "the God." Otherwise, 1:1c will contradict what is expressed in 1:1b–2 and 14:28. Therefore it is needless to translate "divine (in essence) was the Logos."⁴ While "the God" points to "the one true God," the Father, "God," in this context, can only indicate the Logos as the manifestation of that God. "The God" refers to God in his transcendence, while "God" implies the revelation and immanence of that one God. This does not mean that the Logos was the "second God." The Logos is the self-manifestation of God precisely because he exists eternally in oneness with God, the Father. This is reiterated in 1:2.

John describes also the role of the pre-existent Logos in creation: "all things" came into being through him and "not even one that has come into being" came without him (1:3). That is, the totality of creation came into existence through the Logos. This does not mean that the Logos was merely an "instrumental cause" (Philo) in creation. The creative activity of the Logos was the creative activity of God. The Logos and Wisdom are parallels, for Wisdom too pre-existed with God and was engaged in God's creative activity (Prov 3:19–20; 8:22–31; Sir 1:1–10). All things in heaven and on earth were created through Christ and for Christ (1 Cor 8:6b; Col 1:16–17; Heb 1:2; Rev 3:14).

God's creation was community oriented (Gen 1–2), for God created "all things" as families according to their kinds (Gen 1:21, 24–25). John, therefore, begins his Gospel by disclosing the community motif embedded in creation. The whole creation constitutes one household of God. All creatures came to life by God's word, but human beings by God's breath (Gen 2:7; 1:26–27). Since life flows from God to the total creation, John categorically states, "In him was life" (1:4a). The Genesis story connects light with life. So also John presents divine life and light together by writing, "And the life was the Light of humankind" (1:4b). The life of Logos derived from

---

3. Schnackenburg 1980–84: 1.234.
4. Contra Haenchen 1984: 1.108, 110. The Greek word *theos* never means "divine."

the Father and the Light projected from it are essentially the same and they were one in existence eternally.

While narrating creation, John's special attention falls on "humankind" (1:4), God's main focus in creation. The community he envisaged is a community of human beings, while other creatures were subject to them (Gen 1:28–30; Rom 8:19–22). As Light, the life in the Logos is the guiding principle for human life (cf. Ps 27:1; Ps 36:9; Hos 10:12 LXX; Wis 7:26, 27; Sir 17:11). For John the essence of the Logos is life, which gives light to human beings enabling them to experience end-time salvation both now and in future. This idea anticipates the later reference to Jesus as the Light and life (8:12).

The nature of light is to constantly shine and stand against "darkness" (1:5). Light and darkness in John are symbols of good and bad qualities of life, respectively, and they engage in combat against each other. Where there is light there is no darkness and vice versa. Such dualism is reflected in Qumran writings written in the second and first centuries BCE (e.g., 1QS 3.19–22; 1QM 13.5–6, 14–15). These writings use "day" figuratively with "light," and "night" with "darkness" (1QS 10.1–2), and so also John. The nature of the Light in 1:5 is in the present tense, "shines," but that of darkness is in the past tense, "did not overcome." This means that the Light keeps on shining. It exposes evil, guides human beings, illuminates and transforms human life, and judges human works (3:19–21). The nature of darkness, however, is to strive to overcome the Light, but the Light won over darkness once and for all.

Witness of John the Baptist to the Logos (1:6–8, 15)

Following the pre-existence of the Logos-Light, John traces the beginning of salvation history in John the Baptist, who was sent by God to bear witness to the Light (1:6–8; cf. Mark 1:1–5; Acts 1:22; 10:37; 13:23–25).

The Greek verb *egeneto* introduces the Baptist in the statement, "There was a man," and the same word is used to introduce the Word who "became" flesh (1:14a). This sets both Jesus and John the Baptist in the same mission of bringing God's salvation to humankind. The task of John the Baptist, however, is limited only to bearing witness to Jesus so that people may believe in Jesus as the Light. The task of bearing witness to the Logos-Light is repeated in 1:8 with an emphatic denial that John the Baptist himself was the Light. The Baptist was only a lamp whose witness was temporary (5:35).

Prologue

This is to rebut communities that regarded the Baptist toward the end of the first century as the Redeemer sent by God (cf. Luke 3:15) or even as the Light.

The Baptist's testimony prepares the way for the Logos to come in flesh to reveal God's character and to offer eternal life for those who believe. The Baptist confirms that Christ was pre-existent and that he is greater than the Baptist in status and rank (1:15). In fact, 1:15 does not interrupt the flow of thought between 1:14 and 1:16–18. Whereas 1:14 narrates the witness of the believing community to the glory revealed in the Logos-Son, 1:15 expresses the witness of the Baptist to the same glory, which was pre-existing as the Logos, even though temporally the Logos became flesh after the Baptist was born (cf. 1:26–27, 29–30; Matt 3:11 par.).

New humanity Enlightened by the Light (1:9–13)

The third section of the prologue introduces the Logos as "the true Light." That is, he is the "genuine" or "authentic" Light, surpassing any other lights, which are "obsolete, defective, and unreliable."[5] He was coming into the world, the realm of human affairs, to enlighten every human being (1:9). "Enlightenment" means not just the attainment of intellectual knowledge but the insight one may get about God and his purpose for human beings. It is an illumination that transforms people from their evil nature to do good works. The universal implication of this mission is known from the word "every human."

Even though the Light in the Logos came into the world, the world failed to know him (1:10). "Knowing" is a key word used in the Gospel to mean not so much the Hellenistic and Gnostic notion of intellectual perception as an active relationship between God and his people (see Amos 3:2 for God knowing his people in terms of choosing them and caring for them, and Jer 31:33–34 for the humans to know God in terms of their humble obedience and trust in him). The word "world" in John refers mainly to those who reject Jesus and his followers because of their hostility towards them (e.g., 15:18–19; 17:14). God's provision to humankind to become children of God and the world's rejection are prefigured in the prologue (1:9–10).

The Logos-Light was rejected, notably, by his own people. In John, the term "my own" denotes the people chosen by Jesus (or those given by God

---

5. Neyrey 2007: 43.

to Jesus) to be his followers (17:6, 10). The parallel phrase "his own people" (1:11b) confirms that those who did not receive the Light were Jesus' own people, the Jews. It is noteworthy that only those who keep the covenant made by God are his "treasured possession" (Exod 19:5). However, the Jews who received God's covenant belonged to the old and fallen humanity, and therefore they could not perceive the Logos-Light as the Messiah. John, in contrast, will declare in his Gospel that it is the people of God, under the new covenant, who will be "his own possession" (cf. 1:12).

In spite of the world's rejection, God offered opportunity to the Jews and Gentiles to receive the Logos and to become his children. "Receiving" is the receptive aspect of believing. The object of faith is "his name." In the OT, God manifests his character and work by revealing, or sometimes by concealing, his name, YHWH or "I am that I am" (e.g., Gen 32:27–30; Exod 3:13–14; 6:2–3; Isa 42:8). The Johannine Jesus bears this name so that he may manifest it to those who believe in him (17:6, 26). By revealing God's name, Jesus reveals God himself. This powerful name of God enables those who receive him and believe in his name to be born in the family of God as his children, that is, to become members of new covenant community (1:12).

John discloses the source of new birth both in negative terms (i.e., neither of blood nor of the will of flesh nor of the will of man) and in positive term (i.e., of God). The new covenant community comes into being by the Spirit, the life-giving power of God, and not by any human effort (John 1:13; 3:3–8; cf. Deut 32:18; Ps 2:7).[6]

Dwelling of the Logos-in-flesh among humans (1:14, 16–18)

This section constitutes the fifth strophe of the hymn (1:1–18) and is the climax of what John wants to say in the prologue. His statement "the Word became flesh" (1:14a) would have kept many in astonishment in the late first century, since no philosophical or religious thought understood the concept of Logos in this way. The birth narratives of Matthew and Luke are summed up by John in one sentence: "And the Word became flesh."

The conjunction "and" stresses the transition of the Logos from his pre-existent state to human history. Whereas 1:1 shows the transcendence

---

6. While the reference to the blood and flesh indicates mortal humanity (Matt 16:17; 1 Cor 15:50), the expression "the will of man" reflects the Jewish belief that a woman begets a child by a man's initiative.

of the Word, 1:14 describes how he became immanent—the supernatural natural, and the invisible visible.[7] It would have been easier for understanding the incarnation if John had simply written, "The Word was born as a man" (cf. Phil 2:7b). Why should John use two catching words, "became" and "flesh"?

Some in the early church might have believed that by becoming a man Christ put off his divine glory in heaven (cf. Phil 2:7a). As observed above, there were heretics in the late first century who questioned either Christ's divinity or his humanity. The word "became" (*egeneto*) implies that by taking human form the pre-existent Word did not cease to be God, just as Jesus continued to be Jesus of Nazareth even after he *became* a prophet (Luke 24:19; cf. 3 John 8).[8] It does not support a "naïve Docetism"[9] that minimizes the reality of Jesus' humanity. In the earthly life of Jesus, his oneness with the Father continued. Otherwise it would be impossible to see the Father's glory on earth.

The word "flesh" goes beyond mere humanness and points to the frailty and vulnerability of human beings (Isa 40:6; John 6:63).[10] This means that Jesus, by assuming human flesh, experienced the weakness and helplessness of human beings, enabling him to be compassionate toward helpless sinners (cf. Rom 8:3; 2 Cor 8:9; Heb 2:17–18). John's word "flesh" thus displays not merely a polemic purpose, but it also gives the good news that the one God, who is inaccessible (1 Tim 6:16), came to live with the fallen humanity.

This thought is carried forward by the statement "and he dwelt among us" (literally "and he tabernacled in the midst of us"). The Logos becoming flesh and his dwelling among human beings go together, as the conjunction "and" shows. The Greek word *eskēnōsen* ("he tabernacled/dwelt") echoes the dwelling of God among his people in the tabernacle (Exod 25:8–9; 29:45–46; Zech 2:10–11). Besides the wilderness motif, one can also see a Wisdom motif[11]: The Creator chose the people of Israel as the tent where Wisdom can dwell and minister before him (Sir 24:8, 10). What was applied to Wisdom is now applicable to the Logos, though with a conceptual difference. The eschatological motif in 1:14b becomes obvious in its allusion

---

7. Kanagaraj 2005: 53.
8. Kanagaraj 1998b: 80–81.
9. Käsemann 1968: 4–26.
10. Milne 1993: 46.
11. Keener 2005: 1.408–9.

to the Lord's dwelling in the midst of the people of Israel on the day when many nations will join themselves to be his people (Zech 2:10–11; cf. Rev 7:15; 21:3).[12] In this eschatological framework, the phrase "among us" does not indicate only the people of Israel, but broadly all human beings. Thus, in the coming of the Logos in human flesh, the end-time has dawned.

However, the personal pronoun "we" in "we beheld his glory" (1:14c) points exclusively to those who, by faith, could see and experience God's glory in the Logos incarnate. It need not be confined only to eyewitnesses or to the Johannine community. For unbelievers, however, the glory of God revealed in flesh remains hidden.[13] "Seeing God's glory" can be connected with the tabernacle and the temple, where one can see God's presence or his glory (Exod 24:15–17; 25:8; 40:35; 1 Kgs 8:10, 11, 13). The temple is also the place where God put his name to dwell (1 Kgs 8:29; 9:3; 2 Chr 6:20). For John the name of God that dwelt in the tabernacle/temple and God's glory that was seen by the Israelites are the same, and now they are revealed in Jesus, the incarnate Logos (cf. 17:11–12 with 17:22, 26).

Moses saw God's glory in terms of his steadfast love and faithfulness (Exod 33:18–19; 34:6–7), which are equivalent to the twin words "grace and truth" (1:14). Jesus was bearing God's glory even in Jesus' pre-existent state (17:5, 24). It marks the oneness between them, on one hand, and the oneness between the believers, on the other (17:22). In this context, "glory" can mean the eternal relationship of love that exists between the Father and the Son (17:24b).[14] In the light of Lazarus' resurrection (11:4, 40), God's glory may also indicate God's saving power[15] or God's love expressed in his generosity to restore life.[16] The glory seen in the Son was God's splendor, manifested in his love and faithfulness to his covenant to give divine life. The idea of seeing God's glory in flesh could be a polemic against the then-prevalent interest in mystical visions to see God in heaven in his kingly glory and in human form.[17]

The sharing of glory by the Father and the Son, a mark of oneness between them, is confirmed by the Greek word *monogenēs* ("only Son"), used four times in John (1:14, 18; 3:16, 18; cf. Wis 7:22 LXX). The word

12. Cf. Keener 2005: 1.409.
13. Cf. Bultmann 1971: 63–64.
14. Barrett 1978: 514.
15. Bratcher 1991: 23.
16. Pamment 1983: 14–15.
17. Kanagaraj 1998a: 214–47.

means "only one of its kind," but when used in relation to the Father it means the "only Son."[18] After introducing the Logos as God and narrating that the glory revealed is that of the only Son from the Father, John would not have hesitated to call the "only Son" as the "only God" (cf. 1:18 in some manuscripts). In sharing with God oneness in life, glory, name, status, and function, there is no one who is equal to the status of Jesus as God's Son and therefore Jesus is the only Son of God. From 1:14 onwards the pre-existent Logos is spoken in John in terms of the "Son of God."

God's steadfast love and faithfulness to his covenant, which constitute his glory, are termed as "his fullness" in 1:16.[19] All those who believe through the witness of the Johannine community received "grace upon grace." Literally, the phrase "grace upon grace" can be translated as "grace in the place of grace." It does not mean that in place of the Mosaic Law the grace through Jesus was given, for John never opposes the Law in his Gospel. The Law that marks the old covenant was also a gift of God given to his people out of his grace. This means that the OT manifestation of God's gracious love and favor has become accessible to all who believe in Christ, replacing the impossible observance of the OT Law by a personal and unique manifestation through his Son.[20] Thus, "grace upon grace" implies God's *continuous* supply of the same grace, expressed through the Law, from one degree to another by the gracious indwelling of Jesus.[21] All human efforts to keep the Law in order to experience God are thereby made redundant.

The steadfast love and faithfulness of God, given in the OT Law in a shadowy way, have attained reality in the coming of the Logos-in-flesh, "Jesus Christ" (1:17). The phrase "given through Moses" implies the role of mediator played by Moses in giving the Law (cf. Gal 3:19b). The major aspect of God's covenant with his people is God's giving of the Law (Deut 5:1–21), which is the "Book of the Covenant" that was sealed by the offering of the "blood of the covenant" (Exod 24:7–8). The reference to the Law given through Moses (1:17), then, has an implicit reference to the covenant community. However, John looks beyond this old covenant community to a new covenant community that will be established in Jesus Christ, through whom came to humankind God's "grace and truth." These dual words allude

---

18. Dodd 1958: 305 n. 1; Barrett 1978: 166.

19. "Fullness" (*plērōma*) means "the totality of divine powers and attributes" revealed in Jesus; see Lightfoot 1997: 48, 78.

20. Cf. Edwards 1988: 8–9.

21. Lindars 1957: 27; Kanagaraj 2005: 61.

to God's mercy and initiative to forgive the sins of his people, who disobeyed his covenant, and to God's faithfulness to put the Law within their hearts as the mark of making a new covenant (Exod 34:6–7; Jer 31:31–34; Ezek 36:22–32). By being in the "bosom of the Father," Jesus alone knows God in the most intimate way and therefore he alone can reveal God to the world in his mercy and faithfulness (John 1:18; cf. 10:14–15; 14:10–11).

The whole Gospel, according to the prologue, evolves around one theme: *the revelation of the one God in his glory and his encounter with all human beings in the life and mission of Jesus, the pre-existent God-become-flesh, to found and nurture a witnessing new covenant community.*

Excursus: The Understanding of the Logos in the First Century CE

The first-century Jews treated the Logos as Wisdom and the Law in their pre-existence with the Creator (Prov 8:22–31; Sir 1:1–10; 24:3; Prov 3:19–20; Wis 9:1–2; Bar 3:9–4:4; *1 En.* 42; Sir 15:1; 19:20; 39:1; 24:23; 34:8; 39:1; 4 Macc 1:16–17) and as the creative word used by God in creation (Gen 1; cf. Ps 33:6, 9). For them the Logos accomplishes God's mission (Isa 9:8–9; 55:11) and brings healing and deliverance (Ps 107:20), a means by which God's will and message were communicated (Jer 1:4; Ezek 1:3; 6:1; Amos 3:1, 8). They understood the Logos as the Aramaic *memra*, a periphrasis for God and his powerful acts (e.g., *Tg. Exod.* 19:17; 31:13; *Tg. Onq. Gen.* 3:8; *Tg. Isa.* 48:13).

The Greeks understood the Logos as reason or the rational principle that is behind the world to keep it in order and within every human being. For the Stoics, the Logos controls the stars and seasons and pervades all things. Although one can be united with God through the Logos (*Corp. herm.* 13.6–7), reason can be built up in a person only after the immortal soul gets rid of bodily senses by escaping from the prison of the body. This is called "rebirth" (*Corp. herm.* 13.7–8).

The Hellenistic Jewish understanding of the Logos is known from Philo's writings. For Philo the Logos is a real being distinct from God and an intermediary between God and the world (*Her.* 2–5). Logos is the divine reason (*Cher.* 36), the second God (*QG* 2.62), God himself (without the definite article; *Somn.* 1.229–30). To perceive the Logos is to perceive the invisible God, for the Logos is that by which God draws the perfect man from earthly things to himself (*Sac.* 8). The unknowable God is knowable as Light through the

Excursus: The Understanding of the Logos in the First Century CE

Logos (*QE* 68; cf. *Mos.* 2.95–100). As the Logos belongs to the intelligible world (*Opif.* 4, 16; *Mos.* 2.127), it never descends to the sensible world, but one should move to the intelligible world to encounter the Logos.[22] For Philo, mystical union with God in terms of indwelling within the soul's life is possible through the Logos (*Post.* 122, by interpreting Num 14:9).

Although people would have understood the Logos in different ways, the underlying common theme is that the Logos is God and in the Logos one can apprehend God. However, John's insight that the Logos became flesh is missing. No wonder first-century Christians meant by the Logos the "Christian message" (e.g., Mark 2:2; 4:14; Acts 14:25), the content of which is Christ and his glory (2 Cor 4:5–6) or "Christ crucified" (1 Cor 1:23; 2:2; Gal 3:1), in whom one can see God.

Fusing the Horizons

Several years ago, one of my friends confronted me saying that Christianity came into being by the birth of Jesus about two thousand years ago, whereas other major religions had been in existence even before that time. This is an example of how the world thinks of Christ and the time of his existence. The proclamation of Jesus' story as beginning from his pre-existence with the eternal God as God would make it clear that Christ lived even before the time of creation and that God's plan to create a new community in Jesus Christ was in him before anything was created. This message will lead hearers, particularly those from other religious faith, to perceive Jesus as the unique revelation of God.

There is a deep aspiration among many religious groups today to see the one true God. People try to see God by spending a huge amount of money or even by subduing and wounding one's body. The Fourth Gospel proclaims that the one true God revealed his character in Jesus, who is the place in which one can see God now. God's new community is called to bear witness to this by words and deeds.

---

22. Sandmel 1979: 95; Kanagaraj 1998a: 72.

Foundation of the Community of Faith (1:19-51)

Witness of John the Baptist (1:19-28)

The narrative of Jesus' life and ministry begins with the witness of John the Baptist to Jesus (cf. Matt 3:1-12; Mark 1:1-8; Luke 1:1-17). The commencing word "and" in 1:19 marks the continuity between the prologue and the whole Gospel story, by having the testimony of the Baptist as the starting point for the formation of new covenant community around Jesus. There was an apprehension among the religious leaders in Jerusalem about the Baptist's ministry, which drew many to become his disciples. Therefore they sent a delegation of priests and Levites to John the Baptist to gather firsthand information about his real identity and the purpose of his mission. The delegates met the Baptist at "Bethany beyond Jordan," where John was baptizing (1:28).[23]

The term "the Jews" in 1:19, in conjunction with 1:24, indicates "the Pharisees," the "separated ones."[24] These religious leaders had separated themselves politically from Hasmonean rule and religiously from others who were not observing the priestly laws of purity (Lev 1-15). They had vast political and social influence in Jesus' time,[25] but rejected Jesus as the Messiah. Therefore they are identified in John with "the world," which, in general, rejected Jesus (John 1:10; 7:7; 15:18; cf. 8:23). In response to their question, "Who are you?," the Baptist answers, "I am not the Christ" (1:19-20). Probably the leaders suspected that the Baptist could be the long-awaited Messiah, the King and deliverer from the house of David. However, they did not dare to ask him whether he was the Messiah. The Baptist's unreserved denial (cf. 3:28) could be a polemic against those who claimed that he was the Messiah.

In Jesus' time, the scribes taught that Elijah should come first in order to prepare the way for Christ's appearance (Mal 3:1; 4:5-6; Mark 9:11-12). That is why the priests and Levites asked the Baptist, "Are you Elijah?" (John 1:21). After the Baptist's denial that he was Elijah, they asked him,

---

23. Possibly the "Bethany beyond Jordan" was on the eastern side of Jordan up in the northern end of Peraea, closer to Aenon (near Salim), a place of springs in the western bank of Jordan.

24. For various shades of meaning of the term "the Jews" in John see Griffith 2008: 185; Brown 2010: 157-75. The term also refers to the Jews who genuinely believed in Jesus after seeing Jesus' sign (11:45).

25. Cf. Dunn 2003: 265-70.

Foundation of the Community of Faith

"Are you the prophet?," perhaps having in mind Deut 18:15 and 18, which speak of a prophet like Moses whom God will raise up. It is unlikely that the delegates had in mind the prophet mentioned in Qumran writings (4QTest 5–8; 1QS 9.11), as the Qumran community separated itself by revolting against Jerusalem priests and their cultic practices. There is no evidence that, besides Elijah and a Moses-like prophet, the Jews were expecting any other figure as the eschatological prophet. Nor do we have evidence that John's community identified Christ with a prophet-like figure.[26] After stating that he was not the prophet either, the Baptist explains his mission as preparing the way for the coming of the Lord ("Christ"). He was nothing but a voice that cried out in the wilderness in order to purify and prepare a group of people for God by declaring the coming of Christ, as the Scripture testifies (Isa 40:3; cf. Matt 3:3 par.).

The enquiry of the agents gives an opportunity for the Baptist to project Jesus' greatness as the Christ who is present among them but hidden to their eyes (1:26–27).[27] Without comparing his baptism with that of Jesus (Matt 3:11 par.), the Baptist discloses the spiritual blindness of the religious leaders, who, by this time, should have rightly understood such scriptural passages as Isa 40:3 and Mal 3:1; 4:5–6. Although Jesus came to the human scene chronologically after the Baptist (cf. 1:15), the latter acknowledges Jesus' greatness by stating, "the thong of whose sandal I am not worthy to untie." In a teacher-disciple relationship in rabbinic circles, a menial job such as untying the thong of a teacher's sandals was not assigned to any of his pupils and still less to a slave.[28] The Baptist acknowledges his unworthiness even to be a slave to Jesus, who is the Christ, the Son of God (1:34), for Jesus' mission of bringing salvation to humankind by his death and resurrection surpasses any human enterprise.

Content of the Baptist's witness (1:29–34)

In 1:29–34, the Baptist unveils who Jesus is and implicitly what he will accomplish. For the first time the name "Jesus" appears in 1:29 after 1:17. The day after the enquiry of Jerusalem leaders, John gives a picture of the real

---

26. John 6:14; 7:40; 9:17 do not prove that the Johannine community had developed a prophet Christology.

27. This reflects the current belief that the Messiah is concealed in the presence of God's power from the beginning (*1 En.* 62:7; *4 Ezra* 13:2–4, 52; Dan 7:13–14).

28. Barclay 1957: 1.62.

Christ, Jesus, who was coming toward the Baptist (1:29). There is no reference in this section either to the audience to whom Jesus was introduced or to his baptism. Perhaps John intended the audience to be anyone who reads it. The Baptist bears witness to Jesus as "the Lamb of God, who removes the sin of the world."

The book of Revelation (5:6, 8, 12, 13; 6:16; 7:9–10, 14, 17; 22:1, 3) refers to "the Lamb." However, there Greek word used for "lamb" (*arnion*) is different from what is used in John (*amnos*), though there is not much essential difference.[29] There are three OT references to the "Lamb of God" (Gen 22:8; Exod 12:3–6; Isa 53:7). In Isaac's sacrifice (Gen 22) there is no reference to the removal of sin, although it prefigures Jesus' death and resurrection (cf. John 3:16; Heb 11:17–19).

Exodus 12 may give a possible background to John 1:29, since Jesus was identified in Christian circles as the Lamb of God in whose death people receive deliverance just like the people of Israel were delivered from Egyptian bondage by the offering of the paschal lamb (cf. 19:36 with Exod 12:46 and Num 9:12; 1 Cor 5:7). However, Isa 53:4–7 gives a relevant background to interpret "the Lamb of God" in John 1:29, 36. Just like the Servant of the Lord who would heal people by carrying their sorrows and sins (Isa 53:4–6), by offering himself for sin (Isa 53:10), and by pouring his soul to death (Isa 53:12), so also Jesus will take away human sin by pouring himself out to death on the cross. His death will bring deliverance for people from their suffering and eternal destruction. Thus, the Baptist witnesses to Jesus as the Lamb who will be slaughtered on the cross for human sin to bring salvation for all who believe. The readers can see a shadow of the cross in the Baptist's witness.

After publicly acknowledging the superiority of the man Jesus in rank and status as the one who was existing before him (cf. 1:15, 27; 8:58), the Baptist acknowledges twice his ignorance of the identity of Christ, the Son of God (1:31, 33). He states that he came to baptize people with water so that the pre-existent Christ might be revealed to Israel (1:31). The term "Israel" could refer to the Jews who will believe and accept the God-sent Messiah, in contrast to "the Jews" in Jerusalem.[30]

The Baptist could identify that it is Jesus who is the Son of God when he saw the Spirit descending from heaven like a dove and remaining on

---

29. For other arguments against the background of Revelation see Ridderbos 1997: 72; Keener 2005: 1.452.

30. Cf. Michaels 2010: 113.

Foundation of the Community of Faith

Jesus during his baptism (1:32; cf. Matt 3:16 par.). John uses the Synoptic tradition freely with an emphasis on the "remaining" of the Spirit on Jesus (1:32–33).[31] Jesus was revealed to the Baptist by God, who sent John to baptize with water, as the one who baptizes people with the Holy Spirit by means of a vision of the descent of the Spirit that remained upon Jesus (1:33). This echoes Isa 11:1–2 LXX, where the identifying mark of the Christ is the resting of the Spirit of the Lord upon him. That Jesus is "the one who baptizes with the Holy Spirit" implies that Jesus, the bearer of God's Spirit, is the one who fills those who believe in him with the same Spirit. The baptism with water can purify and prepare people to accept Christ, the Son of God, but the baptism with the Holy Spirit will enable believers to experience divine life and to continue his mission in the world (4:14; 7:37–39; 20:21–23).

Soon after the Baptist saw the descent of the Holy Spirit on Jesus, implicitly at the time of Jesus' baptism, he bore witness that Jesus is the Son of God (1:34). In John the title "Son of God" is spoken of equally with God the Father (5:18; 10:30; 14:9–11), in contrast to the Roman emperor, who also was called "son of God." In this sense, Jesus' sonship is the only of its kind. The Jews in Qumran identified the "son" in 2 Sam 7:14 and Ps 2:7 with the Messiah begotten by God (1QSa 2.11–12; 4QFlor 1.1–19), and similarly John identifies the "Son of God" with the Messiah. At first the Baptist cryptically introduces Jesus as "the one standing among you whom you do not know" (1:26), and the veil is removed for the "insiders" when he introduces Jesus as the Lamb of God (1:29), and finally he reveals the one "upon whom the Spirit descends and remains" (1:33) as the Son of God.[32]

Emergence of Jesus' new community (1:35–51)

The next day after the Baptist unveiled who Jesus is, two of his disciples followed Jesus and came into fellowship with him. This initiates the dawn of the new covenant community around Jesus. The Baptist introduced Jesus, who was walking by, to these disciples saying, "Behold, the Lamb of God" (1:36). The name of one of the two is mentioned as Andrew, Simon Peter's brother, but the name of the other is hidden (1:40). Their immediate response of following Jesus proves the convincing effect of the Baptist's

---

31. The word "to remain" (*menein*), which is used about forty times in the Gospel, indicates the intimate union that exists between Jesus and the Father and also between Jesus and his followers.

32. Neyrey 2007: 53.

testimony, which enabled his disciples finally to accept Jesus as the Christ. In John's Gospel, a genuine "seeing" of Jesus is often preceded by "hearing" about Jesus and followed by "believing" and "witnessing."[33] Jesus, on seeing the two walking behind him, questioned them, "What are you seeking?" (1:38). On the surface, Jesus' question asks what they really want from him, but at a deeper level it means whether they are seeking the life that quench their spiritual thirst.[34]

The two disciples, instead of answering the question directly, asked Jesus, "Rabbi, where are you staying?" The question shows that the two wanted to know Jesus more and have intimate friendship with him. The Greek word used for "staying" (*menein*) in John denotes intimacy with Jesus. The knowledge they had gained through the Baptist that Jesus is the Lamb of God, who takes away human sin and who empowers believers with the Holy Spirit, could have created a spiritual longing within them. Therefore they wanted to remain with him and learn from him the Law, which was normally taught by Jewish rabbis even until late at night.[35] This explains why they called him "Rabbi," which means "my great one" or "teacher."

Jesus' answer, "Come and you will see," invites the seekers not only to come and stay with him but also to perceive him as the Messiah to whom the OT points (cf. John 6:37; Matt 11:28). Responding to Jesus' invitation, the two disciples went with him. The time of their stay with Jesus is specified as the "tenth hour," which, as per Jewish reckoning, would be 4:00 p.m. Does it denote the time when the disciples came to Jesus or the time when they left him? The statement "they stayed with him that day" (1:39b) implies that the two stayed with Jesus until 4.00 p.m. If the disciples' stay had fallen on a Friday, as Brown has calculated,[36] then the followers would have left Jesus before the Sabbath started, at 6.00 p.m.[37] In his dialogue with them throughout the day, Jesus convinced them through the Scriptures that he is the Messiah (cf. John 1:41, 45; Luke 24:25–27, 32). The disciples got new revelation about God and the Messiah, which marked a turning point in their lives.

---

33. Kanagaraj 2005: 84–85.
34. Cf. Carson 1991: 154–55.
35. Barrett 1978: 204.
36. Brown 1978: 1.98.

37. The reference to the precise time or day occurs often in John (e.g., 3:2; 4:6; 18:28; 19:39, 42; 20:1, 19), showing that the narrated events happened in history at a particular point of time.

Foundation of the Community of Faith

Their joy and new knowledge of Scripture inspired the two disciples to tell others that they found the Messiah.[38] Andrew shares this good news first to his brother Simon (1:41), who was inspired to see Jesus. Therefore Andrew brought him to Jesus to be a part of Jesus' community. With the Baptist as the origin, the two disciples became the pioneers of Christ's community, the church.

The Greek word *emblepsas* ("having looked at") in 1:42 implies Jesus' deep insight and inner perception into the life of Simon. Jesus had already known Peter by the name "Simon" and his father, John, for he foreknew each human being by name, background, and future destination (1:48; 2:24–25; 4:16–18; 13:38; 20:25, 27; 21:6). Simon will be called "Cephas" (*petros* in Greek), meaning "rock," because at his meeting with Jesus, Simon must have perceived him as the Christ. By changing his name, Jesus hints at a change in Peter's life and ministry thereafter.

Jesus takes the initiative ("Jesus decided") to shift the place of his ministry from the eastern side of Jordan to the western side of the Sea of Galilee, where he finds Philip of Bethsaida (cf. 12:21), a disciple who attains importance in John's Gospel (12:21–22; 14:8–9). Bethsaida is mentioned as the "city of Andrew and Peter" (1:44), whereas according to the Synoptic Gospels Andrew and Peter came from Capernaum (Matt 8:5, 14; Mark 1:21, 29; Luke 4:31, 38). However, both Bethsaida and Capernaum were situated in Galilee and after 70 CE the whole region around the Sea of Galilee was called "Galilee,"[39] and therefore John is not incorrect in mentioning the native place of Philip. He is the only disciple whom Jesus commands in John, "Follow me" (1:43), a command given to other disciples in the Synoptic Gospels (Matt 4:19–22; 8:22; 9:9; Mark 1:17, 20; 2:14). Philip decided to follow Jesus, and this led him to identify Jesus of Nazareth as the Christ to whom the Law of Moses and the OT prophets (the whole of OT) testify (John 1:45).

Philip immediately shared his conviction with Nathanael by witnessing, "We have found him . . ." Thus the circle of God's new community became bigger by the addition of those who believed Jesus as the Christ and bore witness to him enthusiastically. Since the foundation of this new community is faith in Jesus as the Messiah, Jesus, in John, is revealed and

---

38. For the sake of Greek readers the narrator translates the Hebrew "Messiah" into Greek "Christ" (cf. 1:38, 41).

39. Barrett 1978: 183.

confessed as the Messiah in the initial stage of his ministry, whereas in other Gospels it is divulged later (Matt 16:16, 20 par.).

Nathanael's immediate question, "Can any good thing be from Nazareth?" (1:46), reflects perhaps the civic rivalry between Cana, Nathanael's native place (21:2), and the neighboring Nazareth.[40] Philip's response, "Come and see," looks back to the same invitation given by Jesus to the two disciples (1:39). As Nathanael was approaching Jesus, Jesus called him an Israelite in whom there is no craftiness, because Jesus knew his inner thirst to see the Messiah (1:47), and this explains Jesus' foreknowledge of Nathanael even before Philip called him, because Jesus had seen him when Nathanael was under the fig tree (1:48). The statement "I saw you ... when you were under the fig tree" indicates that Nathanael was looking for the Messiah to come and was, therefore, meditating on the Law under the fig tree to search for the Messiah and his activities. Some rabbinic texts claim that the more one studies the words of Law the more relish one finds in them, just like the one who searches on the fig tree finds more fruits on it (e.g., *b. ʿErub.* 54a).[41] Nathanael's action is in line with the Jewish rabbis who studied under fig trees.[42] Jesus' foreknowledge of Philip's meeting with Nathanael and of Nathanel's expectation of the Messiah proves that Jesus was divine even while he was a human.

In his first encounter with Jesus, Nathanael confesses that Jesus is the "Son of God" and the "King of Israel" (1:49). His search of the Scriptures had led him to identify both titles as denoting the Messiah, who will subdue the enemies of Israel and establish his kingdom. That Christ will come as King in the family of David in order to rule over Israelites with justice and peace is an OT concept (Isa 11:1–5; 35:4; Zeph 3:14–17; Zech 9:9–10). Christ is also portrayed as the Son begotten by God (2 Sam 7:14; Ps 2:7). The messianic title "King of Israel," in conjunction with "Son of God," alludes to these OT passages.

Nevertheless, Jesus questioned Nathanael's faith, for he had believed in Jesus as the Christ only by seeing his supernatural knowledge (1:50; cf. 2:23–25; 12:37; 20:29). In John, believing in Jesus just by seeing his supernatural deeds causes only an embryonic faith, and genuine faith comes by hearing his words. After pointing out his faith as based on seeing, Jesus gives him a promise that he will see greater things than Jesus' supernatural

---

40. Keener 2005: 1.484; Barrett 1978: 184.
41. Brown 1978: 1.83; Neyrey 2007: 58.
42. Cf. Barclay 1957: 1.77–78.

knowledge. This promise is given also for all Jesus' followers, as the plural "you [will see]" in 1:51 shows.

The community of disciples will see greater things throughout Jesus' life and ministry. Jesus' promise is introduced with his solemn declaration, "Truly, truly I say to you," which appears twenty-five times in the Johnnine sayings of Jesus. This implies that Jesus pronounces a heavenly truth that is confirmed and unchangeable. He promises a vision that will be seen collectively by all those who believe in Jesus.

God's new community, emerged around Jesus, will see "heaven opened" and get a vision of God's glory (Ezek 1:1; Mark 1:10; Acts 7:56; Rev 4:1; 11:19; cf. 1 Kgs 22:19; Dan 7:13; Matt 26:64; Mark 14:62; Rev 12:1; 15:1; etc.). It will see the angels of God ascending and descending on the Son of Man, just like Jacob saw (Gen 28:12–17). Jacob saw the angels of God ascending and descending on a ladder and at the top of it he saw the Lord God, who revealed himself to Jacob as the God of his fathers.

The Johannine Jesus replaces Jacob's ladder with the Son of Man on whom the angels were ascending and descending. This means that just as Jacob's ladder was the means of communication between earth and heaven, John portrays the Son of Man, Jesus, as the way from earth to heaven (John 14:6) and the means of communication with God. Moreover, there is no reference in John for the presence of God who revealed himself to Jacob (Gen 28:13–15). However, for John one can see the same God in the Son of Man. Thus Jesus, the Son of Man, becomes to all people both the way to heaven and the revelation of God's glory.

The idea of the Son of Man as the mediator between heaven and earth is based on Daniel's vision of "one like a son of man," who is the representative of both God and the saints of the Most High and through whom God's people will possess God's kingdom, dominion, and authority (Dan 7:9–27). It is possible that Jesus picked up the title "Son of Man" for himself from Daniel 7 to denote the communication between God and humanity.[43] At the same time, the term "son of man" was used to refer to the "man of God's right hand," implying the "anointed one of God" (Ps 80:17). When John was written, the Jews understood the title "Son of Man" in terms of the "Elect One" of God or the "Christ" (*1 En.* 37–71; *4 Ezra* 12–13). In John,

---

43. In the OT the term "son of man" means a mere mortal human being (e.g., Ps 8:4; Ezek 2:1; 3:1; 4:1; etc.), but Dan 7:13–14 shows "the son of man" as a heavenly being who comes with the clouds of heaven. In view of John's constant emphasis that Jesus came from heaven (e.g., 3:13; 6:38, 41–42, 50–51; 8:23), we should understand the title "Son of Man" against the background of Dan 7.

"Son of Man" is spoken by the people on par with "Messiah" (12:34). Thus, the "Son of Man" in 1:51 refers to Christ, who came from heaven to reveal God, his love and life-giving power. He is the place where one can see God's glory in human form on earth (John 19:5; cf. Ezek 1:26–28). This could be a polemic against the Jewish mystics who claimed that one can see the kingly glory of God in human form only by ascending to heaven (cf. John 3:13).

The whole Gospel of John hereafter will show how Jesus' promise in 1:51 was fulfilled in the life and ministry of Jesus and how God was creating a new covenant community in the Son of Man. In this sense, 1:51 is a springboard for studying the Gospel of John.

JOHN 2
The Beginning of Jesus' Public Ministry

JESUS' PUBLIC MINISTRY (2:1—12:50)

Some scholars treat John 2 as the beginning of the unit that ends at 4:54, often given the title "From Cana to Cana."[1] This section pictures how the first sign took place in Cana of Galilee (2:1–12) and the second sign, which completes the first sphere of Jesus' Galilean ministry, also took place in Cana (4:46–54). God's new community was expanded by including both the Jews and the Gentiles.

First sign of Jesus in John (2:1–12)

In 2:1–12 a vision of Jesus' glory, promised in 1:51, becomes possible first in a wedding at Cana, the native place of Nathanael, situated in Galilee eight miles north of Nazareth, where Jesus was brought up. The time reference "on the third day" implies not only that Jesus' revelation of his glory took place after three days of his promise (1:50b–51) but also that by this time the circle of twelve disciples was complete. If we count the number of days from the time the Baptist witnessed about Jesus (1:19–2:1), the wedding at Cana falls on the seventh day. Brown sees here an implicit reference to God's creation of the world in seven days (Gen 1:1–2:3) and argues that John is seeing the start of Jesus' ministry as the start of new creation.[2] This symbolic interpretation looks forward to the creation of a new humanity by Jesus who was raised on the third day (20:22).

Galilee had both Jews and Gentiles in it, and the beginning of Jesus' ministry and his first sign performed there may symbolically mean that he loves both Jews and Gentiles and that they have an equal place in the new community he came to create. "The mother of Jesus was there" implies that

---
1. See Brown 1978: 1.95–96; Ridderbos 1997: 97–99.
2. Brown 1978: 1.105–6.

the wedding could have been that of one of her relatives or of a close family friend. That is why Jesus and his disciples also had been invited. Jesus' mother is mentioned throughout John's Gospel without her name. Brown thinks that the absence of the name may be to symbolize her as a new Eve or new Israel, the church.[3] However, most probably the avoidance of her name is just to highlight her earthly relationship to Jesus. Being the mother of Jesus, she too had a place in Jesus' new community (cf. 2:12).

The reference to the invitation of Jesus along with his disciples (2:2) shows how closely the community of Jesus' disciples had been linked with him within a short time. The mother of Jesus, as a woman, plays a key role in the first sign that Jesus does. Wine, as per Jewish custom, was used in festive occasions such as weddings.[4] The wine used in this wedding ran out. Jesus' mother may well have had some responsibility in catering for the guests,[5] therefore she immediately brought the urgent matter to the attention of Jesus by telling him, "They do not have wine" (2:3). Perhaps she believed that Jesus, being the Son of God, was able to provide for the need on any occasion. However, Jesus did not do any miracle as his mother expected. He questioned her, "What is for me and you, O woman?" (2:4a). The word "O woman" is not a word of disrespect (cf. 19:26). Jesus' words "My hour has not yet come" (2:4b) show that Jesus would act to supply wine in accordance with the will and timing of God rather than his physical parent. For him, to do the will of the Father was his food (4:34) and so he did not allow human relationships to direct his steps in his mission. While this meaning is well taken, the term "hour," which occurs twenty-six times in John, has a deeper meaning.

Although Jesus says that his hour has not yet come, later he uses both present and future tenses to say, "The hour is coming, and now is" (4:23; 5:25; 16:32). Eventually he says, "The hour has come" (12:23, 27; 13:1; 17:1). The Johannine terms "the hour," "my hour," and "his hour" indicate the time when Jesus will return to the Father through his death and resurrection. The term "an hour" (the Greek word *hōra* without the definite article) refers to the effects that Jesus' hour would bring in the lives of the believers, and those effects include the manner of worshipping God, persecution, a new understanding of Jesus' words, and the final resurrection of all humans

---

3. Brown 1978: 1.107–9; cf. Schneiders 1993: 128.
4. Keener 2005: 1.501.
5. Carson 1991: 169.

Jesus' Public Ministry

to face judgment (cf. 4:21; 5:25, 28–29; 16:2, 25).[6] Thus, at the deeper level "my hour" in 2:4 means that the Father's time to reveal Jesus' glory through his death and resurrection has not yet come.

Gaining confidence from Jesus' response, his mother instructed the servants, "You do what he would tell you" (2:5). She acted with an exemplary faith and with determination to supply wine through Jesus. However, his disciples were so passive that they were unable to recognize the need of the time.

Jesus started acting in his own time as per God's will. He wished to supply better quality of wine by using the water kept in six stone jars, as per the Jewish rite of purification, each jar containing 80–120 liters (2:6 TNIV).[7] The use of "stone jars" for purification is mentioned not in Lev 11:32–38, but in the Mishnah, a Rabbinic text of the second century that reflects the life situation of the late first century (*m. Kelim* 5:11; *m. Beṣah* 2:3). He asked the servants to fill the jars with water up to the brim and they did it (2:7). In obedience to Jesus' instruction, they drew some water out and took it to the master of the feast (2:7–8).[8]

The text does not mention when the water drawn out of jars was turned into wine. We are only told that the master of the feast tasted the "water which had become wine" without knowing where it was from (2:9). The Greek perfect-tense *gegenēmenon* shows the quality of the water, which perhaps had already become wine before it came to the hands of the master. The water became wine probably when the servants were drawing it from the jars or when they were carrying it. They knew by whom the miracle happened, but not how it happened (2:9). There is a secrecy motif in this first sign of Jesus (2:11a), conveying the truth that the miraculous deeds of Jesus are beyond human comprehension. The focus of the sign, then, is not on how or when the turning of water into wine happened but on why it happened.

This sign also contains non-understanding, a literary feature of John. The master of the feast misunderstood the supply of "good wine" as the work of the bridegroom. Hence he told the bridegroom that he was keeping thus far the good wine in contrast to the usual custom of offering the

---

6. Cf. Brown 1978: 1.517.

7. John gives the capacity of each jar as "two or three measures," one "measure" being equivalent to almost forty liters, and thus six jars will hold 480–720 liters; Schnackenburg 1980–84: 1.332; Ridderbos 1997: 107.

8. The Greek word *architriklinos* means "head waiter, butler" or, more aptly to the context, "master of the feast"; BDAG, 139.

best wine first so that the guests would appreciate the host's provision, and then, after too much drinking, offering the wine of lesser quality (2:10).[9] The master thus never understood the work of Jesus.

By following the Jewish rite of purification to do his first sign (literally "beginning of the signs"), Jesus brings out the truth that the real meaning of the Jewish religious customs is fulfilled only in him, who transforms the old ceremonial system into something that human beings can experience. Jesus replaces the old Jewish ritual order with his own new order.

In the OT, the "sweet wine" supplied by God to his people is the mark of deliverance from exile (Jer 31:12; Amos 9:13–14) and of prosperity (Joel 3:18), and it has an eschatological connotation also. In the light of this, Jesus' conversion of water into wine indicates that the long-awaited kingdom of God has arrived and that God himself has drawn near in the person and ministry of Jesus to fulfill his promise of abundant blessings.[10] The narrative of the wedding at Cana reaches its climax in 2:11, where the manifestation of Jesus' glory through this sign leads the disciples to believe in him, while for others it is only a satisfaction of physical thirst (see comments on 1:14 for understanding "glory"). This sign renews the disciples' commitment to Jesus and leads them into deeper faith.

After this sign, Jesus went to Capernaum with his mother, brothers, and disciples and stayed a few days there (2:12). This is a symbol of the corporate life of the new community, which includes men and women, centered in Jesus.

Jesus' revolutionary act in the temple (2:13–22)

In 2:13 there is an abrupt shift from Capernaum (2:12) to Jerusalem. In the Synoptic accounts, Jesus enters into Jerusalem only once, at the end of his ministry, but in John Jesus makes four visits to Jerusalem, mainly during the Passover (2:13; 5:1; 7:10, 14; 12:9, 12). During one of his visits Jesus cleansed the Jerusalem temple and subsequently confronted the Jewish leaders (2:13–22). In the Synoptic Gospels this event is narrated nearly at the end of Jesus' ministry (Matt 21:12–17 par.), whereas in John it is placed in the beginning of Jesus' ministry. One cannot prove that Jesus cleansed the temple twice. For John chronology has only marginal significance. In

---

9. See Kruse 2008: 95–96.
10. Kruse 2008: 96–97.

Jesus' Public Ministry

both 2:1–11 and 2:13–22 Jesus transforms the Jewish legal custom to do good to people by fulfilling their need.

Jesus went up to Jerusalem just before the Passover, a Jewish festival celebrated every year in commemoration of God's deliverance of the Israelites from slavery in Egypt, having passed over their houses without killing the first-born by seeing the blood of a lamb on their lintels and doorposts (Exod 12). All who went up to Jerusalem used to go to the temple to offer sacrifices and worship God (cf. Ps 122). Naturally Jesus, as a Jew, first went into the temple.

In the temple, Jesus did not see an atmosphere of worship, but a business trend. He found those who were selling oxen, sheep, and pigeons, and money changers sitting (2:14) for exchanging the currency brought by pilgrims who came from other countries into Tyrian coinage, which was the prescribed currency to pay temple dues (*m. Bek.* 8:7). The oxen, sheep, and pigeons were required by the Law to be sacrificed (Lev 1 and 3). Surprisingly, sale of "lambs," the actual Passover sacrifice, is not mentioned in the narrative. The temple authorities apparently did not give priority to the sacrificial lambs, but were primarily concerned with the trade that would bring them economic profit. That is why Jesus became zealous for the house of God and made a whip of cords to chase out the animals and to pour out the coins of the money changers by overturning their tables (2:15). He rebuked them by stating that they should not use "my Father's house" for the purpose of trading (John 2:16; cf. Jer 7:11 and Isa 56:7; see also Matt 21:13 par.).

The business seems to have been carried on in the "Court of the Gentiles," an area beyond which Gentiles were not permitted to go, into the forecourts and the sanctuary, lest they face the death penalty. The ongoing business and profit making consequently prevented the Gentiles from entry into the temple to pray and worship,[11] although the temple was to be the house of prayer for "all nations" (Mark 11:17). John's phrase "a house of trade" alludes to Zech 14:21, where it appears in the context of Zechariah's prophecy about coming of the non-Jews into the temple to worship Yahweh the King (Zech 14:16–17). Thus, one of the reasons, if not the sole reason,[12] for Jesus' vehement action was the preventing of Gentiles by the Jewish authorities from entering the court by making it a commercial place.

---

11. Kruse 2008: 100.
12. Keener 2005: 1.524.

John 2:13–22

The narrator comments that Jesus' disciples remembered what is written in the Scripture, "The zeal for your house will consume me" (John 2:17; cf. Ps 69:9). They realized that Jesus' vehement action to preserve the purification of the house of the Lord was due to his consuming zeal for the Father's house (cf. Luke 2:49). Psalm 69 actually speaks of the suffering of a righteous one and it was used by first-century Christians to proclaim the suffering and death of Jesus (cf. Ps 69:21 with Matt 27:34, 48; Luke 23:36; John 19:30; Rom 11:9–10). Jesus' words "will consume me" anticipate his suffering and death in order to build a new temple, that is, a community with a new life to worship the Father in spirit and in truth (4:23–24).

That Jesus spoke of his death is further confirmed by 2:19, where he asks "the Jews" to destroy "this temple,"[13] his body, with a challenge that he will raise it up in three days (cf. Matt 26:61; 27:40; Mark 14:58; 15:29). He spoke in response to the Jerusalem authorities, who asked for a sign from him to prove that he had authority from God to disrupt the cultic worship by chasing out the animals kept for sacrifice (2:18). In 2:19 Jesus speaks of his death and resurrection in terms of destroying the old temple with all its legal system of animal sacrifices and building a new temple to be a place of life-giving power. In this sense, 2:17–22 foreshadows the death and resurrection of Christ,[14] a "sign" to be seen by his adversaries.

Jesus' cleansing of the temple, as a whole, is a prophetic and symbolic act that points to the "greater reality" that is coming (e.g., Isa 8:16–18; Ezek 4:1–3). It is also Jesus' non-miraculous sign that anticipates his sacrifice on the cross (cf. Matt 12:39–40). John's addition of "sheep and oxen" that were driven out of the temple is to symbolize that Jesus removes the need for animal sacrifices to obtain forgiveness of sins and deliverance. The Jerusalem temple is now replaced by a new Temple, Jesus, in whom the offering of animals has no place (cf. 2:19). Jesus himself is the sacrifice to remove human sin and he is the one who offers it (e.g., Heb 9:11–14). His life and work thus mark the end of the temple worship and the beginning of a new and life-giving worship. The action of Jesus in the temple is not merely that of a Jewish reformer or merely a protest against the irreverence and corruption of Jewish worship, but is a sign to convey the truth that the end of

---

13. The Greek word *naos*, used here and in 2:20, represents the whole temple and not the sanctuary alone.

14. Keener 2005: 1.527–31.

Jesus' Public Ministry

animal sacrifice is at hand.[15] In this act of Jesus, one can see the shadow of the cross again.

This is confirmed in 2:20–22. The temple authorities misunderstood Jesus' statement that he was boasting himself of rebuilding the destroyed temple in three days, while it took originally forty-six years to build (2:19–20).[16] They ridiculed him for saying so (cf. Matt 27:40) without understanding that Jesus would give up his body to be destroyed on the cross and would raise it up in three days (2:21) to restore true spiritual worship for which the Jerusalem temple stood. Even his disciples only understood this after Jesus' resurrection. John displays his literary device of non-understanding to lead his readers to a higher level of understanding.[17]

The resurrection of Jesus opened the eyes of Jesus' community to see the reality behind his signs and symbolic acts. The comment "his disciples remembered" (2:17, 22) means an unveiling of truth by the Spirit after the death and resurrection of Jesus (14:26; 16:14) so that they might believe the Scripture that testifies to Jesus (cf. 1:45; 5:39). Such a new vision of Jesus is a partial fulfillment of "greater things" to be seen by his disciples (1:50–51).

Supernatural knowledge of Jesus (2:23–25)

Jesus was participating in the Passover feast (2:23a). John does not describe how the Passover was celebrated in the temple; his focus is always on Jesus and his deeds and on people's response to him. Many believed in Jesus' name by looking at the signs he performed (2:23b). The plural "signs" informs us that Jesus could have done other signs besides what is narrated in John 2. These could include his healing of many blind and lame people who came to him when he was in the temple (cf. Matt 21:14). Though many believed in Jesus, they did so because they saw signs. This kind of superficial faith springs up from common human nature. Those who saw Jesus' signs were amazed and appreciated him probably as a wonder-worker without making a faith commitment to him.

---

15. Hoskyns 1961: 194.

16. Neither the temple repaired by Herod the Great nor the second temple, built under the leadership of Zerubbabel, took forty-six years to construct. It is probable that the specification of forty-six years includes the whole period of Persian kings, Cyrus and Darius (559–513 BCE), in whose time the second temple was built; see Kanagaraj 2005: 110, 113 n. 34.

17. Carson 1982: 59–91; Kanagaraj 1998a: 305–7.

John 2:23–25

In John faith based on "seeing" rather than on "hearing" the testimony about Jesus or his words is not genuine faith (cf. 1:50). Since Jesus himself knew all human beings and their secret thoughts (cf. 1:42, 47–48; 5:42; 6:15, 26, 61, 64; 16:19, 30), no human needs to bear witness about anyone to Jesus (2:25). The supernatural knowledge of God is portrayed in the OT: it is God alone who observes the deeds of all human beings and their secret thoughts, because he has fashioned their hearts and observes their deeds (Ps 7:9; 33:15; 139:1–24; Jer 17:10; cf. Wis 1:6). What is true with the God of the OT is true with the Jesus that John portrays! Since Jesus is the Son of God who is in oneness with the Father, no wonder he exhibits the same omniscience as God. Therefore Jesus did not entrust himself to those who seemed to believe in him by seeing his signs (2:24). This shows that Jesus expected the members of his society to believe in him with a commitment not just by seeing the miracles he performed but by hearing his words.

Excursus: "Sign" in John

The word "sign" (*sēmeion* in Greek) occurs seventeen times in John's Gospel, out of which thirteen times it occurs in plural. "Signs" denotes the miracles of Jesus. In the Synoptic Gospels, the word "sign" bears mostly a negative connotation, as Jesus refuses his opponents' demand to perform a sign (Matt 12:38–39; 16:1, 4; Mark 8:11–12; Luke 11:16, 29; 23:8; cf. John 2:18). Even false prophets and false Christs perform signs (Matt 24:24; Mark 13:22). Nevertheless, signs foreshadow the coming of Christ in glory (Matt 24:3, 30; Mark 13:4; Luke 21:7, 11, 25). The Greek version of Isa 8:18 has the word *sēmeion* with a non-miraculous connotation and in Ezek 4:3 the word indicates the prophetic activity that anticipates a greater reality of which the sign itself is a part. In Isa 66:18–19, *sēmeion* is used to denote the eschatological gathering of all nations to see his glory and the declaration of his glory among the Gentiles by the survivors of the Jewish nation.[18]

In the same line, in all his signs in John, Jesus reveals God's glory in terms of his love and concern for humanity to fulfill their physical and spiritual needs (e.g., 2:1–11; 6:26–27; 11:4, 40). Jesus' signs (works) in John reveal his oneness with the Father (5:18; 10:38) and his own identity as the Christ, the Son of God, and the Son of Man (9:38; 11:25–27; 20:30–31). Through a sign Jesus strengthened the faith of his disciples in him (2:11) and others

18. Barrett 1978: 75–78.

Excursus: "Sign" in John

could come to believe in him (4:53; 6:69; 9:35–38; 11:45; 12:42). Hence most of the signs are followed by a discourse. However, in some cases the signs cause enmity, which culminates in Jesus' death on the cross (5:16, 18; 11:46–57; 12:9–11, 37). His exaltation on the cross is presented in John as the greatest sign in which the symbol and reality meet each other (2:18–22; 3:14–15).

JOHN 3
Testimonies of Jesus and the Baptist

John next narrates Jesus' ministry to three individuals: Nicodemus, a Samaritan woman, and a royal official, who belong to Judea, Samaria, and Galilee respectively (John 3–4). This shows that Jesus is interested in each individual and his purpose is to bring people of all cultures, regions, and languages into his community.

Jesus' Testimony before Nicodemus (3:1–21)

Jesus' dialogue with Nicodemus (3:1–12)

Nicodemus was a Jew, "a man of the Pharisees" and "a ruler of the Jews" (3:1). The designation "ruler" shows his position in the Jewish council (7:50–51). He was "the teacher of Israel" (3:10) who was searching for heavenly truth. So Nicodemus met Jesus, obviously in Jerusalem. By knowing Nicodemus's inner thirst, Jesus initiates his teaching on the necessity of new birth in order to experience life in the kingdom of God (3:3, 5).

Nicodemus came to Jesus by night. It could have been for secrecy, because many Pharisees were opposing Jesus; or night-time could have been simply a convenient time for him and Jesus; or it could be in line with the custom of the rabbis to study the Law and converse about divine things at night.[1] Nevertheless, the twice-repeated remark that Nicodemus came to Jesus at night (3:2; 19:39) makes the symbolic meaning more probable. In John, "night" denotes darkness, an impossible time to do good work and the absence of light causing people to stumble in life because of their evil deeds (3:19–21; 9:4–5; 11:10; 12:35, 36, 46; 13:30). John thus implies that Nicodemus came from the dark sphere of his life to Jesus, the Light that enlightens every human. Nevertheless, many scholars take Nicodemus negatively.[2] However, John seems to admire the initial stage of Nicodemus's

---

1. Str-B: 2.419–20.

2. E.g., de Jonge 1977: 36; Culpepper 1983: 134–36; Neyrey 2007: 76–78; Hakola 2009: 438–55.

faith and shows him later as the one who spoke for Jesus in the Jewish council (7:45–52) and who gave a royal burial to him (19:30–42).

Nicodemus was impressed with the signs that Jesus performed and hence believed that Jesus was a teacher who came from God with divine power (3:2). In this sense, he represents those who believed in Jesus after seeing his signs (2:23). At the initial stage, Nicodemus had only partial understanding of Jesus (cf. 4:19; 9:30–32, 36).

Jesus knew Nicodemus's imperfect knowledge and equally his inner thirst for heavenly reality. Therefore he tells him, by using the phrase "Truly, truly, I say to you," that only those who are born from above can experience heavenly life under God's rule (3:3). The Greek word *anōthen* used has two meanings: "again" and "from above" (3:31; 19:11, 23; cf. 8:23). Both meanings complement each other, for the experience of being born again ("new birth") comes from God who is above (1:13). The idea of becoming children of God by a new birth (1:12–13) is developed in 3:3 as the prerequisite to enter the kingdom of God (cf. Matt 18:3). The new community of Jesus is a community that comes under God's rule by experiencing new birth from above.

The same idea of being born from above is explained by Jesus in 3:5, after Nicodemus expressed his non-understanding of birth from above by his question, "How can a person be born after having grown old? Can one enter a second time into the mother's womb and be born?" (3:4). John uses the literary technique of non-understanding so that the heavenly truth may be revealed clearly. John 3:3 and 3:5 are mutually interpreting. The word "seeing" in 3:3 is replaced by "entering" and the word "from above" by "of water and Spirit" in 3:5. "Seeing" in John means both physical sight and spiritual perception. It denotes "experiencing" or "tasting" (3:36; 8:51, 53) divine life by the power of God's Spirit. Thus, "seeing" and "entering" are identical in meaning. However, "entering" emphasizes the act of coming into the realm of God's reign and see God as King. What is the meaning of "water and spirit" which interprets "from above"?

The main issue of interpretation concerns whether the term "water" refers to a baptism of repentance or to the Jewish proselyte baptism or to Christian baptism. Almost all scholars agree that "spirit" here means the outpouring of the Holy Spirit which brings regeneration (see Ezek 36:25–27, where "water" symbolizes the Spirit of God). That water baptism is a prerequisite for entering the kingdom of God is found neither in the NT nor in any other Christian writings. Even the Baptist's baptism is a symbol

John 3:1-12

of repentance only and is superseded by the coming of Christ, who will baptize with the Holy Spirit (1:26-27, 33). In John's Gospel, "water" is mainly used as a symbol for the Holy Spirit, who will lead the receipient to eternal life (John 4:14-15; 7:37-39; cf. Ezek 47:9). One can say that in 3:5 water and Spirit are used synonymously, one being the symbol and the other reality. It is the Spirit that enables one to be reborn into the family of God and thus to come under the rule of God. The meaning of 3:3 and 3:5 finally is merged into the phrase "born of the Spirit" (3:8).[3] Why, then, does John write "water and spirit" if both refer to the Holy Spirit as the source of rebirth? By placing both the terms together, John stresses the twofold function of the Holy Spirit: life-giving and empowering. Both are related experiences in the realm of God's rule.

John introduces another dramatic dualism: a life controlled by the flesh against the life controlled by the Holy Spirit (3:6). Anyone who is not born of the Spirit lives still in the realm of flesh, that is, under the rule of the fallen human nature that is prone to sin, and therefore exhibits the deeds of the flesh (cf. Gal 5:19-21). In contrast, those who are born of God by the Spirit exhibit the works of the Spirit. They partake in the divine nature and show divine qualities (cf. Gal 5:22-23).

After exhorting Nicodemus not to marvel at his teaching on new birth (3:7), Jesus clarifies that the origin and work of the Spirit within a person is imperceptible to anyone who lives in the realm of flesh, just like the origin and direction of the blowing wind cannot be perceived (John 3:8; cf. Eccl 11:5), because spirit and flesh are opposed to each other (Gal 5:17). What a natural person can see is the fruit of new life manifested in a person who is born of the Spirit, but no one can comprehend the mode of the Spirit's work within that person. With astonishment, Nicodemus questioned, "How can these things happen?" (3:9). Jesus rebuked him for his lack of understanding, although he was a teacher of the Law in Israel (3:10). Nicodemus must have known about regeneration by the Spirit from the OT itself, which speaks of the Spirit's work that gives a new heart and life (Ps 51:10; Isa 44:3; Ezek 11:19-20; 36:26-27; Joel 2:28-29).

By using the phrase "truly, truly, I say to you," Jesus affirms, "We speak what we know and testify to what we have seen but you do not receive our testimony" (3:11). The plural pronouns "we" and "you" show that Jesus is speaking as the representative of the new covenant community, by

---

3. For the argument that both water and spirit stand for the Holy Spirit see Ridderbos 1997: 127-28; Kruse 2008: 109.

Jesus' Testimony before Nicodemus

treating Nicodemus as the one among the Jewish authorities who rejected the church's testimony to Jesus. First, the sharp conflict between Jesus' community, which was testifying to Jesus, and the synagogue authorities, who did not accept their testimony, in the late first century was the re-enactment of the rejection of Jesus' testimony by the same authorities in his lifetime. Secondly, Jesus' affirmation betrays the dualistic tendency of the Gospel to divide people into two opposing groups: insiders (those who believe in Jesus) and outsiders (those who do not accept Jesus).

Jesus rebukes the unbelieving authorities by questioning how they can understand and believe in him if he speaks of heavenly things directly, while they do not understand his message of God's kingdom spoken in earthly terms such as rebirth and wind (3:12). After this question, Nicodemus disappears from the scene until 7:45–52 and 19:38–42. However, the subjects of Jesus' dialogue, such as believing, experiencing divine life, and a heaven-earth dualism, link 3:1–12 with 3:13–21, and therefore it seems more probable that 3:13–21 is a part of Jesus' discourse to Nicodemus.

Jesus' monologue (3:13–21)

Jesus now teaches, "No one has ascended to heaven except the one who descended from heaven, the Son of Man" (3:13).[4] The statement that no human has ascended to heaven seems to be a polemic against the claims of some Jews, including some rabbis, that they had ascended to heaven and had seen God's glory. However, the emphasis lies on the descent of the Son of Man, Jesus. The Son of Man was pre-existent with God in heaven before he descended by incarnation to earth (John 3:13; cf. Eph 4:9–10) with a mission of revealing God in his glory and to give heavenly life to all who believe in him (cf. John 1:50–51; 3:31; 6:32, 38, 42, 46, 50–51, 58, 62; 8:23; 9:33). At the time when John's Gospel was written, the "Son of Man" was understood as a heavenly figure, the "Elect One" or Christ (see comment on 1:51 for a study on "the Son of Man").

However, Jesus speaks of the divine necessity for the Son of Man to be lifted up (3:14). The verb "lifted up" (*hupsaō*) in John has a double meaning: to be exalted and to be glorified (cf. Isa 52:13 LXX). The verb is connected to the Servant's glorification through his vicarious suffering and death (Isa

---

4. Some manuscripts add "[the Son of Man] who is in heaven," and other manuscripts add "[the Son of Man] who is from heaven." These additions were made perhaps to explain the pre-existence of the Son of Man.

52:13—53:12). Similarly, both meanings in John refer to one event: Jesus' death on the cross, which is an act of being lifted up and exalted/glorified (12:23-24, 32-33). In the glorification of the Son of Man on the cross the Father reveals his glory (13:31-32). Both Jesus' death and ascension after resurrection are merged together in the verb "lifted up."

In order to rectify the Israelites' sin that caused poisonous snakes to bite them to death (Num 21:5-9), Moses made a fiery serpent with bronze and set it on a pole so that anyone bitten by a snake could look up to the bronze serpent and live. Similarly, the Johannine Jesus is the one who, in accordance with God's plan, must be lifted up on a pole, the cross, so that everyone who believes in him may have eternal life. Instead of "looking up" to the bronze serpent, John has "believing in him," and in the place of "would live" John has "eternal life" (3:15). Looking to the lifted-up serpent is the mark of "turning towards" God and so also is believing in the lifted-up Son of Man (Wis 16:7).

That the one who believes in him has eternal life is a recurring theme in John (see 3:15-16; 5:24; 6:40, 47; 20:31). "Believing" means "coming to Jesus" in obedience (6:35-37; cf. 12:35-36), and this is the same as "turning towards God." It also means appropriating Jesus' life that is available on the cross. "Believing" and "eating his flesh and drinking his blood" lead one to eternal life (6:53-54). "Believing" is also used in parallel with "seeing" (12:44-45). The crown and culmination of all Greek words for "seeing" is to be found in the word "believing."[5] "Believing" in John is synonymous to "receiving" and "knowing" in the sense of coming into intimate relationship with Jesus (1:12; 17:8). The purpose of God in exalting Jesus is that those who believe in the Son of Man lifted up on the cross should have eternal life (3:15).

"Eternal life" refers to the "life of the age to come" (cf. Dan 12:2). This life will be given at the resurrection of the believers on the last day (John 6:54) and therefore it is called the "resurrection of life" (5:29; cf. 5:25). Sometimes John uses the word "life" to denote "eternal life" (e.g., 6:33, 51; 20:31). It is the very life of God given by him to Jesus (5:26; 6:57; cf. 1:4) and is obtained now and in future by those who believe in Jesus. Jesus gives life to whom he wills (5:21) and it cannot be destroyed by physical death (11:26). It is the life of the kingdom of God given to those who are born of the Spirit (3:3, 5). Those who obey Jesus' words and believe in the Father who sent him have already passed from death to life (5:24). Since Jesus is

---

5. Phillips 1957: 83–96.

the giver of life (6:27), he himself is life (11:25; 14:6). The words *"whoever believes in him"* in 3:15–16 show the universal effect of Jesus' exaltation on the cross and also the inclusive nature of God's new community.

The universal effect of Jesus' mission is obvious in Jesus' continuous teaching to Nicodemus who remains still a silent listener (3:16–21). The conjunction "for," and the reference to the availability of eternal life to everyone who believes in the Son (3:16) link the whole section with 3:13–15. The word "only Son [of God]" is synonymous to the title "Son of Man" in 3:14 (cf. 5:26–27). Jesus assures of God's intensive love for sinful humanity, which, however, loves darkness rather than light (3:19). "God so loved the world" means "this is how [*houtōs*] God loved the world" (NJB): by handing over the Son of Man to be crucified to remove human sin and give new life (3:16).[6]

The manner and content of God's love is expressed by the statement ". . . that he gave his only son." Abraham's offering of his only and beloved son, Isaac (Gen 22:2, 9–10, 16), prefigures God's gift of his unique Son not only to be offered on the cross as a sacrifice to take away human sin (John 1:29, 36; 8:32; 1 John 4:9–10), but also to raise him up from the dead to grant new life for those who believe (Heb 11:17–19). God's purpose of giving his Son is that everyone who believes in him may not perish but may have eternal life (3:16; cf. 3:15). Both "eternal life" and "perishing," being end-time events, are opposed to each other. The former denotes salvation of the believers and the latter the eternal condemnation of those who do not believe in the Son. Human destiny has only these two ends. Such dualism is used in John to urge human beings to choose life (cf. Deut 30:18–19).

God giving his only Son is parallel to God sending his Son into the world. God did not send his Son to condemn the world, but to save the world through the Son (3:17). The phrase "not to perish" (3:16) is interpreted as "not to condemn," and the phrase "to have eternal life" (3:16) is interpreted as "to save." The term "everyone" is read in 3:17 as a collective term "the world," meaning the sphere of human life. The word "sending" has a missional thrust. The purpose of Jesus' mission in the world is to save all people from eternal destruction and to give heavenly life to those who allow him to direct their lives. "The one who does not believe is condemned already" (3:18) implies that anyone who does not accept God's provision for human salvation is already judged as guilty and hence is given up to death. Jesus did not come to judge the world, but to save it from the power

---

6. Cf. Keener 2005: 1.566–67.

of darkness (12:47). But the reason for eternal condemnation is the refusal to believe in the name of the only Son (cf. 1:12). Unbelief is the root of all evil deeds (cf. 16:9).

John refers to the descent of the Son of Man to the world (3:13–15), and then he speaks of the sending/giving of the Son to the world (3:16–18), and in 3:19–21 he speaks of the coming of the Light into the world (cf. 1:9–11)—all denoting the coming of Jesus into the world. In 3:19–21, John describes the Logos incarnate, Jesus, as the Light who came into the world (cf. 8:12; 9:5; 12:35–36, 46). Since human works are naturally evil, all people love to live in darkness rather than in light. Therefore they themselves fall under God's judgment (3:19), an eschatological event that is in operation at present (3:18; 5:24). The Light not only shines and illumines (1:5, 9), but also exposes the evil deeds of humankind and therefore the world hates the Light and does not come to it (3:20).

In contrast, those who do the truth are recognized as those who love the Light and live in it (3:21). They exhibit their faithfulness to the covenant relationship of God by obeying his commandments. Doing good deeds is the same as doing the truth by living in the Light and in fellowship with God (cf. Matt 5:16). The coming of Jesus thus divides human beings into those who love darkness and perform evil and those who come to the Light and perform good deeds (cf. 1QS 3.1—4.26). Nevertheless, the division was caused not by the coming of Jesus into the world but by the response of the people to his coming.

THE BAPTIST'S TESTIMONY TO JESUS (3:22–30)

The phrase "after these" (3:22) links the mission of the Baptist with the mission of the Son of God (3:16–21). After Jesus' ministry in Jerusalem, Jesus and his disciples went into the Judean land, where he was staying with them and baptizing. Since Jesus was already in Judea, his move into the land of Judea seems irrelevant. Therefore some scholars suggest that 3:22–30 should be read after 2:12 and that 3:1–21 should be followed by verses 31–36. However, the word "land of Judea" can also mean "Judean countryside" (NRSV and ESV).[7] Jesus and his disciples might have moved from Jerusalem into the countryside, where water was available for baptism. Jesus himself was not baptizing, but his disciples were (4:2).

---

7. The meaning of the Greek *gē* in 3:22 is "region, country" (BDAG, 196).

The Baptist's testimony to Jesus

Why should Jesus' disciples baptize people, when the Baptist was already giving baptism at Aenon near Salim where there was much water (3:23)?[8] Probably the crowd, which followed Jesus in larger number than that which followed the Baptist (3:26; 4:1), asked for baptism similar to that given by the Baptist. The disciples gave baptism with Jesus' approval and in his name. The narrator comments that John the Baptist had not yet been put in prison (3:24). This comment means that Jesus' ministry in Judea began before the arrest of the Baptist, whereas his ministry in Galilee began after his imprisonment (Mark 1:14).

There arose a controversy over the rite of purification between the Baptist's disciples and a Jew, who might have been one of "the Jews" (3:25). Since baptism was treated as a rite of purification in Judaism, the Jew might have questioned the credibility of the Baptist's baptism compared to the baptism given by Jesus' disciples, which attracted more people. Because the Baptist's disciples, at least some of them, were provoked to jealousy, they came to their master and complained that many were going to Jesus to be baptized.[9] Without rightly understanding Jesus in spite of the Baptist's earlier witness (1:29–34), they refer to Jesus in the third person, "He who was with you beyond the Jordan, to whom you have testified" (3:26a). They considered Jesus as a rival to the Baptist, whom they mistook as the Christ. This setting gives an occasion for the Baptist to intensify his witness to Jesus.

The Baptist speaks first *proverbially* by saying that no human can receive even one thing unless it is given from heaven (3:27), that is, "from God who dwells above in heaven" (cf. 3:3; 8:23; 19:11). Jesus was involved in God's mission with the authority that comes from God. Then the Baptist speaks *factually* by reminding them of his witness that he was not the Christ, although he was sent chronologically before Jesus (3:28; cf. 1:20, 23, 30). The phrase "you yourself bear me witness" shows that when the Baptist was being probed by the "Jews" on his identity, his disciples had heard his testimony (cf. 1:19–28). The Baptist confirms the greatness of Jesus by speaking *metaphorically* that Jesus is a bridegroom and he himself is the "friend" or the "best man," whose function is to stand and hear the bridegroom's voice on the joyful occasion of the wedding (3:29). The bridegroom is naturally more significant than the best man. In the OT the word

---

8. The name "Aenon" may come from the Hebrew word *'ayin*, "spring," implying that there were more springs of water; Kruse 2008: 121.

9. The complaint that "all are going to him" (3:26b) is an exaggeration, meaning that many people are going to Jesus (cf. 4:1; 11:48; 12:19).

"bridegroom" refers to God who rejoices over his "bride," the people of Israel, by covenant relationship (Isa 62:5b; Jer 2:2; Ezek 16:8-14; Hos 2:16, 19-20). So also, those who go to Jesus are his bride (cf. Matt 25:1; Mark 2:19; 2 Cor 11:2; Eph 5:23-27, 31-32; Rev 21:2; 22:17).

When the bridegroom takes the bride by speaking to her and making his vow, the best man rejoices,[10] or when the friend hears the shout of exultation by the bridegroom when he discovers the bride a virgin in the bridal chamber, he rejoices by hearing the joyful voice of the bridegroom. The work of the best man is then complete.[11] Now the Baptist hears that more people are following Jesus and are baptized. This marks the voice of bridegroom's joy. He, who is subordinate to Jesus, fully rejoices that his mission of testifying to Jesus as the Christ is complete. For the Baptist, Jesus must increase but he must decrease (3:30), implying that Jesus should be projected as the Christ, the Son of God, whereas he himself must become less significant. Thus, the Baptist takes away the rival spirit of his disciples against Jesus.

SUMMARY STATEMENTS (3:31-36)

3:31-36 seems to be the continuation of the Baptist's witness to Jesus. Some find a good transition from 3:30 to 3:31. Others argue that 3:31-36 contain the sayings of Jesus and therefore that it should be placed after 3:21. However, 3:31 does not give a relevant sequence to 3:21. Dodd regards 3:22-36 as an explanatory appendix to 3:1-21.[12] Since 3:31-36 recapitulates the words of Jesus and those of the Baptist (3:1-30), we may treat 3:31-36 as a summary placed by the Evangelist or an editor[13] fittingly at the end of the first phase of Jesus' ministry in Judea.

The greatness of Jesus is underlined again in 3:31-36. The close relationship between the Father, the Son, and the Holy Spirit in terms of their corporate function is also visible. The phrase "he who comes from above" indicates not only the heavenly origin of Jesus (3:31c; cf. 3:2), but also contrasts him with anyone who belongs to the earth. A dualism is presented between the nature of the one who is from above and of the one who is of earth (cf. 3:6; 8:23). Humans, who came out of dust, belong to this earth

---

10. Lindars 1992: 17.
11. Kruse 2008: 123.
12. Dodd 1958: 311; cf. Ridderbos 1997: 148.
13. Cf. Brown 1978: 1.159-60.

and therefore they speak and work seeking for earthly things. In contrast, Jesus, who comes from heaven, bears witness to heavenly things, which he has seen and heard from the Father (3:32a; cf. 6:46; 8:26b; 12:49).

The same idea is expressed in 3:34: "For he whom God has sent speaks the words of God." Jesus is the agent who was sent into the world by God. It is essentially the same as "he who comes from above." He could speak the words of God because God gives the Spirit to him without measure (3:34; cf. 1:32–33). Thus God the Father works together with the Son and the Holy Spirit to reveal himself to the world as true.[14] God, out of his love (17:23b-24), has given all things into Jesus' hand (3:35). "All things," entrusted to the Son, may imply God's own life (5:26), authority to judge (5:22, 27), authority over all humans to give eternal life (17:2), Jesus' followers (6:37; 17:6), the words to speak (12:49; 17:8), God's name (17:6, 11–12) and glory (17:22; cf. 1:14).[15]

Although the Son testifies to what he has seen and heard with the Father, no human receives Jesus' testimony (3:32). This means that no one among Jesus' opponents received his testimony to the one true God. But whoever believes sets the seal on the fact that God is true (3:33). The Greek word *sphragizein*, translated "to set the seal," when it is followed by "that" (*hoti*), means "to attest, certify, acknowledge,"[16] referring to an approval of a legal document by putting a seal on it (cf. Esth 8:8, 10). The one who accepts Jesus' testimony experiences God's love and life-giving power and consequently attests that God is indeed trustworthy.

The summary ends with a reference to heavenly life, which is available to those who believe in the Son, and to God's wrath, which remains on anyone who does not obey the Son (3:36). "Believing in the Son" and "obeying the Son" are parallel terms (see comments on 3:15–16). Similarly, "eternal life" or "life" is set against the eschatological wrath of God, which rests now upon those who do not accept and obey the Son. Both eternal life and the end-time wrath of God are spoken in the present tense ("has eternal life" and "rests upon"), implying that they are already in operation among human beings. At the same time, the future-tense "shall not see life" indicates that the one who does not obey now will not experience the future life with God (cf. 5:24; 8:51, 52). Such dualism urges human beings to choose life now by believing in the Son.

---

14. Gruenler 1986: 32–34.
15. Brown 1978: 1.162.
16. BDAG, 980.

JOHN 4
The Inclusive Nature of Jesus' Community

PROPER SETTING FOR THE DIALOGUE (4:1-6)

The Lord came to know that the Pharisees had heard that he was making and baptizing more disciples than John (4:1).[1] However, the narrator clarifies that Jesus himself did not baptize, but his disciples did (4:2). As there was a possibility for the Pharisees to kill him (cf. 7:1), Jesus left Judea to go again to Galilee (4:3).

It was necessary for Jesus to go through Samaria, the normal route for anyone to go to Galilee from Judea (4:4). Samaria is a region that lies in between Judea in the south and Galilee in the north.[2] Strict Jews hated Samaritans (cf. 4:9) and avoided going through Samaria to enter Galilee. The Greek word *edei* ("it was necessary") refers to the divine necessity for Jesus to pass through Samaria so that he could meet a Samaritan woman and bring salvation through her to many Samaritans. Thus, Jesus crossed the racial, religious, and geographical barriers to enter into Samaria and the gender barrier to have a dialogue with a woman. He went to Sychar, a city in Samaria, and sat beside a well, built up in the field that Jacob gave to his son Joseph (John 4:5-6; cf. Gen 33:19; 48:22; Josh 24:32).

After Pompey, the Roman general who captured Palestine (63 BCE), Sychar replaced Shechem as the most important Samaritan city.[3] Jacob had erected an altar, called El-Elohe-Israel ("God, the God of Israel"), in the land of Shechem (Gen 33:18-20) and he would have dug also a well (literally "a spring of water"). Out of tiredness and thirst, Jesus sat down to rest

---

1. Jesus is mentioned as "the Lord," a divine title, which John uses rarely for earthly Jesus and therefore later manuscripts changed this title to "Jesus."

2. The name Samaria is derived from Shemer, a city built by Omri, the king of Israel, after buying the hill from Shemer in about 870 BCE (1 Kgs 16:24). Eventually the city's name, Samaria, became the name of the region.

3. Köstenberger 2009: 146.

Proper Setting for the Dialogue

in about the "sixth hour" (12 noon) near the well, which was called "Jacob's Well" (4:6), probably by leaning on the wall built around the well. The indication of time is not only to highlight the historical reliability of Jesus' ministry in Samaria, but also the fact that it was a high day when living beings needed water to quench their thirst (cf. Gen 29:7). Jesus' weariness and thirst (4:7) prove his full humanity and his supernatural knowledge (4:1) proves his full divinity (cf. 1:47–48; 2:23–25).

Jesus' Self-Revelation to the Samaritan Woman (4:7–26)

A woman of Samaria came to draw water from the well. She came alone in the midday, when usually not many women come to the well. This shows that the woman had been isolated from other women because of her perversion from moral standard (cf. 4:16–18). Jesus takes the initiative to start his dialogue with her by asking for water (literally "Give me to drink"; 4:7). Truly Jesus needed water to quench his thirst, but at the same time it is ironic that the one who can supply living water to quench her thirst forever is the one who asks her for water to drink (4:14; cf. 19:28). At this point, John comments that Jesus' disciples had gone away into the city to buy food (4:8), providing to the dialogue a relevant setting.

As the woman found Jesus to be a Jew, she said with astonishment, "How do you, being a Jew, ask from me, a Samaritan woman, for a drink?" Then the editor clarifies that the Jews have no dealings with Samaritans (4:9). This indicates that there was hatred among the Jews against Samaritans, to the extent that they would not use the vessels used by the Samaritans for purity reasons.[4] The rabbis taught the Jews not to eat Samaritans' cooking or to have any ritual contact with them.

The Samaritans were the people consisting of five nations whom the Assyrians brought in when they captured Samaritan cities in the eighth century BCE. After a priest, at the command of the Assyrian king, came and lived in Bethel to teach them the law of Yahweh, the Samaritan religion became a mixture of the worship of Yahweh and of different gods brought in by the foreigners. Consequently, there was no fear or obedience to Yahweh and his commandments (2 Kgs 17:24–34, 41). The Jews, who returned from exile in 538 BCE, found the Samaritans political rebels

---

4. Although the Greek expression *ou syngkhrasthai* generally means "to have no dealings with," in this context 4:9 needs to be read as: "Jews do not use (vessels) together with Samaritans"; Daube 1950: 137–47, esp. 137–39, 144 (*m. Nid.* 4:1).

who had corrupted Jewish religion with unacceptable practices.[5] Obviously the Samaritans could not be fully regarded as Jews. The destruction of the Samaritan temple on Mount Gerizim by John Hyrcanus, the Hasmonean ruler, in 128 BCE deepened the hatred between the Jews and Samaritans. The Jews perhaps considered the Samaritans as demoniacs (8:48; cf. 7:20). Since the woman was well aware of such a political and religious background dividing the Samaritans from Jews, she got astonished at a Jewish man's request for water. Initially she, like Nicodemus, understood Jesus purely at human level.

Jesus turns her attention to heavenly things. He points out her non-understanding of the person who is asking for water and then discloses himself as the one who would have given her "living water" had she recognized him as the Christ and asked him (4:10). In the OT, God is described as the "fountain of living waters" from which his people would have received life had they not forsaken him (Jer 2:13; 17:13). The term "living waters" also denotes the life of the end-time, when God will be King over all the earth (Zech 14:8–9). This implies that the gift of God Jesus identifies as "living water" is eternal life, a life with God in heaven, and that it has a flowing nature.

In John "water" mostly symbolizes the Holy Spirit, who gives heavenly life as a present possession and also as future life with God to those who believe in Jesus (John 3:3, 5, 8; 7:37–39; cf. 19:34; 20:22; 1QS 4.21). The water Jesus gives is the life of the Holy Spirit, which, as a spring, wells up to eternal life (4:14), the eschatological life that is available even now. Jesus encourages the Samaritan woman to believe in him as the one who comes from God and as the fountain of living waters that gives heavenly life. Such life satisfies the one who receives it so that they have no further thirst. Even death cannot overcome this life (cf. 11:25b–26a).

The woman questioned the greatness of Jesus by asking where he could get the living water, as Jesus had nothing to draw water from and this well's depth could have been around a hundred feet?[6] Was he greater than "our father" Jacob, who gave this well and drank water out of this himself, his sons and his cattle? (4:11–12). Both questions are ironic in the sense that Jesus' power to give life and his greater status than that of Jacob are unknowingly confessed by a Samaritan woman. Jesus gives to the one who believes in him the rivers of living water (7:37–39), and he is greater than

---

5. Carson 1991: 216.
6. Köstenberger 2009: 147.

Abraham (8:53, 58) and logically than Jacob. The words "our father Jacob" show not only the common origin of Jews and Samaritans, but also the woman's knowledge of the Pentateuch.

The heart of the dialogue lies in 4:13–14: "Every one who drinks of this water will thirst again; but whoever drinks of the water that I shall give him will never thirst, but the water that I shall give him will become in him a spring of water welling up to eternal life." The water from Jacob's Well is physical and hence will quench thirst only temporarily. But the water given by Jesus, being the gift of the Holy Spirit, has a twofold function:

(i) It will permanently satisfy the thirst of anyone who drinks of that water, for it provides everlasting existence with God to the one who receives it (cf. Isa 49:10; Rev 7:16);

(ii) As the water given by Jesus has an outflowing nature (Isa 44:3–4), it will be a fountain of life within the one who receives it and will reach out others to lead them to "eternal life" (cf. Ps 1:3; Ezek 47:9–12).

On hearing these words, the woman progresses in her understanding of Jesus and addresses him as *kyrie* ("sir" or "master" or "teacher"; 4:15). However, she misunderstands him, thinking that he is referring to the earthly water that has magical power, and so she asks him for the water that will never make her thirsty (cf. 6:34). Jesus immediately asks her to go and bring her husband (4:16). Jesus' command means that receiving "living water," the gift of the Spirit, will not be possible for anyone who has affinity with the things of the flesh (cf. 3:5–6). Therefore Jesus expects those who ask for living water to acknowledge first their life attached with earthly things. Otherwise, they cannot understand the things of the Spirit. Jesus seeks to help the woman to acknowledge that her lifestyle is socially and morally unacceptable. The woman honestly accepts that she does not have a husband.

Jesus first appreciates her truthfulness, by stating, "You said well" (4:17), and then unveils her past life, saying that she had had five husbands and that the man she is living with now is not her husband. Jesus had foreknown the truth about the woman's perverted life and therefore he states, "You have said this truly" (4:18). Some argue that the woman might not have been an "immoral person," for she might have married five husbands who all died in succession, or she might have divorced her previous husbands, or they might have divorced her one by one. However, the woman's plain statement "I have no husband," while she had a man whom she could not call her husband, makes this conjecture unacceptable. The word "now *having*" is deliberate to indicate that she was not *living* with a legally married person. In conformity with the oriental view on morality, the Samaritans also must have considered frequent remarriages as dishonorable and illegitimate.[7] Jesus touched the core of her life because he wished to give eternal life to the marginalized woman and admit her into God's new community.

The woman took Jesus' disclosure of her private life positively and saw Jesus in a new light and said, "Sir, I perceive that you are a prophet" (4:19). She came to recognize Jesus as a prophet who had divine knowledge and words, for in Samaritan tradition prophecy was closely connected with the power to know what had happened in the past and what was still to come.[8]

The woman's initiation to discuss about worship on Mount Gerizim confirms her understanding of Jesus as a *taheb*, the "coming one," for the Samaritans believed that the *taheb* will come to restore true worship by purifying Mount Gerizim from all defilement caused by the Jews. For them, Mount Gerizim was the most holy of all mountains (cf. *Ant.* 18.4.1).[9] Her statement "*our* fathers worshipped on this mountain" (4:20) may imply the OT patriarchs and those who started worshipping on Mount Gerizim, where the Samaritans built the temple ca. 388 BCE (cf. Deut 11:29; 27:12–13). However, the Jews regarded Jerusalem as the holy site where one should worship (Deut 12:4–7, 21; 14:22–26; 1 Kgs 14:21; 2 Chr 12:13). The long-time conflict between Jews and Samaritans on the place of worship is visible in the woman's statement, "And you [i.e., the Jews] say that in Jerusalem is the place where one must worship" (4:20b).

In response, by politely calling her "O woman" (cf. 2:4; 19:26), Jesus invites her to believe him and his message (4:21a). Jesus calls her first to listen to his message and then mentions the importance of how and whom one should worship rather than where one should worship. The phrase "an hour is coming," in which "hour" is used without the definite article, means that this coming hour will see a change in the worship of God, with both Gerizim and Jerusalem losing significance after "the hour," the time set by God for Jesus to suffer, die, rise from the dead and finally to ascend to the Father.[10] Jesus' cross, which will bring a revival in worship, is anticipated here.

7. Schnackenburg 1980–84: 1.433.
8. Macdonald 1964: 206–7.
9. See also Keener 2005: 1.611.
10. Brown 1978: 1.517–18.

Jesus' Self-Revelation to the Samaritan Woman

Jesus' reveals that the object of worship is God the Father (4:21b). In the coming hour, after Jesus' death and resurrection, true worship will be offered to the Father in "spirit and truth" (4:23–24). The Samaritans worshipped Yahweh alongside foreign gods, and never as the Father with whom believers can relate as children. As God is spirit (4:24), he cannot be limited to any building or place. Jesus challenges that the Samaritans (plural "you") do not experience an intimacy with God as Father, whereas the believing Jews ("we") experience an intimate relationship with God by the salvation they received in Jesus (4:22). By the neuter "what we know" (4:22), Jesus means the believers' intimate relationship with God as Father. Salvation came to all human beings in Jesus, a Jew, born in the tribe of Judah and in the line of David (*T. Dan* 5:10; *T. Naph.* 8:2; *T. Gad* 8:1). In this sense, salvation is from the Jews (cf. Ps 76:1; Isa 2:3; Rom 9:4–5). Thus, Jesus links worship with God's work in Israel's history, especially with the incarnation of Christ. The place of worship has no significance, but it is the worshippers' personal relationship with the Father that matters.

Jesus explains the manner of worship by using the word "an hour" that is coming and by adding the phrase "and now is" (4:23). He means that the opportune time to worship God, expected to happen at the end-time, has already come by virtue of his death, resurrection, and ascension. The eschatological worship can now be offered only in the church, God's new community, which knows God as Father. This community is constituted by "true worshippers" who will worship the Father in "spirit and truth." God is looking for such people as those who worship him. The word "spirit" denotes not the human spirit,[11] but the Holy Spirit, and this is clear from the phrase "God is spirit" (4:24). The believing community is a worshipping community that is comprised of members who are born of the Spirit, and their new birth enables them to rise above the earthly level and worship God with right attitude.[12] The God who is spirit can be seen and worshipped only in the spiritual realm. The word "truth" is knit together with "spirit" by a single preposition, "in." The OT concept of truth denotes God's faithfulness to his covenant relationship, and in John it was revealed in Jesus (1:14). Thus, true worship happens when the worshipper lives in the spiritual realm and accepts the faithfulness of God to his covenant revealed in Jesus.

---

11. *Contra* Collins 1995: 118–21.
12. Cf. Brown 1978: 1.180; Schnackenburg 1980–84: 1.437.

The woman, who had believed in the coming Messiah, now speaks of the Messiah, who will come and declare everything related to the temple and worship (4:25). The Samaritans believed that the coming Messiah, the *taheb*, as the spokesman for God, would reveal the truth by declaring the divine will.[13] As Jesus was declaring the things connected with worship, the belief dawned within her that Jesus could perhaps be that Messiah. As Jesus perceived her inner mind and also foreknew that his dialogue with her was reaching its culmination, he eventually revealed himself to her as the Messiah by saying, "I, I am, the one who is speaking to you" (4:26).

In John the word "I am," used by Jesus for himself, indicates that he is the Christ, the revelation of the one God who is "I am that I am" (Exod 3:13–14). The prophet Isaiah uses this name to affirm both the uniqueness of Yahweh in relation to all other gods of Babylon and his relationship with his people as their God (Isa 41:4; 42:8; 43:10, 11, 13, 15, 25). By saying, "I am he," Jesus expresses his uniqueness in comparison with other deities of the Samaritans, as the Messiah in whom the only God revealed himself. Jesus, the bearer of God's presence, is the place where one can worship God. Jesus, as the new Temple, replaces the Jewish temple in Jerusalem and also the Samaritan temple on Mount Gerizim.[14] Although the woman's perception of Jesus attains its climax now, at first she had only a tentative belief in his messiahship.

JESUS' INJUNCTION ON HIS DISCIPLES' MISSION (4:27–38)

While Jesus was revealing his identity as the Christ, his disciples came back to him with food. When they saw their teacher talking alone with a woman, they were astonished, but no one had the courage to question Jesus about why he was conversing with a Samaritan woman or what his needs were (4:27). Jewish custom prohibited rabbis from talking with women, even with their own wives, in public places (*m. Nid.* 4:1). At this time the woman dramatically goes away from the scene. In her extreme enthusiasm of having met with the Messiah, she forgot all about the earthly water and left her water jar at the well to go to her people in the city (4:28). She went away to call her people to come and see whether or not the man who supernaturally disclosed her life history could be the Messiah (4:29).

---

13. Macdonald 1964: 204–5, 364–65.

14. Kanagaraj 2005: 152. For the first time in the Gospel Jesus reveals himself by the name of God, "I am (he)," to a woman, a Samaritan hated by the Jews.

Jesus' Injunction on His Disciples' Mission

The woman's encounter with Christ gave her courage to invite others to come to Jesus. In Greek her question, "Can this be the Christ?," begins with a negative particle *mēti*, expecting the answer "no." However, this particle, in 4:29, "puts a suggestion in the most tentative and hesitating way."[15] Before she believes in Jesus fully along with other Samaritans (4:42), she wanted them to ensure whether Jesus could be the long-awaited Christ. The fact that many of them came to believe in Jesus through the woman's word of testimony (4:39) shows that her faith in Jesus was genuine.

While the Samaritans were coming to Jesus (4:30), the disciples were persuading him to eat the food they had brought (4:31). Just like Jesus did not drink the earthly water from the woman, so also he did not eat the earthly food. In conformity with the non-understanding of Nicodemus and of the Samaritan, his disciples too did not understand the spiritual truth in Jesus' statement, "I have food to eat of which you do not know" (4:32). They understood it at the human level and therefore questioned among themselves, "Did anyone bring him food to eat?" (4:33). John's literary pattern where Jesus makes a *statement*, which is *misunderstood*, prompting him to *speak further* for clarification, becomes visible again.[16] Jesus now clarifies by saying, "My food is that I may do the will of him who sent me and may accomplish his work" (4:34). His source of life was in the accomplishment of the Father's work.

The sending of the Son by the Father into the world is a familiar theme in John. The Father sent his Son (cf. 3:17, 34; 6:38; 7:18; 9:4). That is, the Son was sent from heaven (6:38) to save the world. However, John particularizes Jesus' suffering and death on the cross as the means by which he accomplished the work of the Father (cf. 5:36; 17:4; 19:28, 30). Just like food nourishes all living beings, so also accomplishing his Father's plan of salvation gives nourishment to Jesus (cf. Deut 8:3).

Jesus now unveils to his disciples the present possibility for them to fulfill God's mission of bringing many into God's new society (4:35; cf. 20:21). He does this by reminding them of a common saying that there are yet four months for the harvest to come (4:35a).[17] Normally it took four months from the end of sowing to the beginning of harvest.[18] However, in

---

15. Moulton 1906: 193.

16. Neyrey 2007: 78, 90; cf. de Jonge 1970–71: 337–59; Carson 1982: 59–91.

17. The question in the form "Do you not say . . . ?" expects the answer "yes." The term "you" denotes generally the society to which his disciples belong.

18. Barrett 1978: 241.

John 4:27–38

the case of God's mission, the opportunity to liberate people from bondage and to bring them into the new community is already present. The metaphorical saying of Jesus, "Lift up your eyes and see the fields that they are already white for harvest" (4:35b), is to give awareness to his followers of the existing opportunity for ministry. The "fields" may indicate the people and "being white for harvest" metaphorically implies their readiness to receive Jesus' words and believe in him. The word "harvest" denotes the currently available season to involve oneself in Christ's work of compassion (Matt 9:36–38; Luke 10:2). The "harvest" time also indicates the time of judgment given to the evildoers at the end-time (Matt 13:24–30, 36–43; Mark 4:26–29). The salvation in Jesus contains in itself also condemnation for those who do not believe in him. Jesus calls his followers to participate in the harvest.

The eschatological element in the "harvest" is confirmed by Jesus' statement that the one who is involved in the harvest faithfully will receive in future the reward of heavenly life, which is also a present experience (John 4:36; cf. Rev 22:12; John 3:14–15). Two ideas become visible: First, the task of reaping is nothing but gathering fruit of what has already been sown, as per the proverbial saying, "One sows and another reaps" (4:37). Secondly, God's mission includes a prior sowing. The people who believe and join God's new community by the collective labor of the sower and reaper are the "fruit" of the harvest. Jesus sends the members of his society to reap that which they did not sow, but "others" have done the sowing already (4:38).

The mission entrusted by Jesus to his followers involves teamwork, which, at the gathering of fruit, brings joy for all involved. Who does Jesus mean by the "others" who have labored? The reaping of Jesus' followers will be the result of Jesus' accomplishment of the Father's work on the cross. The church's mission ultimately flows from the Father who sent Jesus on a mission of saving the world. The church's mission now is the continuation of Jesus' mission (17:18; 20:21). The ministry of the OT prophets and kings and the preparatory work of John the Baptist all led up to the redemptive work of Jesus. Thus, the seed sown for the harvest to be done by the church is Jesus' labor, accomplished with the authority of the Father. Both the Father and the Son are thus involved in the redemptive work. If so, "others" in 4:38 refers to the labor of sowing already done by the Father and the Son together, who have left the harvest to the members of God's new

Jesus' Injunction on His Disciples' Mission

community.[19] The Samaritan woman who brings her people to Jesus is one of the harvesters and not one of those who labored for the harvest.

INCLUSION OF SAMARITANS INTO GOD'S NEW COMMUNITY (4:39–42)

The Samaritan woman's faith in Jesus as the Messiah, though with some hesitation, and her word of testimony were so powerful that they led many Samaritans to the initial faith in Jesus prior to their meeting with him (4:39)! Jesus accepted people of fickle faith in the beginning stage so that he might reveal himself to them more clearly (see 1:46; 3:9; 4:33; 7:41–42; 11:39; 18:33).

The woman proclaimed Jesus' supernatural knowledge of what all she had done and how she had lived. Such prophetic utterance, according to Samaritan belief, cannot come from any other person than the coming *taheb* who will declare everything. So they immediately came to him and asked him to stay with them. Jesus broke the enmity between Jews and Samaritans by staying with them for two days (4:40), which would have been scandalous for a Jew. The Evangelist's comment that many more believed because of his word (4:41) shows that Jesus, during his two-day stay, had dialogue with the Samaritans on things related to human salvation. Jesus' words convinced many in Sychar that he was the Messiah who came from heaven to save the whole world.

The Samaritans' faith was fully founded on Jesus' words of salvation and not any more on the woman's word of testimony. This implies that Jesus sowed the seed within the Samaritan woman by revealing himself as the long-awaited Messiah, and the woman's testimony made the harvest. In this sense, she may be identified as an apostle. The Samaritans publicly confessed, "we have heard for ourselves, and we know that this man is indeed the Savior of the world" (4:42). In the first century, Hellenistic gods such as Zeus and Asclepius, as well as the gods Isis and Serapis of the mystery religions, were called saviors. The same title was ascribed to the Roman emperors from Nero to Hadrian.[20] But Christians were exalting Jesus as the Savior of the world long before John was written (Luke 1:47; 2:11; Acts 5:31; 13:23; Phil 3:20; 1 Tim 1:1; 2:3; 4:10; 2 Tim 1:10; Titus 2:10, 13). The

---

19. Cf. Whitacre 1999: 112.
20. Keener 2005: 1.627–8; Kanagaraj 2005: 159.

Samaritans' confession of Jesus as the Savior of the world, then, would have provoked the adherents of other religions and the Roman government.

By appreciating Jesus as the one who delivers people from their evil deeds, the woman, along with her fellow citizens, entered into Jesus' new community because of the hard labor of Jesus done without food and drink. *John shows that the new covenant community of Jesus includes Jews, non-Jews, and half-Jews like Samaritans; it is a multiethnic community!*

Entry of a Roman official's family into God's community (4:43–54)

Jesus set his journey to Galilee after two fruitful days in Samaria (4:43). Jesus' departure from Samaria to Galilee is described as a situation that fits the proverb, "A prophet does not have honor in his own hometown" (4:44). Jesus had good response in Sychar of Samaria. Similarly, the Galileans welcomed him when he came to Galilee (4:45). Where was he dishonored? Which country does Jesus refer to as his "own hometown"? In the Synoptic Gospels, the same proverb is used in connection with the unbelief Jesus faced in Nazareth in Galilee, where he was brought up and which is regarded as his hometown (Matt 13:57 par.). The reason for Jesus going to Galilee was that he had no honor in his own hometown (the Greek particle *oun*, "therefore," is used in 4:45).

Some scholars argue that the Greek word used is *patris*, meaning "fatherland," which, for John, is Judea. If so, 4:44 should be read in combination with 4:1–3. But the word *patris* is used in the Synoptic Gospels to indicate Nazareth as Jesus' hometown. We may probably solve the puzzle by observing the geographical location of Nazareth. In first-century Palestine, Nazareth was situated in the southern part of Galilee ("lower Galilee"), where there were descendants of Judean settlers a century earlier.[21] Nazareth almost lies on the road that links south and north. When Jesus traveled to Cana of Galilee (cf. 4:46) from Samaria, going through Nazareth would have been the normal route. But Jesus avoided his "hometown" because of their unbelief and rejection of him and went to upper Galilee, where people welcomed him enthusiastically, as they had seen Jesus' signs performed in Jerusalem. There is an invisible reference, then, to Nazareth in 4:44.

Jesus visited again Cana of Galilee, where he had turned water into wine earlier (4:46). A royal official (*basilikos*) came up from Capernaum

---

21. Dunn 2003: 297.

to meet Jesus at Cana and asked him to come down to heal his son who was about to die due to fever (4:47, 52). The reference to the official's servants (4:51) shows that this man was a government official who was serving Herod Antipas (4 BCE–39 CE), a tetrarch known as "king" (Matt 14:9; Mark 6:14–22).

John records that Jesus had come from Judea to Galilee (4:47, 54), overlooking his journey to Samaria. Due to the deep hatred between Samaritans and Jews, Jesus' successful ministry in Samaria could have been kept secret. Whether the official was a Jew or Gentile is not clear in the text. The similarity of this story with the story of healing of a Gentile centurion's servant (Matt 8:5–13; Luke 7:1–10) gives the clue that the royal official in 4:46–54 might have been a Gentile,[22] for there were many types of royal administrative officials in Capernaum, as it was a commercial town.[23]

Jesus rebuked him by saying, "Unless you see signs and wonders you will never believe" (4:48). Thus Jesus discourages "believing" by merely "seeing" signs. Both "you see" and "you will never believe" are in plural form and thus the official is seen as the representative of Roman officials, rather than the whole of the Galileans,[24] who would always like to see signs from Jesus. Some argue that the mild rebuke is reminiscent of his rebuke directed to the Jewish authorities for asking for a sign (Matt 16:4 par.) and therefore that the officer must be a Galilean Jew.[25] However, the rebuke to the Jews is sharper than the rebuke to the official in John. In the Synoptic Gospels, Jesus did not perform a sign on their request, whereas in John Jesus did heal the official's son. Perhaps Jesus rebuked him in order to bring him to true faith (cf. Matt 15:21–28 par.). The official persistently invited Jesus to come down to Capernaum before his child dies (4:49).[26] He appealed to Jesus humbly, by addressing him as "sir" (*kyrie*; cf. 4:15, 19), with the belief that if only Jesus came and touched, his dying son would receive life. However, unexpectedly Jesus commanded him, "Go, your son lives" (4:50). Jesus' words have power to give life even from a distance, just like God's word brought life (Gen 1).

---

22. Barrett 1978: 247.
23. Brown 1978: 1.190.
24. Kruse 2008: 145; Lincoln 2006: 185.
25. E.g., Karris 1990: 57–65.
26. The word "come down" implies that Capernaum was in the lower of part of Galilee, about two hundred meters below sea level, whereas Cana was situated on a plateau.

On hearing the good news that his son lives, the official believes it and goes down to Capernaum. "Believing" Jesus' *word* is a mark of genuine faith in John. The man did not see immediately that his son was living, but he gave full credence to Jesus' word. Without seeing, he believed (cf. Heb 11:1; 2 Cor 5:7; Rom 8:24-25), unlike Nathanael and Thomas (1:50; 20:29), and thus he became a model of a true disciple of Jesus. Jesus' word that the child is alive came out of his mouth in the "seventh hour" (1:00 p.m.; 4:52-53). The distance from Capernaum to Cana is sixteen miles by the shorter road.[27] As per the Jewish calculation of time, the day ends at 6:00 p.m. and the official was still journeying, perhaps in a cart. As the official was on the way, his servants met him to tell him that his son was living (4:51). Out of pleasant surprise, the officer inquired with curiosity[28] of the hour at which he got better, and they said, "Yesterday at the seventh hour the fever left him" (4:52).

The father of the child realized that his son was healed at the same hour when Jesus told him, "Your son lives" (4:53). The coherence of time convinced the official of the supernatural power of Jesus' word and also of the fact that God was in Jesus. That the officer did not think of Jesus as a "divine man" or a "wonder worker," but as the manifestation of God, is known from the faith he exercised along with his household. The healing power of Jesus led a Gentile officer, along with his family, into Jesus' newly founded community. The sign endorses the truth that the Gentiles too have a role to play in Jesus' community.

John numbers this healing as the second sign that Jesus did, after he came to Galilee from Judea (4:54). John's counting of signs does not mean that he used what is called a "signs source," but it means that Jesus' first phase of ministry in Galilee started with a miracle in Cana and ends with another miracle performed in the same place.

Fusing the Horizons

Several churches are functioning today exclusively for the people of their own region or culture or caste or class or denomination. They do not accept believers who come to their churches from other culture or caste than theirs into full

---

27. Brown (1978: 1.191) calculates the distance as twenty miles.

28. The same Greek verb *pynthanesthai* ("to inquire") in 13:24 carries a sense of curiosity and a strong desire to know some piece of information; Köstenberger 2009: 171.

membership. Sometimes, by their cold attitude shown to visitors, they convey the message that their respective churches belong to them only. In some churches, those who do not belong to their community are allowed to worship with them, but they do not get full membership in the church. This means that the non-members cannot be part of any decision-making body. Moreover, they are not given the right to vote in church elections. Some churches that are dominated by one particular caste treat Christians from other castes only as sources of income to the church without giving them equal participation in worship, church work, and employment.

The main reason for such cold treatment is the fear of the dominating community that its members may lose membership in church councils and thus their identity. One caste prevents the other caste group from superseding it by using their spiritual gifts and skills in the ministry of the church. Fear of oppression and humiliation often grips the new covenant community to the extent that they do not include people from other cultures or ethnic groups. Thus social, political, and communal factors drive the body of Christ into insecurity and exclusivism. They practice discrimination without a global vision to perceive the inclusive nature of God's new community.

The exclusive attitude of the Christian community has been overcome in the past by the firm action taken by pastors and other Christian leaders. They built up good rapport with the majority group and then taught them to include other sheep into the fold. Many churches today arrange for a picnic or excursion or retreat or recreation or Bible study for all the parishioners so that people from one community may intimately relate with people from another. The leaders may keep the church focused on the mission of bringing others into Jesus' community to promote the spirit of love and unity, just like Jesus kept the Samaritan woman involved in bringing her people to him and exhorted his disciples to reap the harvest at the present time. It is the collective and active participation in the outflowing ministry of the church that will make both the sower and the reaper rejoice together and accept each other.

By recording Jesus' positive attitude to the Jews and to the outcasts, John conveys that the church, as a multiethnic community, should accept all sections of people without any discrimination and encourage them to use their gifts and talents for building the church up (cf. Eph 3:3–6).

JOHN 5
Self-Defense of Jesus before His Accusers

John 5 falls within the unit of chapters 5–10, which contains Jesus' three signs and the events that took place during four different feasts of the Jews.

HOLISTIC HEALING GIVEN TO A SICK (5:1–18)

"After this" introduces Jesus' movement from one place to another, not necessarily in chronological order (5:1; cf. 6:1; 7:1). Jesus goes up to Jerusalem for "a feast of the Jews" (5:1). It is puzzling why John did not specify the feast in 5:1, as he does in 6:4; 7:2; and 10:22. Guilding argues that the feast in 5:1 is the feast of the new year.[1] This is probable, for if it meant instead the feast of Tabernacles, John would have mentioned it, as he does in chapter 7. Whatever the name of the feast is, the focus of the story falls on the observance of the Sabbath and Jesus' reinterpretation of the observance by his sign done in Jerusalem.

John introduces a pool called *Bēthzatha* in Hebrew.[2] The Aramaic name *Bēthesdā* ("house of mercy") is attested by the second best manuscript and is also relevant to our context.[3] It was situated at the Sheep Gate in Jerusalem (5:2). Although the Greek version reads "at the sheep," the context necessitates us to understand it not as "Sheep Pool" but as "Sheep Gate," located in the northern part of Jerusalem (Neh 3:1, 32; 12:39). Archaeological excavation shows that there were two large pools at the northeast of the temple, built ca. 200 BCE, and other smaller pools in which people could bathe. These two pools had a central partition, which could have been the central portico, and the other four porticoes may denote two on either side of the double pool.[4] Thus, there were five porticoes in which numerous

---

1. Guilding 1960: 69–91; cf. Neyrey 2007: 102 n. 133; Fenton 1970: 67.
2. Some ancient manuscripts read *Bēthesda* and others *Bēthsaida*.
3. Köstenberger 2009: 178, 195; cf. Brown 1978: 1.206–7.
4. Lincoln 2006: 193.

invalids such as the blind, lame, and paralyzed used to lie (5:3), because people believed that the water in the double pool had healing power.[5]

Some ancient authorities insert verse 4 after 5:3 to read: ". . . waiting for the moving of the water, 4 for an angel went down at a certain season into the pool, and troubled the water; whosoever then first after the troubling of the water stepped in was made whole of whatsoever disease he had." This addition reflects a popular belief at that time and the scribes inserted it to explain 5:7.

There was a man who had been ill for thirty-eight years without having anyone to put him first into the pool before another sick person stepped down into the water ahead of him when it was stirred (5:5, 7). It implies that he was a paralytic or lame and was unable to walk or run. Jesus, who visited the pool on the Sabbath, supernaturally knew that this particular man had been lying there for a long time. He went to the man and asked him, "Do you want to become well?" (5:6b). Jesus' question shows that he does not do anything against human will. Probably the man got the idea that Jesus would heal him. Therefore he unreservedly told Jesus that there is no one to put him in the pool when the water is troubled and that while he is going another invalid person steps down into it before him. On hearing this Jesus told him, "Rise, take up your pallet and walk" (5:8). Immediately the man became well. He took up his pallet and walked (5:9). This incident reveals that Jesus can change any circumstances for human welfare. John deliberately mentions that that day was the Sabbath (5:9b; cf. 9:14).

His purpose in healing the man on the Sabbath is twofold: first, to fulfill the meaning of Sabbath law as to bring freedom to those who are in physical and social bondage (cf. Deut 5:15); second, by foreknowing the conflict that will arise with the Jewish authorities, Jesus wished to prove his oneness with the Father in work and to initiate the process of going to the cross. After his healing, "the Jews" raised their objection and persecuted Jesus for having worked on the Sabbath (5:16). They even planned to kill him (5:18). This would enable the Son to accomplish God's redemptive purpose to which the Law points.[6]

"The Jews," instead of rejoicing over the man who was healed, showed resentment, by quoting the Law, which does not permit anyone to take up the pallet on the Sabbath (5:10). The OT warns that working on the Sabbath

---

5. At the time of Hadrian (early second century CE), the location of the pools was considered a healing sanctuary dedicated to Asclepius or Serapis; Lincoln 2006: 193.

6. For Jesus' reinterpretation of Sabbath ethics, see Kanagaraj 2001: 33–60.

day, including collecting sticks and bearing a burden out of one's house, is liable to the death penalty (Exod 31:14–15; Num 15:32–36; Jer 17:21–22; cf. Neh 13:15–22). The concern of the OT is that people should not be engaged in selfish acts on the Sabbath, but should fulfill God's will. However, this meaning of Sabbath was twisted by the rabbis in strict legal terms in their oral law. They prohibited on the Sabbath the work of carrying a load from one domain into another (*m. Šabb.* 7:2; 10:1–5; 11:1–2). Here is a reference to the onerous nomism of Jewish leaders, who were supposed to seek the welfare of the people. Jesus fulfills the inner meaning of the Law by giving freely the divine life (Lev 18:5), which the Law could not give due to human failure to fulfill the Law (cf. Rom 7). Jesus' healing on the Sabbath exemplifies the truth that God, by sending his own Son, did what the Law could not do to enable people to fulfill the Law (Rom 8:3–4).

The healed man understood Jesus only as a respectable person and hence he addressed him as "sir" or "master." He did not know him as the Son of God who has the power to give life even to the dead (5:19, 21). When the authorities accused the man for having broken the Law, he did not testify to the marvelous way in which he was made well. Instead, the narrative style of John turns to the identity of Jesus—a key feature in John's Gospel! The man testified unknowingly to Jesus by saying, "He who made me well, that man said to me, 'Take up your pallet and walk'" (5:11). When the authorities enquired him who it was who said so (5:12), the man answered that he did not know who it was (5:13a; cf. 9:24–27), because Jesus remained withdrawn from the festival crowd (5:13b). John's narrative technique of presenting non-understanding in order to make a person understand the identity of Jesus becomes visible. By withdrawing himself, Jesus avoided not only popularity, but especially his arrest and death before the "hour" of the Father.

Jesus later found the man in the temple (5:14a). The healed man, who became a part of God's new society, went to the temple probably to give thanks to God and celebrate the feast with others whom he had probably not seen for years. Jesus revealed himself in the temple as the one who healed him, not only by reminding him of his total healing but also by warning him not to sin any more lest worse thing happens to him (5:14b),[7] for anyone who sins after receiving God's gift of healing and salvation

---

7. Not every sickness is due to human sin, but in this man's case probably his long-term illness was connected with his sin.

becomes liable to severe punishment and his guilt remains (cf. 9:41). Thus, Jesus offered the man not only physical healing, but also spiritual welfare.

The man's proclamation of Jesus to "the Jews" (5:15) is often interpreted as an act of betrayal[8] or as his decision to remain in the old world by joining the enemies of Jesus.[9] However, the man could have gone to "the Jews" out of his reverence for them and also out of his excitement of having found out the healer. He testified to the love and power of Jesus before the authorities. Otherwise, Jesus' holistic healing and the healed man's participation in temple worship would be meaningless.

Since Jesus did such signs on the Sabbath, "the Jews" continued persecuting him (5:16). Each sign Jesus did was taking him towards the cross through the resultant conflict between him and the authorities. When "the Jews" raised the issue of having healed on the Sabbath, Jesus answered, "My Father is working until now, and I also am working" (5:17). This is the first reference in John's Gospel for Jesus' oneness with the Father in work. True, God rested from all his work of creation (Gen 2:2–3), but this does not mean that he stopped his work of sustaining his creatures (cf. Ps 121:4, 7–8). Referring to the Sabbath, Philo denies that God ever ceased his creative activity (*Leg.* 1.5–6; *Cher.* 87–90). The rabbis believed that because God fills heaven and earth (Jer 23:24) he can do as he wills in the world without breaking the Sabbath law. God is working to give life to people and therefore Jesus, who shares in God's life, cannot stop working to give life to the sick and suffering.

Jesus had addressed God earlier as "my Father" (2:16). He now addresses him again as "my Father," which, for devout Jews, is a blasphemy, for it makes him to be the Son of God and Messiah,[10] claiming thus equality with God. Such a blasphemy deserved the death penalty (19:7). Jesus' work on the Sabbath and his claim to be God's Son kindled the anger of "the Jews" and they sought to kill him (5:17–18). John gives the first reference to Jesus' death by the hands of "the Jews."

THE SON'S AUTHORITY TO GIVE LIFE AND TO JUDGE (5:19–30)

The word "therefore" (*oun* in Greek) in 5:19 links 5:19–47 with 5:17–18. Jesus' defense begins in 5:19 with the "truly, truly, I say to you" formula.

---

8. Jones 1997: 131–32.
9. Ridderbos 1997: 190.
10. Blomberg 2001: 111.

John 5:19–30

He affirms the unchangeable truth that he, as the Son of God, cannot do anything by himself except what he sees the Father doing. Here is a picture of an apprentice who copies what his master does.[11] Although it appears to be a fitting image, Jesus, unlike an apprentice, works always in unity with the Father in such a way that their works cannot be separated from one another (cf. 5:17; see 1:3 and 8:16 for the corporate work of both Father and Son). Within this unity lies the Son's subordination to and dependence on the Father. The Son does not only the Father's work of healing, but also that of judging (5:22, 30). The Son's act of giving life and rendering judgment is done now (5:21–22, 24) and will also be exercised at the end-time (5:25–29).

The energy behind Jesus' acts is the Father's love for the Son and his demonstration of all his works to him (5:20). Out of his eternal love (17:24), God will show greater works through Jesus than what Jesus had hitherto performed so that those who see them may marvel. These works are: raising the dead at the voice of the Son, and giving them life both now and in future (5:21–29). Not mere works, but the very life of the Son is drawn from God (5:26) and therefore he could raise the dead by his voice and give them life as per his will (5:21, 25). 5:21–24 refers to two kinds of life possible for human beings: receiving divine life that is eternal, or undergoing condemnation under the wrath of God. Anyone who hears Jesus' message of salvation and believes the Father, who sent Jesus, has already passed from the realm of natural life, which leads to eternal death, to the divine realm of life, which leads to eternal life (5:24; cf. 3:16–21). God expects them to hear and obey his words spoken through Jesus and this is how can one observe the Sabbath (cf. Ezek 20:11, 13).

Both giving life and rendering judgment are the whole prerogatives of God. His purpose in entrusting those works to Jesus is that human beings may honor the Son just as they honor the Father. Anyone who does not honor the Son does not honor the Father who sent him from heaven (5:22–23), because they are one. "Honoring" means worshipping and obeying. Jesus speaks these words to "the Jews" who worship Yahweh as the only God, but reject the one sent by him. Therefore 5:23a has plural subject with the present tense, meaning "as they are honoring the Father." It is impossible to worship the one true God without worshipping and obeying Jesus.

The dual idea of giving life and rendering judgment is repeated in 5:25–29 as eschatological. All those who are in tombs will rise up from

---

11. Dodd 1968: 30–40.

the dead to be judged at "an hour" of the Father (5:25, 28). The criterion to judge all human beings is "the hour" of Jesus' death on the cross, which gives choice to people either to accept or reject him. Thus, "an hour" denotes the effects of "the hour" (cf. 2:4). The Son's judgment has both present and future implications, with an emphasis on future life after death (5:25). "Do not marvel at this" (5:28; cf. 3:7) means that mere emotional amazement cannot lead to eternal life.

In an hour of final resurrection at the voice of the Son of God, those who did good works will inherit divine life and those who did evil will face God's eternal punishment (John 5:28–29; cf. Dan 12:2; Rom 2:6–11). The term "works" does not mean works of the Law, but works of faith in the crucified Son of Man. The Son will judge with the authority given to him by the Father (5:30; 8:16), because he is the Son of Man (5:27). The Son of God is identified here with the Son of Man (cf. 3:14–16; for the Son of Man as eschatological judge see Matt 25:31–46; *1 En.* 37–71; *T. Abr.* 11–13; *4 Ezra* 11–13). As the Son of Man, Jesus represents both humanity and God (Dan 7:9–27) and salvation comes to humanity through the same Son of Man by his death on the cross. Since salvation is inseparable from judgment, the Son of Man becomes also the agent of God's judgment.

The Johannine Jesus, who is dependent on the Father, cannot do anything on his own initiative and he judges as he hears from the Father (5:30a). His will to act flows from the Father who sent him (5:21, 30b) and therefore his judgment is right.

Four Witnesses to Jesus who Judges the "Judges" (5:31–47)

The Jewish Law demands two or three witnesses to prove any claim of a crime as true (Deut 19:15; cf. Matt 18:16). Jesus is accused by the authorities that he unlawfully works on the Sabbath and that he makes himself equal to God (5:18). But they, who should prove the charges by witnesses, fail to do so. Now, ironically, the accused puts forward four witnesses against his accusers.

By denying that he bears witness to himself, the Son follows the principle that one's self-witness cannot be accepted as reliable (5:31; cf. 8:13). There is "another," which denotes the Father (cf. 5:37), who bears witness to Jesus. Since God is true (John 17:3; 1 John 5:20; Rev 3:7), his witness to Jesus is trustworthy (5:32; cf. 8:18).

John 5:31–47

1. John the Baptist is the first witness to Jesus' rank and status. "You sent to John," recalls the delegation of priests and Levites sent to the Baptist by Jewish authorities (1:19–28). The Baptist categorically denied that he was the Christ and bore witness to the pre-existent Christ. For him, Jesus' rank and status are far greater and earlier than his. Jesus sums up the Baptist's witness as to the "truth" (5:33), referring to his valid message that Jesus is the Christ, the Son of God[12] (cf. 1:7–8, 15, 29–36; 3:26–30). However, Jesus cautions his adversaries that he never received the testimony from a human (cf. Gal 1:11–12), but that he only reminds them of the Baptist's witness so that they may be saved (5:34). He also affirms that the Baptist was a "burning and shining lamp" in whose light, however, they were rejoicing for "an hour," i.e., for a time as short as an hour (5:35). The Baptist was "an ordinary portable lamp" who gave light by his witness to the Light. That the Baptist was a lamp may be the fulfillment of Ps 132:17b. "The Jews" believed temporarily that he was the long-awaited Christ and hence they were in "exuberant joy." However, their joy quickly faded away after they understood that he was not the Christ.

2. Jesus' own works given to him by the Father to accomplish testify that the Father has sent Jesus (5:36). That is, the authority to heal the sick flows from God and it cannot be bound by mere legal observance of the Sabbath. Jesus' "works" are doubly emphasized and God's purpose in granting those works is to finish doing them (cf. 4:34; 17:4). The plural "works" implies all forms of Jesus' signs, which eventually led him to the greatest sign of dying on the cross to save humanity. In this sense, the witness of Jesus' works is greater than that of the Baptist.

3. Jesus discloses that "there is another" who bears witness to him (5:32) as "the Father who sent me" (5:37) and himself as the one whom the Father sent (5:38). "Sending" hints at the pre-existence of the Son with the Father and at their mutual knowing due to eternal relationship with one another (7:29; 10:15). Since the Son is from the Father, he alone can reveal the unknowable God to human beings (1:18; 6:46).[13] Otherwise they can never see God, just as the people of Israel, who never heard God's voice (Deut 5:24–26) nor saw his form (Exod 20:19, 22; Deut 4:15, 33, 36). Moreover, "sending" expresses the Son's

---

12. Barrett 1978: 264.
13. Haenchen 1962–63: 210; Beasley-Murray 1991: 16–17.

equality with the Father.[14] Therefore the Father bears witness to the Son and attests the signs performed by him on the Sabbath. Jesus accuses his accusers that in spite of all these, they did not believe in the one sent by the Father and therefore that his words were not abiding in them (5:38).

4. The Jewish scriptures, according to Jesus, bear witness to him. The plural "scriptures" indicates various writings in the OT and primarily the five books of the Law (cf. 5:46–47). The Jewish authorities searched the scriptures, as they believed that they have eternal life in them (5:39). The verb "to search" (the scriptures) is a technical term used in first-century Judaism for the study and exposition of the Law (e.g., 1QS 5.11). The Jews believed that the study and interpretation of the scriptures would lead them to the life in the world to come (*Gen Rab.* 1:19). Nevertheless, they have missed out, perhaps due to their legal reading, "the hermeneutical key provided by God's present revelation" in Jesus.[15] Since the whole of the OT testifies to Jesus (5:46), eternal life is in him. They would receive life if they would come to him, but they were not willing to do so (5:40).

From this point onwards, Jesus accuses his opponents for their selfishness and false belief in Moses. In contrast to them, Jesus does not seek to be honored by human beings (5:41), because God has already granted him the honor that he deserves to receive from humans (5:23). Because of their selfish ambition for glory from one another, they do not seek the glory that comes from the only God (John 5:44; cf. Rom 2:29; 2 Cor 10:18; 1 Thess 2:4). "The only God" would remind the authorities of the Jewish faith in one God whose honor alone matters. Jesus categorically states that it is difficult for them to believe in the one sent by the Father if they seek to receive honor from one another. In fact, "the Jews" do not really love God and hence they do not believe Jesus, who has come from the Father with his authority (5:42–43a). Jesus hypothetically says that if any false prophet who speaks in his own name or falsely in the name of the Lord (cf. Jer 23:25; 29:9, 25, 31; Deut 18:20) comes to them, they will accept him, for both the Jewish leaders and false prophets seek their own honor and gain

---

14. The halakic principle says, "An agent is like the one who sent him," in the sense that both are one in will and work (cf. Ashton 1991: 314). However, there is no essential oneness in this principle as we have it in Jesus, God's agent (cf. 12:44–45).

15. Lincoln 2006: 207.

(5:43b). If they do not believe in Jesus, consequently they will fall prey to lying prophets.[16]

Jesus warns his opponents of the forthcoming judgment in which, not Jesus, but Moses himself, in whom they have set their hope, will accuse them of their unbelief in the one sent by their own God (5:45). "Moses" symbolizes here the Law given through him (1:17) and written by him (5:47). In fact, what Moses wrote was a prophecy of the coming of Christ and in this sense, Moses wrote of Jesus (5:46). If they had really believed in the Law that points to Jesus, then they would have accepted him as the Messiah and believed in his words. "His [i.e., Moses'] writings" represents the whole OT, which bears witness to Jesus (5:39). Jesus defends himself that his words are foreshadowed in the OT writings. In Jesus' attack on his accusers as those who are blind to their own Law, the table is turned: the accused becomes the accuser and the judges are judged in this trial-like scene.[17]

---

16. Cf. Schnackenburg 1980–84: 2.128.
17. Lincoln 2006: 205, 208; Neyrey 2007: 115.

JOHN 6
Two Signs and a Discourse

FEEDING OF THE MULTITUDE (JOHN 6:1–15)

The "feeding of the multitude" appears in all four Gospels. According to Matthew and Mark, after the feeding, the disciples crossed to the other side, to the *land* at Gennesaret (Matt 14:34; Mark 6:53) that lies on the western shore south of Capernaum, although Jesus instructed them to go to Bethsaida (Mark 6:45) on the northeastern shore of the Sea of Galilee. In Luke the feeding took place at Bethsaida (Luke 9:10–17). John too indicates the same location, for after the feeding the disciples cross the sea to go to Capernaum on the northwest coast (John 6:17, 24). The Gospel accounts, when put together, show that the feeding miracle happened in the hilly country northeast of Bethsaida and that the disciples rowed back to Capernaum, which was near the land of Gennesaret, with Bethsaida en route.[1]

The phrase "after this" (6:1) links two events allowing room for intervening occurrences.[2] Therefore there is no need to read John 6 after John 4, as some scholars propose.[3] Even if we rearrange the chapters, there is no smooth transition between Jesus' healing in Cana and the scene at the Sea of Galilee. Jesus went across the Sea of Galilee, that is, of Tiberias (Luke 5:1; *J.W.* 3.10.7 identifies it as the "sea of Gennesaret"). The name of the city, Tiberias, which was founded by Herod Antipas (ca. 20 CE) on the southwest side of the Sea of Galilee and named after the emperor Tiberius (14–37 CE), came to be used for the Sea of Galilee. Jesus crossed the sea to go to a mountain situated perhaps near Bethsaida, the hometown of Philip and Andrew (1:44), both of whom had active roles in the feeding miracle (6:5, 8–9). Jesus sat down upon the mountain along with his disciples

---

1. Blomberg 2001: 121 n. 154; McRay 2003: 168–69.
2. Ridderbos 1997: 183.
3. E.g., Bernard 1985: 2.xvi–xix; Bultmann 1971: 203–37; Schnackenburg 1980–84: 2.4–9.

John 6:1-15

(6:3), depicting the Jewish custom of pupils sitting around their teacher for learning.

A crowd of Galilean peasants and fishermen who had seen Jesus healing the sick followed him and reached the place where they were sitting (6:2). "The Passover, the feast of the Jews, was at hand" (6:4) means that the Jewish Passover had almost arrived. Usually Jesus went up to Jerusalem at Passover (2:13; 12:1, 12; 13:1). However, in this year Jesus seems to have remained in Galilee.

"Lifting up his eyes" (6:5a) is a Jewish gesture of prayer (11:41; 17:1). Here it marks Jesus' compassion for the needy (cf. Mark 6:34). His "seeing" of a multitude coming to him implies both his physical sight and his deeper perception of their need for food. Before the crowd reached him, Jesus foreknew how miraculously he would feed them (6:6b)! That is why he asked Philip, to test him, "From where shall we buy bread so that they may eat?" (6:5b). While in the Synoptic Gospels the disciples bring to Jesus the need for food (Matt 14:15 par.), in John Jesus takes the initiative to give food. Jesus' testing of Philip reflects a teacher who would test his pupils to deepen their understanding of truth. Philip was astonished by Jesus' question, because they did not have enough money to feed the multitude. In his estimate, the total cost would be more than two hundred denarii (i.e., two hundred days' wages for a laborer) to give even a little amount of food to each person (6:7). In the process of feeding, Jesus showed his disciples that they are partners in his mission.

Andrew, Simon Peter's brother, found out a little boy who had five barley loaves and two fish[4] and introduced him to Jesus, raising doubt, however, over its sufficiency to feed such a large crowd (6:8-9). A "barley loaf" was a cheap bread used by poorer classes (*Spec.* 3.57). It has an allusion to Elisha's miracle of feeding a hundred men with barley loaves (2 Kgs 4:42-44). The Jews expected that miracles like those of Elisha would happen in the messianic time.[5] If so, John's deliberate use of "barley loaves" indicates that the messianic time had dawned in Jesus.

Responding to Andrew's doubt, Jesus instructed the disciples to make the crowd sit down and they did so (John 6:10; cf. 2:7). John specifies that there was "much grass" (cf. Matt 14:19; Mark 6:39), implying that the feeding took place during the spring. He also specifies the number of men who

---

4. The used Greek word *opsarion* means "preserved fish" (BDAG, 746), especially "pickled fish" (Barrett 1978: 275).

5. Nicol 1972: 89-90.

ate as five thousand (cf. Matt 14:21 par.) to show the intensity of Jesus' sign. Before distributing, Jesus took the loaves and gave thanks, obviously to God, and similarly the fish (John 6:11; Matt 14:19 par.). John focuses on Jesus as the host at the meal who distributed the loaves and fish to the people, unlike the Synoptic Gospels, in which Jesus delegates the responsibility of distribution to the disciples (Matt 14:19 par.).[6]

Since Jesus took the bread and gave thanks before distribution in the Last Supper also (Matt 26:27 par.; 1 Cor 11:24-25), some find eucharistic echoes in John's account of feeding.[7] However, the Jews always used to give thanks to God before eating and the host would distribute the bread. "Giving thanks" for the gift of food is a symbolic act of giving it into the hands of God before distribution. The Eucharist would be observed privately with his twelve disciples and not in public. The event in John only shows that Jesus fed the hungry, and that the abundance of Jesus' supply is beyond human comprehension (6:7, 9).

The people ate as much as they wanted and were satisfied (6:12). Jesus' instruction, after this, to the disciples to gather the fragments left over (cf. Ruth 2:14) so that nothing may be lost shows that he wishes his followers, as per the Jewish custom,[8] to use the food left over responsibly. The gathered fragments of five barley loaves filled twelve baskets (6:13). The precise numbers shows how Jesus can multiply a little thing given in his hands and meet the needs of many. The twelve baskets could be an allusion to the twelve tribes of Israel, which constitute the people of God, leading on to Jesus' twelve disciples, who constitute the core of the new people of God (6:67, 70, 71).[9]

By seeing the sign, people understood Jesus as "truly the prophet who is coming into the world" (6:14; cf. 4:19; 7:40, 52). "The prophet" promised by Moses may refer to the Messiah (Deut 18:15-19; cf. 4QTest 5-8; 1QS 9.11). However, in John, the title "prophet" alone does not identify Jesus as the Messiah. Wherever the term "prophet" occurs, it is superseded by such titles as "Christ," "Son of Man" and "Son of God" (4:25-26; 6:32-58; 7:40-43; 9:35-38).[10] But the phrase, "[the prophet] who is coming into the world" has a messianic connotation (John 11:27; 12:13; cf. Matt 11:3).

6. Cf. Lincoln 2006: 213; Kruse 2008: 163.
7. Brown 1978: 1.247; Guilding 1960: 58-61.
8. Köstenberger 2007: 444.
9. Carson 1991: 271; Lincoln 2006: 213; Köstenberger 2007: 444.
10. de Jonge 1977: 50-66.

John 6:1-15

John combines in 6:14-15 both the "one who is coming" (the Messiah) and "king" (cf. 1:45, 49; 12:13, 15). The crowd confessed Jesus to be the prophet who is coming into the world and wanted to *make* him king, a political figure, without knowing that he *is* already the messianic King. He knew that in their excitement of having eaten their fill, people sought to seize and make him king (6:15). Since his kingship is not of this world (18:36), he withdrew himself to go back to the mountain by himself, probably to pray (Matt 14:23; Mark 6:46). Thus, the messianic secret is displayed in John differently from Mark (see comments on 1:41-45; 7:3-9; 10:24-25).

JESUS WALKING ON THE SEA (6:16-21)

John records the fifth sign in 6:16-21, in which Jesus reveals God's glory in terms of his power to save his disciples from danger by exercising his unique authority over nature. This is the only sign in John that Jesus performed exclusively for the twelve disciples. John seems to follow here a tradition independent of his knowledge of the Synoptic accounts.

After Jesus went to the mountain, the disciples might have been waiting for him until evening, as the comment "Jesus had not *yet* come to them" (6:17) shows. In the evening they decided to row back on the Sea to Capernaum without Jesus (6:16-17; cf. Matt 14:23; Mark 6:47). Josephus gives the breadth of the Sea of Gennesaret as 40 furlongs and its length as 140 (*J.W.* 3.10.7). Although the average breadth was about five miles, from the mountainside south of Bethdaida they might have had to row at least one mile longer. As they were rowing towards Capernaum via Bethsaida, the sun set and it became dark. The Sea of Galilee was often subject to strong winds blowing east, which caused waves to rise up, making it tough to row west (6:18).[11] They had rowed about three or four miles (6:19a), almost to the middle of the sea, where human help was impossible.

Being surrounded by darkness (a temporal reference without symbolic meaning), the disciples became desperate. In this situation, they saw Jesus "walking on the sea and drawing near to the boat" (6:19b). By translating the Greek phrase *epi tēs thalassēs* as "by the sea," Weiss argues that the disciples actually saw Jesus walking along the shore rather than on the sea and that due to darkness they mistook themselves to be in the middle of the sea, while actually they were nearly at the other side.[12] However, the

---

11. Kruse 2008: 165; McRay 2003: 169.
12. Cited by Bultmann 1971: 215 n. 6.

Jesus Walking on the Sea

Greek phrase literally means "*on* the sea" (Job 9:8; John 1:51; Rev 10:5), and Weiss' interpretation fails to explain why, then, Jesus was walking to come nearer to the boat, which was "in the midst of the sea" (Mark 6:47, Greek version). The same phrase is translated as "at the seashore" or "by the Sea of Tiberias" (RSV, ESV) in 21:1, because the disciples were already at the shore and Jesus was standing, not walking, "on the beach" (21:4).

When they saw Jesus walking on the sea, the disciples were frightened. Jesus told them not to be frightened (6:20b). This recalls appearances of God in which the witnesses are so fearful that God had to tell them not to fear (Gen 15:1; 26:24; Judg 6:22–23; Isa 41:10; 43:1; cf. Matt 14:26–27; Luke 1:12–13; 2:9–10; Rev 1:17). God's appearance in Jesus is confirmed by his use of the word "I, I am," the name of the Lord (cf. 4:26). Jesus bears the name of God (17:6) and reveals himself as the very presence of God when his followers are at the point of death (cf. Isa 41:4; 42:6, 8; 43:10, 25; 45:18; 46:4; 51:10–15). Jesus' walking on the sea portrays him as God, the creator (Job 9:8; cf. 38:16), the wisdom of God (Sir 24:5–6), and the Savior (Ps 77:19; Isa 43:16).[13] The scene thus presents itself as a divine epiphany, centered on the expression "I am."[14]

The whole event is performed by Jesus at the Passover (6:4). One of the scripture readings at the Passover was Isa 51:6–16,[15] which refers to God's deliverance of his people by making a way through the sea. The same God makes a way on the sea to deliver Jesus' disciples from danger. Thus, the true meaning of the Passover is fulfilled in Jesus. The sign thus was not mere demonstration of Jesus' authority over nature, but more the revelation of God in Jesus by the name "I am" (Isa 51:12 LXX) and his deliverance.

After seeing Jesus and hearing his comforting words, the disciples "were willing to take him into the boat" (6:21). Immediately, the boat was at the land to which they were going. Some scholars interpret that the boat reached its destination without human effort soon after Jesus got into the boat. If so, it is a "miracle within a miracle."[16] However, the Greek *eutheōs* ("immediately") does not have any miraculous connotation. It only implies that the boat reached the other shore "straightway,"[17] unhindered by the stormy wind and rising waves.

---

13. Lincoln 2006: 218.
14. Brown 1978: 1.254.
15. Guilding 1960: 278.
16. Barrett 1978: 281; Schnackenburg 1980–84: 2.27; Carson 1991: 276.
17. Abbott 1906: 19–22.

John 6:22–59

Jesus' Self-Revelation as the Life-Giving Bread (6:22–59)

Arrival of the people to Capernaum (6:22–25a)

The crowd fed by Jesus was eagerly looking for him. As there were no boats to take them to the other side of the sea, they stayed that night in the place where they had eaten. "On the next day" (6:22), being the day after Jesus walked on the sea, the crowd realized that there was on the shore only one boat, used by Jesus and his disciples. They had also seen Jesus' disciples going to Capernaum on that boat without Jesus and they could not see Jesus either (6:24). On that day some boats came from Tiberias to the place where the people had eaten (6:23). John reiterates that Jesus gave thanks to God before the bread was supplied, reminding the readers of God's work of feeding the hungry in Jesus. They boarded the boats sailing to Capernaum, on the other side of the sea (6:24), and found him there (6:25a).

Jesus' encounter with the crowd (6:25b–34)

After the people found Jesus, they asked him, "Rabbi, when did you come here?" without knowing that he walked on the sea and crossed (6:25b). By means of the "truly, truly, I say to you" formula, Jesus expresses the most reliable truth (6:26) and chides them for seeking him only because they ate their fill. Loaves and fish cannot satisfy human hunger permanently and so the people wanted more. They could not see Jesus' glory and believe in him (6:29, 30, 36). Jesus exhorts them, therefore, not to spend their energy by working for the food that perishes, but to work for the food that gives eternal life (6:27a). The point of this dualism is that the food that leads to eternal life should be primarily sought, although earthly food is needed for human livelihood.

The divine life that Jesus, the Son of Man, gives has both present and future value (cf. 3:14–15; 5:27–29), because "on him God the Father set his seal" (6:27b). God has delegated his authority exclusively to Jesus to give heavenly life to all who believe in him (cf. 3:33; 5:21, 24, 27). He gave his Spirit to Jesus as the stamp of his approval and ownership on Jesus (cf. 2 Cor 1:22; Eph 1:13), not necessarily at Jesus' baptism,[18] but even in his pre-existent state, for the Greek aorist tense "set [his seal]" means God's once-and-for-all action.

---

18. *Contra* Köstenberger 2009: 207.

Jesus' Self-Revelation as the Life-Giving Bread

The people now raise another question: "What shall we to do the works of God?" (6:28). Jesus responds that the work of God is nothing but to believe in him whom God sent (6:29). People thought that they can earn eternal life by good works (cf. Matt 19:16), perhaps works of the Law.[19] But Jesus exhorted them just to believe in him. By using the singular "work," Jesus brings all good works under the umbrella of believing in him. "Believing" is the positive response of humans to Jesus, and good works spring out of that response. That God sent Jesus is a recurring theme in John (see comments on 3:17; 4:34; 5:37–38).

The people raise their third question in two forms: What sign, then, can you do, that we might see and believe you? And what work can you perform (6:30; cf. 2:18)? The same crowd that was fed with five loaves and two fish challenges Jesus to do another sign to lead them to faith! This means that they expected Jesus to keep on giving them food miraculously (cf. 6:34). In support of their desire, they quote the OT and boast of their forefathers who ate manna in the wilderness given from heaven (6:31). It is actually an indirect question: "Can you do for us again what Moses did, that we may believe you?" Some think that the OT quotation is closer to Ps 78:24.[20] However, it seems to be a combination of words found in several OT passages (Exod 16:4, 15; Neh 9:15; Ps 78:23–24; 105:40).

The people's reference to "the bread from heaven to eat" (Exod 16:4, 14–15) becomes the key for Jesus to unlock the meaning of the manna given in the wilderness. He responds with the phrase "Truly, truly, I say to you" to introduce the reliable heavenly truth. At first, he refutes their understanding that it was Moses who gave them bread from heaven.[21] Then he assures them that "my Father" gives them *now* the *true* bread from heaven (6:32). Unlike the manna, which satisfied the people's physical hunger only temporarily, Jesus says that this *authentic* bread, which also comes down from heaven, gives life *now* to the world at large (6:33). The *true* bread which God gives now is Jesus (cf. 6:35), who came down from heaven to give divine life to all humans (cf. 3:13–16; 5:24–26, 29; 6:27). Jesus' saying in 6:32–33 may also indicate the present fulfillment in him of the Jewish

---

19. Beasley-Murray 1987: 91.

20. Borgen 1968: 41; Daly-Denton 2000: 5–9, 131–44.

21. Jesus uses the plural "you" as recipients of the heavenly manna, because, as per Jewish belief, the present generation is in solidarity with their forefathers physically.

expectation that the Messiah, the second Redeemer, would give manna just like Moses, the first redeemer, did.[22]

The people who earlier questioned Jesus' credibility to give bread from heaven now beseech him, "Lord, always give us this bread" (6:34; cf. 4:15). The question-answer format used in 6:25-34 is another use of John's literary technique of non-understanding to project his Christology. The crowd is led from its earthly understanding of "bread" to know Jesus as the life-giving bread from heaven.

Jesus' discourse on the living bread (6:35-59)

Jesus' heavenly origin (6:35-51)

6:35-51 has the first "I am" saying with a predicate in John (6:35, 41, 48, 51). The reference to Jesus having come down from heaven/God occurs seven times.

To the people's request to give them the bread of life, Jesus emphatically says, "I am the bread of life" (6:35; cf. 6:48, 51; see comments on 4:26 and 6:20 on the "I am" saying). "I am" basically means the self-revelation of God in Jesus, denoting God's eternal existence. The predicate indicates, in addition, God's communication with human beings. God communicates himself in Jesus as life-giving food, the food that endures to eternal life (6:27). People expected Jesus to supply them bread from heaven for their livelihood. But Jesus' affirmation "I am the bread of life" discloses that the bread of God has already come down in human form to manifest God's love for humanity and give them divine life. What was expected to come at the end of the age (Dan 12:2) is available now in Jesus!

"The one who comes to me" and "the one who believes in me" (6:35) are parallels that interpret each other. The expressions "shall never hunger" and "shall never thirst" convey the same idea: those who come to Jesus and believe in him will have complete satisfaction in life without being dominated by worldly desires or worries. This idea recalls God's invitation to come to him to eat and drink without money (Isa 55:1-2) and that of Wisdom to come to her to eat and drink so that people may walk with insight (Prov 9:1-6). Jesus, the Wisdom of God, calls people to come to him by faith so that they may have life in abundance (10:10b) without further need for hunger or thirst for earthly things (cf. Sir 24:12). Thus, Jesus reveals and

---

22. Barrett 1978: 288-89; Kruse 2008: 169.

Jesus' Self-Revelation as the Life-Giving Bread

fulfills the role of God. However, he admonishes his audience by saying, "You have seen me, but do not believe" (6:36). They should have perceived Jesus as God's self-revelation in his signs, but they failed to see due to their affinity with earthly things. Even after they saw the sign of feeding the multitude, they did not believe and receive him. Their unbelief is reflected in their murmuring and disputing among themselves (6:41, 42, 52).

All whom the Father has given to the Son will come to him and the Son will not cast them out (6:37; cf. 6:39; 10:29; 17:2, 6; 18:9), because what the Father does he also does (5:17, 19–21). Jesus highlights the Father's initiative to bring people to him (cf. 6:44, 65). Does it mean that God has predestined some to be given to Jesus and others not to? 6:37 shows not so much God's predestination as the co-operation between the Father and the Son: God takes the initiative to enable people to believe in and come to Jesus and the Son fully accepts them. God, who has a universal vision (3:16–17), cannot be selective in admitting them into his community. It is the hearers who should decide on God's offer of eternal life in Jesus.

Such initiative act of God also proves that the Son has come down from heaven to do the will of the Father rather than his own will (6:38; cf. 4:34; 5:30). The will of the Father is that not even one person whom God gave to Jesus should perish eternally, but that Jesus should raise them up at the last day (6:39; cf. 5:28–29). The neuter singular "it" ("raise it up") refers to the *community* of those who believed in Jesus by the work of God within them. "The last day" indicates the time of final judgment of God, when he will render to people according to their deeds (John 12:48; cf. 5:28–29; Rom 2:6–11; "the day of Yahweh" in Amos 5:18–20; "that day" in Isa 2:11, 17, 20; *1 En.* 45:3–6). The statement "everyone whom he has given to me" (6:39) is interpreted in 6:40 as "everyone who sees the Son and believes in him," and "that I may lose nothing of all that he has given me" is interpreted as "that the one (who is raised up) may have eternal life." Those who perceive God's glory in the Son and believe in him will enjoy life with God and Jesus will raise them up at the end-time.

The Galilean Jews became indignant on Jesus' assertion of his heavenly origin and therefore murmured at him (6:41). They, who eagerly went to Capernaum to see Jesus, are now called "the Jews." In their murmuring, which shows their unbelief in Jesus and rejection of his teaching, they resemble the Jewish authorities. They reflect the same character of their forefathers in the wilderness who became rebellious and murmured against Moses (Exod 16:2, 7–12; cf. Exod 15:24; 17:3; Num 11:1; 14:2, 27). This

John 6:35–59

shows ironically that *"our fathers,"* who ate manna in the wilderness (6:31), are indeed their fathers in showing unbelief and grumbling.

They understood Jesus and his coming into the world in earthly terms, for they questioned among themselves, "Is not this Jesus the son of Joseph, whose father and mother we know? How does he now say, 'I have come down from heaven'?" (6:42; cf. Matt 13:55–57a par.). The claim of having come down from heaven implies Jesus' pre-existence with God and hence his oneness with the Father. "The Jews" are offended at this claim and show thus their unbelief in the virginal conception of Jesus.

Knowing their murmuring, Jesus admonishes them not to murmur among themselves (6:43). He reiterates in 6:44 what he spoke in 6:39–40 and thereby confirms his pre-existence in heaven whence he came down. Jesus speaks of the magnetic power of God to draw people to him, by saying, "No one can come to me unless the Father who sent me draws him" (6:44; cf. 6:65). The rabbis used the word "to draw" or "to bring nigh" to speak of bringing a person to the Law for conversion (*m. 'Abot* 1:12), making them sharers in the knowledge of God.[23] John uses the same word to refer to God drawing people to Jesus, in whom they can fulfill the Law and share in the knowledge of God. The correlation between God's everlasting love and his power to draw people unto himself is found in Jer 38:3 LXX (31:3 in English).[24] The work of drawing people unto Jesus belongs to the Father who sent Jesus. God works in oneness with the Son. In fact, the word "drawing" people to Jesus looks forward to the cross (12:32), and also to the future resurrection of those who are thus drawn (cf. 6:39–40). The task of raising the dead to life is the sole prerogative of God (cf. 5:21), and it is given to the Son.

Although the Father draws people to Jesus, human beings have the responsibility to come to Jesus by hearing and learning from the Father (6:45). This is in accordance with what is written in the prophets. The plural "the prophets" occurs only here in John, while he cites the writing of only one prophet, Isa 54:13, perhaps as an example. John changes the particularity found in Isa 54:13 MT ("All your sons shall be taught by the Lord") and LXX ("And I shall make your sons to be taught by God") into universality by using the indefinite plural in 6:45. What was applicable to the people of Israel is now made applicable to every one. The idea that all shall be taught by God in the scriptures is related to the new covenant, for one of the marks

---

23. Brown 1978: 1.271; Köstenberger 2009: 213.
24. Kanagaraj 2005: 212.

of the new covenant is that God will put his Law within the hearts of his people so that they may know the Lord without having to be taught by others (Jer 31:33–34; cf. Ps 78:1–8) but by the Lord (Isa 54:7, 13). These prophecies are fulfilled in Jesus (cf. 5:39, 46), especially in his exaltation on the cross, when the Father will draw all, taught by God, to Jesus. Those who are thus drawn to Jesus constitute the new covenant community.

Jesus reiterates that he is from God and claims that no one has seen the Father except the one who is from God. He makes an absolute claim, "he has seen the Father" (6:46), in which the subject "he" is put in an emphatic position in Greek (cf. 1:18; 3:32). While "[he] who is from God" implies Jesus' pre-existence with God, the statement "he has seen the Father" implies his intimate and eternal relationship with the Father. Therefore Jesus could solemnly affirm that anyone who receives him by faith has eternal life, the life of communion with God, even in this age (6:47). By categorically stating, "I am the bread of life" (6:48), Jesus presents himself as the revelation of the life-giving God (cf. 6:33, 35).

Jesus counteracts to the boastful statement of "the Jews," "Our fathers ate manna in the wilderness" (6:31), by stating that all their fathers who ate manna died (6:49). By saying "*your* fathers," Jesus distances himself from the unbelieving Jews who sought Jesus for earthly food alone. The manna satisfied the physical hunger of Israelites, but they all died without enjoying the needed life with God. Similarly, the loaves supplied by Jesus satisfied the Galileans' physical hunger, but they could not believe him and experience eternal life.

In contrast to the bread eaten in the wilderness, Jesus is "the bread that comes down from heaven." He connects his heavenly origin with the human response of "eating" lest those who eat it are overcome by death (6:50). For the first time the word "eating" is introduced (cf. 6:51), anticipating its link with "drinking." If anyone eats of the bread from heaven, that person will have heavenly life without undergoing the eternal punishment of death both now and in future (cf. 3:16; 6:27, 35, 40). "Eating" metaphorically means "coming" to Jesus and "believing" in him (6:35).[25]

The content of 6:48, 50 is interpreted in 6:51 with the addition of "and the bread that I shall give for the life of the world is my flesh." John uses the adjectival participle to identify Jesus as "the living bread." His "coming down from heaven" means his eternal existence in heaven with God and his entry into the world in human flesh, as the word "my flesh," used first time

---

25. Neyrey (2007: 127) comments that "eating" means believing and consuming food.

in this section, shows. The conditional clause, "If anyone eats of this bread, that person will live for ever," means that the one who eats of the bread from heaven is not bound by death (6:50), but will have the end-time life forever (6:51). Jesus defines the bread as his flesh, which he will give for the life of the world. This statement links 6:36-51 with 6:52-59 and looks forward to the cross, where Jesus will give himself as a sacrifice to conquer death and make divine life available for the "world," i.e., for all people. The word "flesh" is used perhaps to combat Docetism, a belief that the Logos only appeared to be a man, by counter-arguing that Jesus was fully and really a human being (John 1:14; 1 John 4:2). Thus, Jesus redefines the Passover in terms of himself as the Passover lamb whose flesh will be sacrificed on the cross for the life of whole humanity.

The necessity to eat his flesh and drink his blood (6:52-59)

"The Jews" again took offence at Jesus' identification of his flesh with the bread that is to be eaten. Therefore they disputed among themselves by questioning, "How can this fellow give us his flesh to eat?" (6:52). This question arose due to their partial understanding of what Jesus actually meant. They picked up the phrase "(eating) of my flesh" but ignored that his flesh will be given "for the life of the world." On hearing their dispute, Jesus reiterates his statement by adding two important themes: the title "Son of Man" and "drink his blood." He solemnly affirms the heavenly truth by his "truly, truly, I say to you" phrase that "unless you eat the flesh of the Son of Man and drink his blood, you have no life in you" (6:53). In 6:54 "Son of Man" is replaced with the first-person personal pronoun "my" and the promise "I will raise him up at the last day" is added. Eating blood, in which is the life of the flesh, is strictly prohibited in the Law (Lev 17:10-12) and therefore the Jews got offended.

Eating Jesus' flesh and drinking his blood have often been interpreted as denoting the Eucharist.[26] Lincoln thinks that the "Words of Institution" from the Synoptic Gospels of the Last Supper have influenced the formation in 6:53.[27] But in 6:53-58 Jesus answers that he will offer his whole person, flesh and blood, in death on the cross so that those who eat and drink will have divine life within themselves.[28] Eating his flesh and drinking his

26. E.g., Fenton 1970: 84; Bultmann 1971:234-37; Brown 1978: 1.284-85, 292.
27. Lincoln 2006: 232.
28. Cf. Dunn 1970-71: 331. John does not seem to replace faith with partaking of

Jesus' Self-Revelation as the Life-Giving Bread

blood symbolize the response of human beings for Jesus' giving himself on the cross in terms of coming to him to satisfy their hunger and believing in him to quench their thirst (cf. 6:35). They signify "the believing appropriation—by the mouth of faith—of Jesus' self-offering in death."[29] Though the terms cannot be interpreted in terms of eating and drinking in the Eucharist, Christians in the late first century possibly understood the significance of the Eucharist by reading 6:53–58.[30]

The title "the Son of Man" is mainly used to denote Jesus' glorification on the cross (cf. 3:14; 8:28; 12:23, 32–34), and in 6:53 also it indicates Jesus' self-sacrifice on the cross, which leads those who eat his flesh and drink his blood to partake in his life. The present tense "has eternal life" and the future "I will raise him up at the last day" are put together in 6:54 to convey the idea that believing in Jesus as the bread of life leads the believer to possess eternal life now (6:47; 3:36; 5:24) and to participate in the future life of resurrection even after physical death (cf. 5:29). The adverb "truly" (6:55) shows that Jesus' flesh as food and blood as drink are authentic, since they belong to the heavenly sphere.[31]

Those who absorb the life of the Son of Man by faith abide in him and he in them in the sense that they mutually dwell within one another (6:56). This means that the believers absorb Jesus' life by being knit together with him by faith and bear fruit for the glory of the Father (15:1–11). Both the Father and the Son are in one another (14:10–11) and so the one who is united with Jesus actually abides in the Father through Jesus.[32] Thus, mutual union with Jesus enables one to receive God's life even now (cf. the present tense "abides"). This union becomes possible by the Holy Spirit, an idea implied in 6:56 (cf. 6:63). The interrelation between believers, Jesus, and God through the Spirit is a life-sharing relationship (6:57) without the notion of deification. Those who come into union with Jesus will live because of him, as the Son lives by sharing in the Father's life (5:21, 26).

In 6:58 Jesus sums up his discourse by referring back to the people's indirect question in 6:31. He reveals himself again as the bread that came down from heaven so that those who eat of it may live forever even after

---

sacraments; Blomberg 2001: 126–27.

29. Ridderbos 1997: 242. The different Greek word used in 6:54 for "eating" does not affect the meaning.

30. Beasley-Murray 1987: 95; Carson 1991: 296.

31. Fenton 1970: 85.

32. Kanagaraj 1998a: 264.

their physical death, unlike the bread eaten by their forefathers, who died without enjoying eternal life. John concludes the discourse by stating that Jesus taught these things in the synagogue at Capernaum (6:59; cf. 1:28; 8:20).

JESUS' DIALOGUE WITH HIS DISCIPLES (6:60–71)

Many of Jesus' disciples did not accept his discourse due to their non-understanding. They murmured by saying, "This is a hard saying; who can hear it?" (6:60–61). The hard and offensive saying, for them, was Jesus' heavenly origin and his teaching on eating his flesh and drinking his blood, for eating human flesh and drinking blood were both forbidden in the Law. Their question was how the things legally forbidden could lead one to eternal life. They did not understand the significance of Jesus' incarnation (i.e., his coming down from heaven) and of the need to come to and believe in the Word-become-flesh who was sacrificed on the cross (i.e., eating his flesh and drinking his blood), if they were to enjoy his life.[33] Their conclusion was that no one could accept such teachings. Jesus, by his supernatural knowledge, knew of their grumbling at his teaching and asked them, "Do you take offense at this?" (6:61).

If they take offense at his teaching on his coming down from heaven and the need for humans to eat his flesh and drink his blood, they would be even more be offended if they were to see the Son of Man ascending to the place of his origin (6:62). Jesus thus reaffirms his heavenly origin and assures that he will ascend to heaven, the place where he was before, through his death and resurrection (cf. 20:17). As his ascension will exhibit a greater glory than his incarnation and death did, they will not believe his ascension to the Father's glory either (cf. 17:5). For Jesus the mystery of his incarnation and manifestation of his glory on the cross can be comprehended only in the Spirit (cf. John 4:14; 20:22; Gen 2:7).

The term "flesh" in 6:63 means the fallen human nature in whose control people are living. Flesh is of no avail for understanding Jesus' words, for his words spoken are "spirit and life" (6:63b). The whole discourse hangs on 6:63, which speaks of Jesus' words as of the Spirit who gives life (cf. Ezek 37:1–14; Ps 104:29–30). What is true of "eating his flesh and drinking his blood," which leads to eternal life, is also true with the Spirit's activity in human lives!

33. Dunn 1970–71: 331, 333.

Jesus' Dialogue with His Disciples

However, Jesus says that some of them do not believe (6:64) and hence they take offense at spiritual things. The expression "some of you" refers to "many of his disciples" (6:60, 66) as well as the disciple among the Twelve who will betray Jesus. He foreknew "from the beginning" (i.e., from the beginning of Jesus' ministry and his choosing of the disciples[34]) those who would not believe and the one who would betray him. Jesus' foreknowledge of the people proves that he came from heaven, where he was with the Father. The readers will know later that Judas Iscariot is the one who would betray him (cf. 6:70–71; 13:2, 21–30). The reference to Judas' betrayal shows that Jesus' journey to the cross has already begun.

As some of the hearers, including "his disciples," did not actually believe in Jesus and his words, but took offense at them, Jesus reminds them of the initiative of the Father in drawing believers unto him (6:37, 44, 45). Surprisingly, many of his disciples did not accept Jesus' sayings, and this proves that no one can come to him unless the enabling power of God is granted to them (6:65).

All the disciples who did not receive Jesus' words turned back and would no longer walk with him (6:66). Unbelief leads eventually to losing communion with Jesus and to denying that the Son of God came in the flesh (1 John 2:19, 22; 4:2–3; 2 John 7). With great concern, Jesus asks the twelve disciples whether they also wish to depart (6:67).[35] On behalf of the disciples, Simon Peter confirms their allegiance to their Master by answering, "Lord, to whom shall we go?" Though it is a question, it is actually a statement that there is no one whom they can follow except Jesus, not because he performs signs, but because he has the words that give eternal life (6:68). A faith anchored in Jesus as Lord and in his words leads the believer to have divine life.

In their encounter with Jesus, Peter and his fellow disciples came to the knowledge and acceptance that Jesus is the "Holy One of God" (6:69). The confession that Jesus is the "Holy One of God" is unique to John. The title makes Jesus equal to the Lord God, who is the "Holy One of Israel" and who chose the people of Israel to fulfill his purpose on earth (Isa 43:14; 47:4; 49:7; 54:5). Jesus, similarly, chose a new people of God to fulfill God's purpose of redeeming the world and therefore he is the "Holy One of God" (6:69–70). The Greek word for "holy" means consecrated or separated for

---

34. Ridderbos 1997: 248.

35. It seems the term "the Twelve" (6:67, 70, 71) became, by the time John was written, a standard title for the inner circles of Jesus' disciples, including Judas Iscariot.

the service of God (cf. Lev 21:6–8, 15; 22:9; 2 Chr 23:6; 35:3). Jesus was set apart to fulfill God's mission in the world. In this sense, Jesus is the "Holy One of God," the Christ.

Jesus had foreknown that one of the Twelve was a devil (6:70; cf. 13:2), the prince of evil and the ruler of this world (12:31; 14:30; 16:11). The "devil" is also "Satan" (13:27), who instigated Judas to betray Jesus. The narrator explains that Jesus was speaking of Judas, the son of Simon Iscariot and one of the Twelve, who would betray Jesus (6:71).[36] Judas was not merely to be used by the devil, but he himself was a devil, for finally he chose to be a tool of the devil, who always stands in opposition to Jesus. By mentioning Judas' betrayal, the beginning of Jesus' suffering and death on the cross, John gives a fitting end to the whole discourse.

---

36. "Iscariot" may mean "man of Kerioth," Kerioth being a town in southern Judea (Brown 1978: 1.298). Cf. Jer 48:24, 41; Amos 2:2.

JOHN 7
Is Jesus the Christ?: Conflict with "the Jews"

John 7 is apparently Jesus' continuous response to the accusation raised by the Jewish authorities in John 5. We have in it Jesus' words spoken at the feast of Tabernacles, and then his words spoken at the feast of the Dedication follow in John 10. On each occasion, the conflict between Jesus and the Jewish authorities is intensified so as to bring him nearer to the cross. John 7:53, together with 8:1–11, seems to be a later addition and therefore it needs to be studied with John 8.

JESUS, HIS BROTHERS, AND "THE JEWS" (7:1–13)

"After this" gives a transition from one narrative to another without chronological sequence (cf. 5:1; 6:1). Jesus foreknew that "the Jews" were seeking to kill him and therefore, deciding against going to Judea, he continued his ministry in Galilee (7:1; cf. 4:1, 3). The Jewish feast of Tabernacles had arrived (7:2; cf. 2:13; 6:4; 11:55). This feast, known also as the "festival of Booths," was celebrated in late September as "a most holy and most eminent feast" (*Ant.* 8.4.1). It commemorated the time when the Israelites lived in booths in the wilderness (Lev 23:33–43). At this feast, the ark of the covenant of the Lord and all the vessels in the tent were brought into Solomon's temple from Zion and therefore it came to be known as the "feast of Tabernacles" (1 Kgs 8:1–8). Water and light were dominant themes in the feast of Tabernacles, expressing the ritual libation with the water drawn from Siloam (*m. Sukkah* 4:9) and the illumination of the temple with lights (*m. Sukkah* 5:1–4).[1]

Jesus' brothers urged him to go to Judea and show himself to his disciples by doing the works he was doing in Galilee. By saying that no one works in secret if he would become popular, they tempted him to show himself to "the world" (the Roman world at large). Even his brothers did

---

1. Malina and Rohrbaugh 1998: 140–41.

not believe in Jesus (7:3-5). Jesus' answer, "My time has not yet come" (7:6), implies that Jesus' fulfillment of God's work cannot be controlled by family or earthly relationships (cf. 2:4). He tells his brothers that "your time" is always available for you. Jesus' "my time" refers to the time set by God for which he has to wait, whereas "your time" implies his brothers' readiness to act at any time, as they are not governed by the God-appointed mission but by their own convenience. Jesus contends that the world cannot hate his brothers, because they are on the side of the world in their unbelief, but that the world hates him because by his testimony he exposes the world's evil deeds (7:7; cf. 3:19-20; 15:18, 23). By refusing to follow his brothers' advice, Jesus tells them, "you go to the feast," for his time, appointed by the Father, to reveal his messianic identity has not yet fully come. So saying, he remained in Galilee (7:8-9). Jesus' messianic identity in John was kept secret to the unbelievers like Jesus' brothers, but was revealed to those who believed in him (e.g., 6:69). There is a concealed manifestation of Jesus as the Christ in John.

After his brothers had gone up to the feast, Jesus goes up not publicly but secretly (7:10). "The Jews," who had come for the feast, were searching for him at the feast and started muttering among themselves about Jesus' identity. Some appreciated him as a good man, probably because they had seen his healing done in Jerusalem, but others accused him of leading the crowd astray (John 7:11-12; cf. Luke 23:2), probably because he broke the Sabbath law and made himself equal with God (5:18).[2] However, the people feared the Jewish leaders, who had imposed punishment on those who believed in Jesus (cf. 9:22; 12:42), and did not speak openly about Jesus (7:13).

VEILED REFERENCES TO JESUS AS THE CHRIST (7:14-36)

Soon after Jesus joined the feast in the middle of the eight-day celebration, he went up to the temple to teach (7:14). He must have taught on the significance of the feast of Tabernacles from the scriptures, pointing out how they testify to him as the Christ (5:39-40, 45-47), and this explains why the Jewish crowd was amazed at Jesus' knowledge of the scriptures. In their view, Jesus never studied the scriptures under a rabbi (7:15). In response,

---

2. In the late first century the Jewish authorities accused Christians of leading people astray from monotheism. John finds Jesus as having already faced the same charge during his lifetime.

Veiled References to Jesus as the Christ

Jesus denies that his teaching is his own, but confesses that it is of "the one who sent me" (7:16). "Teaching" in John is a collective term denoting the "words of revelation" received from God and spoken by Jesus (cf. 3:32, 34; 8:26–28; 12:49; 14:24; 18:19–20). By saying this, Jesus indirectly reveals his heavenly origin and status as the Christ, who pre-existed with God. However, human beings, at the natural level, cannot grasp whether Jesus' teaching comes from God or he speaks on his own accord,[3] unless they wish to do God's will (7:17).

Anyone who speaks on his own authority naturally wishes his own name to be honored. In contrast, he who speaks for the one who sent him seeks the sender's name to be exalted. Jesus does not seek his own glory (5:41; 8:50, 54) but the glory of the Father who sent him (cf. 5:44). If God is true to his words, the one who speaks God's words also must be true to his words (7:18; cf. 3:33; 7:28). Thus there is no wickedness in Jesus. While he is guiltless, Jesus asks, "Why do you seek to kill me?" (7:19). If they plan to kill him (7:25; cf. 5:18), then they are not really obeying the Law given to them by Moses, who wrote of Jesus (5:46). The people immediately accuse Jesus of being demon possessed (cf. 8:48, 52; 10:20) and ask him sarcastically, "Who is seeking to kill you?" (7:20). "Having a demon" means "being out of one's mind" or "being controlled by evil spirits."[4]

Jesus refers to the healing of the paralytic done on the Sabbath as "one deed" at which all were marveling (7:21). He argues that Moses gave the law of circumcision not merely for purification (Lev 12:1–3), but for the sake of restoring human lives, as the phrase "because of this" (7:22) shows. In fact, the law of circumcision was given earlier than Moses to the patriarchs like Abraham as a mark of covenant with God to preserve one's life (Gen 17:10–14; 21:4). Thus, circumcision actually was not from Moses, but from the patriarchs, each of whom was called "our father" (4:12; 8:39).

The rabbis permitted circumcision to be done on the Sabbath if the child had been born on the previous Sabbath (*m. Šabb.* 18:3; 19:1–2; *m. Ned.* 3:11; *t. Šabb.* 15:16; *b. Yoma* 85b),[5] by treating this as the fulfillment of Mosaic Law. Jesus argues that if on the Sabbath circumcision of a single part of the body can be done as per Moses' Law, which cannot be broken, how

---

3. The Greek phrase translated "on his own" (7:17b, 18a) can mean either "on his own authority" or "on his own initiative"; Zerwick and Grosvenor 1988: 308.

4. Lindars 1972: 290.

5. Blomberg 2001: 135; Lincoln 2006: 250.

much more the healing of the whole person should be accepted (7:23).[6] He questions why his opponents are angry while he has thus fulfilled the Sabbath law. Jesus' questions (7:19, 23) are to enable them to judge him and his works soberly and not to accuse him by seeing his work outwardly (7:24).

Jesus' public admonition led some people in Jerusalem to doubt whether he was the man whom the religious authorities were seeking to kill (7:25; the indefinite plural "they" refers to Jewish authorities; cf. 7:26b). They questioned among themselves whether the authorities themselves are convinced that "this man" (Jesus) is the Christ (7:26).[7] The Jerusalemites had known the place whence Jesus came, alluding to Nazareth (7:27a; 7:41b; cf. 6:42). They had also learned that no one will know the origin of the Christ when he appears (7:27b). Although, according to the scriptures, Christ will come from Bethlehem, the city of David (Mic 5:2; cf. 7:42), there was a belief in the late first century that the Messiah would be kept hidden before God until he reveals himself "in the time of his day" (1 En. 38:2-3; 4 Ezra 12:32). A Qumran writing refers to "a holy branch" that is to be hidden (1QH 8.4-36; cf. Isa 11:1; Jer 23:5, where "a righteous branch" denotes the messianic King) and this hiddenness will be until the time when he would reveal to the Teacher his salvation (1QH 5.11-12). The crowd reflects in 7:27 the first-century belief on the hidden origin of the Messiah.

Since people did not believe that he is the Christ who came from God, as he taught in the temple he told them that they knew his origin only in terms of his physical birth or residence and clarified that he did not come on his own authority or initiative (cf. 7:17; 5:19). He admonished the unbelievers that they did not know God, the trustworthy and faithful one, who sent him (7:28; cf. 7:18). He claimed that since he comes from God, who sent him, he alone intimately knows him (7:29; cf. 6:46). Thus, Jesus reveals himself as the pre-existent Christ hidden to human eyes.

The unbelieving Jews took Jesus' claims as blasphemous and therefore sought to "lay hands on" him (7:30). But no one could seize him, because the time of the Father to glorify his Son on the cross had not yet come (cf. 2:4; 8:20, 59; 10:39). The "many" who believed in him did so only with the question, "When Christ appears, will he do more signs than this man did?" (7:31). Their faith obviously was based on Jesus' signs alone (cf. 2:23;

---

6. The Greek *holon anthrōpon* means "the whole person," implying Jesus' holistic healing of the paralytic in John 5.

7. Their question is put in a tentative and hesitating way, as it starts with the Greek *mēpote* (cf. 4:29).

11:45). There is no evidence in Jewish literature for the belief that when the Christ appears he will perform miracles. However, the OT refers to the miracles that will happen at the time of final salvation (Isa 35:5–6; 61:1). But it is natural for the Jews to wonder whether such a miracle worker as Jesus might not be the Messiah[8] (cf. Matt 11:2–5; 12:22–23, 28; Mark 8:11; 13:21–22; Luke 11:16, which identify doing signs as a mark of the Messiah).

The Pharisees heard the mutterings about Jesus' messianic identity. Seeking to maintain order in the temple, the chief priests and the Pharisees sent the temple police to arrest Jesus (7:32). Foreknowing this, Jesus hinted at his death and resurrection. "I shall be with you a little longer" (7:33; cf. 12:25–26; 13:3, 33, 36) is Jesus' prediction on his brief time on earth before he goes to the Father through the cross and resurrection (cf. 12:35; 13:33; 14:19; 16:16). After he goes to the Father, the people will seek him but they will neither find him nor be able to go to him (7:34).

The Jews could not grasp the meaning of Jesus' sayings, "You will seek me and you will not find me" and "Where I am you cannot come" (7:36). They sarcastically asked one another, "Where is this man about to go that we shall not find him? He is not going to the Dispersion among the Greeks to teach the Greeks; is he?" (7:35; cf. 8:22). Though the word "dispersion" denotes the Jews who were living outside Palestine (cf. Deut 28:25; 30:4; Isa 49:6; Ps 147:2; 2 Macc 1:27; *Pss. Sol.* 8:34), the "Greeks" to whom Jesus may go to teach could refer to the Greek-speaking natives rather than the Greek-speaking Jews.[9] Ironically, the crowd's sarcastic question, which expects the answer "no," becomes in John an unconscious prophecy for Jesus' ministry to the Greeks (12:20–26), which will be followed by his apostles after his ascension (e.g., Acts 11:20–21).

THE AUTHORITIES' REJECTION OF JESUS' PROCLAMATION (7:37–52)

The last day of the feast, being the eighth day, was the "great day" and praising and rejoicing continued (*m. Sukkah* 4:8). People offered food offerings and lived in booths for seven days (Lev 23:34, 36a, 41, 42). On the seventh day, there used to be a procession of the priests and people, with the water drawn from the pool of Siloam, to the temple where the priests would pour out the water and wine at the base of the altar (*m. Mid.* 2:7; *m.*

---

8. Barrett 1978: 323.

9. Köstenberger (2009: 239) comments that the term "Greeks" could be an umbrella term to mean the Gentiles in the Greco-Roman world at large.

Sukkah 4:9; etc.), probably for securing rain.[10] This ritual pouring of water and the lighting of the lamps ceased on the seventh day (*m. Sukkah* 4:1, 9–10). The eighth day of the feast was a day for "solemn assembly" and for a special food offering to be given to the Lord (Lev 23:36). Jesus would have chosen the eighth day as the right time to proclaim about the living water (7:37-38) and light (8:12) to the people assembled. On this day, Jesus stood up and cried out (7:37). Jesus' standing posture indicates that his message is a public prophetic announcement more than his earlier proclamation in the temple (7:28). Jesus' act of crying out marks his proclamation to all pilgrims about his gift of outflowing life (cf. 1:15; 7:28; 12:44).

Jesus' proclamation in 7:37b-38 may be understood in two ways, depending upon the placement of the full stop:

1. "Let anyone who is thirsty come to me, and let the one who believes in me drink. As the Scripture has said..." (NRSV). This rendering would mean that the rivers of living water will flow from Jesus.

2. "If anyone thirsts, let him come to me and drink. Whoever believes in me, as the Scripture has said, ..." (ESV, RSV, NIV). This reading would mean that the rivers of living water will flow from the heart of the believer.

Some scholars think that Jesus' "heart" (literally "belly") means his inmost part[11] from where the living water flows (cf. 4:10, 14a; 6:35b; 19:34; 20:22). Jesus is the source and giver of living water and the one who believes in him will never thirst (John 4:14; 6:35; cf. Prov 9:5; Sir 24:19-21; 51:23-24). They point out its appropriateness for the feast of Tabernacles when the water is poured for ritual cleansing and the lights are lit to illuminate the temple. Jesus calls people to *receive* the living water from him instead of pouring out the ritual water and reveals himself as the Light of the world. However, it does not explain how the water received by the believer outflows to give life to others (cf. 4:14b).

The phrase "rivers of living water" symbolizes the Spirit, which those who believe in him will receive by virtue of Jesus' exaltation on the cross and ascent to the Father (7:39). Jesus calls each person to come to him and drink (7:37). "Drinking" is the same as believing in him (7:38a; 4:14b). When believers receive it, it will flow out through them as saving power, just like the water that flows from the temple gives life to all creatures wherever

---

10. Keener 2005: 1.722-23.
11. Behm 1977: 788 n. 16; cf. Ps 39:9 LXX (in English Ps 40:8).

it goes (Ezek 47:1–12; cf. Zech 14:8). The life of the Spirit received by the believer is dynamic to reach out many others. In 7:37–38a, Jesus refers to himself in the first-person personal pronoun, "me," but in the scriptural quotation he uses the third-person personal pronoun, "Out of *his* heart shall flow rivers of living water" (7:38b), obviously denoting the inward being of the one who by faith receives the Spirit and becomes a life-giving source to others.[12] We are justified, then, if we put the full stop after "drink" and take "the one who believes in me" with 7:38.

The phrase "as the scripture said" (7:38b) points to any relevant OT passage rather than the rabbinic writings, which Jesus never recognized as "the scripture." The exact wording of the scriptural quotation in 7:38 cannot be confined to one OT passage alone. The notion of living water that flows from God's presence into the believers, who, in turn, become the rivers of life-giving water, may be a blending of such OT passages as Ezek 47:1–12; Zech 14:8; and Isa 58:11, perhaps with an allusion to Joel 3:18.[13]

The pouring of the Spirit into people's hearts is expressed by the sprinkling of water upon God's people so that they may walk in his ways and that other nations may know the greatness of the Lord (Ezek 36:23, 25–27; 37:14). This is the essence of God's new covenant made with his people so that they may become a new covenant community (Jer 31:31–34). Against this background, 7:38–39 anticipates God's new covenant community, founded by Jesus and stabilized by the Spirit. The rivers of living water will flow from this community to give new life to others.

Opinions are divided among people on Jesus' messianic status (7:40–44; cf. 7:25–27, 31). When people heard Jesus' words, some confessed that Jesus is really "the prophet" (7:40), perhaps like Moses (Deut 18:15, 18) or Elijah (Mal 3:1; 4:5). In John, the titles "the prophet" and "the Christ" do not refer to the same figure (1:20–21), although both of them are associated with the end-time salvation. Others, however, believed that he is the Christ. The crowd, which said that no one will know where Christ comes from (7:27), now raises the question, "Does the Christ come from Galilee?," which expects the answer "no" (7:41; cf. 7:52), for such a powerful political figure as Christ cannot come from the backward region of Galilee, particularly from Nazareth (cf. 1:45–46).

Nevertheless, some who had known the scriptures rightly said that Christ comes from the seed of David (cf. 2 Sam 7:12–16; Ps 18:50; 89:3–4,

---

12. Kruse 2008: 192; Köstenberger 2009: 240–41.
13. Isa 44:3 and Joel 2:28 too may throw light on 7:38; Keener 2005: 1.726.

John 7:37–52

35–37; Isa 11:1, 10; Jer 23:5) and from Bethlehem, the village where David was (John 7:42; cf. Mic 5:2). Thus, there was a division among people over the identity of Jesus (7:43). Some, probably the unbelieving Jews and the temple officers, wished to arrest Jesus, but no one laid hands on him (7:44; cf. 7:30).

The chief priests and the Pharisees were waiting for the temple police to seize Jesus and bring him back to them. But, to their disappointment, the police returned without Jesus. The leaders questioned them indignantly, "Why did you not bring him?" (7:45). The temple employees, who had experienced the drawing power of Jesus' words, said, "No one ever spoke like this man" (7:46). Jesus' teaching was so convincing that they could not do any harm to him. For the religious authorities any one who follows Jesus or even sympathizes with him has gone astray from the Law. Therefore they asked the officers, "And you have not gone astray, have you?" (7:47). This reflects the popular accusation that Jesus and, after him, late first-century Christians were leading people astray (cf. 7:12).

The authorities further questioned them, "Did any of the authorities or of the Pharisees believe in him?," expecting the answer "no" (7:48). Then they admonished the officials to follow the examples of their leaders rather than troublesome preachers like Jesus. The leaders' question betrays their own ignorance, for they were unaware that Nicodemus, one among them, had already been taught by Jesus with the result that he almost believed in him and that many of the authorities themselves secretly believed in Jesus (12:42). Their anger now turns against the crowd that believed Jesus as the Christ. They pronounce a curse on those who ignorantly disobey the Law (cf. Deut 27:26; 28:15; Ps 119:21) by accepting someone who breaks the Sabbath law (7:49).

The people accursed are not "the people of the land," the mixed pagan-Jewish population, who were thought of being ignorant of the Law. The accursed are rather the Jewish pilgrims who had come to Jerusalem for the feast, some of whom had proper understanding of Jesus. The Pharisees regarded them equal to "the people of the land." John ironically says that those who were judged as scripturally illiterate understood Jesus correctly as the Messiah.[14]

Nicodemus is introduced here again after the narrator left him abruptly in John 3 as the one who had gone to Jesus before and as one of the authorities (7:50; cf. 19:39). The epithet "one of them" does not necessarily picture

---

14. Köstenberger 2009: 243.

The Authorities' Rejection of Jesus' Proclamation

Nicodemus as one of the Pharisees who rejected Jesus. His claim "our law" (7:51) does not show him as identifying himself with the unbelieving Pharisees, but generally with Jewish people. Nicodemus indirectly defends Jesus by means of the Law. Thus, he calls into question the Pharisees' knowledge of the Law[15] by asking, "Does our law judge the man unless first one hears from him and knows what he does?" (7:51). Actually the Law does not allow judges to judge a man without hearing him and inquiring diligently into the case (Deut 1:16–17; 17:4; 19:18). Nicodemus not only demands for a fair trial, but also accuses the authorities, who exhibit a prejudgmental attitude towards others without following the Law.

Nicodemus exhorts his colleagues to hear first Jesus' words and learn the significance of his works, after which they may judge him fairly. Nicodemus' saying gives the authorities the impression that he believes Jesus as the end-time prophet, the Messiah, whose words and deeds should be properly understood. Therefore they respond, "You are not from Galilee, are you? Search and see that a prophet does not arise from Galilee" (7:52).[16] Their words show that Nicodemus spoke in favor of Jesus. This, in turn, proves that what Jesus spoke to Nicodemus earlier (3:1–21) must have convinced him that Jesus represents the rule of God and that by believing in him as the Christ, the Son of God, one can receive eternal life.[17]

The chief priests and the Pharisees were wrong in saying that no prophet will arise from Galilee. They were unaware that prophets such as Jonah (2 Kgs 14:25), possibly Elijah (1 Kgs 17:1), and Nahum (Nah 1:1) came from Galilee.[18] They were ignorant of the rabbinic tradition that says, "R. Eliezer (ca. 90 CE) said: Thou hast no single tribe in Israel from which a prophet has not come forth" (*b. Sukkah* 27b).[19] Above all, they forgot that Jesus was not from Galilee, but from Bethlehem in Judea (Mic 5:2; cf. 7:42). The religious leaders, who should have learnt this by searching the scriptures, show their own blindness as they ignore Nicodemus' appeal to the Law and seek to kill Jesus.

---

15. Lincoln 2006: 259.

16. The early manuscripts P⁶⁶ and P⁷⁵ read "*the* prophet" and this may be the original reading in 7:52; Brown 1978: 1.325; Blomberg 2001: 139.

17. Cf. Ridderbos 1997: 285.

18. Köstenberger 2009: 244. Blomberg (2001:139) adds Hosea too among the Galilean prophets.

19. Barrett 1978: 333.

JOHN 8
Intensification of Jesus' Conflict with "the Jews"

7:53–8:11 is not found in the earliest and most reliable Greek manuscripts. No Greek commentator before twelfth century seems to make any reference to this passage. Bultmann omits this passage in his commentary, stating that it belongs neither to John's Gospel nor to the ecclesiastical redaction.[1] Many commentators think that it interrupts the events and discourse at the feast of Tabernacles. Most of the vocabularies used in 8:1–11 are not Johannine,[2] but Lucan (cf. Luke 7:36–50). This does not mean that the story in 7:53—8:11 is not historical. Papias, for example, mentions of a woman who was accused of many sins before the Lord, which the *Gospel according to the Hebrews* contains (*Hist. eccl.* 3.39). The story of Jesus forgiving the sins of adulterous women was already in circulation. Perhaps it was not accepted into NT canon for a long time lest it encourage the sin of adultery in the early church. John inserts the story at this point probably to illustrate the transforming power of Jesus, the Light, to forgive and warn sinners, by overturning the condemnation pronounced by the Law (8:5, 11).

REVERSAL OF THE LAW'S CONDEMNATION (7:53–8:11)

The opening statement, "And they went each to his home" (7:53), followed by Jesus going to the Mount of Olives (8:1), presupposes a concluded assembly of people in which Jesus had taught. In the early morning Jesus came to the temple again to teach and the whole people came to listen to him (John 8:2; cf. Luke 19:47; 20:1; 21:37–38). Jesus sat down and taught, as Jewish teachers used to do. At this point the scribes and the Pharisees brought before him a woman, probably a married woman, whom they said was caught in adultery (8:3–4).

---

1. Bultmann 1971: 312 n. 2.
2. See the details in Köstenberger 2009: 245–46.

Reversal of the Law's Condemnation

The pair "the scribes and the Pharisees," which appears in the Synoptic Gospels, is strange in 8:3. Moreover, throughout his Gospel, John places the Pharisees functionally in a higher rank of authority to the extent that people feared them (1:19, 24; 4:1; 7:13, 32, 45–52; 9:22; 12:42), but in 8:3 they do the work of temple police! They placed the woman in the midst of the crowd and accused her before Jesus of adultery, which, as per Moses' Law, deserves death by stoning (8:5). They did not bring the adulterous man as an accused. This shows their bias mind and disobedience to the Law (cf. Lev 20:10–12, 14; 21:9; Deut 22:2–24).

Their question "What, then, do you say of her?" (8:5) was to test Jesus. They could bring a charge against him that he was not observing the Law if he acquitted her (8:6a), and if he instructed them to put her to death they could accuse him of infringing on the authority of the Roman governor, who was the only one normally to issue a death sentence. The scribes and the Pharisees thus attempted to bring religious and political charge against Jesus and put him to death.[3] Even Jesus' opponents, who were teachers of the Law, unknowingly accepted him as the judge whose judgment is just (5:30) and as a "teacher" (8:4).

Jesus' response to them was puzzling. He simply bent down and wrote with his finger on the ground (8:6b), and John narrates that he did the same again (8:8). This is the only reference in the whole of NT to Jesus writing. What and why did he write? Four interpretations are proposed.[4] However, the solution for such questions probably lies in the phrase "with his finger." In the Synoptic Gospels, the finger of Jesus is identified with the power of the Holy Spirit by which he casts out demons (Luke 11:26; cf. Matt 12:28; Mark 3:22–30). The OT describes God's finger as having written the Ten Commandments (Exod 31:18; 32:16; Deut 9:10) and as having performed miraculous power (Deut 8:19).

The more relevant image that may underlie Jesus' writing with his finger is Dan 5:5–9, 24–28, where the fingers of a human hand appeared and wrote on the wall disclosing God's displeasure over the acts of the Babylonian king, Belshazzar, and the impending judgment on him. In 8:6, 8 the same God acts by writing on the ground with the finger of human hand to convict the accusers of their own sins and of the resultant judgment of God that has already fallen on them. Jesus' opponents would not have understood the words written on the ground, but they were powerful enough to

---

3. Brown 1978: 1.338.
4. Keener 2005: 1.737–8.

John 7:53–8:11

disturb them. Jesus' subsequent command that any one who was without sin may first throw a stone at her (8:7) convicted them of their own sins. Jesus' words, along with the power of his writing done on the ground with his finger (8:8), persuaded them, beginning from the elders, to leave the place fast. Jesus easily turned the table against his enemies and made those who judged others dishonestly themselves become the accused. Thereby he not only acquitted the woman from condemnation (8:11), but also brought the accusers under condemnation. Jesus' authority to judge (5:22, 27) reversed the condemnation of sinners (cf. 3:17).

Although Jesus delivered the woman from condemnation, he did not condone her sin. He commanded her to go and sin no more (8:11). The divine forgiveness and liberation from condemnation mercifully granted by Jesus persuades and enables forgiven sinners not to remain in sin. By acquitting and transforming the woman's life, Jesus enabled her to obey the commandment not to commit adultery!

JESUS, THE LIGHT OF THE WORLD (8:12–20)

The word "again" may link Jesus' sayings in 8:12–20 with his sayings in John 7. The forensic language used does not mean that the trial of Jesus continues here from John 7.[5] We have here the dialogue, in severe conflicting terms, between Jesus and the crowd, and not a formal trial.[6] The audience is a mixed group of Pharisees (8:13), "the Jews" (8:22, 48, 52, 57), and the believing Jews (8:31).

Jesus claims himself as the Light of the world by using "I am," the second of the seven such sayings in John. The proposed Isaianic background of Yahweh's lawsuit against Israel[7] does not fit into Jesus' "I am" saying in 8:12. It should be understood as denoting God, whose name is "I am who I am" (Exod 3:13–14) and who communicates himself as light (cf. Gen 1:3–8; Ps 27:1; 36:9; etc.), not only of Judeans but of the whole world. Jesus' self-manifestation as the Light of the world is made here relevant to the feast of Tabernacles. On the first day of the feast four large lampstands were lit up in the court of women and the young priests held in their hands the candlesticks alight. The lights were so bright that the court was visible to the whole city of Jerusalem (*m. Sukkah* 5:2–4). However, on the last day

---

5. *Contra* Neyrey 2007: 153.
6. Cf. Motyer 1997: 144–45.
7. Motyer 1997: 145–46.

these lights were extinguished, and Jesus declared, "I am the Light of the world" (8:12a), meaning that this Light shines in the darkness (1:5) and replaces the ritual lights. The feast of Tabernacles commemorated God's presence in the pillar of fire and cloud that saved the Israelites from their enemies and led them in the wilderness (Exod 13:21–22; 14:19–25; 40:38). Similarly, Jesus, the Light of the world, reveals God in his dazzling light and saves from danger all those who follow him.

Each "I am" saying with a predicate in John demands some form of human response: Just like Jesus as the bread of life is to be "eaten," as the Light he is to be followed (8:12b). The verb "to follow" in Judaism, means "leading an ethical life in accordance with the Law." In Jesus' time, it had an added notion of becoming a disciple. The one who would follow Jesus, the Light, will become his disciple and obey his words. The life in the Word (1:4), now incarnate, is the Light of humankind. It enlightens every one who believes and obeys him (1:9, 12–13; 12:36, 46). In this sense, those who follow Jesus can have even now the "light of life," the divine life believed to be given at the end-time (1QS 3.7). They will reflect the light of God in their works (3:21) and know their goal in life, unlike those who remain in wickedness (3:20; 12:35).

For the Jews, any claim of a crime should be attested by two or three witnesses (Num 35:30; Deut 17:6; 19:15; cf. 8:17). Later they applied the same rule for other legal cases also (*m. Ketub.* 2:9; cf. *m. Roš Haš.* 3:1).[8] Ignoring that Jesus' claims have already been attested by at least four witnesses (5:31–47), the Pharisees took Jesus' declaration of himself as the Light to be a self-witness and accused him that his testimony (to himself) is not trustworthy (8:13). As Jesus does the works of God in oneness with him, both the Father and the Son witness together (5:19–20; 8:18). Therefore, even if it seems outwardly that Jesus alone bears witness to himself, his witness is genuine and trustworthy (8:14a). He attacked the Pharisees that they did not understand that he came from the Father and that he goes back to the Father (8:14b). That is why they did not perceive that Jesus' testimony to himself as the Light of the world is genuine, for Jesus testifies to what he has seen and heard from the Father (3:31–32; 6:46; 8:26).

Jesus charged the leaders that they judge according to the flesh (8:15). Flesh belongs to the earth, and those who belong to the earthly domain cannot grasp spiritual things (3:6; 6:63) and they judge only by appearances (7:24), in contrast to Jesus, who does not judge anyone according to the

---

8. Köstenberger 2009: 254.

flesh. Jesus' judgment is genuine, because it is not he who alone judges, but he and the Father who sent him judge (8:16; cf. 5:22; 27–29). The phrase "I and he [i.e., the Father] who sent me" betrays Semitism, denoting the solidarity between Israel and Yahweh (*m. Sukkah* 4:5).[9] In John, Jesus replaces Israel in his solidarity with the Father,[10] because Israel failed to maintain its relationship with Yahweh by her disobedience. By reminding them of the requirement of the Law for at least two witnesses, Jesus reiterated that he bears witness to himself, because the Father who sent him bears witness to him (8:17–18; 5:31–32). The term "*your* law" means the Law the Pharisees themselves accept. By using it, Jesus distanced himself from the unbelieving Jews (cf. 10:34; 15:25).

Jesus' address of God as "the Father who sent me" triggered the sarcastic question from his opponents, "Where is your Father?" (8:19), which may mean, "Who is your Father?," implying that Jesus does not have a legitimate earthly father. Their question indicates that they were unable to understand the oneness that exists between Jesus and their "one Father, God" (8:41; cf. 5:18). Therefore Jesus accused them that they did not know him, who comes from the Father, and consequently they did not know their own God, whom Jesus addressed as "my Father" (8:19). They perhaps had a theoretical knowledge of God of which they were proud (Deut 4:7; Rom 2:17),[11] but not an intimate relationship with him, as the term "knowing" means.[12]

Jesus confronted "the Jews" with these words in the treasury, near the women's court in the temple and the hall where the Sanhedrin met.[13] Jewish officials would have heard Jesus' words spoken in this key place, but no one arrested him, for his hour, determined by God, had not yet come (8:20).

Jesus' oneness with and submission to the Father (8:21–30)

The word "again" (8:21) may either point to similar words already spoken by Jesus (7:33–36) or to another layer of Jesus' teaching. Jesus says "I go away" without mentioning his destination, but the reader will know that

---

9. Köstenberger 2009: 255–56.
10. Dodd 1958: 94.
11. Kruse 2008: 203.
12. "Knowing God" is possible by seeing Jesus (12:45; 14:9) and believing in him (12:44; 1:12).
13. Morris 1995: 394; Köstenberger 2009: 257.

Jesus' Oneness with and Submission to the Father

Jesus is going to the Father who sent him (cf. 7:33; 8:14, 16b). Jesus rebukes "the Jews," "You will seek me, and you will die in your sin" (8:21). "Sin" in John indicates not so much individual actions as unbelief (3:18; 16:9). Seeking Jesus without faith eventually brings eternal death instead of heavenly life with God, both now and in future (8:24; 3:16; 5:24). As unbelievers, where Jesus goes they cannot come. When they heard it, they ridiculed him saying, "Will he kill himself, because he says, 'Where I am going, you cannot come'?" (8:22; cf. 7:35-36). There is an irony that when Jesus warns them that they will die due to their sin, "the Jews" ignore this warning and speak of Jesus killing himself. Committing suicide belongs to the earthly realm and self-murder is an instance of crime against God our Creator (J.W. 3.8.5). Therefore Jesus responds in dualistic terms that his opponents are from "below," whereas he is from "above" from the Father (8:23).

To be from below is to be attached with this world, which is unspiritual, devilish, and full of selfish ambition and evil practices (Jas 3:15-16). Those who are from below, therefore, live in alienation from God (John 1:10; 7:7; 14:17, 27; 15:18-19), and they cannot understand divine things. In contrast, to be "from above" denotes to being "from God who is in heaven" (3:3). Jesus comes from above (cf. 6:46; 8:42) and therefore he does not bear the nature of this world. "The Jews," being from this earth, live for earthly things and they cannot believe that Jesus is the "I am" who has delivered people from bondage. Those who do not believe cannot be delivered from sin but will die in it (8:24).

The closest parallel to the "I am" statement in 8:24 is in Isa 43. In his lawsuit against the world, Yahweh declares that he has chosen his people so that they may know, and believe . . . that "I am [he]" (Isa 43:10 LXX) and promises, "I, even I, am he that blots out . . . your sins" (43:25 LXX). This means that if they do not believe in Yahweh that he is "I am," their sins will not be blotted out and they will perish in their sins.[14] By picking up this image, Jesus reveals himself as God in his name "I am" and fulfills God's role of forgiving people of their sins lest they die in them. "The Jews" will not seek Jesus as long as he is on earth. They may seek him for salvation, after he goes away to the Father, but their delayed search will cause them to die in their sin (8:21).

Although Jesus' opponents know that "I am" is the name of God, which Jesus used for himself, they are unable to comprehend the nature of his claim and hence ask him, "You, who are you?" (8:25a). Jesus seems to

---

14. Cf. Ball 1996: 188-94.

confirm his identity in terms of his oneness with the Father by answering, "Why do I even speak to you at all?"[15] (8:25b). It does not mean that Jesus has nothing to tell them. He has always been identifying himself as the one who is "from above" (8:14, 23) or "I am [he]" (8:12, 24, 28, 59) or "I and the Father who sent me" (8:16, 18) and ascribing to himself and the Father the common task of judging, bearing witness, and speaking (8:16, 18, 23, 26). But still "the Jews" do not understand, because of their unbelief and earthly inclinations, that Jesus speaks about the Father who is true (8:26–27). Jesus thus has actually much to say and judge about his opponents, but he speaks to the world only what he hears from the Father (8:26).

Jesus predicts that his critics will come to perceive Jesus' oneness with the Father after they lift him up on the cross (8:28a). The idea of the Son of Man being lifted up on the cross (3:14) appears again here, but with a reference to the Jewish authorities who will lift him up. Once they crucify Jesus, "the Jews" will realize that he is the "I am," the revelation of God's love and salvation. Jesus' exaltation will put them to shame by showing that they could not destroy him and that he did not speak on his own authority, but spoke what the Father taught him (8:28b). Jesus thus reveals his submission to the Father within his oneness.

Jesus emphasizes again that he who sent him is with him always (8:29). The cross may *prima facie* show that Jesus is left alone by God. But because Jesus always performs what is pleasing to God, the oneness between Jesus and the Father and Jesus' submission to accomplish God's mission cannot be broken. Jesus' words led many to believe in him (8:30).

Jesus' verbal attack on the hostile Jews (8:31–47)

Jesus exhorts the Jews who believe in him to remain in his word in order to be his true disciples (8:31). This is the same instruction given to the twelve disciples (15:7). In John, "believing" and "abiding in" are interrelated: those who do not believe the one sent by God cannot have his word abiding in them (5:38). The truth, which they will experience in him (1:14, 17), Jesus continues, will make them free (8:32). Obedience to Jesus' word will lead the believers to know the truth, the divine reality, and will free them from the bondage of sin (8:34, 36).

---

15. See Lincoln 2006: 261 n. 1.

Jesus' Verbal Attack on the Hostile Jews

Some commentators take 8:33 onwards as Jesus' rebuke against the believing Jews.[16] However, it is impossible to imagine that those who received Jesus' exhortation (8:31–32) came immediately under a serious attack by Jesus, who himself said that those who hear his words and believe in the one who sent him do not come under condemnation (5:24). It seems probable that in 8:33–47 Jesus addresses the hostile Jews, who constituted a major part of the audience. As Jesus' teaching took place in the temple (8:20, 59), the audience could have been a mixed group.[17] The unbelieving Jews, including the Jewish authorities, understood Jesus' teaching on freedom in earthly terms. Forgetting the bondage in which their forefathers were in Egypt and in Babylon, and the Roman yoke under which they were living, they proudly claimed that they, who are descendants of Abraham, have never been in bondage to anyone (8:33). They were also ignorant that those who believe in Jesus are the real descendants of Abraham (Gal 3:6–7). Naturally they asked Jesus, "How do you say that you will be made free?"

In response, Jesus solemnly affirmed the heavenly truth, by using the expression "truly, truly, I say to you," that every one who commits sin is a slave to sin (8:34). For Jesus all are slaves to their selfish nature. Freedom from egoism cannot be attained by one's own efforts, but it is a gift of God given to all who believe in Jesus, whom the Father sent to remove human sin (John 1:29, 36; cf. Rom 6:16–23). Jesus clarified it further in a parabolic form: a slave does not have a permanent place in the family, but a son, by virtue of his birth, belongs to that family for ever (8:35).[18] In Jewish society, to be called a "slave" was one of the worst possible insults.[19] Slaves could be sold and so had no right to be in a household permanently. As the only Son of the Father, Jesus remains in the house of God forever (14:2–3). Just as a son has authority to free his slaves, Jesus has the authority to liberate those who are slaves to sin and make them "children of God" (1:12). Therefore Jesus promised that if only the Son makes them free from sin will they become truly free (8:36).

Jesus accepts that the Jews genetically originate from Abraham. However, his accusers do not exhibit Abraham's moral qualities such as a

---

16. E.g., Bultmann 1971: 433; Carson 1991: 347–48; Lincoln 2006: 270. Köstenberger 2009: 261.

17. Kanagaraj 2005: 281–84.

18. Cf. Köstenberger 2009: 263.

19. Jeremias 1975: 110–11, 312–16, 345–51.

modest mind, a humble heart, and compassion, as the rabbis regarded.[20] Instead of recognizing that the day of Christ has dawned in Jesus, which Abraham himself could see and rejoice (8:56), his opponents seek to arrest and kill him (7:1, 19, 25, 32; 8:20). They neither believe in him nor receive his word of salvation and therefore Jesus' word has no place in them (8:37, 43). They, who are proud of Abraham's paternity, are attempting to kill the one who did good by preaching the truth heard from God (8:39-40, 45). If they were Abraham's children, they would do what Abraham did to men who conveyed the word of God (8:39; cf. Gen 18:1-19). Indeed, Jesus' accusers are descended neither from Abraham nor from God (8:41-43) but from the devil (8:44).[21] Jesus speaks of what he has seen with his Father, but his opponents do what they have heard from their father, the devil (8:38). Different paternity is the basic cause of Jesus' conflict with "the Jews." He deliberately contrasts himself and what he has *seen* from "my Father" with "the Jews" who have only *heard* from "your father."

Jesus' contrast of "*my* Father" and "*your* father" makes "the Jews" to feel that they are being identified as children of fornication. So they respond that they were not born of fornication and that they have one Father, God (8:41). This could be an indirect attack on Jesus' birth, which, Jesus' accusers thought, could have been by fornication since he lacked a biological father.[22] However, the opponents' main stress is that they have God as their only Father. In Jewish tradition, "fornication" was sometimes a metaphor for idolatry. If so, their defense would be that they are not unfaithful idolaters (cf. Hos 1:2; 2:4-5 LXX) but that they are faithful to the one God (Deut 6:4).[23]

In response, Jesus argues that if God were their Father they would love Jesus, who came by being sent by God rather than on his own initiative (8:42). The four verbs "came forth," "I am present," "have come," and "sent" denote Jesus' heavenly origin and his God-given mission to the world (3:17; 7:28). So speaking, Jesus attacks his accusers that they cannot even bear to hear his word (8:43) because they are like their father, the devil, and they are committed to fulfill their father's desires. The devil was a murderer from the beginning; he does not have the truth in him and so has no association with truth, and he is a liar by nature and father of lies (8:44).

20. Str-B 2.523.
21. Keener 2005: 1.757.
22. Blomberg 2001: 146.
23. Lincoln 2006: 271-72; Keener 2005: 1.759-60.

The Greek word *diabolos* ("devil") means "the one who separates," "the enemy," or "the seducer." He vigorously attempts to separate people from God and make them to worship him. He seduces people by his lies, makes them believe falsehood to be the truth, and drives people to sin by fulfilling his desires (cf. 1 John 3:8). Thus a liar becomes the father of those who speak lies. That he was a "murderer from the beginning" may allude to his act of separating Adam and Eve from their Maker even in the beginning of the world and bringing sin and death upon every one (Rom 5:12–14; Wis 2:24; Sir 25:24). It may also recall the first physical murder, committed by Cain against his brother Abel (Gen 4:8; 1 John 3:12).[24] The devil does not live in the sphere of truth and therefore his children do not believe the one who came to disclose the truth, the heavenly reality (8:45).

At this point, Jesus challenges them by asking which of them convicts him of sin. The implied answer is that no one can, because he is from above and possesses the life of God. Jesus also asks them why they do not believe him if he speaks the truth (8:46). Jesus' answer for his own question is that "the Jews" are not born of God (8:47), for any one who is born of God hears and obeys the words of God spoken by him (cf. John 1:12–13; 1 John 3:9, 10; 4:4, 6; 5:18–19). The conflict between Jesus and "the Jews" anticipates the conflict between Christians and the religious authorities in the late first century.

EXISTENCE OF JESUS BEFORE ABRAHAM (8:48–59)

Jesus' verbal attack on his opponents aggravate them and to justify themselves they call Jesus a Samaritan who has a demon (8:48, 52; cf. 4:9). However, Jesus denies emphatically that he has a demon. They thus dishonor him, but Jesus honors his Father (8:49). Anyone who does not honor the Son does not honor the Father either (5:23). Jesus' rebuke against their dishonor does not mean that he seeks glory for himself. For him, God, who judges fairly, seeks his glory (8:50; cf. 5:41; 7:18).

On the surface, Jesus uses the image of a lawsuit with his adversaries before the tribunal of God[25] to say that God is the ultimate judge, who will bring glory to Jesus. At a deeper level, Jesus declares that the way in which God seeks to glorify his Son is through his death on the cross (12:23, 32, 33; 13:31–32; 17:1, 4, 5). Jesus' enemies, due to their unbelief, have placed

---

24. Keener 2005: 1.761.
25. Bultmann 1971: 300 n. 2; cf. Lincoln 2006: 275.

themselves under the death sentence pronounced by God.[26] However, by using the expression "truly, truly, I say to you," Jesus says that any one who accepts his word of salvation will never experience death (8:51). "The Jews" reiterate now that Jesus has a demon and ask how, if Abraham and other OT prophets have already died, Jesus can say that any one who obeys his word will never taste death. "Seeing death" (8:51) means "tasting death" (8:52).

They ask him, "Are you greater than our father Abraham?" (8:53; cf. 4:12). They see Jesus as no more than a human and not worthy to be compared with such esteemed patriarchs as Abraham and the prophets, who all died. Their question "Who do you make yourself to be?" divulges their thought that Jesus is making himself equal to God, who alone can protect a person from death (Deut 32:39; 1 Sam 2:6; 2 Kgs 5:7). Jesus repeatedly says that if he glorified himself it would have no value, but that it is his Father who glorifies him (8:54; cf. 8:50; 13:31–34).

"The Jews" boastfully claim Yahweh, Jesus' Father, as their God, but without an intimate relationship with him (cf. 1:10; 7:28; 8:19). But Jesus affirms twice that he knows the Father in the sense that he obeys God's word (8:55; cf. 10:15). Jesus cannot hide his intimacy with God, lest he becomes a liar like his opponents, who falsely claim that Jesus' Father is their God (8:54–55). "Your father Abraham" (8:56) indicates that "the Jews" are the physical descendants of Abraham. But they do not share Abraham's attitude towards Jesus. Abraham rejoiced when God revealed himself to him with a promise to give him a son (Gen 17:17; cf. *Jub.* 14:21; 15:17; 16:19). Similar promises given to Abraham (Gen 12:1–4, 7; 15:4–6; 17:6–8) have come to complete fulfillment with the coming of Christ in the flesh (Gal 3:16) and Abraham lived in joyful hope of seeing the day of the Messiah, for the gospel was preached beforehand to Abraham (Gal 3:8). He saw that day, by faith, in his lifetime, just as Isaiah saw Christ's glory (12:41). After his death, he watched Jesus' life and ministry from heaven and rejoiced to see it clearly (John 8:56; cf. Heb 11:13).

Jesus' opponents, with earthly understanding, contemptuously question him, "You have not (attained) yet fifty years and have you seen Abraham?" (8:57). Their question provides Jesus an occasion to claim for himself the absolute "I am" (cf. 8:24, 28) as the climax of the dialogue. By means of the phrase "truly, truly, I say to you," Jesus affirms the heavenly truth, "Before Abraham came into being, I am" (8:58). The divine name "I am"

---

26. Hoskyns 1961: 346.

Existence of Jesus before Abraham

shows Jesus as the one who transcends time and space, unlike Abraham, a human being, who came into existence at a specific time. His affirmation resembles Yahweh's statement about his incomparable status to other gods (Isa 43:10), implying that Jesus, who pre-existed in oneness with God, is indeed greater in status and function than any of the patriarchs, including Abraham (1:15, 27; 3:31; 8:53).

Unfortunately, Jesus' accusers reject his divine status and treat his claim as blasphemy (cf. 19:7) that deserves the death penalty by stoning (Lev 24:11–16; 1 Kgs 21:9, 10, 13). So they take up stones, which could have been kept at the Gentile court for rebuilding the temple,[27] to throw at him. This public attempt by "the Jews" to kill Jesus brings him nearer to the cross. However, since the Father's time had not yet come, he secretly goes out of the temple (8:59).

27. Jeremias 1975: 118.

JOHN 9
The Holistic Healing of a Man Born Blind

The healing of a blind man takes place soon after the feast of Tabernacles, marking the messianic day when there will be recovery of sight for the blind (Isa 61:1). John's presentation of this sixth sign contains eight scenes (9:1–5, 6–7, 8–12, 13–17, 18–23, 24–34, 35–39, 40–41).[1] A study of John 9 in three parts will reveal to us how a man born blind received holistic healing from Jesus and how, in the process, he came to perceive Jesus as the Son of Man who is to be worshipped.

RECOVERY OF SIGHT FOR A BLIND MAN (9:1–12)

After Jesus left the temple, he saw a man born blind begging (9:1, 8). Jewish society believed that sickness and sufferings often come because of the sins of the individuals (2 Kgs 14:6; Mark 2:5; John 5:14) or because of the sins of the parents (Exod 20:5; Deut 5:9). Therefore, the disciples ask Jesus whose sin was the cause of the man being born blind (9:2). Jesus answers that the man's blindness is not due to his or his parents' sins, but is due to the manifestation of works of God in him (9:3). God sent Jesus into the world to accomplish his work of deliverance (4:34; 5:17, 36; 17:4), which is to be performed on the blind man so that God might reveal himself through his healing of the man born blind.

Jesus' injunction, "*We* must work the works of him who sent me" (9:4), includes also his followers in doing God's works. The plural "works" denotes not only physical healing, but also spiritual insight. The work of bringing holistic healing to the sick and suffering is not optional, but is divine commandment, as the word "must [work]" shows. This divine work cannot be done on their own, but only with Jesus (15:5). It needs to be done during the day when light is available. Jesus hints at his departure from the world (7:33; 8:21), as he warns that night comes when no one can work in

---

1. Kruse 2008: 217–29; cf. Lincoln 2006: 280.

Recovery of Sight for a Blind Man

dark hours (9:4). This is confirmed by Jesus' statement, "As long as I am in the world, I am the Light of the world" (9:5; cf. 8:12; 12:35–36). Thus, Jesus thrusts the urgency to illuminate the world by bringing holistic healing to the suffering humanity.

Jesus spat on the ground, made clay out of the spittle, anointed the man's eyes with the clay, and sent him to the pool of Siloam to wash himself. The man followed Jesus' instruction fully and came back to him after regaining his physical sight (9:6–7)! John does not attach any magical power to the spittle, though saliva was regarded later by some rabbis as containing healing properties (*b. B. Bat.* 126b),[2] and so also was the water of Siloam. The healing took place only when the blind man washed his eyes in the pool of Siloam, and this shows the man's complete trust in Jesus and obedience to his instruction. The narrator gives the meaning of "Siloam" as "sent one" (9:7), pointing to Jesus, who was sent by God, as the source of healing. John deliberately connects Jesus with the pool of Siloam, from where water was drawn for the purifying ceremony at the feast of Tabernacles, to reveal him as the one who replaces the water in Siloam with his power to bring wholeness to human life.

The neighbors, who had seen him blind and begging, were astonished at his healing (9:8). While some were certain that the healed man was the one who had been sitting and begging, others hesitantly said that he looked like the blind beggar (9:9). However, the man confirmed his identity by telling that he was the same man who had been sitting and begging. John puts the phrase "I, I am [he]" in the mouth of the healed man this time to reveal his social identity, but without any divine significance. On people's further enquiry about his healing (9:10), the man witnessed about Jesus and the manner in which he healed him. He had understood Jesus only as a man (9:11), but was not aware of his whereabouts (9:12; cf. 5:11–13).

The Pharisees' investigation on the healing (9:13–34)

Unlike the healed paralytic who went to "the Jews" to identify Jesus as the healer (5:15), the man born blind was brought by his neighbors to the Pharisees to narrate the healing story (9:13), for it was on the Sabbath when Jesus opened the man's eyes (9:14). The Pharisees asked the man how he received his sight and the man testified, "He put clay on my eyes, and I washed, and I see" (9:15). The rabbis forbade both washing and mixing or kneading of

---

2. Köstenberger 2009: 283.

clay on the Sabbath (*m. Šabb.* 7:2). Some Pharisees concluded that Jesus was not from God, as he transgressed the Sabbath law by performing healing. Other Pharisees questioned how Jesus, who had sinned, could do such signs, and thus there was a division among the Pharisees (9:16).[3] Now the discussion turns from healing to the healer. They enquired the healed man of his view about the man who opened his eyes (9:17). Ironically, the religious leaders, who should have glorified God for the healing of a man born blind, trouble him to give his opinion on the healer!

The healed man confessed Jesus to be a "prophet," a word that does not mean the Messiah here. Popularly, a prophet was known as someone close to God who has supernatural knowledge (cf. John 4:19; Luke 7:39) and is endowed with extraordinary power from God to do miracles (Matt 21:46; Mark 6:15; Luke 24:19). The understanding of the healed man about Jesus attains progress.

But the Pharisees, who are called "the Jews," did not believe that the man who was blind received his sight. Hence they called the man's parents for further investigation (9:18). They asked the parents whether or not the healed man is their son who was born blind and, if so, how he is able to see now (9:19). His parents accepted that the man is their son who was born blind, but denied any knowledge either of the manner in which he got his sight or of the healer. They suggest that "the Jews" question their son instead, who is of age[4] and who can speak for himself (9:20-21). They answered thus out of fear for the religious authorities, who had already officially decided to put those who confess Jesus as the Messiah out of the synagogue (9:22-23; 12:42), which would involve permanent excommunication from the people of Israel and from all religious services.

Some scholars maintain that the reference to the Pharisees' decision is an anachronism, written back to the time of Jesus, for such a formal decision took place only after 85 CE, when the "twelfth benediction," which cursed all heretics, including Christians, was pronounced. Arguing so, Martyn reads the story as a two-level drama in which the healed man represents not only those who were healed by Jesus in Jerusalem, but also those

---

3. This is the first time that John reports about the division among the Pharisees.

4. As per Jewish law, the age to make legal response is at least thirteen; Barrett 1978: 361.

The Pharisees' Investigation on the Healing

who were cast out of the synagogue because of their faith in Jesus as the Christ after 70 CE.[5]

The word "already" seems to indicate that the excommunication that was officially enforced in the late first century is already seen in the Jewish rejection of Jesus and his followers in Jesus' time. The two temporal perspectives—the pre-resurrection life of Jesus and the post-resurrection perspective of the evangelist—are telescoped together in the telling of the story.[6] Actually, John brings the believers' excommunication back to Jesus' time, just as he brings Jesus' glorification back to the cross or even earlier to the incarnation. He sees the reality of Jesus' crucifixion happening already in the early attempts of his opponents to arrest and kill Jesus (7:1, 19, 25, 30, 32, 45; 8:20, 40, 59; 8:44; 11:57). Similarly, he brings backward the gift of the Holy Spirit to the day of resurrection (20:19–23). Since John finds it difficult to separate the events of salvation in time, he does not stress the chronology of the saving events as much as he does the events themselves. For him God's salvific events together constitute one compound event.[7] The persecution inflicted upon Christians in Jesus' time anticipates the sufferings that God's new community will undergo in the world at all times (cf. 16:2).

In 9:24 the scene changes to the conflicting dialogue between the healed man and the authorities. The Pharisees called him a second time and insisted that he give glory to God, probably by worshipping him alone (cf. 1 Chr 16:28–29) and by denying that Jesus is the Messiah. Since they were convinced that the man received his sight through Jesus, they labeled Jesus contemptuously as "this man" who is a sinner. This may mean either that Jesus is, like any other human, liable to sin or that since Jesus healed on the Sabbath he is a sinner.

There is a play on the word "to know" in 9:25. The Pharisees affirm, "We know that this man is a sinner," but they do not know that only by giving glory to Jesus can one bring glory to God (5:23). The healed man also speaks of what he knows and what he does not know: he does not know whether Jesus is a sinner or not in the pharisaic standard, but he knows that his darkness was transformed by Jesus into light and that he, who was blind, can now see. When they see the man's admiration for Jesus, "the Jews" ask him, "What did he do to you? How did he open your eyes?"

---

5. Martyn 2003: 37–62.
6. Lincoln 2006: 284.
7. Kanagaraj 2005: 309–11.

(9:26). They already knew the manner in which Jesus opened the man's eyes (9:15). However, they try to prevent him from believing Jesus by convincing him that Jesus is a sinner.

The healed man turns the table against the authorities by chiding them for their non-understanding and their unwillingness to listen to what he already told them. He prudently refuses to repeat the whole story. He counter-questions, "Why do you wish to hear it again? You do not want to become his disciples, do you?" (9:27). "You did not listen" means that the Pharisees neither accept the reality of healing nor believe in the healer. Investigation done with this mindset will be in vain. His second question is sarcastic, expecting the answer "no," for he knows that they do not wish to become Jesus' disciples even after knowing of Jesus' sign. Ironically, a blind beggar, by virtue of his sight received from Jesus, is turned to do the function of a religious leader to admonish the "religious leaders" themselves. They, not the man born blind, are defective in sight.[8]

The officials told him angrily, with an emphatic "you," "*You* are his disciple" (9:28a). They took the man's question "Do you also want to become his disciples?" as an admission that he is his disciple.[9] They boastfully said, with an emphatic "we," "But *we* are the disciples of Moses," assuming that to be Moses' disciples is superior to being Jesus' disciples (9:28b). They set Moses and Jesus in opposition to each other without grasping that Moses wrote of Jesus (5:46). They were proud of observing Moses' Law, ignoring that Moses, on whom they had set their hope, himself will accuse them before the Father (5:45).

The subject of the dialogue now turns to the origin of Jesus. They rightly believed that God spoke to Moses, even face to face (Exod 33:11; Num 12:8; cf. Deut 34:10–11), but belittled Jesus by confessing their ignorance of the place where "this man" comes from (9:29). In fact they had heard from Jesus several times about his origin (3:13; 6:38, 41, 42, 51; 7:29; 8:23). "The Jews" tried to impress upon the mind of the healed man a wrong notion that Moses is greater than Jesus. The man's personal experience of Jesus' healing gave him courage to point out the irrelevant speech of the religious leaders by telling them, "There is marvel in this, because you do not know where he is from, but he opened my eyes!" (9:30).

The man starts teaching the teachers of the Law the common truth: They all know, including the Pharisees, that God does not listen to the

---

8. Neyrey 2007: 173.
9. Kruse 2008: 225.

The Pharisees' Investigation on the Healing

works and prayers of sinners, but that he approves the works and prayers of anyone who worships God and does his will (9:31). Thereby their claim that Jesus is a sinner is refuted by a man who was born blind. Worship of God and doing his will are two inseparable acts of God's new community.

The healed man's second logical point is that since the beginning of the world no one has ever heard, if not seen, any human who has opened the eyes of a man born blind (9:32), and yet that is what Jesus did, so he must be from God, and cannot be classified as a sinner. The man is convinced that unless Jesus had come from God, he could do nothing such as opening of a blind man's eyes (9:33). Instead of accepting the man's testimony, the teachers of the Law reject his words by saying, "You were born fully with sins and are you teaching us?" (9:34). Jesus' healing of the man from his blindness shows God's love to forgive his sins, but the Pharisees treat him as one who was born in complete sin. In their pride, they are not willing to accept the teaching given by a man who got new insight from Jesus, but cast him out of Jewish community and rob his religious freedom. This action foreshadows the expulsion of Christians from the synagogue in the late first century[10] and the persecution faced by them even today.

JESUS' SELF-REVELATION AS THE SON OF MAN (9:35–41)

The last scene brings Jesus in to reveal himself fully to the healed man and to disclose the blindness of the Jewish leaders. Soon after they cast the healed man out, Jesus found him (9:35) and gave him wholeness by bringing him to the right understanding of himself. Abruptly Jesus asks him, "Do you believe in the Son of Man?" Probably he wanted to assure the man that Jesus descended from heaven, where he was before (3:13; 6:62), and that he will not cast out anyone who comes to him (6:37).

Jesus divulges that the purpose of his coming from God into the world is for judgment (5:27), which is paradoxically twofold: he came so that those who do not see may see and those who see may become blind (9:39).[11] He came to give sight to those who would believe him as the Son of Man who came from God. The healed man exemplifies this. However, those who do not accept this truth may physically see, but they lack spiritual insight to see

---

10. Kanagaraj 2005: 315.

11. Jesus' statement that he came into this world for judgment does not contradict his statements in 3:17 and 12:47. Jesus' coming is generally for the salvation of the world, but those who do not believe in him keep themselves under judgment (3:18) and thus Jesus' salvation turns to be the judgment for unbelievers.

God in Jesus and his heavenly origin. Some of the Pharisees ask him, "We are not blind. Are we too?" (9:40). Jesus' answer implies that the Pharisees are actually blind to the truth that Jesus is the Christ who came down from God and who was prior to and greater than Moses. Were they to accept that they are blind to this truth, they would have no sin, because they would, then, humble themselves and be freed from sin. However, until now they bear their sin because they claim proudly, "We see" (9:41).

The climax of Jesus' dialogue with the healed man comes as the latter asks Jesus to identify the Son of Man so that he may believe in him (9:36), and Jesus reveals himself by saying, "You have seen him, and it is he who speaks to you" (9:37; cf. 4:26). Since the man believes him, eventually he acknowledges Jesus as "Lord" and worships him (9:38). We can observe a growth in the man's understanding of Jesus, as it was with the Samaritan woman: he understood him first as a man (9:11), then as a prophet (9:17), afterwards as "the man from God" (9:33), and finally as the Son of Man who came from heaven to render judgment and as the Lord who is to be worshipped (9:37).[12]

---

12. The man would not have necessarily understood the Son of Man to be the Messiah, but John's readers would have.

JOHN 10
The Impact of Jesus on His Community and on Others

JESUS, THE SELF-GIVING SHEPHERD (10:1–21)

Scholars treat 10:1–21 as a unified sequence with John 9, as Jesus has the same audience with a similar confrontation.[1] Jesus declares himself the good shepherd, who truly cares for his people to the extent of sacrificing himself for them, in contrast to the Pharisees, the false shepherds, who cast people away (cf. 9:34). Jesus' discourse in 10:1–18 is a figurative speech or a parable (10:6) on the shepherd-sheep relationship. He took this parable from the life-situation in Palestine.

At first, there is a picture of a sheepfold, the place to house the sheep, with a door to enter. In the Palestinian context, the door is for the shepherd to enter in to take care of the sheep and lead them out and in. Anyone who climbs up and enters the sheepfold is a thief and robber (10:1). By this imagery, Jesus reproves the Pharisees who did not care for the man who received his sight, but who tried to take away his faith. They would not enter by the door, who is Jesus himself (10:7, 9), but used wrong methods to steal the healed man who now belongs to Jesus' flock. Moreover, they expelled him out of Jewish society without care for his welfare. Such leaders are condemned by Yahweh himself (Ezek 34:1–10) and Jesus calls them "thieves and robbers" (10:1, 8), "strangers" (10:5) and "hirelings" (10:12).

In contrast, the shepherd of the sheep enters the fold through the door, the proper way to get access to the sheep (10:2). The shepherd mentioned is Jesus (10:11, 14) and the sheep are the members of the community he founded. Obviously the door of the sheepfold is kept locked to protect the sheep from false shepherds. The gatekeeper, who guards the entry to the sheepfold, opens the door to the true shepherd. The sheep can easily

---

1. Keener 2005: 1.775–820; Lincoln 2006: 291–92.

recognize the shepherd's voice, as he calls them by name in order to assemble them and lead them out for food and drink (John 10:3; cf. Num 27:17; Ps 23:2; 80:1).

The sheep of Jesus are "his own" possession (10:4, 14) for whom he has unfailing love. When all his sheep come out of the fold, the shepherd goes before them and the sheep follow him by recognizing rightly their shepherd's voice. They will not go after false shepherds, because they are not familiar with the voice of such strangers (10:5). Surprisingly, they (i.e., the Pharisees) did not understand about what he was speaking to them. Based on Ezekiel 34, they should have understood the imagery as picturing the intimate relationship that exists between God and his people. This again proves how blind they were to Jesus' teachings, though they claimed, "We see" (9:41).

It is 10:7–18 that explains who the door of the sheep is and who the shepherd is. It does not seem to hinder a smooth reading of the passage,[2] but gives proper continuity to 10:1–6. The word "door" stands for Jesus, the protector of the sheep from "thieves and robbers" (10:1, 8), and this unchangeable truth is brought out with a solemn affirmation, "truly, truly, I say to you" (10:7). In this context, the "thieves and robbers" denote the Jewish rulers who came "before" Jesus to steal the faith of his sheep, as it is illustrated in their vain attempt to drag the healed man away from his faith in Jesus. Thus, the phrase "before me" has a spatial connotation rather than a temporal connotation.[3]

Jesus interprets the parable further by revealing himself as "I am the door (of the sheep)" (10:7, 9) and thus reveals God, who is "I am that I am," as the door to protect his people and lead them out in paths of righteousness, goodness, and prosperity (Ps 23). In the OT, the word "gate [of heaven]" indicates God's self-revelation and his bestowal of gifts to his chosen ones (Gen 28:17; Ps 78:23; Ps 118:19, 20). In the NT, the "door" or "gate" indicates the point of entrance into heavenly life or eternal destruction at the end-time and the revelation of heavenly secrets to his devotee (Matt 7:13, 14; 25:10; Mark 9:43, 45, 47; Luke 13:24, 25; Rev 4:1). The affirmation that Jesus is the door implies God's self-manifestation and the means of imparting God's gifts and heavenly secrets to human beings, particularly to those who belong to his sheepfold. In this sense, those who have Jesus as the only way to enter will be delivered from eternal damnation.

---

2. Contra von Wahlde 2010: 1.10–12.
3. Michaels 2010: 582–83.

Jesus, the Self-Giving Shepherd

"I came" in 10:10 is a missiological term that denotes Jesus' mission in the world to give heavenly life in abundance to those who become his sheep by receiving him. In contrast, the "thief" comes to steal the faith of Jesus' sheep, to kill and to lead humanity to final destruction. The singular "the thief" is a collective term that denotes Jesus' opponents, whose purpose is to snatch away those who confess Jesus as the Christ from him and from the synagogue fellowship (9:22, 34). Their murderous act and theft (10:12) are stressed in the purpose clause with a double negative in Greek (10:10). Their purpose is in contrast to Jesus' purpose of coming into the world to give his life as a sacrifice to remove human sin, fulfilling thus the temple sacrifice of sheep.[4] Therefore Jesus claims himself as the good shepherd by using God's self-revelatory name "I am" (10:11). It shows himself as the shepherd in the line of David, the Davidic Messiah (2 Sam 5:2; Ps 78:70–72; Jer 3:15; Ezek 34:23–24; 37:24; Mic 5:2, 4; cf. *Pss. Sol.* 17:40–42), who will sacrifice his life for the welfare of others (Isa 53:12; Zech 12:10; 13:7–9).[5]

Jesus is "good" because he is the model of what a shepherd should be.[6] Therefore we may call him the "noble shepherd."[7] Jesus again contrasts himself with the false religious leaders, who are figuratively and collectively called a "hireling." Like a hireling, they forsake Jesus' sheep to be snatched and scattered by "the wolf" and flee to save their own life (10:12–13; cf. Ezek 22:27). "The wolf," in a church context, implies collectively the false apostles and teachers (Acts 20:29–30). In the OT, Yahweh is portrayed as the caring shepherd over against the shepherds of Israel who were destroying and scattering the sheep of his pasture (Jer 23:1–4; Ezek 34:11–16). In John, Jesus takes up the role of Yahweh to be a loving shepherd and to have intimate relationship with his sheep, because what belonged to God are now "his own" sheep (10:14; cf. 6:37, 39–40). Jesus knows his sheep as the ones who were given to him by God in order to communicate God's words to them, to consecrate them in truth and to keep them one (17:6–19). The

---

4. The idea of sacrifice is known from the phrase "laying down his life *for* the sheep" (John 10:11; cf. Zech 13:7–9; Isa 53:10) and by the Greek term *thyein*, "to kill" (10:10), which anticipates "the Jews" who would kill Jesus.

5. Köstenberger 2009: 304–5, esp. n. 36; Jeremias 1978: 489. Philo mentions of Moses' prayer for a good shepherd (*Agr.* 10.44; cf. *Agr.* 12.49) and ascribes shepherding, in the context of God's "I Am" statement, to God and his firstborn Son, the true Word (*Agr.* 12.50–52).

6. Michaels 2010: 585.

7. Neyrey 2007: 180–81.

sheep, in turn, will know their shepherd by receiving his words and believing that he is from God and that he was sent by God (17:8).

As they know each other mutually, their mutual relationship gives Jesus, the owner, a claim on the sheep that no hireling can make.[8] Their intimacy is essentially the same as that of the Son with the Father, and Jesus sacrifices his life for the prosperity of the sheep out of his relationship established by a new covenant (10:15).

The shepherd's goodness is also reflected in his remembrance of "other sheep," the non-Jews, to bring them into his sheepfold. They also will become his own sheep who will recognize and obey his voice. In Jesus, the eschatological ingathering of Jews and Gentiles is dawned (cf. Isa 56:6-8; 66:18-21; Zech 14:16). Eventually, the flock will have both Jews and non-Jews who believe in Jesus and they all will become "one flock" having "one shepherd" (10:16). Jesus' love and care are not limited to Jews alone, but they include the Gentiles also. This oneness goes beyond "one stick/nation" and "one king/shepherd," which refer to the unity of Israelites alone (Ezek 37:15-24; cf. Zech 14:9), to all nationalities. The oneness, created by the sacrificial death of Jesus, is the hallmark of God's new community, which progresses under "one shepherd," Jesus.

The declaration "Because of this the Father loves me, because I lay down my life" (10:17) does not mean that the Father's love for the Son is conditioned by Son's obedience to sacrifice his life. It is entirely the Son's voluntary act ("I have authority to lay it down and I have authority to take it again"; 10:18), which is anchored on the Father's love for him (3:16). The idea of taking back the life laid down, which occurs twice (10:17-18), anticipates Jesus' resurrection. His death, followed by his resurrection, is indeed a command received from the Father out of his love (10:18b). Where there is love relationship, there is a command to obey to preserve intimacy (cf. Gen 3; Rom 5:12-21).

Jesus' words cause division among the Jewish people (10:19; cf. 7:43; 9:16). Without understanding the imagery used by Jesus, many of them accuse, "He has a demon and he is mad" (cf. 7:20; 8:48), and therefore they need not listen to his words (10:20). Both the accusations, "he has a demon" and "he is mad," are interrelated, meaning, "he is out of his mind" (Mark 3:21-22). Others, however, do not accept Jesus' words as those of a demoniac, because a demon could not have opened the eyes of the blind (10:21; 9:32).

---

8. Bultmann 1971: 371.

JEWISH REJECTION OF JESUS INTENSIFIED (10:22–42)

Now John moves on to narrate Jesus' conflict with his Jewish accusers in Jerusalem, this time at the feast of the Dedication, which was celebrated within three months after the feast of Tabernacles. By openly attacking "the Jews" that they are not his sheep because of their unbelief, Jesus assures once more of his love for "my sheep" and that he will give them eternal life and protect them from anyone who would snatch them away from the Father's hand (10:26–29). The point of contention, however, is on Jesus' identity.

Is Jesus the Christ? (10:22–31)

The feast of the Dedication (*Hanukkah*), a festival called "Lights" (*Ant.* 12.7.7), was celebrated in Jerusalem (10:22) during winter, commemorating the cleansing of the temple and relighting of the altar fire by Judas Maccabaeus in 164 BCE, three years to the day after the desecration by Antiochus Epiphanes (2 Macc 10:1–9; cf. 1 Macc 1:54). On the day of this feast Jesus was walking in the temple, in the portico of Solomon (10:23), which could be the eastern cloister built by King Solomon (*J.W.* 5.5.1; *Ant.* 15.11.3; 20.9.7). This was a traditional place for teaching and disputation (Acts 3:11; 5:12).[9]

"The Jews" gathered around Jesus with a hostile intention (cf. Ps 118:10–12) and insisted that he openly confess if he was the Christ (10:24).[10] Jesus had already revealed himself as the shepherd-king who will come in the line of David. His opponents could not grasp it, but attempted to make him confess his messiahship plainly so that they might accuse him of blasphemy and condemn him to death (cf. Mark 14:61–64). Jesus' answer, "I told you, and you do not believe" (10:25a), looks back to all he had taught thus far. His words were spoken and his works were done with the authority of God (5:43) and as a witness to himself that he was sent by God (10:25b; 5:36). However, they did not believe. Thus Jesus implicitly accepts that he is the Christ and that only those who believe his words and works can perceive this "Messianic Secret."[11] Believing Jesus as the Christ is fundamental

---

9. Michaels 2010: 595.

10. They asked Jesus, "Until how long would you seize our spirit/soul?" ("How long will you keep us in suspense?" [ESV]), implying a state of anxiety (cf. Ps 25:1 LXX; 86:4 LXX); von Wahlde 2010: 2.471.

11. Keener 2005: 1.824.

to enter his sheepfold (cf. 1:41, 45; 4:25-26; 9:35-37; 12:34; 20:31), but "the Jews" are not his sheep because of their unbelief (10:26).

The sheep owned by Jesus obey his voice and follow him wherever he leads (10:3-4, 27). Jesus knows them, as he has an intimate relationship of love with them (10:27, 14). Since he knows them, he gives them the life of the age to come, even now, and they will be delivered from final destruction and from the thieves who would try to snatch his sheep from his hand (10:28, 10, 12-15). Jesus assures that no one, even a Jewish authority, is able to snatch his sheep out of his Father's hand, because the Father, who has given them to Jesus, is greater than all powers (10:29).[12]

"Out of my hand" and "out of the Father's hand" are the same, for the sheep are under the protection and care of the Father and the Son, who are one in works (5:17), words (3:34; 8:26), glory (1:14; 13:31-32), name (17:6, 11), life (5:21, 26), and authority to judge (5:22, 27). Therefore the one who sees the Son sees the Father (12:45; 14:9), and the one who believes in Jesus believes in God (12:44). Both the Father and the Son mutually indwell one another (14:10-11). Therefore the Johannine Jesus plainly affirms, "I and the Father are one" (10:30). Father and Son pre-existed in oneness with each other, although they are two personalities and therefore the Son alone can reveal God who otherwise cannot be seen with human eyes (1:1, 18; 6:46). Jesus' reclaim for equality with the Father so kindled the anger of his opponents that they took up stones to stone and kill him (10:31; cf. 8:59).

Is Jesus the Son of God? (10:32-39)

Without leaving the temple this time, Jesus confronts his enemies. He asks them ironically for which of the good works he did are they going to stone him (10:32). Jesus' works, including the two signs done on the Sabbath (5:9, 16; 9:14), are good because they involve the giving, not taking, of life.[13] But "the Jews" responded by saying that Jesus, being a man, made himself God and thus spoke blasphemy that deserved death by stoning (John 10:33; cf. Lev 24:16). They could not perceive the divine truth behind Jesus' declaration, "I and the Father are one" (10:30).

In response, Jesus appeals to the Scripture by saying, "Is it not written in your law, 'I said, you are gods?,'" a question that expects the answer "yes" (10:34). "Your law" means the Law that the Jews themselves uphold

---

12. Cf. Lincoln 2006: 305-6.
13. Michaels 2010: 602.

Jewish Rejection of Jesus Intensified

(cf. 5:39; 8:17; 15:25). By saying so, Jesus is distancing himself from the Jews who wrongly understood the Law. The quotation comes from Ps 82:6, where the term "gods" means the divine council whose members are the "sons of the Most High" (Ps 82:1, 6b). The context implies that Yahweh, the judge, will bring justice to the weak, the fatherless, and the needy (Ps 82:1b, 3–4), but will pronounce destruction on the judges and leaders who failed to do justice (Ps 82:2–7). Jesus argues that if God, who made Moses a god to Pharoah (Exod 7:1) and who called even the unjust judges and false leaders "gods," how can they accuse Jesus, who was consecrated and sent into the world, that he blasphemes by saying, "I am the Son of God" (10:34–36)? If Scripture itself, which cannot be disobeyed, uses the term "god" of someone besides God himself, how much more appropriate is the use of the term for Jesus?[14]

Jesus challenges his accusers that they need not believe him, if his works are not the works of "my Father" (10:37). Then he invites them to believe his works so that they may perceive that the Father is in him and he in the Father (10:38; cf. 14:10–11), for his signs themselves will show to them his oneness with the Father in terms of their mutual indwelling. In spite of Jesus' teaching, the authorities seek to arrest him (10:39; cf. 7:30; 11:57), but Jesus escapes from their hands.

Others who believed in Jesus (10:40-42)

Jesus crossed the Jordan again and went to "Bethany beyond Jordan," a place of springs, situated perhaps on the eastern side of Jordan in northern Peraea, and this is the place where John was baptizing at first (10:40; cf. 1:28; 3:23). Jesus remained there and many who had seen his signs came to hear his words. They were so influenced by Jesus' life and words that they exclaimed that whatever John, without doing any sign, said about Jesus was true (10:41). No wonder many believed in Jesus there, perhaps as the Christ, the Son of God.

The whole ministry of Jesus narrated in 1:19—10:39 is concerned with Jesus' words and works that led him to a conflict with his Jewish opponents basically on the issue of who Jesus is. The conflict eventually led Jesus to the cross, which becomes clear in the subsequent chapters, particularly after Lazarus was raised from the dead (11:47–53; 12:7, 23; 13:1–3; etc.). The cross will project Jesus as Christ, the King of the Jews and the Son of God,

---

14. See Keener 2005: 1.829.

who came to the world to reveal God's love and faithfulness to his own covenant with his people.

Fusing the Horizons

The imagery of sheep and shepherd is used in the OT to describe the covenantal relationship between Yahweh and his people, and in the NT it explains the intimate relationship that exists between Jesus and God's new community. Today it shows us the characteristics of a Christian leader/pastor in relation to his/her people (cf. Eph 4:11 where "pastors" are known as *poimenas*, "shepherds"; 1 Pet 5:4). As a model shepherd-leader, Jesus shows love for his people and equally does justice by punishing the wicked and leading the believers in spiritual warfare.[15]

I know a pastor in India who used to carry food, clothing, and other needed things to the people of his congregation when they were caught by natural calamities such as flood and drought. He used to help the poor by giving money, clothing, and textbooks for children whenever they needed them. At the same time, he used to be strict in administering the institutions that were under his management, punishing wrongdoers and admiring those who performed well. Most of the people loved him and I have appreciated his care for his own flock.

Another pastor whom I know used to go to meet with his people, risking his own life, whenever they were in danger of being attacked by their adversaries belonging to another caste group in the village. The pastor's presence has saved his congregation members several times from the hands of their enemies. Still another pastor saved one of his congregation members from the hands of police when he was dragged into the police station with false accusations. He delivered the man by talking with the concerned police officers and explaining what actually happened.

These are the glimpses of Christian leaders who, by following Jesus, have demonstrated themselves as model shepherds by giving themselves for the welfare of the people given to them.

---

15. Newbigin 1977: 14.

JOHN 11
Lazarus' Resurrection and Its Implications

RAISING OF LAZARUS FROM THE DEAD (11:1-44)

John 11, which has Jesus' seventh sign, links the events that happened at the Jewish feasts and the events of Jesus' suffering and death. It is Lazarus' resurrection, followed by Jesus' triumphant entry into Jerusalem (12:12-19), that eventually lead Jesus to death. There are several events that link John 11 with previous chapters: Jesus' staying two days longer in the place where John at first baptized (10:40) even after hearing of Lazarus' illness (11:6), the attempt to stone at Jesus (11:8), the reference to light and life (11:9-10, 25-26) and to the healing of the man born blind (11:37), the authorities' plan to kill Jesus (11:46-53), and their order to arrest him (11:57).[1]

The death of Lazarus (11:1-16)

Lazarus, of Bethany, the village of Mary and her sister Martha, is introduced as "certain man" who was ill (11:1). John takes it for granted that his audience knew that Lazarus was the brother of Martha and Mary. Mary attained significance because she anointed Jesus with a costly ointment and wiped his feet with her hair. Lazarus, who is mentioned now as her brother, was ill (11:2). The two sisters sent a message to Jesus, who was ministering in Bethany beyond Jordan, saying, "Lord, behold, he whom you love is ill" (11:3). The sisters obviously expected Jesus to come and heal Lazarus (cf. 11:21, 32). The description of Lazarus as "the one whom you love" shows Lazarus' intimacy with Jesus. It is difficult, however, to prove that Lazarus is "the disciple whom Jesus loved" (13:23), as the name of this disciple is completely hidden in John.

---

1. Kanagaraj 2005: 355.

After hearing of Lazarus' sickness, Jesus comments that Lazarus' sickness is not unto death. Although he foreknew that Lazarus would die (11:11, 14), for him death will have no power over Lazarus, because Jesus will raise him up to life to manifest God's glory. In the manifestation of God's glory, the Son of God will be glorified (11:4).[2] Whatever glorifies God glorifies Jesus also (13:31-32). Jesus' raising of Lazarus, the seventh sign in John, will demonstrate God's life-giving power and also will lead to Jesus' arrest, suffering, and death on the cross (11:46-53), where God's glory will be manifested in Jesus.

Out of his love for Martha, Mary, and Lazarus, Jesus stayed two more days in his place even after he learned that Lazarus was ill (11:5-6). This delay is due to Jesus' commitment to work in God's time so that God's glory may be revealed magnificently in human powerlessness and that his disciples may believe in him (11:15, 40, 42, 45; cf. 11:48). After two days, Jesus, as the mark of his willingness to be put to death, said, "Let us go into Judea again" (11:7). In response, his disciples, who understood the circumstances in human terms, said, "Rabbi, the Jews were now seeking to stone you, and are you going there again?" (11:8). They knew what happened at the feast of the Dedication (10:31) and so wanted to protect Jesus' life.

Jesus responded in terms of metaphors: "day," implying light, and "night," implying darkness. His counter-question, "Are there not twelve hours in the day?," expects the answer "yes" (11:9a). The twelve hours from sunrise to sunset has enough light so that no one may stumble on the way. In contrast, those who perform activities at night stumble on the way due to the dominating darkness and absence of light in them. The metaphor means, at the natural level, that in the sunlight, available at daytime, peoples' works are exposed and they find their direction, but that at night, when there is darkness, they cannot work and find their way to reach their destination (cf. 9:4). However, at the supernatural level, it means that Jesus is the Light of the world (8:12; 9:5) in whose light peoples' deeds are exposed (3:20-21) and that his absence will cause darkness in the world. As a result, people become ignorant of Jesus and keep doing evil (3:19-20). Jesus' statements on walking in the day and walking in the night (11:9b-10) have ethical connotations, as the verb "to walk" shows, and therefore make a supernatural meaning possible. That is, the time appointed by the Father for Jesus to depart from the world is fast approaching and he must go to Judea to face suffering and death. Therefore, Jesus exhorted them to believe

---

2. The title "Son of God" is used only in 11:4 to denote the glorification of Jesus.

Raising of Lazarus from the Dead

in the Light and do good works while the Light is with them for a little while (12:35–36), lest they miss God's way and purpose.

Jesus enigmatically states that Lazarus, "our friend," has fallen asleep and that he goes to awake him (11:11). "To fall asleep" was used in Judaism and in Christian circles as a euphemism for death (1 Cor 15:6; 1 Thess 4:14–16). The narrator clarifies that Jesus means that Lazarus is dead (11:13a). However, his disciples tell Jesus that Lazarus would be restored if he had fallen asleep, thinking that Jesus meant Lazarus' physical sleep (11:12–13). Now Jesus himself clarifies that Lazarus is dead (11:14). Jesus expresses his gladness for not having been in Bethany for the sake of his disciples, for Lazarus' death will enable the disciples to see God's glory in Jesus and to believe in him as the giver of life (11:4, 15). Thus saying, he exhorts them to go to Lazarus (11:15). Thomas, who was called Didymos, a nickname for a twin,[3] invites his codisciples to go with Jesus to die with him (11:16; 14:5). Thomas unconsciously predicts Jesus' death in Judea without, however, grasping its redemptive significance. He also unconsciously predicts that all the twelve disciples would eventually die as martyrs for Jesus.

Martha's confession of Jesus as the Christ (11:17–27)

In 11:17, the scene shifts to Bethany of Judea, two miles away from Jerusalem in the southeast, on the way to Jericho (11:18). From now on, Jesus becomes the focus in this chapter, without any reference to his disciples. When Jesus arrives there, he finds Lazarus having been in the tomb for four days, a length of time by which, as per Jewish belief, the soul would have left the body and the body would have fully decayed, making it impossible to recognize the person.[4] The reference to the decay of Lazarus' body is to prepare the readers to perceive the glorious power of God.

Many Judeans were consoling Martha and Mary over Lazarus' death (11:19). At this time, Martha hears that Jesus was coming. Immediately she went out and met him (11:20) while he was still outside the village (11:30). Mary was sitting in the house mourning (cf. Job 2:8, 13; Ezek 8:14). Martha's act shows the family's faith in and love for Jesus. Her statement of anguish, "Lord, if you were here, my brother would not have died" (11:21), shows her preliminary faith in the lordship of Jesus. However, her conviction that "even now I know that whatever you ask from God, God will give

---

3. Michaels 2010: 623 n. 42.
4. Lindars 1972: 392–93; Ridderbos 1997: 393.

you" (11:22) shows her deeper faith that if Jesus prays to the Father who sent him, Lazarus will be brought back to life. On seeing Martha's faith, Jesus promises that her brother will be raised (11:23).

Martha misunderstands Jesus' promise as referring to Lazarus' resurrection at the end-time (11:24; cf. 5:28-29; 6:40, 44, 54, 58). Jesus corrects her by affirming, "I am the resurrection and the life" (11:25a). This means that in Jesus the eternally existing God reveals himself as the one who offers to those who believe in Jesus the life of resurrection now and at the end-time. The present possession of resurrection life in Jesus is known by the use of present tenses "I am" and "the one who believes," while its future inheritance is envisaged in Jesus' assurance, "Even if [those who believe in me] die, they *shall* live" (11:25b). The present and future experiences of resurrection life are intertwined in 11:26 (cf. 5:24-25). Every one who lives and believes in Jesus *now shall* never experience death. With this clarification, Jesus asks Martha, "Do you believe this?" (11:26b).

Martha's answer, "Yes, Lord, I have believed that you are the Christ, the Son of God, who is coming into the world" (11:27), is highly charged with christological meaning. The intensive perfect, "I have believed," means, "I have come to believe," and indicates a settled conviction.[5] Martha's confession is the basic belief of God's new community. The credit of confessing Jesus as the Christ, the Son of God, goes to a woman in John, whereas in the Synoptic Gospels it goes to a man, Simon Peter (Matt 16:16 par.). In John, the title "Christ" is used synonymously with "the Holy One of God" (6:69), "the one of whom Moses in the Law and also the prophets wrote" (1:41, 45), the "Son of God" and "the King of Israel" (1:49). The additional confession "He who is coming into the world" implies Jesus' whole incarnate life in the world (1:9). In the Synoptic Gospels it refers to the Messiah (Matt 11:3; Luke 7:19). The title "the Son of God," which is used in synonymous terms with "Christ," emphasizes Jesus' equality with the Father (5:18; 19:7). Thus, Martha's confession has three different titles for Jesus, each with different emphasis, but conveying the same truth.

Jesus' mourning over Lazarus' death (11:28-37)

After confessing Jesus as the Messiah, the Son of God, Martha rushed home to call her sister and said to her privately, "The teacher is here and is calling you" (11:28). It is more reasonable to take the Greek word *lathra*

---

5. Köstenberger 2009: 336 n. 71.

Raising of Lazarus from the Dead

("privately") with Martha speaking to Mary than with Martha calling her,[6] for only after Mary heard Martha did Mary rise quickly and go out to meet Jesus (11:29, 31). This shows that Martha must have spoken with Mary secretly in the midst of other mourners so that she too might go and welcome Jesus, who was still outside the village in the place where Martha met him (11:30). The use of the word "the teacher" shows that Martha, and possibly Mary too, considered themselves as learners from Jesus. The expression "is here" does not indicate in this context the coming (*parousia*) of Jesus.[7] It simply conveys the nearness of Jesus outside the village. The text does not say that Jesus was calling for Mary. However, Martha's words "The teacher is here and is calling you" could be a euphemism used to get Mary to meet with Jesus. Mary's quick response to go to Jesus shows her love and high regard for him. Most probably Martha also followed her, as both of them were at Lazarus' tomb (10:39–40).

The neighbors who were sitting with Mary (11:19) saw her rise quickly and go out. They thought that she was departing to the tomb to weep there and therefore they followed her (11:31). Their underlying concern was that they should not leave a bereaved person alone. Mary, however, came to the place where Jesus was. When she saw him, she fell at his feet and said almost verbatim what Martha had told in 11:21 (11:32). She thus expressed her belief in the life-giving power of Jesus! "Falling at Jesus' feet," in Mary's case, is a symbolic act of paying homage (cf. 12:1–8) and of pouring her grief to him with tears (11:33). Mary's humble act so moved the hearts of her friends that they wept. When Jesus saw Mary and the Jews weeping out of sorrow, he became greatly agitated in his spirit and troubled (11:33, 38). He expressed his fierce indignation toward death by his inner groaning (cf. Lam 2:6).

With grief, Jesus asked for the place where Lazarus' body was laid and they led him to the tomb by saying, "Lord, come and see" (11:34). The word "they" could refer to the two sisters who were accompanied by their friends. It does not seem that they had yet reached Lazarus' tomb, but Jesus' emotion, mixed with his compassion for the bereaved, made him weep along with them. The Greek word *dokruein*, used in the aorist tense for Jesus' weeping, is different from the word that is used in the present tense for Mary's and the Jews' weeping (*klaiein*). This means that Jesus did not join in the mourners' continual crying, but that he "burst into tears" out

---

6. Contra Köstenberger 2009: 336 n. 73.
7. Contra Michaels 2010: 634.

John 11:28-37

of his pity for the bereaved (11:35).[8] He wept with those who wept (Rom 12:15)! Jesus' emotions of compassion and deep distress as a human and his self-identification with the grieving humanity are intermingled in the shortest verse, "Jesus wept" (11:35).

On seeing Jesus weeping, some mourners were astonished at the love Jesus had habitually for Lazarus (11:36). However, others raised the question, "Could not this man, who opened the eyes of the blind, have done something that he would not even die?" (11:37). Though this is reasonable question, it shows their unbelief in the healing power of Jesus, even after seeing his opening of eyes of a man born blind.[9] They were also ignorant of God's way and time of performing signs.

Exit of Lazarus from the tomb (11:38-44)

With an agitated heart, Jesus came to the tomb. The word "again" indicates that this is the second time that Jesus was emotionally moved (cf. 11:33). Lazarus' tomb was a cave with a stone laid upon it. The Jews usually buried their dead in natural caves outside the village. Archaeological evidence suggests that Lazarus' tomb was horizontal with a square stone laid upon it.[10] It was probably an antechamber with an opening in the ground leading to the actual burial chamber. The stone was laid at this opening. Jesus asked the bystanders to take the stone away (11:39). Martha, the sister of the "dead man," prevented the removal of the stone by reminding that it was four days since he died and therefore there will be an odor. Martha shows here her little faith, in contrast to her faith shown earlier (11:22). John confirms through Martha's objection the reality of Lazarus' death four days ago. This, in turn, leads to the reality of his resurrection.

Jesus reminds Martha of his earlier injunction that if she would believe she would see the glory of God (11:40). This assurance given to Martha is not recorded by John, though he assured his disciples of the revelation of the glory of God through Lazarus' death (11:4). Possibly Jesus gave this promise to Martha during his encounter with her outside the village. "Seeing the glory of God" in Jesus' signs and supremely on the cross is a recurring theme in John, probably as a polemic against the then-prevalent interest in the ascent to heaven to see God's kingly glory on the throne in

---

8. Cf. Michaels 2010: 640; Köstenberger 2009: 341 n. 94.
9. Carson 1991: 417; Köstenberger 2009: 342.
10. Cf. Schnackenburg 1980-84: 2.517 n. 63.

human form. Those who believe, not those who claim to have ascended to heaven, would see God's love and saving power in Jesus' deeds, though sometimes people come to believe in Jesus after seeing God's love in Jesus' signs (2:11; 9:36–38; 11:45).

After they removed the stone, Jesus prays to the Father by lifting up his eyes, a gesture by which the Jews used to pray (John 11:41; cf. 17:1; Ps 121:1–2). Jesus thus shows his dependence on God and his appeal to the Father to work (5:17). By calling God "Father" (cf. 12:27–28; 17:1, 5, 11, 21, 24), Jesus first of all gives thanks to God (cf. 6:11, 23) by foreseeing that God has already heard his prayer to bring Lazarus back to life (cf. "you *heard*" in 11:41). Jesus knew that the Father always hears his petitions (11:42a), just like the Son always does what the Father does. In the Godhead, the Father and the Son mutually fulfill one another's will. Although God hears his Son's prayer always, Jesus utters a formal prayer at Lazarus' tomb for the sake of the bystanders so that they might see his sign and come to believe that God sent him into the world (11:42b) to deliver those who believe in him from eternal condemnation and give them divine life (3:16–17).

After his prayer, Jesus cries with a loud voice, "Lazarus, come out!" (11:43). At the voice of Jesus, the dead man comes out of the tomb in the same condition in which he was buried, having his hands and feet bound and his face wrapped with a cloth. The Jewish manner of burial reflected here confirms the historical reliability of the story. Jesus' command, "Unbind him and allow him to go" (11:44), indicates the victory of Jesus over physical death and the freedom from bondage he gives to people even now. Jesus' loud voice asking the dead man to come out marks his authority to raise the dead and anticipates the eschatological resurrection of the dead by the same voice (5:28–29). The coming out of Lazarus from the tomb with cloths unbound is different from Jesus' resurrection, with his cloths left behind in the tomb and the napkin of his head rolled up in the place by itself (20:6–7), indicating Jesus' sovereignty in his resurrection, unlike Lazarus' dependence on Jesus to be raised.[11] The link between Lazarus' death and resurrection and the resolution of Jewish authorities, after Lazarus' resurrection, to murder Jesus shows that Lazarus' episode prefigures Jesus' death and resurrection.

---

11. Cf. Lincoln 2006: 329; Keener 2005: 2.848.

John 11:45-57

DECISION OF THE JEWISH COUNCIL TO KILL JESUS (11:45-57)

There was a double response to Jesus' sign of raising Lazarus. Many Judeans who had come with Mary looked at the sign and started believing in Jesus (11:45). However, some of them went and told the Pharisees, who were already looking for an opportunity to arrest Jesus and put him to death (5:18; 7:1, 30, 32; 8:20, 59; 10:31, 39; 11:8), what Jesus did to Lazarus (11:46). Being aggravated with what they heard, the chief priests and the Pharisees, who constituted the Sanhedrin (the Jewish council), gathered the council to discuss on what they should do with Jesus who was performing many signs (20:30; 21:25) and drawing many to believe in him. They feared that if every one starts believing in Jesus,[12] then the believers would make him king (cf. 6:14-15), which would mean rebellion against the Roman governance. It would then provoke the Romans to come and take away their place, the Jerusalem temple (cf. 2 Macc 1:29; 5:19; Acts 6:14; 21:28), and nation, the people of Israel (11:48). Thus, they were troubled by the religious and political consequences of the mass following Jesus. This could be a political prophecy concerning the Romans, who would seize Jerusalem in 66-70 CE to destroy the temple and take away the Jews as slaves.[13]

Caiaphas, the high priest of that year, is the spokesperson in this discussion. In 18-36 CE he was the high priest, the *ex officio* president of the Sanhedrin, and thus he was "one of them." The phrase "of that year" does not mean that the high priests were appointed annually, though in some cases that happened. It means "in that year," that is, "in the year when Jesus was arrested and crucified."[14] Caiaphas chides the council members that they know nothing (11:49), for they do not reckon that it is advantageous for them if one man dies for the people instead of the whole nation perishing (11:50). Though Caiaphas' counsel is politically motivated, it is within God's redemptive plan for the welfare of all nations and therefore he is later reminded of what he suggested (18:14).

There was a belief that the high priests had a gift of prophecy[15] and therefore the narrator comments that, being the high priest in that year, Caiaphas himself unknowingly prophesied that Jesus was going to die not only for the salvation of Jewish nation but also for the ingathering of the

---

12. The word "every one" is an exaggerated form for "many."
13. Kanagaraj 2005: 377.
14. Kanagaraj 2005: 377-78; cf. Keener 2005: 2.854.
15. Lincoln, 2006: 330 (e.g., *Ant.* 6.12.4-5).

Decision of the Jewish Council to Kill Jesus

dispersed Jews, the "children of God" (11:51–52). The term "the children of God" in John refers widely to all those who believe in Jesus (1:12–13). The statement that the benefit of Jesus' death is for all humans ironically came from the mouth of someone who stood against Jesus. He unconsciously acknowledged that Jesus will gather "other sheep" into his sheepfold so that they may become "one flock, one shepherd" (10:7–16).

The council agreed to what was said by Caiaphas and took an official resolution to kill Jesus (11:53). Since it was an official decision of the Jewish council, Jesus was no longer ministering (literally "walking") openly among the Jews, but went away from there to Ephraim (cf. 2 Sam 13:23; 2 Chr 13:19), a town in the country near the wilderness lying about fifteen miles to the northeast of Jerusalem. Jesus stayed there with his disciples (11:54), for the hour of the Father had not yet come for him to hand himself over to "the Jews."

In accordance with their decision, the chief priests and the Pharisees gave orders that any one who knew where Jesus was should inform them so that they might arrest him (11:57). At this time the Passover of the Jews came. Many from the countryside of Judea went up to Jerusalem to purify themselves (cf. Num 9:6–13; 2 Chr 30:15–19) before entering into the court of the priests to sacrifice the Passover lambs (11:55; cf. 18:28). The pilgrims were expecting Jesus to come to Jerusalem for the Passover. Some who were in the temple questioned among themselves, "What do you think? That he will never come to the feast?" (11:56). Probably the people expected from Jesus more signs, which on previous occasions were followed by references to his death and resurrection (2:13–22; 6:4–71). Their expectation and the leaders' decision to murder Jesus foreshadow Jesus' death and resurrection in Jerusalem to stabilize God's new community.

JOHN 12
The Final Journey of Jesus to Jerusalem

MARY'S ANOINTING OF JESUS (12:1–11)

Six days before the Passover, Jesus came to Bethany where he had raised Lazarus from the dead (12:1). John 12 thus provides continuity to John 11 and echoes the Synoptic tradition on Jesus' stay in Bethany in his last days on earth (Matt 21:17; Mark 11:12). There they made for him a "dinner," an evening meal. The hosts were Lazarus and his sisters. Martha was serving and Mary anointed Jesus' feet, while Lazarus was reclining with Jesus (12:2–3a). The feast could have been an occasion to mark their love and gratitude to Jesus. Mary took a pound of costly ointment produced from the roots of the spikenard plant (pure nard),[1] anointed the feet of Jesus, and wiped his feet with her hair (cf. 11:2). A *litra* of ointment, in Roman measurement, was 12 ounces[2] or 326 grams,[3] costing about 300 denarii (12:5), the unit of a day's earnings for a laborer. This means that the ointment had been prepared from a large quantity of the aromatic plant.

Anointing the feet of guests was not a common Jewish custom during the meal. Other Gospels speak of a woman who anointed Jesus' head two days before the Passover at Bethany (Matt 26:6–13; Mark 14:3–9) and of another woman who wet Jesus' feet with her tears and wiped them with her hair (Luke 7:36–50). John seems to fuse both these traditions, identifying the woman as Mary of Bethany, and focuses on Jesus' feet rather than his head.

She wiped the ointment she had poured on Jesus' feet with her hair rather than with any of her clothes. This too was not a normal Jewish custom. A woman unbinding her hair in public was considered a sign of loose

---

1. This nard may be an extract from an aromatic Nepalese plant, *Nardostachys jatamansi*; Kruse 2009: 258.
2. Michaels 2010: 664 n. 19.
3. Kruse 2009: 258.

Mary's Anointing of Jesus

morals.[4] However, Mary might have been allowed to do anointing in this fashion in order to fill the house with the fragrance of the perfume (12:3b) and thus to share the family's joy with other guests. There could be royal overtones in Mary's anointing, an event followed by Jesus' entry into Jerusalem, where he is hailed as "he who comes in the name of the Lord, even the King of Israel" (12:13).[5] Mary's act, then, acknowledges Jesus as the King of Israel, the Messiah who is to come. What Jesus will do before the feast of the Passover (13:1–17) is prefigured in Mary's act of humility!

However, Judas Iscariot, one of his disciples, who would betray Jesus, views Mary's act as a waste and suggests that the ointment could have been sold and the money given to the poor (12:4–5). Unlike Matthew (26:8–9) and Mark (14:4–5), John specifies Judas Iscariot as the one who murmured. Although he may seem right, his motive was wrong, for he did not say it with real care for the poor, but because he was a thief, the one who was holding the money box and who took what was put in it (12:6). Perhaps he used to steal money put in the box (cf. 13:29).[6] His covetousness made him to betray Jesus for thirty pieces of silver (Matt 26:15–16).

Jesus defends Mary by saying, "Leave her alone, so that she might keep it for the day of my burial" (12:7). He reminds the guests that they have the poor always with them (cf. Deut 15:11) and adds, "But you do not always have me" (12:8), hinting at his departure to the Father through the cross (13:1). For Jesus, the priority is to acknowledge him as the messianic King and to spend anything costly for him rather than to give money to the poor without real care for them. Mary's act of sacrificial anointing looks forward to the day of Jesus' burial. The outcome of Jesus' death, which will spread the fragrance of God's sacrificial love to the world, is already exhibited in Mary's anointing of his feet. Mary unknowingly performs a prophetic act.[7] For the Johannine Jesus, Mary's annointing is neither an act of penitence (Luke) nor a preparatory act for future burial (Matthew and Mark), but an act performed *on the day of his burial*. Thus he brings the meaning of his death to be seen in the sacrifice made by one of his female disciples even before the Passover.[8] Mary's anointing proclaims Jesus' enthronement as King on the cross in fulfillment of God's redemptive plan for humanity.

4. Köstenberger 2009: 362.
5. Köstenberger 2009: 361; cf. Koester 2003: 130.
6. As Judas Iscariot is labeled as a thief, the statement "he used to take away" (*ebastazen*) should be understood in terms of taking away for oneself from the money box.
7. Lindars 1972: 419.
8. Kanagaraj 2005: 391–92.

John 12:1–11

A great crowd of Jewish people heard that Jesus was in Bethany and came there to see Jesus and also Lazarus, whom he had raised from the dead (12:9). On account of Lazarus many Jews went to Jesus and believed in him (12:11). Thus Lazarus became the means of drawing people to Jesus. The mass following behind Jesus made the chief priests to plan to kill Lazarus also (12:10). It is ironic that the Jewish leaders were seeking to kill the innocents during the Passover, which commemorates God's gift of freedom and new life.[9]

REVOLUTIONARY ENTRY OF JESUS INTO JERUSALEM (12:12–19)

On the next day of the anointing, a great crowd of pilgrims (cf. 12:9) heard that Jesus was coming to Jerusalem. Out of joy they took the branches of palm trees and went out to meet him. John alone specifies the palm branches used by the crowd and not the garments that were spread along the road before Jesus (Matt 21:8; Mark 11:8). Palm branches were mainly used to give a jubilant welcome to a king or warrior and as a mark of joy and thanksgiving for God's deliverance (1 Macc 13:51; 2 Macc 10:7; cf. Rev 7:9; *T. Naph.* 5:4).

The crowd acclaims that Jesus is "the one who comes in the name of the Lord" and "the King of Israel" (12:13; cf. Zeph 3:15). It implies that Jesus is the Christ (11:27) and Son of God (1:49), who enters into Jerusalem to overcome his enemies revolutionarily by his suffering, death, and resurrection. They cry "Hosanna," which means, "Save now, we pray" (cf. 2 Sam 14:4 MT), a prayer that was turned into a cry of praise to the messianic King. The greeting "Blessed is he who comes in the name of the Lord" was used to give thanks to the Lord for his salvation and also as a prayer for the coming Messiah (Ps 118:25–27; the epithet "he who comes" denotes the expected Messiah in Matt 3:11; 11:3; 23:39; John 11:27). Unknowingly, the crowd acclaims the truth that Jesus is the Davidic Messiah, the King.

In John, Jesus sits on a young ass *after* the crowd's acclamation (12:14) to exhibit that he comes as a humble and accessible king rather than as a political figure with military power and glory. Jesus' riding on a young ass is presented as the fulfillment of Zech 9:9, which refers to the coming King of the Jews humbly seated on an ass's colt (12:15). John changes the OT command "Rejoice greatly" to "Fear not" (cf. Zeph 3:14–17; Isa 35:4; 44:6–8). It assures people not to fear, as they used to the Roman authoritarianism, for

---

9. Kanagaraj 2005: 393.

Revolutionary Entry of Jesus into Jerusalem

the King of the Jews is coming in humility to deliver Israel and bring peace to the whole earth.[10]

Jesus' disciples could not understand at first that his riding on an ass was the fulfillment of the OT prophecy. But after Jesus was glorified on the cross, they remembered the humble nature of Jesus' kingship and what the pilgrims had done to him as already written in Scripture (12:16; cf. 2:22; 4:33-34; 11:11-16). The disciples' remembrance could be due to the coming of the Holy Spirit (7:39; 16:7), who will remind them of all that Jesus had told them (14:26).[11] Some in the crowd who went to greet Jesus had been with Jesus when he raised Lazarus. These people bore witness to what they had seen and heard (12:17). Obviously this crowd believed in Jesus after seeing the sign, for in John's Gospel bearing witness is always done by those who believe in Jesus (1:7-8, 15; 5:31-37). Some people went to meet Jesus because they heard of Jesus' sign (12:18).

Bewildered by the mass following after Jesus, the Pharisees were unable to do anything to Jesus in spite of their public arrest warrant (11:57). They said to one another, "You see that you accomplish nothing; look, the world went after him" (12:19). The term "world" is an exaggerated word for "many" (cf. 11:48). It conveys the universal effect of the life and ministry of Jesus. Their words could be an unconscious prophecy that in future many more will believe and join God's community of believers. Jesus' entry into Jerusalem was revolutionary because the King of Israel was riding on an ass and his entry shook the hearts of religious leadership with a sense of defeat.

COMING OF THE GREEKS TO JESUS (12:20-36)

Dying for oneself (12:20-26)

There were some Greeks who had gone up to Jerusalem to worship at the Passover feast (12:20). These Greeks are not the Greek-speaking Jews.[12] These devout Greeks might be "God-fearers," who liked Judaism because of its monotheism and strong ethical teachings but who would not accept circumcision and break with their families (Acts 10:1-2; 13:16; 17:4; cf. Acts

---

10. Barrett 1978: 419; Kanagaraj 2005: 396-97.

11. The Jesus tradition in the Gospels is the result of the disciples' remembrance of what Jesus said and did and of their sharing among themselves after the resurrection; Dunn 2003: 128-33, 177-86, 404-7, etc.

12. *Contra* Robinson 1959-60: 120.

8:27–28; Luke 7:2–5).[13] They came to Philip of Bethsaida (1:44) and said, "Sir, we wish to see Jesus" (12:21). Philip, along with Andrew, told Jesus (12:22). The Greeks who came to Jerusalem to worship Yahweh wished to see Jesus. Theologically, it implies that real worship during the Passover lies in seeing Jesus, the paschal lamb.

At the end-time Yahweh will gather the Gentiles with the Jews to worship Yahweh and celebrate feast at Jerusalem, for his house is a house of prayer for all nations (Isa 56:6–8; Zech 14:16–19; Mic 4:2–4). Jesus sees in the coming of the Greeks the ingathering of the Gentiles with the Jews to form in him a new community that will worship him, and so he answers, "The hour has come that the Son of Man might be glorified" (12:23). The "hour" of Jesus' death attests to the end-time at which Jews and Gentiles will be united together to worship and serve the one God revealed in Jesus. Jesus uses a parable to bring out the divine necessity for him to die and bring forth a new community. By means of the "truly, truly, I say to you" formula he teaches that if a seed does not die in the soil, it cannot become productive. It should give up its own life to bring forth life (12:24; cf. 2 Kgs 19:30). Similarly, Jesus will give up his life on the cross and will draw to himself all who believe in him so that they may reflect his life now and in future.

The same principle applies to each person: those who love their life will lose it and those who hate their life will keep it for eternal life (12:25). This paradoxical principle brings out the cost of being a disciple to Jesus. "Hating one's life" involves dying to one's own desires constantly. This will allow Jesus to control his disciples' lives so that they may do good deeds (2 Cor 4:10–12). They will exhibit the divine character, which cannot be destroyed by physical death.

Giving up oneself to die daily will lead a person to become a servant to Jesus. Jesus challenges the Greeks and his disciples that if anyone would serve him, let that person follow him (12:26a; cf. 8:12). Those who would serve Jesus will be where Jesus is and the Father will honor them (12:26b). Jesus promised that he will come and take his followers to himself that "where I am you may be also" (14:3; cf. 17:24). By taking up Jesus' disciples to be with him in the Father's house (14:2), the Father honors them, because they served him in the world by exhibiting Jesus' lifestyle! The message to

---

13. Lindars 1972: 427; Köstenberger 2009: 377.

Coming of the Greeks to Jesus

the Greeks is this: "Seeing Jesus," as an act of worship, demands the cost of their own lives, and it involves serving Jesus and following his life pattern.[14]

The lifting-up of the Son of Man (12:27-36)

In the coming of the Greeks to him, Jesus sees his fast-approaching death. Therefore he divulges his inner struggle by saying, "Now my soul is troubled. And what would I say, 'Father, save me from this hour?'" (12:27; cf. Matt 26:38; Mark 14:34). The implied answer is "no." He immediately affirms, "But on account of this I came to this hour." He realizes that since the "hour" of the Father for his crucifixion has come (12:23), he cannot avoid it. He prays to the Father to glorify his name through his death (12:28a). When the Son is exalted on the cross, he reveals the Father's love and life-giving power to humanity and thus the Father is glorified (13:31–32; 17:1, 4–5).

While Jesus was praying, a voice came from heaven, "I glorified and again I will glorify it" (12:28b; cf. Mark 1:11; 9:7). The double promise assures that God has glorified his name throughout the life and ministry of Jesus (2:11; 11:4, 40) and that he will glorify it in his death and resurrection. Without recognizing the voice as God's voice, some of the bystanders said that it was a thunder. Others thought that an angel had spoken to him probably to strengthen him in his trouble (12:29). But Jesus explained that the voice came not for his benefit but for theirs (12:30). He does not need heavenly help to keep his faith and strengthen him, but the crowd needed to know that the Father is at work in the Son[15] and that in the Son's self-sacrifice on the cross the Father is glorified.

The twice-repeated "now" in 12:31 indicates the hour of Jesus' death, which has already dawned (cf. 12:27, 33). It has brought judgment of this world and the overthrow of the "ruler of this world." "This world," the sphere of human affairs, is under evil (1 John 5:19). The people of this world, because of their unbelief and love for darkness (3:19), reject Jesus and his followers (15:18–25; 17:14–16) and thus put themselves under God's judgment (3:18–21), which is both present and future (5:25, 27–29, 12:48).

The "ruler of this world" confronts Jesus (14:30; 16:11), because he is the evil one (1 John 2:13–14; 3:12; 5:18), the devil (6:70; 8:44; 13:2) and

---

14. Cf. Kanagaraj 2005: 404.
15. Fenton 1970: 135; cf. Lincoln 2006: 352.

Satan (13:27).[16] He causes people to do evil against Jesus and his followers (e.g., 8:44; 13:2). Humans can be liberated from evil, when the "ruler of this world" is cast out by Jesus' power generated from his death and resurrection. By using the present "now" and the future "shall be cast out," John merges into one the present effect of Jesus' crucifixion to make the devil powerless and to annihilate him at the end-time (Rev 12:9; 20:10).

With an emphatic "I" Jesus then says, "And *I*, when I am lifted up from the earth, will draw all to myself." "To be lifted up" implies "to be exalted, glorified" (Isa 52:13), and it echoes Moses' lifting up of the serpent to give life to the dying (Num 21:9; 3:14–15). Jesus will be lifted up on a pole by crucifixion, the Roman form of execution. From the cross, Jesus will draw all people unto himself to form a new community (12:32). "All people" bears the universal effect of Jesus' death. It is the Father who draws all those who believe in Jesus lifted up on the cross (cf. 6:44, 37). The narrator explains plainly that by "being lifted up" Jesus means the nature of his death, that is, by crucifixion (12:33).

The crowd seems to have understood the term "being lifted up" as denoting Jesus' death. Therefore they asked, "We have heard from the Law that the Christ remains for ever, and how do you say that the Son of Man must be lifted up? Who is this Son of Man?" (12:34). Jesus did not link the title "Son of Man" here with his being lifted up. However, he has already spoken of the Son of Man being glorified (12:23) by being lifted up on the cross (3:14; 8:28). The people could have heard those words. The "Law" indicates the OT from which they had known that the Christ will remain forever. Ps 89:36 reads that David's offspring (the Christ) shall endure forever and that his throne is established forever (cf. Ps 89:51; cf. 2 Sam 7:1; Gal 3:16). A messianic psalm has, "You are a priest for ever" (Ps 110:4). The Jewish crowd might have thought of such verses.

There is an intermingling of two christological titles in 12:34: Christ and the Son of Man. The crowd obviously identifies the Christ with the Son of Man, for when Jesus speaks of the death of the Son of Man the crowd responds that Christ remains forever. In the late first century, some Jews identified the Son of Man with the pre-existent Messiah, the Elect One of God, who would be on the throne of glory and render judgment (*1 En.* 45:3; 51:3; 55:4; 61:8; cf. 48:6; 49; etc.). They understood the "one like a son of

16. He is the personified power of evil, called "Belial" (e.g., 1QM 1.1, 5, 13; 4.2; 11.8; 1QS 1.18, 24; 2.5, 19). In the first century CE, he was also called "Berial" or "Beliar" (*Ascen. Isa.* 2:4) and "the prince of the world" (*Ascen. Isa.* 1:3; 10:9); Schnackenburg 1980–84: 2.391, 527 n. 88.

man" of Dan 7:13–14 as the Christ-like figure who, with full of honor and glory, will establish the eternal kingdom. Possibly, the crowd was familiar with these traditions and thought that Jesus must be wrong in saying that the Son of Man must die. Jesus did not answer directly to the question, "Who is this Son of Man?" However, he implicitly said that the Son of Man is the messianic King who will establish his rule by being lifted up on the cross, followed by his resurrection.

On several occasions, Jesus has said that he, the Light, will be in the world for a little longer before he goes to the Father (7:33; 9:4–5; 11:9–10). He reiterates the same in 12:35 by indicating the nearness of his departure and urges the crowd to walk in the Light while they still have it with them. That is, people should live by believing in the Light (12:36) and consequently by doing good works (3:19–21; 9:4–5). Otherwise, the power of darkness will dominate them making them to do wickedness (3:20; 12:46) and lose their vision. Humankind, in this world of dualism, should choose one way of life, either walking in the darkness or believing in the Light so that they might become children of light (1:4–5, 9–12).[17] With these words, Jesus departs and hides himself from the people, probably to prepare himself for death.

UNBELIEF AND JUDGMENT (12:37–50)

Jesus did many signs in Jerusalem so that people might see his glory and believe in him. However, even after seeing the signs they did not believe in him (12:37). For John even unbelief is within God's plan of salvation, fulfilling the prophet's saying in Isa 53:1 LXX (12:38; cf. Rom 10:16). Isaiah was frustrated to see people not believing his message, although the mighty works of God ("the arm of the Lord") were revealed. So John cites Isaiah's prophecy (Isa 6:10) again to give reason for the unbelief of Jesus' audience. They could not believe, because God blinded their eyes and hardened their heart lest they could see with their eyes and understand in their heart, and turn to God for healing (12:39–40).[18] There is no reference to God's predestination to cause some to understand his message and believe and others not. At all times, including the time of Isaiah, some hear God's words and

---

17. The Qumran community identified itself as the children of light and all others as children of darkness (1QM 1.11–16; 1QS 1.9–10; 3.13–26).

18. The quotation in 12:40 may follow the Aramaic text, or the Hebrew text quoted from memory, or an ancient Greek translation of Isaiah; Kanagaraj 2005: 414–15.

believe in him, and others, by hardening their hearts, do not believe. Such a double response is inevitable whenever God's words are preached and signs performed.

Isaiah uttered such words because he saw his glory and spoke of him (John 12:41; cf. Acts 2:31). "His glory" indicates Jesus' glory (cf. 12:37, 42). Obviously, 12:41 looks back to Isaiah's vision in the temple (Isa 6:1–7) and reinterprets the "glory of Yahweh" (*Tg. Isa.* 6:1) as the glory of Jesus. Isaiah, who ministered in the eighth/seventh century BCE, saw the pre-existent Christ who was with God (1:1; 5:46; 8:56, 58) and proclaimed him. In this context, the citation from Isa 6:9–10 in John 12:40 proves that although Jesus, who was foreseen by Isaiah and who existed before Abraham, performed several signs, many did not believe in him. Nevertheless, many, even of the Jewish authorities, believed in Jesus, although they were not bold enough to publicly confess their faith, because they feared that the Pharisees would put them out of the synagogue (12:42; cf. 9:22). Those who feared excommunication treated it as humiliation rather than an opportunity to bear witness to Jesus. They loved to have reputation from human beings rather than the praise from God (12:43).

Jesus "cried out"—a verb used to indicate Jesus' identity or origin or his gift to humans (cf. 1:15; 7:28, 37; 12:44)—that he is the reflection of the Father who sent him, because they are one (10:30, 38; 14:10–11). Therefore those who believe in him believe in God and those who see Jesus can see God, who sent him into the world (12:44–45). The Jewish *shaliah* principle says that an agent represents the one who sends him (*m. Ber.* 5:5). This principle does not imply that Jesus is an emissary of the Father.[19] Jesus' statements show that the Son manifests God, the Sender, not as his emissary, but as the one who pre-existed with him and as the one who shares equality with him.[20] Jesus' reminder, "I have come as light into the world" (12:46a), recalls the coming of the Logos-Light into the world and of the need to believe in him (1:9–12; 8:12; 9:5). He came to free those who believe in Jesus from their attachment with darkness, the realm of evil that leads to final condemnation (12:46b; 35–36; 3:18–19).

"Believing" involves hearing Jesus' words and obeying them. Rejecting Jesus means not believing in him and hence not receiving his sayings. Jesus warns those who disobey his sayings now that they will be judged on the last day by the same word spoken by him, although he himself did not

---

19. *Contra* Köstenberger 2009: 393.
20. For distinctive elements in Johannine sending-motif see Kanagaraj 1998a: 260.

come to judge but to save human beings (12:47–48; 3:17). Jesus' words are collectively personified as a judge (12:48), because he did not speak anything on his own initiative or authority (cf. 5:19; 8:26, 28), but the Father who sent him has himself given the commandment of what to say and what to speak (12:49). The phrases "what to say" and "what to speak" emphasize the divine necessity for Jesus to speak words given only by God. Though he is one with the Father, within that equality the Son is subordinate,[21] without which their oneness would be impossible.

Jesus discloses that God's commandment, the object of obedience, is eternal life (12:50a; cf. 6:68), for obedience to God's commandment leads one to inherit the life of the age to come now and at the end-time (cf. 5:24–25). Therefore as the Father has told him, so does Jesus speak what he speaks (12:50b).

Fusing the Horizons

There is a need for believers to fall down and die so that they may yield much fruit. Jesus explains that we should lose our lives in order to keep it for eternal life. This means, in the light of the Synoptic parallels, that we are called to carry the cross and follow him. The people of God's community are to carry in their bodies the death of Jesus always so that the life of Jesus may be manifested from within them (2 Cor 4:10–12; cf. Rom 6:1–14). We must go through spiritually what Jesus went through physically: we need to die to our own intentions and purposes and gain a new perspective on life.[22] The church today is not aware of the need to die to itself and receive new life to serve the world effectively. This is the cost to be paid by any one who would follow Jesus.

Several years ago, I heard a Christian leader speaking of two pieces of wheat grain, one put inside the showcase and another sown on the ground. The grain placed inside the glass looked good and beautiful, but it was without growth, whereas the other grain that was sown went into the ground and died before it yielded fruit. Similarly, he said, the members of God's community should either remain showy or die and yield fruit. From that time on, I committed myself to fall and die in order to lead a life that will be useful for others.

---

21. Cf. Keener 2005: 2.889 n. 187.
22. Hughes 2007: 274.

Fusing the Horizons

God led me to the ministry and to places I never planned to go. I had to pass through the experience of dying to my own interests often through disappointments, fears, uncertainties, others' cheating and misunderstanding, false accusations, provocations, unexpected events, both good and bad, etc. They all worked together to enable me die to myself and renew my commitment to live for others. Previously I did not know the value of forgiveness, but after having a vision of Jesus' cross I understood what God's forgiveness means and how much I owe to forgive those who wrong me. In the course of time, the cross became the source of life and refuge for me, and there is joy in carrying the sufferings of Jesus so that I may be a blessing for many.

JOHN 13
Jesus' Last Supper with His Disciples

JESUS' PRIVATE MINISTRY (13:1—17:26)

With John 13, there begins another major section of John's Gospel, which contains Jesus' private ministry to his followers (13:1–17:26). Jesus' sayings recorded in this section are meant for the believers to make them stand firm in faith in the face of trials and affliction in this evil world. Jesus teaches that the new covenant community needs to overcome evil with love, humble service, and good works done in union with him (i.e., by bearing fruit). The members of the community need not be troubled either by the world's hatred or over Jesus' departure, for he will send them the Spirit of truth to be with them in his absence, to teach them and to guide them unto all truth. The Spirit will also enable them to love one another within and outside the community. Indeed, Jesus' ethical instruction "Love one another" is a new commandment given to the new community. He also instructs them to pray to the Father in his name, and he himself prayed to the Father that his followers might be protected from the evil in the world and that the church might grow with more believers added through the words preached by them. Finally, Jesus himself will come to take his followers to the Father's house, where they will be with him forever. This section, then, has several distinctive features of God's new community!

WASHING OF THE DISCIPLES' FEET (13:1–20)

13:1–3 gives the setting for Jesus' act of washing his disciples' feet. He had the Last Supper (13:2, 4) with his disciples one day earlier than the Passover. In the Synoptic accounts (Mark 14:12; Luke 22:15), Jesus has the Passover meal with his disciples on the day of Passover (Friday, the 15th of Nisan). But John sets the meal on the evening that begins the Day of Preparation (Thursday, the 14th of Nisan), on which Jesus was betrayed and crucified

(18:28; 19:14, 31, 36, 42).¹ It raises the question: which version gives the correct date for Jesus' celebration of the Passover? Scholars are divided in answering. The Passover, as per the Lord's commandment, is to begin at twilight on the 14th of Nisan with the eating of unleavened bread, with the feast on the 15th (Exod 12:18; Lev 23:5–6). John narrates that Jesus had the "Passover meal" before the day of Passover. Historically, John is not wrong, because the eating of unleavened bread begins on the evening of Nisan 14 itself. It also fulfills his theological purpose of merging Jesus' crucifixion with the time when the priests slaughtered Passover lambs in the temple (at about 3:00 p.m. on Nisan 14) and thereby he presents Jesus as the Passover lamb whose blood was shed on the cross for human deliverance (John 19:36; cf. 1 Cor 5:7).

Before the Passover, Jesus supernaturally knew that "his hour," the appointed time of the Father, had come to depart from the world (13:1a; cf. 12:23, 27). The verb "to depart" literally means "to ascend," implying Jesus' ascent to the Father by crucifixion.² His disciples are termed as "his own" (10:4, 14, 29; 17:6, 9, 10), which marks Jesus' ownership on them. The verb "to love" is repeated twice emphasizing Jesus' love for his followers until the end of his earthly life and beyond (13:1b). His act of love is set against the act of the devil, who laid in Judas Iscariot's heart the determination to betray Jesus (13:2). There is no reference in John that Judas betrayed Jesus for the sake of money (cf. Matt 26:14–16 par.).

Jesus knew that the Father had given all things into his hands (cf. 3:35), which includes God's authority to destroy the power of the devil. He also knew that he came from God and was departing to God (13:3).³ At this point, Jesus (i) rose from the meal, (ii) put off his garments, (iii) took a towel, (iv) girded himself with it, (v) poured water into the basin, (vi) began to wash the feet of the disciples, and (vii) wiped them with his towel (13:4–5). Foot washing, in Jewish society, was considered too menial a job for even a Jewish slave to undertake, appropriate only for a Gentile slave and his wife and children.⁴ Occasionally disciples would render such service to their teacher as a sign of devotion.⁵ Here Jesus takes up the form of a slave (Phil 2:7) and humbles himself to serve his disciples by washing

1. Cf. Lincoln 2006: 365; Köstenberger 2009: 401.
2. Nicholson 1983: 98–103.
3. The descent-ascent motif is common in John (cf. 3:13, 31; 6:38, 41, 62; 8:23).
4. *Mek.* on Exod 21:2; Lev 25:9; cf. Beasley-Murray 1999: 233.
5. Brown 1978: 2.564.

their feet. Jesus' act of wiping their feet with his towel recalls Mary's act of wiping Jesus' feet by her hair (11:2; 12:3) and symbolizes his offering of himself to cleanse his followers from sin.

When Jesus came to Peter to wash his feet, he, with astonishment, responded, "Lord, do you wash my feet?" (13:6), "You will never wash my feet" (13:8a). Peter's refusal shows his misunderstanding that Jesus, the teacher, should not do a menial job generally. The worldly view of leadership expects the leader to sit in a place of honor during the meal and allow others to wash his feet and serve him. Jesus reverses the role of patrons from whom the inferiors would not expect service[6] and thereby defines his lordship in terms of serving others. Jesus' response, "What I am doing you do not know now, but after these events you will understand" (13:7), anticipates his death and resurrection, which will bring to his followers the right understanding of his life, suffering, and death (2:22; 12:16). Jesus' shedding of his blood on the cross was necessary to cleanse those who are received into God's new community. Disallowing Jesus to wash amounts to unbelief in the suffering Messiah and denial of having partnership with him (13:8b). Thus, Jesus' foot washing is a symbol of cleansing with his blood and of having fellowship with him.

Wishing to have fellowship with Jesus, Peter said that Jesus might wash not only his feet, but also his hands and head (13:9). Jesus answered, "The one who has been bathed does not need to be washed, except for the feet, but he is wholly clean; and you are clean, but not all" (13:10). We may take 13:10a as a little parable and 13:10b as its application to all disciples (cf. 13:16; 4:35a; 8:35),[7] for the statement "You are clean" has a plural "you." Guests are already clean and they do not need to take a complete bath during supper. However, they may need a slave to wash their feet to remove the dust.[8] Similarly, the disciples are already clean by Jesus' words (15:3), but they need continuous cleansing by the same words (17:17) to remain united in his love. However, foreknowing that Judas would soon betray him, Jesus said, "But not all [are clean]" (13:11; cf. 6:70–71). The washing was ineffective to make Judas clean, because he allowed the devil to control him (cf. 13:2, 18). One interpretation of Jesus' foot washing thus points to his work of cleansing his community.

---

6. Keener 2005: 2.909.
7. Schnackenburg 1980–84: 3.22.
8. Ridderbos 1997: 460.

The other related interpretation is that it is an exemplary act of the Teacher before his pupils to emulate (13:12-20). The theme that only those who are cleansed by Jesus can perform foot washing links both 13:1-11 and 13:12-20. After washing of the disciples' feet, including those of Judas Iscariot, Jesus put on his outer garments and resumed his place. His question, "Do you know what I have done to you?" (13:12), made the disciples perplexed and they could not answer anything. Therefore Jesus took the initiative to answer. He reminded them that they address Jesus as "Teacher" and "Lord" (13:13).

Many people regarded Jesus as "Teacher" more highly than they regarded the rabbis (1:38; 3:2; 11:28; 20:16). By virtue of listening to Jesus' teaching, his disciples soon accepted him as their "Teacher" (9:2; 13:13, 14). The Greek word *kyrios* generally means "sir" or "master" (4:11, 15, 19, 49; 5:7; 6:34; 8:11; 9:36; 20:15), but it denotes Jesus, who bears the name of God, as "Lord" (6:23, 68, 69; 9:38; 11:27; 13:13-14; 20:20, 28; 21:7, 12). The first Christians did not hesitate to offer worship, due to God alone, to the risen Jesus, for they saw God's glory in Jesus' incarnate life, death, and resurrection. Jesus accepted these titles, but argued, "If . . . your Lord and Teacher has washed your feet, you also ought to wash one another's feet" (13:14). He makes washing others' feet an obligation to all those who were cleansed by him. Jesus presents it as an example to follow by his disciples (13:15). The act of foot washing decides the daily relationship with one another in society, for it involves forgiving each other, clearing the hurts caused to one another, confessing the mistakes to each other, performing hospitality and acts of kindness, caring for the afflicted, etc. (cf. 1 Tim 5:10).

Jesus, by means of "truly, truly, I say to you," refers to a proverbial saying well-known to his disciples (13:17a): "A slave is not greater than his master nor the sent one than the one who sent him" (John 13:16; cf. Matt 10:24 par.). Jesus is the master, and his pupils, who are to serve their master, are not greater than him. If the master himself washes the feet of his subordinates, how much more his students should do what he did? Jesus' saying that the sent one is not greater than the one who sent him conveys the same point and supports Jesus' beatitude, "Blessed are you if you do them" (13:17b). An ambassador is only a plenipotentiary, but the sender has greater value and status than the sent agents. Jesus is the one who sends the disciples into the world (17:18; 20:21). If the sender has shown God to the world by love and humble service, the sent ones too should do the same so that they may have the joy of the kingdom of God.[9]

Jesus' immediate statement "I am not speaking of you all" (13:18a), refers to those who inherited God's blessings by imitating Jesus. However, not all can inherit divine blessings. He knows each disciple whom he chose (15:16). Judas will lose God's end-time blessings because of his self-surrender to the devil to betray Jesus (cf. 6:70–71; 13:2, 27). Judas' betrayal is supported by the quotation from Ps 41:9 (cf. Ps 55:12–13), where the psalmist groans to the Lord that his close friend, who ate his bread, turned hostile to him.[10] Judas is described as the one who ate bread with Jesus, for he was with Jesus closely, heard his message, and experienced God's love in him. But eventually he violently acted against Jesus! He lifted up against him the very heel washed by Jesus![11] The fulfillment of the Scripture implies that Judas' treachery against Jesus was within the written will of God.

The statement "From now on, I am telling you before it happens" points to the forthcoming betrayal by Judas. Judas' treacherous act will indeed lead other disciples to believe Jesus as "I am" (13:19), the revelation of the eternally existent and incomparable God, for Judas' act sets the stage for Jesus to be lifted up on the cross (8:24, 28, 58). The "I am" statement is followed by a mission-focused statement with the "truly, truly, I say to you" formula as a confirmed truth: "The one who receives some one whom I will send receives me, and the one who receives me receives the one who sent me" (13:20). Jesus' "I am" statement in 13:19 expresses his oneness with God in revelatory terms, whereas 13:20 expresses this oneness in functional terms.[12] Anyone who, in the course of Christian mission, receives Jesus receives the God who sent him (cf. Matt 10:40 par.). This anticipates 20:21, where Jesus, after his glorification, will send his followers into the world on his mission.

---

9. In the NT, the word *makarioi* ("blessed") has the idea of joy in the future kingdom of God, which can be possessed even now; Brown 1978: 2.553.

10. "Lifting one's heel against" someone means "lifting up one's hand against" another person or "rising up against" someone (2 Sam 18:28, 31; 20:21).

11. Thomas 1991: 113.

12. Kanagaraj 2005: 444.

John 13:21-38

Two predictions sandwiched by Jesus' new commandment (13:21-38)

Judas' betrayal predicted (13:21-30)

Next we see that Jesus is troubled in spirit (cf. 11:33; 12:27) because he knows that he is going to be betrayed by a member of his own community. He testifies to the truth solemnly that one of them will betray him (13:21). Obviously, the disciples did not understand Jesus' use of the Scripture to say that his own friend lifted his heel against him. Therefore they looked at one another, being uncertain of the identity of that person (13:22).

For the first time, one of his disciples is introduced as the one whom Jesus loved, and he was lying close to the chest of Jesus during the supper (13:23). The identity of this disciple, who is not named at all, has been the subject of differing views. He is the disciple who was at the cross and who bore witness to what he had seen (19:35). To him was Jesus' mother entrusted (19:27). Eventually, we are told that he is the one who wrote the Gospel events (21:20-24). His intimacy with Jesus, closeness to Peter, his presence at the cross, his participation in the Passover meal with Jesus and other disciples (cf. Matt 26:20-24 par.; John 13:1), and his witness to the life of Jesus by writing give us clues that he was one of the Twelve. According to the Synoptic tradition, Peter, James, and John constituted the inner circle of the disciples (Mark 9:2; 14:33). The disciple whom Jesus loved is distinguished from Peter (13:24; 20:1-10). Among James and John, James was martyred early (Acts 12:2) and therefore there is a high probability for John, the son of Zebedee, to be the front candidate to be called "the disciple whom Jesus loved."[13] His anonymity may indicate that this disciple is an ideal disciple representing all believers who experience Jesus' love.

In banquets, the participants reclined according to their status. In many banquets, three persons were assigned to recline at one table. The one reclined at Jesus' right would have the opportunity to lean his head near Jesus' chest and thus the beloved disciple would have been sitting at the right side of Jesus. This does not mean that John exalts the beloved disciple over against Peter, who did not recline nearer to Jesus. Probably Judas was reclining to Jesus' left, which is a more honorable position, and this would

---

13. Michaels 2010: 749-50; Keener 2005: 2.917-18. The beloved disciple could have been a former disciple of John the Baptist who began to follow Jesus in Judea (1:35-40) up to and beyond the cross; Cullmann 1976: 71-78.

have enabled Jesus easily to give the dipped morsel to him (13:26)[14] and talk to him without being overheard by other disciples (13:27–29). Simon Peter, who might have been sitting at a speaking distance to the beloved disciple, signaled him to enquire who it is of whom Jesus speaks as betrayer (13:24). This leads the beloved disciple to lie close to the chest of Jesus to ask him, "Lord, who is it?" (13:25).

Jesus identifies the person to the beloved disciple by saying, "It is that man to whom I shall dip the morsel and give it." When he had dipped the morsel, he gave to Judas, the son of Iscariot (13:26). "Morsel" could be a piece of bread rather than a bunch of the bitter herbs that were dipped into fruit purée at the Passover meal. Dipping bread into a sauce dish and giving it to a guest was a favor done by the host.[15] Jesus' special favor done to Judas exemplifies that he loved his own until the end (13:1). Judas accepted the bread, but he did not change his decision to betray Jesus. It shows how deliberately Judas became a traitor (Luke 6:16) and treacherous. Soon after he received the bread, Satan, the power of evil, entered into him to hasten to do what had already been put in his mind (13:2). By sending Judas out with a command to betray him quickly (13:27), Jesus proves that he is in full control of his hour and that even Satan operates with his permission.[16]

The other disciples could hear Jesus commanding Judas, "What you are going to do, do quickly," but they did not know why he spoke thus to him (13:28). Some thought that because Judas was holding the money box (cf. 12:6) Jesus had asked him to buy the needed things for the feast or to give some help to the poor (13:29). It was customary to give alms to the poor on the Passover night.[17] Judas was actually going to sell his master for his own monetary profit (cf. Matt 26:14–16; Mark 14:10–11) rather than spending money to buy anything for others. The unintended result of his action will be to procure for the feast the true Lamb of God, who will be killed for removing the sins of humanity.[18]

After he received the morsel, Judas left the place *immediately* (13:30). We can see a picture of Satan taking full control of Judas, but obeying Jesus' command to do it "quickly." The narrator adds the comment, "And it was

---

14. Keener 2005: 2.915–16; cf. Malina and Rohrbaugh 1998: 220.
15. Keener 2005: 2.918.
16. Kanagaraj 2005: 447.
17. Jeremias 1966: 53–54.
18. Kanagaraj 2005: 447.

night." It is a symbol of Judas entering into darkness by leaving the Light of the world.

The new commandment (13:31-35)

As there are several themes that link this passage with John 14–16, some commentators treat 13:31–38 as part of Jesus' farewell discourse.[19] When Judas had gone out, Jesus said to the remaining eleven disciples, "Now is the Son of Man glorified, and God is glorified in him" (13:31). The temporal "now" is in an emphatic position to emphasize that the hour of glorification is already in operation. Jesus, the Son of Man, will be glorified on the cross (3:14; cf. 8:54; 11:4; 12:23). In the crucified Son of Man, God is glorified in the sense that God's love and life-giving power are revealed.[20] The glorification of God and of Jesus is always mutual, because they share one glory (1:14; 5:23). This mutuality is confirmed in 13:32 with an added reference to the end-time glorification of both of them. If God is glorified in the suffering and death of the Son of Man, he will also glorify him in himself. The future "he will glorify him" implies that God will accept Jesus in his own presence immediately ("at once") with the same glory that he had possessed with God before the existence of the world (17:5, 24).

Jesus addresses his disciples as "little children" (*teknia*) in 13:33. It shows his affection for his own and their unity as a family. Then he discloses that yet a little while he will be with them and that they will seek him, but they will not be able to find him and also they cannot go to the place where Jesus will go (13:33; cf. 7:33–34).

Jesus gives them a new commandment that "you love one another, just as I loved you, that you also love one another" (13:34; cf. 15:17). The Greek word *agapān*, translated "to love," implies "divine love," for it denotes the self-giving love of God (3:16). The word "commandment" points to the divine necessity and carries moral overtones. It is called the "new commandment" because "loving one another," which is repeated thrice in 13:34–35, is the fulfillment of all the Law and the prophets (Deut 6:5; Lev 19:18; Matt 22:35–40 par.; Luke 10:25–28; Rom 13:8–10). It is the essence of life in God's new community, for it is only by seeing the love shared among the

---

19. E.g., Carson 1991: 476–510; Köstenberger 2009: 419; Lincoln 2006: 381–83. Michaels (2010: 761–63) takes 13:36–38 along with 14:1–31.

20. The word "glorified" is put in aorist tense in Greek, meaning that in Judas' plan to betray Jesus the Son of Man and God have been glorified once and for all.

Two Predictions Sandwiched by Jesus' New Commandment

believers will all people recognize them as Jesus' followers (13:35). Love is not just an emotional expression, but it involves helping the needy (1 John 3:17–18). It is sacrificial love to the extent of giving one's life for the welfare of others, just as Jesus did (15:12–13; 1 John 3:16; 4:7–12). Love and self-sacrifice are reciprocal actions.[21] Jesus' love for his followers is the ground on which they can love one another. It is essential to experience Jesus' love before we love our fellow-beings.

Peter's denial foretold (13:36–38)

Jesus' saying "Where I am going, you cannot come" (13:33) and the reference to Peter's laying down of his life for Jesus (13:37) link 13:36–38 with 7:33–34. For Simon Peter's question "Lord, where are you going?," Jesus gives a ray of hope by assuring that Peter will follow him afterward, if not now, to the place where he is going (13:36). Jesus already said that he will go to God who sent him (7:33; cf. 14:2–3), but his disciples did not understand it (13:36a; 14:5). Jesus' statement that Peter will follow *afterward* highlights Jesus' ascension to the Father, to be followed by his disciples later.

Peter is hasty to follow Jesus *now*, without understanding Jesus' redemptive death by which he would go to the Father. Therefore he questions Jesus, "Lord, why cannot I follow you now?" He confirms his love for Jesus by promising that he will lay down his life for his Master (13:37). Jesus will lay down his life for the salvation of humankind (10:11, 15), whereas Peter wants to prove emotionally his loyalty for his Master by dying for him (cf. Matt 26:35 par.)! Peter's words embody "an absurd parody of Jesus' own," putting him in control of his own life.[22] However, ironically what he promised at human level will happen later when the risen Jesus will ask Peter to follow him (21:18–19). Peter cannot go, at the natural level, through the same death and resurrection as Jesus, but he can die for Jesus while serving him.

As Jesus knew the impossibility of Peter to die for him, he predicted with the solemn affirmation "truly, truly, I say to you" that the cock would not crow until Peter denies him thrice (13:38). Jesus indicates that the human fallen nature is weak and insufficient to follow him and that it will soon be proved true in Peter's life. Jesus' sarcastic question, "Will you lay down your life for me?," which expects the answer, "no," confirms this. Jesus

---

21. Koester 2003: 134.
22. Michaels 2010: 765.

foreknew that out of Peter's own weakness he would soon deny his Master three times. "Thrice" indicates the certainty of his denial and the extent of human vulnerability to become victims of circumstances to deny Jesus.

JOHN 14
Jesus' Pastoral Speech I

The content of John 14:1—16:33 is normally called Jesus' "Farewell Discourse" delivered to his disciples. However, Jesus is not going to leave them permanently. He promises to come back to take them to his Father's house (14:3, 28). Also, he will meet them after his resurrection for commissioning them (20:13–29).[1] John 14:1—16:33 contains Jesus' exhortation, admonition, encouragement, promises, and warnings. Therefore it is appropriate to understand the section as Jesus' "Pastoral Speech" given to his disciples. It fits well into his Pastoral/Priestly Prayer in John 17.

THE SON'S REVELATION OF THE FATHER (14:1–14)

Judas having left the community of disciples, Jesus now has an exclusive session with the eleven disciples. He encourages them, saying, "Let your hearts not be troubled" (14:1a), which looks back to Jesus' statements about his departure (13:33, 36) and his prediction of Peter's denial (13:38), besides his foretelling of Judas' betrayal (13:21). The plural *"your* hearts" includes all disciples who were agitated at what Jesus had predicted. Jesus exhorts them to continue believing in God and in him (14:1b). In this context, "believing" means "trusting firmly" in times of distress. One cannot believe in God without believing in Jesus, because Jesus is the revelation of God (12:44).

As Jesus is from above (8:23; 6:46) and has come down from heaven (6:33, 38, 51), he has seen that there are many dwelling places "in my Father's house." He confirms this truth by his question, "if it were not so, would I have told you that I go to prepare a place for you?" (14:2). The phrase "my Father's house" could denote the temple (2:16). Possibly there is a temple motif here that identifies the Father's house as a heavenly temple into which Jesus, the high priest, will enter with his own blood after his

---

1. Carson 1991: 480; Ridderbos 1997: 481–82.

John 14:1-14

death and resurrection to offer eternal redemption (Heb 9:12, 24). "Many dwelling places" has an inclusive sense of accommodating all members of Jesus' community.[2]

There is no trace in John that Jesus told them earlier that he was going to prepare a place for them. Perhaps it is a traditional saying known to his readers but not included in the narrative.[3] Probably Jesus said this when he spoke of his leaving the world (13:33, 36). Jesus is going to the Father's house to prepare a place for all his disciples. This is repeated in 14:3 with the promise that he will come again. There is no indication of the time of his second coming, but the purpose of his coming is to take the disciples to himself so that where he is they also may be (cf. 17:24). "Taking to myself" implies "taking up his followers along with him." "To be with Jesus where he is" is an eschatological expression that assures them that they will remain with Jesus forever (cf. 1 Thess 4:16-17). Living in the Father's house in 14:2-3 has a family connotation: they will live as children of God. The people of God's community relate with one another as members of one family.

Jesus reminds his disciples that during their association with him they know the way to the Father's house (14:4). However, John uses his literary device of non-understanding. Thomas asks, "How can we know the way?" (14:5), and confesses their ignorance of the place where Jesus is going to and the way to it. Jesus removes their non-understanding by affirming, "I am the way, the truth, and the life; no one comes to the Father, except through me" (14:6). This explains where Jesus is going to and the way there, and indicates that there is a possibility for any person to go to the Father in heaven by following Jesus alone.

Jesus has already taught that he is the way to heaven from the earth (1:51). In 14:6 he adds two more characteristics, "the truth" and "the life." Ps 86:11 links the Lord's way with truth and Ps 119:30 refers to the way of faithfulness. Prov 15:24 and Jer 21:8 speak of the way of life. For Qumran community the study of the Law and its lifestyle is "the way" (1QS 8.14-15; 9.17-18; 10.21; CD-A 1.13).[4] The closer parallel, however, is in Isa 30:20-21, where a word calling, "This is the way, walk in it," is that of the Teacher who is now revealed. John depicts Jesus, the way personified,

---

2. Cf. Kruse 2008: 291.
3. Lincoln 2006: 389.
4. Lincoln 2006: 390; Keener 2005: 2.941-42.

as the fulfillment of this prophecy.[5] For him the way for true life, promised by the Law, is in Jesus. He is the way that leads humankind to God, as he is embodied with truth (1:14c, 17) and divine life.[6] Through him alone can one come to God, the Father, and know him. By their intimate relationship with Jesus his disciples have already experienced the Father. They have known him and seen him (14:7), though they themselves were not aware of this truth. Their ignorance becomes visible in Philip's appeal, "Lord, show us the Father and it suffices us" (14:8). This kind of non-understanding is a springboard for John to explain heavenly truth.

After mildly rebuking Philip, "I have been with you so much time and have you not known me, Philip?," Jesus reveals that one who has seen him has seen the Father; then he strongly rebukes, "How do you say 'Show us the Father'?" (14:9). "So much time" indicates the extent of time that Jesus was with them to reveal God by his words and works and to show them the unity of the Father and the Son (14:8–11).[7] The theme that the one who has seen Jesus has seen God (cf. 12:44–45) is developed in 14:10–11, in terms of mutual indwelling of Jesus and God. Jesus admonishes Philip by questioning him, "Do you not believe that I am in the Father and the Father in me?" (14:10a). Seeing God in Jesus is possible only by "believing" that both Jesus and God mutually dwell within one another. Unity does not mean unification of Jesus with God, but the reciprocal relationship of love that exists between them.

Jesus speaks of his words and works in inseparable terms (14:10). He does not speak on his own initiative and the corollary is that he speaks the words received from God (3:34; 8:28b; 12:49). Jesus' works are the works of the Father, who dwells in oneness with him (4:34; 5:17, 19; 17:4). The disciples who have experienced Jesus, then, have already seen the Father. Therefore Philip's appeal "Show us the Father" is redundant. The existing mutuality between the Father and the Son needs to be believed and accepted, particularly by seeing his works/signs, which bear witness to the Father who sent him (5:36; 10:38). In 14:8–11 "seeing" leads to the theme of mutual indwelling of the Father and the Son, which, in turn, leads to Jesus' persuasion to believe. The content of faith is: "I am in the Father and the Father in me."

Jesus uses the "truly, truly, I say to you" formula to explain the outcome of "believing." Those who continually believe in him will do the works that

5. Kanagaraj 2005: 465–66.
6. Cf. Carson 1991: 491.
7. Köstenberger 2009: 431.

Jesus does and, in fact, greater works than these, because Jesus is going to the Father (14:12). Faith without doing Jesus' works is dead (Jas 2:14-26). The believers will not only perform miracles, but also will speak words of salvation to the world. Thus they will make the community founded by Jesus grow. Doing "greater works" does not make his followers greater than Jesus, because those works will be done actually by the Holy Spirit, who will be bestowed on them after Jesus goes to the Father (7:39; 16:7). The "greater works" include convicting the world of sin, judgment, and righteousness (16:7-11) and forgiving or retaining the sins of others (20:23). Jesus' work of salvation will be done through his community in greater glory by the power of the Spirit.[8]

Nevertheless, greater works cannot be done unless the church prays to God through Jesus. If his followers pray for anything in Jesus' name, Jesus promises that he will do it. This idea is repeated twice (14:13-14) to confirm the effect of prayer, an outward expression of inward faith and dependence. The terms "whatever you ask," and "if you ask me anything" denote the content of prayers. The context of 14:13-14 suggests that the content of prayer is related to "our part in God's plans."[9] God's new community may pray for power and wisdom to do his works and show Jesus to the world as God's self-manifestation. "In my name" implies prayer offered by relying upon Jesus' work of salvation accomplished on the cross. Jesus' name is God's name delegated on him (5:43; 10:25; 12:13; 17:6, 11-12, 26). Therefore when the church prays in Jesus' name, it claims the authority of God to grant what it asks for. With God-given authority Jesus promises, "I will do it." Both receiving prayers and granting what are asked for are collective responsibilities of the Father and the Son (14:13-14; 15:16; 16:23).

JESUS' PROMISE TO SEND THE *PARAKLĒTOS* (14:15-31)

Besides his command to love one another, Jesus speaks of his disciples' love for him. If they love him, they will obey his commandments (14:15, 23-24). The plural "commandments" includes his command to wash one another's feet (13:14-15), to love one another (13:34; 15:12), to believe in the oneness of the Father and the Son (14:8-11), and to ask him anything in his name (14:13-14). Jesus' love for his followers is expressed in his prayer to God for them (cf. 6:11; 11:41-42; 17:1-26). He promises that he will pray to

---

8. Cf. Kanagaraj 2005: 471.
9. Kruse 2008: 298.

Jesus' Promise to Send the Paraklētos

the Father to give them "another helper" (*allos paraklētos*) to be with them forever (14:16).[10]

The word *allos paraklētos* is identified as "the Spirit of truth" (14:17; cf. 15:26; 16:13) and the Holy Spirit (14:26).[11] The Spirit will be with Jesus' disciples not merely in his absence, but until the end of this age and beyond ("forever"). Jesus is the *paraklētos* who, as our advocate, intercedes for us with the Father (1 John 2:1), and the Holy Spirit is *allos paraklētos*, in which the word *allos* indicates "another of the same quality." Jesus and the Spirit, thus, have the same task of dwelling within Jesus' followers and of interceding for them with the Father.[12] *Paraklētos* can also mean "comforter," a term that the rabbis used as a title for the Messiah.[13] The *paraklētos* is the one who carries truth and who communicates truth (1:14, 16; 14:6). That is, the Spirit communicates the faithfulness of God to all human beings and particularly to God's own community. The Spirit of truth is given by the Father by hearing the prayer of his Son (14:16).

The world, being the realm of unbelief and evil, cannot receive the Spirit, because it neither sees him nor knows him due to its rejection of Jesus (14:17a; cf. 1:10; 3:19; 15:18–25; 17:14–16). In contrast, since the *paraklētos* dwells within Jesus' community, it can have an intimate relationship with Jesus through the Spirit and with God through Jesus (14:17b). In this sense, Jesus will not leave them as orphans and he will come to them (14:18).

Jesus draws another contrast between the world and his disciples in their relationship with Jesus (14:19). "Yet a little while, and the world will see me no more" indicates a very little time left before Jesus will be hung on the cross and the impossibility for the world to see him physically afterwards (cf. 7:33; 12:35; 16:16–19). In contrast, Jesus' disciples will be able to see him. The disciples will continue seeing him as risen Jesus within a short time after his death through his Spirit bestowed on them. Jesus uses again the present tense, "Because I live," foreseeing his immediate resurrection from the dead. Then he uses future tense to say, "You also will live." This

---

10. Köstenberger (2009: 421, 434) translates *allos paraklētos* aptly as "another helping presence."

11. "The spirit of truth" is opposed to "the spirit of deceit or of injustice"; both are placed within humankind to make them walk in wisdom or in folly, in justice and truth or in injustice (1QS 3.18–19; 4.23; cf. *T. Jud.* 20:1–5); Lincoln 2006: 394.

12. The Greek word *paraklētos* is made up of *para* ("beside") and *klētos* ("the called one"), meaning "the one who is called beside" to help and support.

13. Wijingaards 1988: 58.

future living denotes not merely the Spirit-empowered life soon after Jesus' resurrection, but also the end-time life with him (14:3; 17:24).

Jesus' resurrection will unveil the tripartite relationship between himself and the Father and his followers ("I am in my Father, and you in me, and I in you"). It will enable them to perceive the mutual indwelling that exists between the Father, the Son, and the community of believers (14:20). It is not the believers' deification, but a collective participation in divine life (cf. 6:56; 14:17; 15:4; 17:21). This participation brings a responsibility to God's community to show their love for Jesus by obeying his commandments (cf. 14:15). Those who do so will be loved by the Father and the Son, and out of love the Son will manifest himself to them (14:21).

Now John introduces another disciple, Judas (not Iscariot), as the spokesperson (cf. Luke 6:16; Acts 1:13). He asks Jesus, "Lord, how is it that you will manifest yourself to us, and not to the world?" (14:22). Judas misunderstands that Jesus' self-revelation is confined to the believers alone, although he came to reveal himself to every human (e.g., 1:9, 18; 3:16; 6:37, 51). Perhaps, like his fellow Jews, Judas longed for the manifestation of the Messiah in the world.[14] But he did not know God's plan that a handful of disciples would reach out to the world to bear witness to Jesus and keep God's community growing.

In response to Judas' question, Jesus reiterates that obeying his word is the mark of one's love for him. What was told exclusively to his disciples (14:15) is now made applicable to anyone who would love Jesus (14:23). "My word" and "my commandments" are essentially the same, denoting Jesus' message of salvation (cf. 1 John 3:23). "My Father" will love anyone who loves Jesus and obeys his word, and both the Father and the Son will come and make their dwelling with such persons (14:23b). The Jews expected God to dwell among his people in the age to come (Ezek 37:26–27; Rev 21:3)[15]. What was expected at the end-time is possible now for anyone who loves and obeys Jesus. Those who do not love Jesus do not obey his words and those who disobey Jesus' words do not love God, for the word that Jesus speaks is not his, but the Father's (14:24; cf. 3:34; 8:28b; 14:10; 12:49).

Jesus' statement "These things I have spoken to you, while I am dwelling with you" (14:25) introduces two other functions of the Holy Spirit, whom the Father will send in Jesus' authority as the bearer of God's name:

---

14. Kruse 2008: 305.
15. Kruse 2008: 305.

Jesus' Promise to Send the Paraklētos

he will teach his disciples all things, and he will remind them all that Jesus said (14:26). "Teaching all things" and "Reminding all that Jesus said" convey the same meaning. The remembrance of the disciples of the significance of Jesus' acts and sayings after his departure is the work of the Spirit (2:22; 12:16).

At this point, Jesus pronounces "peace" that he leaves with them, defining it as "my peace," which is different from the peace that the world gives (14:27a). Jesus' peace is not a mere farewell greeting used in Jewish and Greek circles[16] or a state of welfare free from worldly sufferings, but it is a gift of God's presence, salvation and life to be enjoyed at present and at the end-time (cf. Ps 29:11; Isa 52:7; 57:19; Ezek 37:26). Therefore the hearts of the disciples need not be troubled or be afraid (14:27b; 14:1a). This double assurance with the same meaning gives hope for Jesus' community to have peace in the midst of persecution in the world. Jesus goes to the Father who is greater than him (14:28b). However, he will come to them, as he already told them, to make his home with them by the Spirit and eventually to take them to the Father's house (14:28a; cf. 14:3, 18, 23).

When there is oneness between the Father and the Son (10:30), how do we understand Jesus' statement, "The Father is greater than I?" Certainly Jesus spoke and worked in subjection to the Father (5:19, 30; 11:41–42; 12:49; 14:31; 15:10), even while he spoke and worked in oneness with the Father (e.g., 1:1c, 14; 3:34; 5:17; 8:28; 12:49). Jesus could not have lived with his two natures separately—divine nature to show his oneness with God and human nature to speak of his subordination. Both equality with and subjection to the Father existed in Jesus. Real equality is manifested, even in human relationships, in one's submission to another person. Within the spectrum of equality there is an element of the Son's subordination to the Father to fulfill the mission of saving the world.[17] Both unity and subordination, and divinity and humanity dwelling together, are two facets of one truth. This paradox is the "mystery of incarnation."[18] The Son, who was equal with the Father (Phil 2:6), voluntarily accepted subordinate role to minister to humankind. Since Jesus is going to the Father, who is greater than he, the disciples would have rejoiced if they loved him, for it is to their advantage that he is going (14:2–3; 16:7a).

16. Lincoln 2006: 397.
17. Kanagaraj 2005: 487.
18. Guthrie 1985: 314.

Jesus' purpose in telling is that when it takes place they may believe (14:29). The object of faith is not specified. In this context, it means that the disciples, by seeing all things happening as Jesus foretold, will believe his words and come to a new understanding of Jesus and his mission. At the end of the first part of his speech, Jesus refers to the "ruler of this world" (cf. 12:31) who is coming. Therefore, he tells them that he will no longer talk much with them. In the coming of the ruler of the world, Jesus sees that the hour of his death, which is the climax of his combat with the devil, is approaching. The devil succeeded in coming into Judas Iscariot to make him betray his Master (6:70–71; 13:2, 18, 27), but he cannot overpower Jesus to prevent him from going to the Father through the cross. In this sense, the ruler of the world has no authority or claim on Jesus (literally, "he has nothing over me"; 14:30).

In spite of the coming of the powerless evil one, Jesus does as the Father has commanded him and this obedience proves that he loves the Father (14:31a). Jesus' death, resurrection, ascension, and his coming again are in accordance with the Father's command. Immediately Jesus says, "Rise, let us go from here" (14:31b). This instruction gives the sense that Jesus' Pastoral Speech is concluded. However, 18:1 indicates that Jesus and his disciples left the place only after his discourse and prayer. Moreover, it is unlikely that Jesus' further discourse that contains such important subjects (John 15 and 16) and his intensive prayer (John 17), would have been said on the way in a casual setting. Jesus' instruction is simply to rise from the place of reclining and go to a convenient place in the same hall so that Jesus might continue his discourse on other pertinent matters.

JOHN 15
Jesus' Pastoral Speech II

THE TRUE VINE AND THE BRANCHES (15:1–17)

John 15 opens abruptly, without any phrase of transition, with Jesus' final "I am" saying: "I am the true vine" (15:1a). This implies that Jesus is still giving instruction in the supper hall. He uses the metaphor of vine and branches to describe the tripartite relationship between the Father, the Son, and their new community. Jesus is the true vine, meaning that he is the genuine and authentic vine in contrast to the earthly vine, for Jesus is from God who is true (7:28; 17:3; cf. 1:9; 6:32).

Several OT passages speak of the people of Israel and Judah, who were supposed to be fruit-bearing vine or vineyard but failed to give the fruit expected by Yahweh (Ps 80:8–19; Isa 5:1–7; 27:2–6; Jer 2:21; 6:9; 8:13; 12:10; Ezek 15:1–8; 17:1–10; 19:10–14 and Hos 10:1). However, we can hardly argue along with Barrett that Jesus bore the fruit Israel failed to,[1] for Jesus, in John, is pictured as the source of life to all those who live in union with him so that *they* may bear fruit. John 15 shows that whereas Israel and Judah failed to bear fruit and glorify God, those who remain in Jesus' love and words can bear fruit and glorify God. Israel's failure can be turned into victory if anyone remains in Jesus.[2]

Jesus asserts, "My Father is the vinedresser" (15:1b), meaning that God is the planter and protector of the vine and its branches in his garden.[3] He does everything to keep the branches in union with the vine. Any branch that is not united with Jesus does not yield fruit and God takes away such branches, but he enables the fruit-bearing branches to bear more fruit by pruning them (15:2). This metaphor shows that God enables the believer

---

1. Barrett 1978: 471–73.
2. Kanagaraj 2005: 495.
3. The Greek word *geōrgos* could mean "vine dresser," who spades, clears, plants, and takes care of the vineyard; Köstenberger 2009: 451.

to live in union with Jesus and bear much fruit. Just as God, the owner of the vineyard and planter of the vine, judges Israel by looking for its fruit, so also he does in the new community centered on Jesus.[4] The Father thus plays active role to keep his community in his Son.

Jesus encourages his disciples that they have already been made clean by the "word" he spoke to them (15:3). This "word," which is Jesus' message of salvation, is the Father's word (8:28; 12:49; 14:24), which sanctifies Jesus' disciples (17:17). However, they are asked to maintain their given purity by always remaining in Jesus, as Jesus remains in them (15:4a). "Abiding in" and "bearing fruit" are inseparable. The mutual union will keep the disciples clean and enable them to yield fruit, which is nothing but reproducing the life of Jesus. Just as sap flows from the vine to all its branches, making them to yield fruit, so also the life of Jesus flows from him to all those who are attached with him by faith. It is a progressive act that, without deification of the believers, shows Jesus to the world by good works.

Jesus' followers, as branches, cannot reproduce his life unless they remain in him, the vine, and he in them (15:5). The term "the branches" confirms the community motif underlying in John. The members of God's chosen community should be so linked with Jesus that his life may flow through them to show him to society. "Abiding in Jesus" may denote our hidden life that is rooted in private prayers and meditation on God's Word.[5] "Apart from me you cannot do anything" implies that we cannot reflect Jesus' character and work by living independent of him. If anyone lives independent of Jesus, that person is cast forth and withers. All those who do not live in union with him will eventually be destroyed, just like the branches that are not linked with the vine are gathered, thrown into the fire, and burnt (15:6; cf. Matt 13:41–42). The passive voice used implies that God is the agent of casting out the fruitless branches. The language used in 15:6 indicates the final judgment of God (Matt 3:10; 7:19; 13:40, 42, 50). This warning underlines the urgency to live in union with Jesus by obeying his word (8:31; 15:7, 9) and by appropriating his life that flows from the cross (6:56).

If Jesus' words abide in Jesus' followers, as they abide in Jesus, whatever they wish will be done for them (15:7; cf. 14:13–14). The more they obey Jesus' words, the more they become intimate with him. In their daily communion with Jesus through his words, a blending of wills takes place[6]

---

4. Lincoln 2006: 403.
5. Newbigin 1977: 140–41.
6. Brodie 1993: 481.

and hence those who are attached with Jesus ask for things that Jesus wills. The reproduction of Jesus' character always glorifies the Father. It projects them as Jesus' disciples before those who will see God's glory in them (15:8). Honoring God in daily life is possible only by bearing much fruit, that is, by exhibiting Jesus' character.

The descriptions of abiding "in me" and "in you" are spoken by Jesus in parallel with abiding "in his love" (15:9). Jesus loved his own until the end (13:1), just as the Father loved him. The Father's love for the Son is eternal and is the core of their relationship and work (3:35; 5:20; 10:17; 17:24). The same love is the uniting force between Jesus and his followers. It is Jesus who first loved his people to show that God is love (cf. 1 John 4:8, 16). He asks them now to remain in the love he has already demonstrated. Jesus himself kept his Father's commandments as the mark of abiding in his love. Similarly, the outward expression of remaining in Jesus' love for his disciples is to obey his commandments (15:10; cf. 14:15, 21, 23–24), which are not burdensome (1 John 5:3). The prerequisite for the disciples' fruit-bearing is to keep themselves in the threefold relationship of love and obedience. The purpose of what Jesus spoke in 15:1–10 was that his joy may be within his pupils. Abiding in Jesus, in his words and in his love, will result in experiencing Jesus' joy in all its fullness (15:11). Jesus' complete joy takes away worldly sorrows and brings peace in the midst of troubles[7] (cf. 17:13).

Jesus now reminds of his commandment that his people should love one another in the same pattern as he has (15:12). Jesus explains the greatest degree of divine love as laying down one's life for friends (15:13). "Laying down one's life" refers to voluntary self-sacrifice for the welfare of others (10:11, 15, 17–18). Thus, self-sacrifice is the highest form of love that one can show. Then Jesus says to his followers, "You are my friends," (15:14) instead of "servants" (15:15). In the OT, God identifies Abraham as "my friend" (Isa 41:8; 2 Chr 20:7; Jas 2:23; cf. Exod 33:11 for Moses) to convey his intimate relationship and revelation of secrets to him (Gen 18:17). Similarly, a king's friends were nobles who were closely associated with him in taking royal decisions (1 Esd 8:11, 13, 26; 3 Macc 5:19, 26, 29, 34, 44).[8] By calling his own "my friends," Jesus attests his ownership and intimate relationship with them, to whom he revealed all he heard from the Father (8:26, 28b; 12:49).

---

7. Cf. Lincoln 2006: 405.

8. For an understanding of friendship in the ancient world see Keener 2005: 2.1006–11.

Jesus' disciples can be his friends only if they observe his command to love one another as he has loved them (15:12, 17). As Jesus' divine love drew them together with him, relevantly he calls them "my friends." While in 15:15 Jesus gives the reason for calling them "friends," in 15:16 he reminds them of how he took the initiative to make them his friends and the purpose of his friendship. 15:15a can be rendered, "No longer do I speak to you as slaves," because a slave does not know what his master is doing and why. He has to fully obey the master. Jesus has not treated his disciples as slaves, but as friends, for he himself has demonstrated to them how to serve one another with love (13:1, 14–15).

Out of his love as *philos* ("friend"), Jesus took the initiative to choose his disciples; they did not choose him first (15:16a). God, out of his love and faithfulness to his covenant (Deut 7:7–8), chose people always to accomplish his task through which he will be glorified (e.g., Deut 7:6; 14:2; 18:5; Isa 41:8–9; 43:10; 44:1; 45:4; 49:3). Similarly, Jesus chose his disciples to be commissioned to go and bear fruit that will remain (15:16b). In their bearing fruit, the Father's glory is manifested (15:8). It also prompts the Father to give whatever the disciples will ask in the authority of Jesus' name (15:16c), just like the disciples' abiding in Jesus and his words in them cause the Father to answer their prayers (15:7). The insertion of the verb "to go [and bring fruit]" in 15:16 is deliberate, and it denotes the movement of the disciples to go into the world to fulfill Jesus' mission (17:18; 20:21). If so, the idea of bringing fruit could imply bringing many to Christ.[9] One purpose of Jesus in choosing his followers, then, is to continue his mission in the world. "Your fruit should remain" indicates this continuous process of bearing and bringing fruit. Jesus eventually highlights his command to his community to live in love with one another (15:17). Why is love emphasized? 15:18–25 will shed light on this.

THE WORLD'S HATRED AND JESUS' REMEDY (15:18–27)

Loving one another is imperative within God's new community, and only then can they withstand the world's hatred (1 John 3:11–15). Jesus chose his disciples and separated them out of the world (15:19b). Although the term "world" in John denotes evil forces that make human beings to hate Jesus, in a few cases it means the whole creation of God (e.g., 21:25), particularly the sphere of human affairs (e.g., 1:10; 3:16–17). As it hated Jesus, it will

---

9. Barrett 1978: 478; Brown 1978: 2.665.

definitely hate his disciples (15:18). Jesus' followers receive Jesus, the Light, and hence perform good works, unlike the people of the world, who love darkness to constantly practice evil (3:19–21). This dualism makes Jesus' people not belong to this world or support evildoers. Therefore the people of the world hate them. If Jesus' community conformed to the world, the world would love it (15:19a). If the world persecuted Jesus, it will also persecute those who belong to him, and if it obeyed Jesus' message of salvation, it would obey the words preached by his people as well. This is in accordance with the proverb, "A servant is not greater than his master" (15:20; cf. 13:16). What happened to Jesus, their Master, will also happen to his pupils, since they are knit together, along with the Father, by love. The community of Jesus was facing the world's hatred and persecution in the late first century, as it is even today.

Jesus' community will face all kinds of persecution because of "my name" (15:21). The name of Jesus is the name of God given to him to exhibit his glory to humanity. The world's hatred of Jesus and his disciples is due to its ignorance of the Father, who sent him to the world to reveal the unknown God. If the world hates Jesus, it hates his Father also (15:23). It is impossible to experience God the Father without experiencing Jesus the Son. In this oneness the believers also participate (15:1–11). Therefore the world persecutes the church as it persecuted Jesus.

Jesus argues both in 15:22 and 15:24 that people who are of the world have no excuse for their sin (cf. Rom 1:20–21). If Jesus had not come and manifested God by his words received from him (3:34; 8:26, 28; 12:49), then humans cannot be held accountable for their sin and ignorance of God. However, since God has spoken through his Son to the world persuading it to come out of darkness to the Light, the people cannot say that they are without sin in rejecting Jesus. The statement "They have no excuse for their sin" echoes God's judgment in the last day (cf. Rom 2:15–16), but the particles "but now" (15:22) attest the present reality of God's judgment against human sin. The Johannine Jesus puts forward also his works as evidence for the world's permanent guilt (15:24). Jesus' works, including his signs, demonstrated God's glory to human beings, but yet the world did not believe. If Jesus did not perform the works that no human had done, then people could not have seen the God who worked through Jesus and they would not be guilty of sin (cf. 9:41). But people have seen God revealing himself in Jesus, yet still they hated Jesus and the Father. As Jesus and his Father are one, his words and works are those of the Father (5:36; 14:10). By not acknowledging Jesus, then, humankind has rejected both of them.

John 15:18-27

Even the world's hatred of both Jesus and the Father is due to the *divine necessity* for fulfilling what is written in "their Law," which refers to the whole OT (15:25a). By "their Law," Jesus means the Law observed by "the Jews," who do not perceive that their own Law witnesses to Jesus (5:39; see comments on 8:17; 10:34). Jesus quotes, "They hated me without a cause" (15:25b), which might have been taken either from Ps 35:19 or from Ps 69:4 (cf. Ps 109:3; 119:161), although none of these passages have the same wordings. It seems it is a common statement used by the Jews in their prayers referring to the unjust persecution they faced in the hands of their enemies, particularly the Gentiles (*Pss. Sol.* 7:1).

Jesus' followers, however, are not without help in a hostile situation. Jesus assures them of the coming of the *paraklētos*, the presence of the Spirit of truth, to help. In 14:16 and 26 the origin of the Spirit of truth is the Father, whereas in 15:26 Jesus asserts, "I shall send (the *paraklētos*) from the Father" and "the Spirit of truth who proceeds from the Father." Sending the *paraklētos* is the corporate function of the Father and the Son. What the Father does, the Son also does (5:17, 19). The Son sends the Spirit of truth from the Father and the Spirit proceeds from the Father (15:26). There is not only oneness and function shared between the Father, the Son, and the Holy Spirit, but also submission to one another. The Father listens to the prayer of Jesus (14:16) and sends the *paraklētos* in Jesus' name (14:26a), whereas the Son sends the *paraklētos* from the Father (15:26a). The Spirit of truth will bear witness to the Son in the world that hates him and his people (15:26b).

The Spirit will bear witness to Jesus in and through God's new community ("You also are my witnesses"; 15:27a). Bearing witness to someone is always in favor of that person in a forensic context. Jesus' community bears witness to him,[10] as they had been with Jesus "from the beginning" (15:27b), that is, "from the start of Jesus' ministry to its close"[11] (cf. Acts 1:22). The community of Jesus' disciples witnesses to Jesus not in its own strength, but by the power of the Spirit (15:26-27).

---

10. The Greek word *martureite* ("You are witnessing") should be taken as an indicative verb rather than an imperative, because the disciples were already bearing witness to Jesus (e.g., 1:41-48) and they did not need to be commanded to testify about Jesus.

11. Beasely-Murray 1999: 277.

JOHN 16
Jesus' Pastoral Speech III

INTENSIFICATION OF THE WORLD'S HATRED (16:1–4)

Jesus' opening statement, "I have said all these to you," refers back to 15:18–27, and his purpose of saying it is that they do not go astray (16:1; cf. Mark 14:27–31). Jesus wants his disciples to stand firm in faith in the phase of affliction. He warns them specifically that they will be put out of the synagogue by the Jewish authorities (9:22; 12:42) and that they will even kill them, assuming that by doing so they are rendering service to God (16:2; cf. Num 25:7–13). The teachers of the Law will kill Jesus' followers, mistaking them for heretics and breakers of the Law. This prediction is linked with the statement, "An hour is coming," which looks forward to the time of Christians being killed and their exclusion from Jewish society, after Jesus' hour of self-sacrifice on the cross. Such murderous act of Jesus' opponents against Christians took place after his ascension (e.g., Acts 7:58–60; 12:1–3; *Ant.* 20.9.1).

The reason for such persecution was that the authorities had no intimate relationship with the Father and with Jesus (16:3; cf. 15:21). "Knowing Jesus" will lead to know also the Father (8:19). The persecutors did not know both because of their unbelief in Jesus (5:38) and their hatred towards Jesus' community (15:18). Jesus was saying all things in advance to his followers so that when they are killed by Jesus' enemies at "their hour" they may remember that Jesus had already said those things and believe in him (16:4a; 13:19; 14:29). "Remembering what Jesus said" will give them new insight into Jesus' sayings and courage to face suffering and death. He did not tell them about his departure and the world's hatred from the time they had joined him (cf. 15:27 for "from the beginning"), because he was with them (16:4b). In his presence, the disciples experienced Jesus' love and protection, and there was no need to speak of such matters in the early stage lest they drift away from faith.

The Functions of the Spirit (16:5–15)

"But now" indicates a chronological change and links 16:5 with 16:4b. Jesus tells his disciples that he is going to the Father who sent him, because now the Father's hour has come (12:23; 13:1). He notes that none of them asks him, "Where are you departing?" (16:5). Then he himself affirms that since he talked about the forthcoming persecution to his disciples and his departure to the Father, grief has filled their hearts (16:6). Peter had earlier asked, "Lord, where are you going?" (13:36). Thomas too questioned Jesus about the way to the place where Jesus was going to (14:5). Yet Jesus says, "And none of you asks me, 'Where are you departing?'" Some scholars find two versions of a farewell discourse (13:31—14:31 and 15:1—16:33) that have been combined together without bothering about contradictions.[1] Others suggest that Jesus was not saying that the question was not asked before, but that *now* no one was asking. However, the word "now" is to be read with Jesus' departure to the Father and not with the disciples' asking.[2] As the disciples' hearts were filled with sorrow over Jesus' departure, they could not ask where he was going. Also, Jesus had already told them that he was going to the Father who sent him (7:33; 14:2–7, 28)[3] and so there is no need to ask now about Jesus' destination.

The adversative conjunction "but" that begins 16:7 shows that Jesus' departure is not a matter of sorrow, but of joy, for it is to their advantage that he goes away. If only he goes, then he will send the Paraclete (the Spirit of truth), the helping presence of God, to be with them, and if he does not go away, the Spirit will not come to them. The emphatic statement, "But I tell you the truth," means that Jesus' sending of the Spirit is a confirmed heavenly truth, which he normally expresses by the statement "truly, truly, I say to you." The functions of the Spirit are expressed now in relation to the world (16:8–11). "When he comes" (16:8) indicates the voluntariness of the Spirit to come to the disciples.

The Paraclete will convict the world about sin, righteousness, and judgment (16:8). The Greek verb *elenkhein* ("to convict, convince") has a forensic tone, meaning "to expose" one's evil deeds (3:20) or "to prove someone guilty" or "to convict" someone as ungodly or a transgressor (8:46; 1 Cor 14:24; Jas 2:9; Jude 15) or "to rebuke" (1QH 9.23). The word

---

1. Lincoln 2006: 381–430; Köstenberger 2009: 419–81.
2. Kruse 2008: 324.
3. Dodd 1958: 412–13 n. 1; Barrett 1978: 485–86; Beasley-Murray 1999: 279.

The Functions of the Spirit

carries the sense of persuading the wrongdoer to change his mind (1QS 9.16–17). As Greek moralists believed, the word has an appeal to one's conscience (e.g., *Det.* 146). Thus the work of the Spirit is to convict the world's conscience of its sin and to convince humanity to change their minds to receive either God's righteousness or his judgment. Since the world cannot receive the Holy Spirit (14:17), the work of conviction is mediated through God's new community.[4]

The Spirit of truth will convict the world that sin consists in its unbelief in Jesus (16:9; cf. 3:18; 8:24; 15:22), for unbelief is the root of all evil deeds. Secondly, he will convince the world to receive God's gift of righteousness, which became possible because of Jesus' departure to the Father through the cross and Jesus' disciples will see him no more on earth (16:10). The Spirit offers God's righteousness (justification) for those who believe in Jesus. Thirdly, the Spirit will convict the world of condemnation, in both present and future experience, if they fail to believe and receive God's righteous status in Jesus. God's verdict will be either to make a sinner righteous or to keep the sinner under judgment. Just like God's righteousness, his condemnation also is assured because the ruler of this world is already judged on the cross (16:11; 12:31). That is, the devil's power is defeated. Since the disciples are filled with grief over Jesus' departure and their persecution, they cannot bear now the "many things" Jesus would like to say, perhaps about the nature of his death and of his community's similar fate (16:12). Jesus turns again to the functions of the Spirit of truth in relation to his followers (16:13–14):

(i) He will guide them into all truth. The verb "to guide" means "to lead on one's way" (cf. Ps 143:10). When situation becomes dark, the Spirit will lead them on the way in all truth. "All truth" could mean Jesus (14:6) and God's word (17:17). He will guide them unto Jesus, who communicates God's word to tell them the way they should go (Isa 30:20–21).

(ii) He will speak whatever he hears from the Father and not on his own authority or initiative (3:34; 7:17; 8:26, 28; 12:49; 14:10).

(iii) The Spirit will proclaim the things that are to come (16:13b) and will reiterate what Jesus has already said (16:14b, 15b; cf. 14:26). The Spirit will declare the events that will happen at the end of this age. "Telling what is to come" is possible only for the true God and for the coming

---

4. Barrett 1978: 486–87.

Messiah (cf. 4:25-26) rather than for the idols (Isa 41:22-23). This will be done by the Spirit in the believers' life at present. Therefore Jesus said, "All that the Father has is mine... and he will take what is mine and declare it to you" (16:15). Just like the Father gave authority to the Son to speak his words, the Son has given authority to the Spirit to declare his words. The message of the Father, the Son, and the Holy Spirit is identical because they, being essentially one, hear one another in essential agreement.[5]

(iv) By speaking Jesus' words, the Spirit brings glory to Jesus. The Spirit's work of glorifying Jesus (16:14a) has present and future dimensions. In the present, the glory of Jesus, his love and faithfulness, is manifested by the work of the Holy Spirit through the new covenant community (cf. 17:10), and in the future the same Spirit will lead the church to see Jesus' glory for ever in the Father's house (17:24).

JOY AND PEACE AFTER TRIBULATION (16:16-33)

After declaring the functions of the Holy Spirit, Jesus now plainly says, "A little while, and you will see me no more; again a little while, and you will see me" (16:16). The first "a little while" implies the time when Jesus will go to the Father through his death on the cross and his disciples will see him no more (16:17; cf. 16:5, 10). The same phrase used again implies Jesus' resurrection appearances when they will see him. The disciples, however, express their puzzlement particularly over the phrase "a little while" (16:18), told twice, referring to two forthcoming events in Jesus' mission.

In the midst of non-understanding, Jesus' supernatural knowledge is highlighted: by knowing his followers' wish to ask him of the meaning of his statement (16:19), Jesus, by his oft-repeated phrase "truly, truly, I say to you," assures that their sorrow will be turned into joy. At Jesus' betrayal, trial, and crucifixion the community of believers will weep and lament and become sorrowful, but the world, which hates Jesus and his own, will rejoice by wrongly thinking that it has destroyed a "lawbreaker" (16:20). The words "weeping" and "lamenting" often denote the mourning for the dead (Jer 22:10; Luke 23:27; John 11:31, 33; 20:11) and they point to Jesus' fast-approaching death. Nevertheless, Jesus' resurrection, which will impart new life, will turn the disciples' sorrow into an exceeding joy.

---

5. Gruenler 1986: 117.

Joy and Peace after Tribulation

The turning of sorrow into joy is compared to the turning of the pain of a woman in labor into joy at the birth of her child (16:21). A woman undergoes travail, anguish, and sorrow at the hour when she has to deliver a child. However, after she delivers, she forgets her anguish because of the joy that a child is born in the world. The link between the statement "because her hour came" and her sorrow is deliberate. It denotes metaphorically the hour of Jesus' death on the cross, which will be a time of sorrow and grief to his dear ones. However, just like the sorrow of the woman in travail is turned into joy at the genesis of a new life, so also Jesus' death on the cross will turn into heartfelt joy for his disciples when Jesus sees them again and gives them new life (cf. Isa 26:16–19; 66:7–14). No one can take away their exuberant joy by persecution or hatred (16:22). It is possible that Jesus will see them in three stages: at his appearances soon after his resurrection, at his coming back as the Holy Spirit (20:22), and at his second coming to take them to the Father's house (14:1–3).

Jesus predicts that in the day of their joy of seeing Jesus again, his disciples will not ask him anything (16:23a). In 16:23–24 the verb "to ask" occurs four times, but in 16:23a the Greek word *erōtaō* is used. This word could mean either "to ask a question" (cf. 16:5, 19, 30) or "to ask for" something (cf. 16:26b). The former meaning will imply that as Jesus speaks plainly now (16:25) and as the disciples' hearts rejoice on seeing Jesus, there is no need for them to question him any more.[6] The latter meaning occurs in 16:23b–24 by the Greek word *aiteō*, which refers to the disciples asking the Father for anything. Jesus solemnly affirms ("truly, truly, I say to you") that whatever they ask the Father will give it to them in Jesus' authoritative name.[7] The context in 16:23–24 demands the meaning "to ask for" something for both the Greek verbs.[8]

Until the point of Jesus' death and resurrection they had asked nothing in Jesus' name, because Jesus was with them and he prayed for them on several occasions (e.g., John 17). Now he promises, "Ask, and you will receive" (cf. Matt 7:7–11; Luke 11:9–13). The disciples' communication with and access to the Father by virtue of what Jesus did on the cross will enable them to have their joy complete (16:24; cf. 15:11). The phrase "in my name"

---

6. Lincoln 2006: 424–25; Ridderbos 1997: 539 n. 190.

7. John 14:14 implies that prayers need to be offered to Jesus who will do what is asked. Since Jesus' works are the Father's works, there is no contradiction between 16:23 and 14:14.

8. Bruce 1992: 323; Carson 1991: 545.

in 16:23 may be read either with asking the Father or with the Father's giving. In the light of 16:24 it is sensible to read the phrase with asking the Father who gives what is asked in Jesus' name and not on the merit of the petitioners. Both asking in Jesus' name and God's giving in Jesus' name complement each other.

Jesus acknowledges that he has spoken "these things" in figures (16:25a). "These things" may refer not only to Jesus' speech in 16:16-24, but to the whole Pastoral Speech.[9] He refers to the forthcoming "hour" when he will no longer speak with his disciples in cryptic words, but will tell them plainly of the Father (16:25b). The term "hour," without the definite article in Greek, indicates the period after the resurrection when the church will receive the Holy Spirit[10] and Jesus will speak plainly of the Father through the Spirit.

Jesus says further that after his death and resurrection ("in that day"), his disciples will ask the Father by claiming the authority of Jesus' name, and they will have direct access to the Father. There will be no need, then, for Jesus to pray for them to receive something (16:26). Jesus assures of the Father's continuous love for his community, because they have loved Jesus and have believed that he came from the Father (16:27; 17:8). God himself grants their prayers out of his love for them. Love and faith are thus the binding factors of the believers with God and Jesus. Jesus reiterates that he has come into the world from the Father (cf. 1:9; 3:19; 6:38; 8:23) and that he is leaving the world to return to the Father after his mission is completed (16:28; cf. 13:1). This reflects the Jewish principle that an agent should return to his sender to give an account of the mission for which he was sent.

Jesus' promise that in the coming "hour" he will speak with them plainly of the Father (16:25), his assurance that the Father himself loves them (16:27), and his mission statement (16:28) made the disciples exclaim, "Behold, now you are speaking plainly and not in any figure!" (16:29). They believed that Jesus' promise to speak plainly of the Father in the hour that is coming was already being fulfilled.[11] At the end of Jesus' Pastoral Speech, the disciples began to perceive that Jesus knows all things about God and that there is no need for anyone to question him unlike they questioned him previously (13:36-37; 14:5, 8). Therefore they affirm their faith, saying,

---

9. Cf. Köstenberger 2009: 477.

10. "An hour" indicates the effects of Jesus' hour of glorification on the cross to those who believe in him; Brown 1978: 2.518.

11. Kruse 2008: 331.

Joy and Peace after Tribulation

"By this we believe that you came from God" (16:30). "By this" looks back to all the plain statements of Jesus in 16:25–28. However, Jesus questions them, "Do you now believe?" (16:31). The particle "now," which is put in an emphatic position in Greek, indicates Jesus' exclamation that in spite of his earlier disclosure that he came from the Father and goes back to the Father (8:14; 13:3, 33; 14:2–7; 16:5), his followers believe only now, just before the "hour" of his exaltation on the cross (16:32)! They were unaware how fickle was their belief and hence Jesus' question has both irony and exasperation.[12]

Jesus predicts that at the coming of an hour, which has already come, all his disciples will go scattered by leaving him alone (16:32). Although the word "hour" occurs here without the definite article, the context refers to the time of Jesus' arrest and death rather than the life of the church after Jesus' resurrection. When Jesus will be put to death, those who confessed their faith will be scattered (cf. Matt 26:31; Mark 14:27) and go "every one to his own home." That is, by leaving Jesus alone, each person will go to his own works[13] (cf. Matt 26:56b; Mark 14:50).

Nevertheless, Jesus reminds his followers, "And I am not alone, for the Father is with me" (16:32b). The Father has always been with Jesus (cf. 5:17; 8:16, 29). Even when Jesus enters into the hour set by the Father to glorify him by his death, the Father is with him. The concluding verse draws the key points from the whole Pastoral Speech, as the opening sentence, "I have spoken these things to you," shows. He tells them that he delivered his speech so that in him they may have peace. They may experience peace ("prosperity and God's salvation") as they live in communion with Jesus. In contrast, in the world Jesus' followers have "tribulation," a word which refers to the birthpangs that God's people will undergo at the end of the age (Mark 13:7–8, 19, 24–25) as well as now (16:33a).

Jesus encourages his own to be of good cheer in the phase of tribulation by assuring that he has already overcome the evil in the world (16:33b). This means that persecution will have no power over them, as Jesus will have won victory on the cross (12:31). Those who believe Jesus also will overcome the evil in the world by the power of Jesus' cross (1 John 2:13–14; 4:4; 5:4–5).

---

12. Köstenberger 2009: 479.
13. The Greek plural *ta idia* could mean "his own works or affairs."

JOHN 17
Pastoral Prayer of Jesus

The Pastoral Speech of Jesus is appended in John 17 with his prayer for his disciples and for the future believing community. David Chyträus (1531–1600 CE) called this the "High-Priestly Prayer."[1] The word "high-priestly" is a Jewish term. It is also inappropriate to call the prayer the "Testament of Jesus,"[2] for it overlooks Jesus' resurrection. It is more sensible in our times to call it Jesus' "Pastoral Prayer."[3] The current location of the prayer is in accordance with the Jewish custom of concluding a farewell speech with a prayer.[4]

JESUS' PRAYER FOR HIS GLORIFICATION (17:1–5)

The opening phrase, "after Jesus spoke these," concludes Jesus' Pastoral Speech and begins his prayer directed to the Father (11:41; 12:27; 17:5, 11, 21, 24–25), claiming the petitioner's filial relationship with God. Jesus' gesture of lifting his eyes up to heaven is the normal Jewish way of prayer (Ps 121:1–2; 123:1–4; Dan 4:34; John 6:5; 11:41). Jesus realizes that the time appointed by the Father for his crucifixion has come (12:23; 13:1). This is the event in which the Father will reveal the glory of his Son supremely. The Son's glory is the Father's glory (1:14; 17:22) and thus his glorification will bring honor to the Father (17:1; 13:31–32). This mutual glorification is possible because God has given Jesus authority over all people ("all flesh") to give the life of the age to come ("eternal life") to all whom God has given him (17:2; cf. 5:21, 29).

Eternal life, for Jesus, is to know the only true God and Jesus Christ whom God sent (17:3). He avoids the gnostic term "knowledge," but uses

---

1. Keener 2005: 2.1051.
2. Käsemann 1968.
3. Michaels' (2010: 857) point that this prayer can be viewed as the "Shepherd's prayer" that has both pastoral and priestly concerns fits into our view.
4. Brown 1978: 2.744–45.

Jesus' Prayer for His Glorification

"knowing," which is essentially the same as "believing." "The only true God" refers to Yahweh (the Lord), who is the Creator and Redeemer of all humanity. "Knowing" (17:3) refers to having intimate relationship with God, who is one (Deut 6:4; John 5:44; 1 Cor 8:6) and true (3:33; 7:28; 8:26), and to one's personal experience with Jesus Christ, whom the same God sent into the world to give heavenly life to those who believe.[5]

God's sending of the Son is followed by Jesus' triumphant statement, "I glorified you on earth, having finished the work that you gave me to do" (17:4). Jesus was sent into the world with the work of revealing God in his glory throughout his ministry (1:14, 18; 2:11; 11:40; 13:31). Though the given task will be fully accomplished on the cross (12:23, 27, 28; 13:32; 19:30), Jesus, who has perceived that the "hour" is already set in operation (17:1), prays confidently that he has finished the work of glorifying the Father. He therefore asks the Father to glorify him in God's own presence with the glory that he had with God before the world came into being (17:5; cf. 1:1–2; 17:24; Wis 7:25; 9:10–11) and before his incarnation (12:41). Now Jesus asks for that pre-existent glory to be given to him after he ascends to God's presence (6:62; 13:32).

JESUS' PRAYER FOR HIS DISCIPLES (17:6–19)

Before Jesus prays for his disciples, he gives to God, who sent him, an account of what he has done for them (17:6–8). First, he acknowledges that the people of God's community were given to Jesus by God (17:2, 9, 11). Throughout his earthly ministry, he manifested God's name to them. God's glory was revealed to Moses in terms of God's name (Exod 3:13–14; 33:18–19; 34:5–6). In John too "name" and "glory" are used interchangeably (cf. 17:11–12 with 17:22, 24; the verb "to manifest" alludes to the manifestation of his glory in 2:11). God's name or glory implies his character, eternal existence, and work of salvation among humans. Jesus revealed to his followers God's character of love and life-giving work by his name, "I Am" (cf. 14:8–11). In the OT, God's name dwelt in his temple (Deut 12:5, 11; 1 Kgs 8:13, 17–20, 29; 9:3; 2 Chr 6:20), which was filled with his glory (1 Kgs 8:10–11). Jesus made known God's name (17:6, 26) in the sense that he revealed himself as the Tabernacle/Temple where God put his name/glory

---

5. "Knowing the Lord" means also "turning to the Lord" so that his people may live before him (Hos 6:1–3); Dodd 1958: 163.

to dwell.⁶ Revelation of God's name demands obedience to God's word, and Jesus submits to the Father that his disciples have obeyed his word (17:6).

Jesus commends his disciples for understanding God as the origin of all gifts that Jesus holds when they saw God's name/glory in him (17:7). The words that Jesus gave to them are God's words (3:34; 8:28; 12:49). Jesus acknowledges before God that his disciples have received those words. In consequence, they knew genuinely that Jesus came from God and believed that it is the Father who sent Jesus (17:8). Here "knowing" and "believing" are used in parallel terms, and the word "truly" means "genuinely." Jesus prays for the twelve disciples, and not for the world, because the former have to be built up first as God's own people who have entered into the covenantal relationship with God through Jesus (John 17:9; cf. Exod 19:5-6). Jesus and the Father are one and therefore all those who belong to Jesus (literally "all things," meaning "all possession") are God's and all those who belong to God are Jesus'. Into this mutual relationship the believing community also is grafted, and therefore Jesus is glorified in them (17:10). They have seen God's glory in Jesus throughout his earthly ministry.

As his departure is at hand, Jesus says, "I am no longer in the world, but they are in the world." Therefore he prays to the Father to protect his followers in the authority of his name, which God has given to Jesus (17:11a). Jesus calls God "the Holy Father," highlighting the truth that God's character is morally pure and separated from the world (Ps 111:9; Isa 6:3; Lev 11:44; cf. 2 Macc 14:36; 3 Macc 2:2).⁷ Both God and Jesus are one in love and glory (17:22), and Jesus prays that his disciples also may similarly be one (17:11b).

Jesus has kept the disciples in God's powerful name that was given to him while he was with them (17:12a). This is paralleled with "I guarded them" so well that none of them were lost (17:12b). Here is a picture of a good shepherd who protects his sheep from perishing (10:10-14, 28). However, Jesus exempts one disciple, called "the son of perdition," a Semitic expression for the one who is irrevocably lost.⁸ He is Judas Iscariot, who turned against Jesus (6:70; 13:18) and who was lost in fulfillment of the Scriptures. That is, Judas' betrayal took place as per the written will of God. John probably had in mind Pss 41:9; 69:25; and 109:8 (cf. Acts 1:20). The loss of one disciple cannot stop Jesus from returning to the Father (17:13a).

6. Cf. Köstenberger 2009: 491.
7. Cf. Köstenberger 2009: 493.
8. Cf. Michaels 2010: 869 n. 47.

Jesus' Prayer for His Disciples

Jesus has sought the fullness of his joy to be within his disciples (15:11; 16:24) by speaking "these things" in the world (17:13b). "These things" does not refer to what he speaks in his prayer alone, but to Jesus' message *in toto* given to his disciples thus far.[9]

Jesus relates both God's word given to his disciples and the world's hatred of them (17:14). The total message of Jesus is from God and the disciples have received them and believed in Jesus as the one sent by God (17:8). Consequently, their lifestyle is different from the worldly standard of life that is dominated by the evil one and thus they do not belong to the world, as Jesus is not of this world. Therefore the world has hated them. Jesus makes this point in his prayer not with the desire that the Father should take them out of the world, but that he should protect them from the evil one (17:15; cf. 17:11–12). The "evil" mentioned is the personification of cosmic evil, known as "the ruler of this world" (12:31; 14:30; 16:11).[10] He has been tempting Jesus' adherents to follow the selfish nature of the world. There is a danger for Jesus' followers to fall as a prey to him and perish (e.g., 6:70; 13:2, 27). Therefore, Jesus prays the Father to protect them from this evil one.

Keeping oneself away from evil leads to "sanctification" or "holiness," which denotes God's character of moral purity and a life separated from the world (Lev 11:44–45). God's word, communicated through Jesus, is the heavenly truth that has power to sanctify the disciples. Therefore Jesus prays, "Sanctify them in the truth; your word is truth" (17:17). The disciples' consecration is inseparable from their mission to the world, for after beseeching the Father to sanctify his followers, Jesus states, "As you sent me into the world, I also sent them into the world" (17:18). Sanctifying believers is God's work and doing God's mission is the work of the church sent by Jesus.

Jesus declares, "And I consecrate myself for them so that they also may be consecrated in truth" (17:19). The phrase "for them," in John, conveys the idea of dying for the welfare of others (10:11, 15, 17–18; 11:51; 15:13), echoing the Lord's Servant who poured out his soul to death bearing the sin of many (Isa 53:10, 12). Jesus' self-consecration involves offering himself for taking away human sin (cf. Isa 53:4–10). Jesus consecrates himself for the benefit of his disciples so that they also may be consecrated by the word of truth in Jesus (17:17; cf. 10:36).

9. Cf. Keener 2005: 2.1059.
10. Lincoln 2006: 437.

Jesus' Prayer for His Expanding Community (17:20-26)

Jesus does not pray only for his first disciples, but also for those who will believe the message of salvation preached by them (17:20; cf. 4:39). When the believing community expands, one may expect disunity due to different gifts and views of its members, and therefore Jesus prays first that they all may be one. This will be possible only by showing love for one another and by the indwelling power of the Father and the Son within them (17:21). The mutual indwelling of the Father and Son is to bring all the believers into one (10:38; 14:10-11, 23) so that the world may see Jesus in them and believe that he, the one sent by the Father, has heavenly origin (cf. 17:8, 23). The perfect unity within God's community is the centripetal force to bring the "outsiders" unto faith in Jesus (10:16). The same oneness is described in 17:22 as caused by God's glory, which Jesus possessed and gave to the believers (cf. 17:6). Now God's community is progressing towards completeness, which will make the world to comprehend that God loves his community with the same love that he has for Jesus (17:23).

By calling God again "Father," Jesus expresses his desire that the disciples whom God gave to him may be with him in the place where he is (17:24a; cf. 14:2-3). This will enable the disciples to see Jesus' glory, which God gave him out of his love for Jesus before the foundation of the world (cf. 17:24b, 5). The expression "they whom you have given me," though it focuses on the twelve disciples, refers also to others who believed in Jesus during his ministry (e.g., 4:42; 9:35-38) and who will believe in future by the preaching of eyewitnesses (17:20). Jesus' glory is God's glory (1:14), which has already been given and manifested to Jesus' disciples (17:22; 2:11), and at the end of the age they will see Jesus in his full glory by being in the place where he is (cf. 1 John 3:2). The prayer thus gives a vision of the believers' eschatological destiny.[11]

At the end of his Pastoral Prayer, Jesus calls the Father, "O righteous Father," perhaps to emphasize God's righteousness to make sinners righteous if they believe in Jesus (16:8, 10). The world, which rejected Jesus, did not know God (1:10; 8:19), but Jesus knows God, because he comes from God and has seen him (17:25a; 6:46; 10:15). His disciples ("these men" in Greek) too know that the Father sent Jesus (17:25b), the verb "to know" implying "to believe." The content of faith is that the Father sent Jesus, which

---

11. Lincoln 2006: 439.

Jesus' Prayer for His Expanding Community

speaks for Jesus' heavenly origin, his descent to earth by incarnation, and his departure to the Father through crucifixion and resurrection.

Jesus submits that he made God's name known to his disciples (cf. 17:6), and he vows that he will continue to make it known until and even after he departs from the world (17:26a). The purpose of revealing God's name is that God's love with which he loved Jesus may be in the community of believers and that Jesus may be in them (17:26b). This recalls 15:9: "As my Father loved me, I also have loved you; remain in my love." The threefold relationship of love between the Father, the Son, and their community (17:23) is reiterated in final words of Jesus' prayer.

Fusing the Horizons

Prayer is the crown of Jesus' Pastoral Speech and the nerve of life in God's community. Jesus often exhorted his disciples to ask the Father in his name so that they may receive (14:13–14; 15:7, 16; 16:23–24). He himself demonstrated the power of prayer (6:11; 11:41–42). Therefore organizing communal and individual prayers in churches is as much necessary as worship. Today's Baptist church originated from a prayer meeting held in a small house in Zurich, and an active mission organization in India, Friends Missionary Prayer Band, found its root in prayer.

My mother opened our house in 1962 for women's prayer fellowship on the initiation of the wife of our pastor. The fellowship grew and many more came for prayer. In course of time, men too joined. It became a prayer meeting in which the worshippers used to sing, bear witness, preach, and pray. This prayer fellowship began to attract some people from Hindu faith to attend the meetings. By the Word of God that was preached and through counseling, the Spirit worked in the hearts of many Hindus who ultimately became Christians and received baptism in the Church of South India. Each year about fifteen people from all sections of the society were added to the church and even now they are remaining in God's grace and Christian faith. It was a small beginning as a home church in which prayer attained importance to make God's new community grow!

Believers' unity with one another and with God in Jesus has a key place in Jesus' prayer. Though unity in the church does not mean uniformity, the oneness that can be exhibited by people from various backgrounds and with various gifts (Eph 4:1–7) is powerful enough to make the world believe that

Fusing the Horizons

Jesus is the one sent by God (17:21) to give eternal life. With the aim of expressing Christian unity to the world, the Church of South India was born by the union of several Protestant churches in south India in September 27, 1947, with the motto, "That they all may be one." In similar fashion, the Church of North India came into being in November 29, 1970, with the motto, "Unity–Witness–Service." The oneness that Jesus envisages is not mere organizational, doctrinal, and sacramental in nature, but it is the unity of love (15:9; 17:26), based on the Father's love for Jesus, and of the Spirit (Eph 4:3).

When Christians were severely persecuted in India in the early part of the first decade of the twenty-first century, all churches were united together to condemn the attacks. There were special meetings and processions to show Christian solidarity with one another by breaking down the denominational barriers. Several appeals were made to the concerned authorities to take immediate steps to stop persecuting churches. The unity shown by Christians prompted other nations to interfere and make appeal to the government to stop harming Christians and bring justice to those affected. Some Christian leaders wrote in newspapers, magazines, and journals defending Christian faith in response to a few individuals who wrote against Christians and Christian faith. Efforts were made through the Minority Commission to take the voice of Christians to the governments concerned. All these attempts became channels to proclaim the good news of Jesus Christ so that the world may know who Jesus is. Persecution helped in some places the churches to grow rather than to subside. We may easily understand why Jesus prayed for oneness to prevail among his followers in the pattern of the oneness that prevails between the Father and the Son by the Spirit.

JOHN 18
Arrest and Trials Faced by Jesus

JESUS' PASSION AND RESURRECTION (18:1—20:31)

John 18:1—20:31 constitutes one unit, since it witnesses to the conjoined events of Jesus' passion and resurrection. However, two full chapters (18:1—19:42) are devoted to the passion narrative.

THE BETRAYAL OF JESUS (18:1–11)

After Jesus' Pastoral Speech and Prayer, he went out with his disciples across Kidron valley, a brook situated in the east of Jerusalem. They entered into the garden (18:1), the garden of Gethsemane, meaning "oil press," situated on the Mount of Olives (Matt 26:30, 36 par.). This was the usual place where Jesus met with the Twelve especially for prayer (Matt 26:36 par.) and therefore Judas had known this place (18:2). As it was a place away from the crowd, it was easier for him to betray Jesus and for the cohort[1] and officers from the chief priests and the Pharisees to arrest Jesus without any tumult among people (18:3). Jesus had a large following and therefore it is possible that Pilate had put a cohort of Roman soldiers at the disposal of Jewish authorities for security reasons.[2] "The Jews" must have used the Romans and Jewish officials (the "temple police") so that they could easily bring political charge against Jesus.

Judas was leading the squad of Roman cohort and the temple guards to seize Jesus. They came with lanterns, torches, and weapons (18:3) and thus treated Jesus as a robber (Matt 26:55 par.; cf. Isa 53:12). This shows that Judas' betrayal took place at night (cf. 1 Cor 11:23) when they could arrest Jesus easily without public riot. Jesus, in his foreknowledge, knew all

---

1. A "cohort" (Greek *speira*) is the tenth part of a legion, normally with six hundred Roman soldiers with a commander, though the number varied.

2. Brown 1978: 2.808.

the events that would happen to him, for "the hour" had come. Therefore instead of leaving the place, he came forward to ask, "Whom do you seek?" (18:4). They answered him, "Jesus, the Nazarene," that is, "Jesus who comes from Nazareth" (cf. Matt 2:23). Without reservation, Jesus said, "I am he," (literally "I, I am") meaning that he is the presence and revealer of God whose name is "I Am That I Am" (18:5a). This is confirmed by the captors' reaction of drawing back and falling to the ground (18:6), a common reaction to God's appearance. John's specific comment that Judas, who betrayed him, was standing with them (18:5b) shows that Judas has shifted himself from the love of Jesus to the hatred of the world. This final reference in John to Judas puts him along with those who rejected and crucified Jesus!

When the soldiers and officials remained speechless, Jesus takes the initiative to ask them again, "Whom do you seek?," and the same response, "Jesus, the Nazarene," comes from them (18:7). Jesus uses the same words of self-revelation, "I am he," but with the emphatic statement "I told you." He takes control of the situation and voluntarily surrenders himself to God's will to be arrested (cf. 16:31–32), rather than by Judas' betrayal of Jesus by a kiss (Matt 26:48–50 par.). Therefore he told them, "If you seek me, allow these men go" (18:8). Jesus thus proves himself as the good shepherd who would save the lives of his sheep by voluntarily offering his life (10:11–15, 28; cf. 17:12). Jesus said so to fulfill his own saying, "Of those whom you have given me, I lost no one" (18:9; cf. 17:12; 6:39). Jesus omits the phrase "except the son of perdition" because Judas is already lost by taking the side of Jesus' enemies. The fulfillment of Jesus' words is found only in 18:9, 32, whereas in other places Jesus' life events and words were in fulfillment of the Scriptures. That is, both the Scriptures' words and Jesus' words are God's words.[3]

Peter realized that Jesus was going to be arrested and reacted violently by striking the high priest's slave with a sword, cutting off his right ear (18:10). Among the four evangelists, only John gives the slave's name as "Malchus," reflecting his historical accuracy.[4] Possibly, in John, Peter had a short sword, which could easily be concealed inside the garment.[5] Since Peter knew that the officials were sent by the chief priests and the Pharisees, he struck the right ear of the high priest's slave with a vengeful attitude. Like Matthew, John records Jesus' command, "Put your sword into its sheath"

3. Lincoln 2006: 445.
4. Dodd 1965: 77–80; Blomberg 2001: 232.
5. Köstenberger 2009: 509.

(18:11a; cf. Matt 26:52a). Jesus calls Peter to exercise patience and non-violence even when others act violently, for his kingdom is not to be established by swords and weapons, but by love and non-violence (cf. 18:36).

Jesus voluntarily submitted to face sufferings, betrayal, arrest and crucifixion. Therefore he questions Peter, "Shall I not drink the cup which the Father has given me?" (18:11b), which expects the answer "yes." "Cup" here is a metaphor for Jesus' suffering and death (Matt 20:22–23; 26:42 par.). The term implies in the OT "cup of God's wrath," which evildoers should drink (Ps 75:8; Isa 51:17, 22; Jer 25:15–17; Ezek 23:31–34; Hab 2:16).[6] Jesus must taste God's wrath in terms of suffering and death as a propitiation for human sin (Rom 3:25). He was willing to do so.

The Jewish Trial and Peter's Denial (18:12–27)

Since Jesus voluntary submitted himself, the cohort of soldiers, its commander,[7] and the temple officials could seize Jesus easily and bind him (18:12). First they led him to Annas, the father-in-law of Caiaphas who was the high priest that year (18:13; cf. 11:49, 51). Annas was the high priest in 6–15 CE and his son-in-law, Caiaphas, functioned as high priest in 15–36 CE. No wonder Annas was still an influential figure to interrogate Jesus.[8] Caiaphas will be remembered by John's readers from his unconscious prophecy made in the council that it was expedient that one man should die for the people (18:14; 11:49–50). John's reminder looks forward to the vicarious and beneficial death of Jesus for all people groups.

Leaving what happened in Annas' court to narrate in 18:19–24, John shifts the scene to the first denial of Peter made outside the high priest's palace. The Greek word *aulēn* means "sheepfold" (10:1, 16), but here it means "the central courtyard of the palace."[9] Simon Peter was following Jesus along with "another disciple," who could enter into the court of the high priest along with Jesus because he was known to the high priest (18:15). Unlike in the Synoptic accounts (Matt 26:58 par.), Peter could not enter the courtyard on his own, but stood outside the door until the "other disciple"

---

6. Köstenberger 2009: 509.

7. The Greek *khiliarkhos* means "leader of a thousand soldiers" or "commander of a cohort."

8. When the Romans appointed and replaced the high priests, the Jews regarded high priesthood as lifetime office (cf. Num 35:25). Josephus recognizes Jonathan as high priest even fifteen years after of his deposition (*J.W.* 2.12.6).

9. Quast 1989: 72.

brought Peter in after speaking with the maid who kept the door (18:16). Obviously he was familiar to the doorkeeper and to other servants in the high priest's palace. Who is this "other disciple"? Many scholars believe that he is "the disciple whom Jesus loved," mainly because of his association with Peter. John 20:2, where the "other disciple" is mentioned in apposition to "the one whom Jesus loved," seems to confirm this view.

Nevertheless, wherever John speaks of the beloved disciple, he plainly mentions it. In 20:2 John mentions "the other disciple, the one whom Jesus loved," whereas in 18:15-16 he speaks of "the other disciple who was known to the high priest." If the beloved disciple is John the son of Zebedee, as is likely, then it is difficult to explain how a Galilean fisherman was known to the high priest. Some suggest that Zebedee and his sons were purveyors of fish by appointment to the high priest, but the Jews generally did not regard the trade highly.[10] The Greek *gnōstos*, which also means "related [to the high priest]," makes it improbable that the "other disciple" in 18:15-16 is the beloved disciple. A mere business contact would not have prompted the maid to permit Peter enter the courtyard during trial proceedings. If she could easily recognize Peter as the one who was with Jesus (18:17), how easily would she have recognized the "other disciple," if he was the beloved disciple, as the one who was with Jesus?

There is no definite ground for identifying the disciple with the beloved disciple.[11] There are several characters whose names are hidden in John. For example, one of the disciples of John the Baptist who followed Jesus remains hidden (1:37-41). The mother of Jesus is not mentioned by name throughout the Gospel. John introduces some nameless characters that play their part in key places and then disappear (e.g., 4:4-42; 6:9; 21:2). Similarly, the "other disciple," though not one of the Twelve, was a follower of Jesus and could have belonged to a priestly family in Jerusalem and thereby had "acquaintance" with the high priest. Therefore he could enter through the chief priest's "courtyard" and help Peter to come in (cf. Matt 26:58 par.).[12] Possibly he is one of the unnamed disciples of Jesus (21:2), John the Elder, the real author of the Gospel.

---

10. Sanders 1957: 76; cf. Carson 1991: 74-75.

11. Barrett 1978: 525; Keener 2005: 2.1090-91; Michaels 2010: 898. For other scholars who deny that the "other disciple" in 18:15-16 is the beloved disciple, see Quast 1989: 77-79, though Quast himself identifies him with the beloved disciple.

12. Michaels 2010: 897-900.

The Jewish Trial and Peter's Denial

After bringing Peter into the courtyard, the unnamed disciple disappears. The door-keeping maid recognizes Peter as the disciple of the "accused" Jesus who was on trial and hence poses the doubtful question, "Are you also not one of this man's disciples?" Peter categorically denies the first time, "I am not," perhaps in order to save himself (18:17). He leaves the place immediately and soon joins the high priest's servants and the temple police who had gone to arrest Jesus and who were then standing and warming themselves within the courtyard around the charcoal fire, because it was cold (18:18; cf. Mark 14:54). John alone gives the weather as being cold. Peter is ignorant that those who came to arrest could better identify him as a close associate of Jesus than the maid. We need to wait until 18:25 for the continuation of this story.

John shifts the scene from Peter's denial of Jesus to Jesus' trial before Annas (cf. 18:13), who was questioning Jesus about his disciples and his teaching (18:19). It is Johannine pattern to shift between scenes that take place outside and inside alternately in the passion narrative. The Johannine Jesus does not answer concerning his disciples, but only about his teaching. He answers that he has spoken openly to all humans in the world, and that he spoke nothing secretly. As witnesses Jesus points to all Jewish people who came together in the synagogues and in the remple, where Jesus always taught (18:20). Without disclosing the content of his teaching, Jesus boldly questions Annas, "Why do you ask me? Ask those who have heard what I have spoken to them; behold, they know what I said" (18:21).

While Jesus' teaching was given to all people publicly, Annas should have asked those who heard him, because in official proceedings it was not the accused who was interrogated, but the witnesses for and against the accused.[13] Jesus thus unveils the ignorance of Annas of Jewish Law. Jesus' question causes a temple guard, a bystander, to become so annoyed that he slaps Jesus with his hand (cf. 19:3), the first physical attack on Jesus in John's passion narrative! His angry statement, "Do you answer like this to a high priest?" (18:22), shows that the bystanders took Jesus' words as containing disrespect to a top religious authority.

Jesus did not repay violence for violence, but confronted the official by saying, "If I have spoken wrongly, bear witness to the wrong, but if I have spoken rightly, why do you strike me?" (18:23). "If I have spoken wrongly" reads literally, "if I spoke in an evil manner," meaning, "if I said something

---

13. Kruse 2008: 349. Rabbinic law prohibited anyone from being sentenced to death based on the accused person's confession (*m. Sanh.* 6:2).

John 18:12-27

that dishonored the high priest."[14] Jesus challenges the official to prove that he broke the law, "You shall not . . . curse a ruler of your people" (Exod 22:28; cf. Acts 23:5). If he is unable to prove it, then there is no ground for striking Jesus. No one can convict Jesus of having spoken evil (cf. 8:46). Annas sees the illegal assault on Jesus but fails to do justice in the trial. He sends Jesus bound to Caiaphas, the high priest of that year (18:24, cf. 18:13). Without mentioning what happened in Caiaphas' palace, the scene now turns to the events happening outside (18:25-27). This is the Gospel's characteristic "vestigial scenes," in which a stage is set but nothing happens (e.g., 2:12; 11:54; 12:9, 20-22).[15]

18:25 resumes Peter's act of standing and warming himself (18:18) to give continuity to Peter's first denial. The servants and the temple guards question Peter with suspicion, "And you are not one of his disciples, are you?," and Peter denies the second time by assuring, "I am not" (18:25). However, a servant of the high priest who was the relative of Malchus and who had seen Peter cutting Malchus' ear questions him, "Did I not see you in the garden with him?" (18:26). Peter denies the third time. Immediately a cock crows (18:27; cf. 13:38).

Peter denied Jesus three times to save his own life, although he promised that he would lay down his life for his Master (13:37). But Jesus predicted that the cock would not crow till Peter had denied him three times (13:38), and his prediction was fulfilled (18:17-18, 25-27). Such fulfillment shows that Jesus is the revealer of God and his words. John follows Matthew in this narrative rather than Mark, who refers to the rooster crowing twice before Peter's denial of Jesus (Matt 26:34, 74; Mark 14:30, 71). Also, the reference to Peter's weeping bitterly by remembering what Jesus already told him (Matt 26:75; Mark 14:71) is missing in John. What Peter promised in human strength is proved by Jesus to be useless (cf. 6:63). Since Jesus had known the weakness of his disciples, he did not answer Annas about them, but only about his teaching. John presents Peter's denial dramatically and ironically as taking place outside at the time when the high priest was interrogating Jesus about his disciples inside! John does not refer to Peter again until after Jesus' resurrection.

---

14. Köstenberger 2009: 518.
15. Michaels 2010: 897.

THE ROMAN TRIAL, PART 1 (18:28–40)

By leaving Jesus' trial before Caiaphas abruptly, now John narrates Jesus' trial before Pilate, the Roman governor. Jesus was led from Caiaphas to the praetorium, the official residence of the Roman governor of Judea both in Caesarea (Acts 23:33–36) and in Jerusalem (18:28a). It was a large building in Jerusalem with an outside courtyard where the Jewish crowd could assemble. The specification "It was early" is attested by the crowing of the rooster, probably at 6:00 a.m., when Pilate would attend to the judicial business of the day.[16] "The Jews," who joined the crowd to accuse Jesus before Pilate, did not enter the praetorium (18:28b–29). The Passover was to begin at 6:00 p.m. and "the Jews" would keep themselves pure before they ate the Passover by not entering the praetorium, a Gentile dwelling, which they considered an unclean place. Their act of staying outside the praetorium governs seven scenes that take place outside (18:29–32, 38b-40; 19:4–8, 12-16) and inside the praetorium (18:33–38a; 19:1–3, 9–11).[17]

In the first scene, Pilate came out to "the Jews" to enquire them, as per Roman law, of the nature of their accusation against Jesus (18:29; cf. Mark 15:14). Without specifying any charge, they told contemptuously that if "this man" was not doing evil, they would not have handed him over to Pilate (18:30). They expected Pilate to declare Jesus a criminal. However, Pilate realized that the charge of "the Jews" was pertaining to Jewish law and therefore he sought to dismiss the case by asking, "You take him and judge him according to your law." But the accusers responded saying, "It is not lawful for us to put anyone to death" (18:31). This shows that "the Jews" brought Jesus to Pilate just to get his approval to put Jesus to death.

There is little evidence that the Jewish council had legal authority to put the offenders to death between 6 CE and 70 CE. Even in the case of adultery, which deserved death by stoning, the decision needed to be ratified later by the governor.[18] Thus, "the Jews" correctly said that "it is not lawful" for them to put anyone to death. Although it was "the Jews" who were responsible to kill Jesus, it was Jesus who was in control of the whole proceedings. His death by crucifixion was the fulfillment of what he himself had already predicted (18:32; cf. 12:32–33).

---

16. Brown 1978: 2.844.

17. Cf. Michaels 2010: 913–14.

18. Brown 1978: 2.848. The Jews, however, were permitted to execute Gentiles who entered the inner part of Jerusalem temple; Schnackenburg 1980–84: 3.246, 447 n. 20.

The second scene takes place inside. Pilate came in to Jesus to inquire whether he is the King of the Jews (18:33), a central theme in the passion narrative. This question is abruptly raised, as Jesus' claim to be the King of the Jews is nowhere recorded in John's passion narrative (cf. Matt 27:11 par.). Pilate raised this question probably by guessing that the accusation could be of political nature, if not concerned with Jewish religion. He himself asked Jesus, "What did you do?" (18:35), to ascertain the exact nature of accusation. However, Jesus' counter-question, "Do you say this on your own accord or did others tell you about me?" (18:34), presupposes that Pilate had probably been apprised of Jesus' mission with a politically subversive interpretation by his accusers.[19] Jesus' description of the nature of his kingship (18:36) affirms indirectly that he is the King of the Jews, but with a different nature from the world's understanding of a king.

Jesus' counter-question provokes Pilate to say, "I am not a Jew, am I? Your own nation and the chief priests have handed you over to me; what did you do?" (18:35). Pilate uses the word "Jew" purely in an ethnic sense, though the word in 18:36 could denote the unbelieving world. John, in his literary style, brings out from a Gentile ruler the truth that it was his own people, the Jewish nation and its religious authorities, who handed over Jesus to him and who eventually were responsible to crucify Jesus (cf. 1:11). Since Jesus is a Jew, and not Pilate, he should clarify if he has done evil against his own people who seek to kill him lawfully. In answer, Jesus periphrastically acknowledges that he is the King of the Jews, but openly clarifies that his kingship is not "of this world," that is, it does not have the worldly splendor and military empowerment. If it were, then his "servants," those who believed and followed him, would have fought with swords that Jesus would not be delivered to "the Jews," who accused him religiously and politically (cf. 18:10–11). However, his reign does not have its origin in this world (the Greek *enteuthen* means "from here," denoting "from the world"), but in heaven (18:36). That is, his kingship is God's kingship, which is to be established by Jesus' divine love, suffering, a shameful death on the cross, and his final ascension to the Father.

Pilate could grasp that Jesus is the king and therefore asks him, "So you are a king, aren't you?" (18:37a). After hearing of the humble nature of Jesus' kingship, which has no political aspirations, the Gentile governor declares that Jesus is a king. Though Jesus avoided being made king earlier (6:15), he accepts before Pilate that he is a king, for the "hour" has come to

19. Lincoln 2006: 461.

unveil his identity as King. The reference to Jesus' mission occurs twice in Jesus' statements: "For this I have been born," and "For this I have come into the world" (18:37b). The phrase "for this" refers to Jesus' task of establishing his kingship and to the manner in which he will establish his kingship, that is, by bearing witness to the truth.

"Bearing witness" and "truth" are two important themes in John. While "bearing witness" indicates Jesus' proclamation of his self-identity (5:31–38; 8:13–18; cf. 1:6–8), "truth" means God's faithfulness to his covenant to reveal his glory to humans and relate with them (1:14). Jesus was born in the world to establish his kingship by testifying to what he had seen and heard from the Father (3:32–33) and by revealing God's glory in terms of his love and faithful relationship with human beings. However, only those who choose to live in the realm of truth (those who are of the truth) will hear his voice (18:37c). They are known as Jesus' sheep (10:3, 16, 27) who obey his voice and follow him.

Now Pilate is challenged to decide for himself as to whether or not he belongs to the truth to hear Jesus' voice.[20] It is not Jesus who is on trial, but Pilate, who is confronted with the "Light of the world" to decide whether he is on the side of darkness or light.[21] With this challenge, Pilate asks Jesus, "What is truth?" (18:38a). The irony here is that although Pilate had the embodiment of truth standing before him and was interacting with the truth, he could not experience truth due to his unbelief in Jesus.[22] After raising the question, he did not wait to listen to the voice of truth, but went out to "the Jews" again to tell them that he found no crime in Jesus (18:38b). Pilate, after his interrogation, did not find Jesus a criminal who has a political agenda (cf. 19:4, 6) and therefore he was willing to release him. He mentions that the Jews have the custom that the governor should release a prisoner for them at the Passover and asks the crowd whether he can release for them the King of the Jews (18:39).

There is no convincing reference to the Jewish custom of getting a prisoner released by the governor anywhere outside the Gospel narratives. However, the *Mishna* speaks of a person whom the Roman authorities promised to bring out of prison at the Passover, implicitly at the request of the Jews (*m. Pesaḥ.* 8:6). This rabbinic reference suggests that the release of

---

20. Michaels 2010: 925; Köstenberger 2009: 529.
21. Brown 1978: 2.868; Köstenberger 2009: 529.
22. Kanagaraj 2005: 593.

a prisoner happened with some regularity.[23] Matthew and Mark read that it was the custom of the governor to release any one prisoner whom the Jews wanted (Matt 27:15; Mark 15:6). This means that there was a Jewish custom to ask the governor to release a prisoner of their choice.[24] Since Pilate was convinced that Jesus did not claim to be a king in a political sense, he did not hesitate to use the title "King of the Jews" (19:14-15, 19-22) and release him.

The Jewish opponents, however, did not want Jesus to be released, because they had already decided to put him to death by instigating the Roman officials. They cried again, "Not this man, but Barabbas." John mentions that Barabbas was a robber (cf. Mark 15:7; Luke 23:19) to sharply contrast him from Jesus, the King of the Jews (18:40). Ironically, "the Jews" wanted Jesus to be put to death as if he was posing a political threat, but asked to release a man who was truly a political criminal.[25] Jesus takes the place of Barabbas who represents sinful humanity as a whole!

---

23. Barrett 1978: 538.
24. See Luke 23:17 in Codex Alexandrinus (fifth century CE).
25. Duke 1985: 131.

JOHN 19
The Supreme Revelation of God's Glory

THE ROMAN TRIAL, PART 2 (19:1–16)

In 19:1–3, which constitutes the fourth scene, we are led inside the praetorium, as the Roman trial continues. Although Pilate found no crime in Jesus, he gave him up to the soldiers to find out who Jesus is by scourging (19:1; cf. Acts 22:24). Jesus was given the most severe form of punishments: scourging, beating, and flogging.

Jesus becomes a "mock king" in the hands of the soldiers. They plaited a crown of thorns, put it on his head, and clothed him with a purple robe, and kept going up to him, saying, "Hail, O King of the Jews!," and inflicted him with blows (19:2–3). The crown of thorns consisted of the long spikes of the date palm with some branches twisted together. The thorns may have come from the common thorn bush (Isa 34:13; Nah 1:10) or from date palms with twelve-inch-long thorns near the base, and these thorns would sink into the victim's skull, causing considerable pain.[1] By greeting Jesus as "the King of the Jews," a title that was normally used to greet Caesar, the soldiers unconsciously acknowledged him as King in his humiliation and suffering, anticipating his reign from the cross. Scourging, slapping, and spitting (Matt 27:30 par.) recapitulate Isaiah's experience (Isa 50:6). Since the "mock king" scene depicts that Jesus is the King of the Jews in his humiliation and suffering, John puts this scene at the center of Jesus' trial before Pilate.

The fifth scene shows Pilate's interaction with "the Jews" outside. Pilate brings the humiliated Jesus out to them to make them know that he found no crime in Jesus (19:4) When Jesus comes out wearing the crown of thorns and the purple robe, Pilate says to them, "Behold the man!" (19:5). Pilate's acclamation recalls Samuel's introduction of Saul as king, "Behold the man

---

1. Köstenberger 2009: 532.

of whom I spoke to you" (1 Sam 9:17 LXX),[2] and the Lord's attestation of the Messiah, the Branch, as "Behold, the man . . ." (Zech 6:12).[3] Pilate unknowingly and ironically declares the Man of Suffering as the messianic King (cf. 19:14), who came to establish his kingdom and deliver humankind from the evil one. The chief priests and the officers, who should have understood this from the OT, could not see in the blood-stained Jesus the kingly glory of God. Therefore they cried out, "Crucify him, crucify him!" (19:6a; cf. 19:15).

Pilate therefore became frustrated and said, "You take him and crucify" (19:6b). While the Jews themselves do not have authority to put anyone to death, particularly by crucifixion, Pilate's statement shows his dejection rather than his permission. He throws their own demand back in their face. He means, "*You* take him, I do not care what you do with him! As for me, *I* find in him no probable cause."[4] Without listening to Pilate's judgment, "the Jews" bring another charge: If there is no political crime, for them, Jesus has committed religious crime by making himself the Son of God which, as per the Jewish Law, is a blasphemy that deserves death (19:7; 10:30–33; cf. Lev 24:16), for it amounts to make himself God (5:18). The ruler became more fearful when he heard their words (19:8), for he took Jesus as a "divine man" who had divine origin and occult powers.[5]

With fear, Pilate probably takes Jesus into the praetorium (sixth scene) and asks him, "Where are you from?" But this time Jesus does not give any answer (19:9). Jesus confirms his heavenly origin when Pilate angrily responds to Jesus' silence, "Do you not speak to me? You know that I have authority to release you and to crucify you, don't you?" (19:10). He asserts that he is "from above" from where authority has been given to Pilate either to release him or to crucify him (19:11). Pilate lacks boldness, for he expresses his anger to Jesus, who stands as a powerless man, rather than to the crowd, which demands a guiltless man to be put to death.

Jesus warns Pilate, however, that although God has given authority to him over Jesus, the one who delivered him to Pilate has "the greater sin" (19:11b). The reference may be to Judas, the betrayer. However, although Judas initiated the process, it was the Jewish accusers who handed over Jesus to the religious and political authorities. Thus the singular "the one

2. Keener 2005: 2.1123.
3. Köstenberger 2009: 533.
4. Michaels 2010: 932.
5. Dodd 1965: 114.

The Roman Trial, Part 2

who delivered" is a collective singular referring to all Jewish opponents, including Judas, who are under greater punishment for delivering Jesus to be crucified.[6] Upon Jesus' reference to his origin as from God and to the final punishment on those who delivered him, Pilate becomes so fearful that he seeks to release Jesus (19:12a). Pilate's persuasion to release Jesus obviously takes place outside as the seventh and last scene in the Roman trial.

Without allowing Pilate to release Jesus, "the Jews" caution Pilate, saying, "If you release this man, you are not Caesar's friend; everyone who makes himself a king opposes Caesar" (19:12b). "Friend of Caesar" could be an official honor conferred on Pilate as one of the trusted associates from whom the Roman emperors drew advice[7] (cf. 1 Macc 2:18; 3:38; 6:14; 3 Macc 5:3, 19, 26, 29, 34, 44 for "friends of the king"). "The Jews" argue that if Pilate would show favor to someone who makes himself a king, then it amounts to treason, which may cause Pilate to lose the honor "friend of Caesar" and even suffer execution. On hearing this, Pilate brought Jesus out and sat him down on the judgment seat at a place called "the Pavement" (Hebrew *Gabbatha*; 19:13). The Greek term *bēma* means "stone pavement," and in Aramaic it means a "high place," with steps leading up, situated in the forecourt of the governor's palace.

The Greek word *ekathisen* (19:13) can be taken either transitively (Pilate made Jesus to sit on the judgment seat) or intransitively (Pilate sat on the judgment seat). While in Matt 27:19 it is Pilate who sat down, John uses the active voice instead of Matthew's middle voice. The verb, if transitively understood, gives good sequence to Pilate's act of leading Jesus. It is highly possible, then, that he made Jesus sit on the judgment seat, not to mock at him, but to make a final attempt to exhibit Jesus as the King of the Jews, ironically as a suffering Man and as the judge of all humans (5:22, 27). This interpretation gives good sense to Pilate's statement "Behold your King!" (19:14b) and to the cry of "the Jews" to lift up Jesus (apparently from the judgment seat) and crucify him (19:15).[8] The theological motif is that by bringing Jesus to be judged "the Jews" were passing judgment upon themselves.

Pilate's demonstration of Jesus as King is at the sixth hour (noon) on the day of preparation of the Passover (Nisan 14, Thursday; 19:14a).

---

6. Kanagaraj 2005: 601.

7. Brown 1978: 2.879; Keener 2005: 2.1128.

8. Meeks 1967: 73–76; Haenchen 1984: 2.183; Brodie 1993: 538–89 favor transitive interpretation; against this Keener 2005: 2.1129; Köstenberger 2009: 536–67 n. 78.

The instigation to crucify Jesus comes from "the Jews," who are altogether responsible for having crucified Jesus. However, Pilate makes his last attempt to release Jesus by asking, "Shall I crucify your king?" (19:15b) in which "your king" is emphasized in Greek. The chief priests, on behalf of all accusers, answer, "We have no king except Caesar" (19:15c). In fact, Yahweh alone is the King of Israel (e.g., Judg 8:2; 1 Sam 8:7). The eleventh of the "eighteen benedictions" prays, "May you [i.e., God] be our King, you alone!," for the Jews expected God's kingdom to be set up through his Messiah, the King of Israel (12:13). By confessing Caesar alone as their king, "the Jews" deny in practice God's kingship over them and their messianic hope. Politically, they do not accept Caesar's kingship over them. However, they confess him as king hypocritically to get Jesus crucified. Pilate finally surrenders to the demands of "the Jews" and hands over Jesus to them to be crucified. They then receive Jesus from the Roman court. For Pilate, Jesus is the King of the Jews who deserves no death penalty. Thus Jesus wins in the trial by witnessing to truth.

JESUS' REIGN FROM THE CROSS (19:17-30)

Although "the Jews" received Jesus in their custody and possibly handed him over to the soldiers (19:18, 23), it was Jesus who voluntarily "went out" of the praetorium. He carried his "own cross," the cross on which he was to be crucified, and went to the place called Golgotha, or *gulgoltā*, which means in Aramaic "a skull" (John19:17; cf. Matt 27:33 par.). The place was called so because it looked like the top of a skull.[9] By carrying the cross, Jesus was carrying the sins of the world to put them to death (John 1:29; cf. Rom 3:23-26). On Golgotha, a higher place outside Jerusalem, they (i.e., the Roman soldiers) crucified him on behalf of "the Jews." That is, they nailed Jesus' forearms stretched on both sides and his feet held together on the cross. Normally crucifixion nails were driven higher up on the arms to enable the crucified ones to keep hanging on the cross.[10] Crucifixion was the most shameful and physically agonizing form of death sanctioned by the emperor himself for slaves, bandits, prisoners of war, and revolutionaries.[11]

---

9. Lincoln 2006: 474. It is called *calvaria* in Latin and thus the place of Jesus' crucifixion is widely known as "Calvary."

10. Keener 2005: 2.1202.

11. Köstenberger 2009: 543.

Jesus' Reign from the Cross

The absolute statement "There they crucified him" (19:18a) and the mention of the place of crucifixion as near to the city of Jerusalem (John 19:20; Heb 13:13) have historical significance, for the whole episode specifies the place, time, and the rulers of the day. Two others, one on either side, were crucified with him. They were bandits (Matt 27:38; Mark 15:27) and criminals (Luke 23:33). Jesus was exalted on the cross between them (19:18b) in order to identify himself with the criminals in fulfillment of the OT prophecy (cf. Isa 53:12; Ps 22:16; Luke 22:37). As the Lamb that bears human sins, Jesus was sacrificed on the cross (John 1:29, 36; Isa 53:4–7). Jesus thus revealed God's love supremely on the cross. Paul interpreted Jesus' crucifixion in terms of crucifixion of human selfishness along with Jesus so that the glorious self may be raised with him (Rom 6:2–11; Gal 2:20).

That Jesus is the King who reigns from the cross is confirmed by the title "Jesus of Nazareth, the King of the Jews," written and set up on the cross by Pilate (19:19). "Jesus of Nazareth" refers to the man Jesus who lived in Nazareth. That this humiliated man is the King of the Jews puts Jesus on the highest side of the social spectrum. This paradox can be grasped only by those who see the reality of the cross and believe! Many of the Jewish people could read this title, as it was written in three major languages (Hebrew, Latin, and Greek; 19:20), symbolizing that Jesus was exalted on the cross as the King of the people of all languages.[12] The title set up on Jesus' cross reflects Pilate's final verdict, although he would not have perceived that Jesus is the King who, paradoxically, reigns from the cross. The chief priests, among "the Jews," were intrigued by the writing of Pilate. They urged him to rewrite it, accusing that "this man" Jesus claimed himself to be the King of the Jews (19:21). Their attempt was foiled by Pilate's firm statement, "What I have written, I have written" (19:22), implying that the verdict cannot be changed by inducement.

When the soldiers had crucified Jesus, they took his outer garments and tore them into four pieces to share among themselves, one for each, as per Roman law. This shows that four soldiers were assigned for Jesus. They removed Jesus' undergarment, a long tunic worn next to the skin.[13] This tunic was seamless, woven into one piece from top to bottom (19:23) and so they could not tear it into four parts, but, as per the Roman military custom, they cast lots to decide who should take it (19:24a). John sees both acts of the soldiers as fulfillment of the Scripture (Ps 22:18). In fact, he

---

12. The three languages suggest the universality of Jesus' reign; Keener 2005: 2.1137.
13. Kruse 2008: 361.

John 19:17–30

presents the whole episode of Jesus' passion and death as the fulfillment of OT prophecies (2:19–22; 13:18; 19:24, 28, 36–37) to prove that Jesus is the Christ to whom the OT points. What all the soldiers did to Jesus was within God's plan of salvation, which they themselves did not know (19:24b). Their removal of Jesus' outer and inner garments makes it possible that Jesus was crucified naked, as Romans normally did for any person crucified. However, in deference to the Jewish aversion to public nudity Jesus would have been left with his underclothing.[14]

There were three women (i.e., Jesus' mother, her sister, who was Mary the wife of Clopas, and Mary Magdalene) standing by the cross (19:25).[15] Mary the wife of Clopas could be, to use the modern term, the "co-sister" of Jesus' mother, for Hegesippus (early 2nd century CE) asserted that Cleophas was the brother of Joseph, the husband of Jesus' mother.[16] Probably both Marys were from closely related families. Unlike in the Synoptic Gospels, the women in John were not standing afar, but by the cross, as the beloved disciple also was. As Jesus' mother and the beloved disciple were standing nearer to each other (19:26a), Jesus could see both of them from the cross.

As part of his care to his mother, Jesus said to her, "Woman, behold, your son!" (19:26b). He told his disciple, "Behold, your mother!" and immediately ("from that hour") the disciple accepted her into his care (19:27). The one who loves Jesus obeys his word (14:15, 21, 23–24; 1 John 5:3; 2 John 6). The love of Jesus and of the disciple was mutual. Adoptive ties held significant legal force in Roman culture and intimate friendship also could make functional kinship ties.[17] Jesus had his own brothers (2:12), but he did not entrust his mother with them, probably because they were unbelievers (7:5). Therefore Jesus made his beloved disciple his successor as son to his mother. Both the figures are nameless. Most probably, for John, Jesus' mother represents the church, God's new community of believers, in which the beloved disciple represents the witness par excellence and in which the family bond is stronger than natural familial bonds.[18] Both constitute now

---

14. Brown 1978: 2.902; Köstenberger 2009: 546.

15. For arguments in favor of three women see Kanagaraj 2005: 615–16. Cf. Matt 27:55–56 par.

16. *Hist. eccl.* 3.11.

17. Keener 2005: 2.1144.

18. Cf. Lincoln 2006: 477; Keener 2005: 2.1145.

Jesus' Reign from the Cross

a new family of God, incepted at the cross,[19] in which men and women have equal roles to play.

After symbolically making his newly founded community stabilized at the cross, by his divine knowledge, Jesus knew that all was now accomplished (4:34; 17:4)[20] and said, "I thirst," to fulfill the Scriptures (19:28). Against the backdrop of soldiers who gave Jesus vinegar or savor wine, the saying may be an enactment of Pss 69:21 and 22:15 (cf. Ps 42:2; 63:1). Ironically, the one who gives water that will never make one thirsty (4:14) says on the cross, "I thirst!" Jesus definitely must have been thirsty physically in the process of crucifixion. It proves that Jesus was really a human (cf. 4:6–7). John specifies that there was a vessel with vinegar in the midst, implying that it was customary to keep sour wine or vinegar in the place of crucifixion to quench the thirst of those crucified. When the soldiers put a sponge full of vinegar on the hyssop and held it to Jesus' mouth, perhaps to mock at him (Mark 15:36), there is no reference that Jesus drank it (cf. Mark 15:23). This means that Jesus' thirst was not so much for water as for God and for God's cup of suffering and death (18:11) to be drunk.[21]

The reference to "hyssop" is deliberate in John. It was a small plant whose stem is not lengthy.[22] It is possible that the sponge of vinegar was tied in the hyssop and held to Jesus' mouth by a reed (cf. Matt 27:48; Mark 15:36). Hyssop reminds that Jesus is the Passover Lamb (cf. 18:28; 19:36), for the Israelites sprinkled on their doorposts by dipping hyssop in the blood of the Passover lamb when they were delivered from bondage (Exod 12:21–22). After receiving the vinegar, Jesus saw that he has fulfilled God's redemptive plan for humanity and said victoriously, "It has been finished," the last word before his death in John (19:30a). The purpose of Jesus' coming into the world was to give divine life to human beings, by bearing their sins on the cross, and to establish a new humanity (1:29; 3:16–17; 4:34; 5:36; 10:10; 17:4). Jesus made "the prince of the world" powerless on the cross (12:31; 14:30; 16:11). He completed all these functions successfully!

After Jesus' word of victory, he bowed his head and handed over his spirit (19:30b). Neither "the Jews" nor the Roman soldiers took away Jesus' life, but he himself handed over his spirit, obviously to the Father (Matt

---

19. Cf. Koester 2003: 239–41.

20. This shows that the purpose of Jesus' coming into the world goes beyond his gift of salvation to form God's new community.

21. Cf. Michaels 2010: 961–63.

22. Lincoln 2006: 478.

John 19:17-30

27:50; Luke 23:46). Strictly speaking, Jesus' work continues still. He will send his Spirit (15:26; 16:7) and empower his followers to continue his work of building up God's new society (20:21-23). Therefore Jesus' handing over of his spirit to the Father anticipates his resurrection (10:18) so that he might give divine life to all who believe in him. Thus, Jesus' death denotes an open-ended mission!

THE AFTERMATH OF JESUS' DEATH (19:31-42)

Jesus, the Passover lamb (19:31-37)

In 19:31, "the day of Preparation" means "the day of Preparation of the Sabbath," for John comments that that Sabbath was a "great day." This means that for John the next day (6:00 p.m. Friday to 6:00 p.m. Saturday) was the Sabbath and also the Passover day. Therefore it was called "the great day." The Jews did not allow the bodies of the crucified to remain hanging on the cross all night, for a hanged one is cursed by God (Deut 21:22-23; cf. Gal 3:13). It was essential to remove their bodies before the feast day. Therefore the Jewish authorities asked Pilate to break the legs of the crucified ones to make them die so that their bodies might be removed. Pilate granted their request. The soldiers came and first broke the legs of the two who had been crucified with Jesus (19:32). Then they came to Jesus, but they did not break his legs because they found him already dead (19:33). This special reference is to separate Jesus from the two criminals. Jesus' death before his legs were broken makes the time of his death coincide with the time when the Passover lambs were sacrificed in the temple, at 3:00 p.m. That Jesus' legs were not broken fulfills the Passover law that the bones of the paschal lamb should not be broken (Exod 12:46; Num 9:12).

Nevertheless, one of the soldiers, desiring to ensure Jesus' death, pierced his side with a spear, and immediately blood and water came out (19:34). "Piercing" alludes to Zech 12:10 (cf. John 19:37; Ps 22:16), which refers to the mourners who will look on him whom they have pierced. The word "spear" in Greek (*logkhē*) originally meant an iron spearhead of a three-and-a-half-foot javelin.[23] Immediately after piercing, blood and water came from Jesus' side. Medically, the scourging could have caused a hemorrhage between Jesus' ribs and lungs. With Jesus' body held upright on the cross, the hemorrhagic fluid could have separated into a light serum above

---

23. Keener 2005: 2.1151; Köstenberger 2009: 552 n. 65.

and a thick red fluid below. The spear would have pierced the pleural cavity (i.e., between the rib cage and the lung), and the two parts of the blood could have come out unmixed.[24]

The flow of blood and water from Jesus' side is important because it shows that the one who saw it has borne witness so that the readers may believe (19:35). By recording this, John may prove the humanity of Jesus (cf. 1 John 5:6). However, John's point goes beyond this interpretation. Some understand the blood against the background of 6:52–59 and the water in light of 7:38–39.[25] Others see it against the background of Isa 53 and still others see the blood and water as representing the sacraments by which the church is built up.[26] Most of the interpretations proposed do not take up "blood and water" together as one entity.

19:34b can better be understood in the light of 1 John 5:6–10,[27] which speaks of Jesus' incarnation as his coming by water and blood. This theme is linked with the testimony of the Spirit and with the necessity of believing in the Son of God of whom God has testified. The same motifs occur in 19:34–35. That the Spirit, the water, and the blood are "to the one" (1 John 5:8) means that the Spirit, the water, and the blood agree together to proclaim the truth that Jesus is the Christ, the Son of God, by believing in whom one can have eternal life.[28]

The flow of blood and water proves not only that the Logos came in flesh, but also that the Spirit (symbolized by "water"), which is to be given after Jesus' glorification (7:39), brings new life (symbolized by "blood"), which flows from the crucified Christ.[29] Those who believe will experience the love and new life of the Spirit found on the cross. Thus, the Spirit, blood, and water bear witness together to Jesus as the giver of life. This witness is done through the disciple who was an eyewitness to what happened on the cross (19:35). The Johannine community attests that the content of the disciple's witness is true, because he speaks the truth (cf. 21:24). "Bearing witness" could be not only by words, but also by putting such a vision in writing (cf. 21:25) so that those who hear and read might believe (cf. 20:31).

---

24. Brown 1978: 2.946–47; Kruse 2008: 366.
25. E.g., Lincoln 2006: 479.
26. E.g., Hoskyns 1961: 535.
27. Kanagaraj 2005: 623–25.
28. Smalley 1984: 282.
29. Cf. Koester 2003: 200–201.

Jesus' life, particularly his suffering and death, took place in human history in fulfillment of God's will written in Scripture (19:24, 28, 36, 37). John summarizes the passion story by citing two OT prophecies that Jesus fulfilled. "These things," which includes the suffering and death of Jesus before his legs were broken, happened to fulfill the scripture, "Not a bone of him shall be broken" (19:36). The quotation alludes to Ps 34:20, which mentions that not one of the righteous person's bones will be broken. This proves that Jesus suffered and died as a righteous man. Jesus' death echoes, more than anything, the Passover statute according to which the Passover lamb should be eaten without breaking any of its bones and without leaving any part of it until the morning (Exod 12:46; Num 9:12). If Jesus was killed as a paschal lamb, then lawfully his legs were not to be broken and his body should be removed before the next day, the "high day," that is, Sabbath.

The crucified Jesus fulfilled "another scripture," Zech 12:10, which predicts that when the Lord pours upon Judeans a spirit of grace and pleas for mercy, they shall look on him whom they have pierced. Jesus fulfilled the role of Yahweh who will be pierced by the evil deeds of Jewish nation, but on whom the nation will look with mourning for their evil (19:37). Since a Roman soldier pierced Jesus' side on behalf of "the Jews," it is they who pierced him. The prophecy "they shall look on him" predicts that those who pierced Jesus would come to know through the witness of the church that Jesus is the Messiah who came to deliver them from their wickedness (cf. 8:28). "Piercing" symbolizes the opening of the fountain on the cross to cleanse people of their sin (cf. Zech 13:1) and give them heavenly life (cf. 3:14–15; 7:37–38).

Jesus' Burial (19:38–42)

As per the Roman custom, the bodies of executed criminals were left to be devoured by vultures without burial. However, the Jews used to bury criminals' bodies in a common grave provided by the Sanhedrin (*m. Sanh.* 6:5).[30] In John, however, Jesus was buried as a king. After he died, Joseph of Arimathea, a secret disciple of Jesus for fear of "the Jews," asked Pilate to hand over Jesus' body to him. With Pilate's permission, he came to the place of crucifixion and took away Jesus' body (19:38). Joseph of Arimathea, mentioned in all four Gospels, was from a Jewish town called Arimathea (Luke 23:50), which was in the northwestern part of Judea at its border

---

30. Kruse 2008: 367.

The Aftermath of Jesus' Death

with Samaria. He was a rich man (Matt 27:57), a respected member of the Sanhedrin, and a good and righteous man, who himself was looking for the kingdom of God (Mark 15:43; Luke 23:50). However, out of his fear for Jewish authorities, he did not confess Jesus openly as the Christ lest he be excommunicated from the synagogue (cf. 7:13; 9:22; 12:42; 20:19). But after crucifixion, he got courage to show himself a disciple of Jesus and took away Jesus' body with the knowledge of "the Jews" and Roman soldiers. Jesus, exalted on the cross, drew such a fearful disciple unto him (cf. 12:32)!

Nicodemus, who came to Jesus earlier at night (3:2), came now obviously during daytime and joined Joseph in burying Jesus by bringing about a hundred pounds[31] of a mixture of myrrh and aloes to be applied on Jesus' body before his burial (19:39). This large amount of spices suggests that Jesus was given a royal burial (cf. 2 Chr 16:14; Jer 34:5; *Ant.* 17.8.3), confirming Pilate's writing on the cross that Jesus is the King.[32] This suggests that Nicodemus believed that Jesus is the coming King after he heard Jesus' teaching on the kingdom of God. Mary anointed Jesus six days before the Passover, marking the day of Jesus' burial as King (12:3, 7), whereas Joseph and Nicodemus did so on the day of burial.

Both Joseph and Nicodemus bound Jesus' body in linen cloths (cf. 20:6–7) with spices. The narrator explains, for the sake of Gentile readers, that this was the burial custom of the Jews (19:40). The powdered myrrh and aloes were spread between the linen cloths, while the spices and aromatic oils were applied to the body. Jesus' face must have been bound over the head by a napkin (cf. 20:7). In the place of Jesus' crucifixion, Golgotha, there was a garden and a new tomb, where no one had ever been laid, was situated in the garden (19:41). The tomb was at hand and so they laid Jesus there. As the day of preparation for the Passover was about to end, they had to bury Jesus' body quickly in the nearby tomb (19:42). It was also a day of preparation for the disciples to see the risen Jesus!

The fact that Jesus was buried in a garden again exhibits him as the King of the Jews. The tomb belonged to Joseph of Arimathea (Matt 27:57, 60). This may fulfill Isa 53:9, which predicted that the Lord's Servant was with a rich man in his death. The newness of the tomb reminds us of the newness of the young donkey on which Jesus rode as King (12:14–15; Mark 11:2, 10; Luke 19:30, 38). Undoubtedly, John pictures Jesus as King in his exaltation on the cross, whence he reigns, and his burial confirms it. The

---

31. Or nearly thirty-three kilograms.
32. Cf. Daly-Denton 2000: 299–300.

John 19:38-42

tomb was closed with a stone, though it is not plainly mentioned at this point (cf. 20:1; Luke 24:2).

Fusing the Horizons

John's passion narrative presents Jesus sacrificed on the cross for the deliverance of humankind from sin and eternal death. The idea of sacrifice to get rid of one's sins is present particularly in Hinduism. For example, the Vedas speak of *prajāpati*, the God-become-man and the Lord of creatures offering himself mystically for creatures in a body fit for sacrifice. The *Tāndya-brāhmana* refers to "the Lord of creatures" (*prajāpati*), who offered himself a sacrifice for the gods and thus the Vedic *prajāpati* is both a priest and victim.[33] Thus, Hinduism recognizes the institution of sacrifice as a divinely appointed ordinance in the same way as the institution of sacrifice appears in the OT. John pictures Jesus voluntarily giving himself to be sacrificed on the cross to give fullness of life to humanity. By being both the sacrifice and the priest who offers it, Jesus fulfills the role of *prajāpati* of Rig Veda. K. M. Banerjea (nineteenth century CE) rightly observed that the pure faith to which the Vedas testify is found in its fullness in Jesus, the agent of creation and the true self-sacrificing *prajāpati*.[34] Therefore we no longer need human or animal sacrifices to please God or to be expiation for human sins. We may see in John, then, that Jesus, who came into the world to offer himself as a sacrifice for human sin, is the fulfillment not merely of the Jewish scriptures, but also of the Hindu scriptures and of the aspirations of all other religions.[35]

Jesus testified before Pilate that he came to bear witness to the truth. Many sages, philosophers, and freedom fighters, like Mahatma Gandhi, who wrote his book *My Experiment with Truth*, have searched for and examined truth. They have also practiced truth at the human level and on an experimental basis. But they themselves could not experience the heavenly truth revealed in Jesus. John projects Jesus himself as the truth (14:6) and the one who communicates truth. Jesus came from heaven to testify to the truth by giving firsthand testimony of God's character, the truth. For John, truth

---

33. Slater 1903: 67; Boyd 1989: 282.
34. Boyd 1989: 280-83; Slater 1903: 66-68.
35. Cf. Kanagaraj 2005: 610-11.

Fusing the Horizons

is not something for which one should search alone, but is something to be experienced by believing in Jesus and obeying his voice (18:37).

JOHN 20
Visions of the Risen Jesus

The Resurrection of Jesus (20:1–10)

The resurrection narrative begins with a reference to Mary Magdalene, who went to Jesus' tomb early, while it was still dark, on the first day of the week, that is, the day after the Sabbath (Sunday), and who was shocked to see the stone removed from the tomb (20:1). She came to the tomb alone, probably to see the tomb (Matt 28:1) or to anoint Jesus' body with spices (Mark 16:1; Luke 24:1), or to lament at the tomb, as Jewish women used to do for their dear ones who had died (11:31; *Gospel of Peter* 50). With great anxiety and fear, she ran and went to Peter and the beloved disciple.

Mary told them, "They took the Lord out of the tomb, and we do not know where they have laid him" (20:2). "They" may imply Jesus' enemies or tomb robbers. She identifies Jesus as "the Lord," which is God's name, used for the risen Jesus by the first Christians (cf. 20:13, 18, 25, 28; 21:7, 12). The plural "we" in her report may imply that there were other women with her.[1] In the late-first-century context, it could denote collectively the Johannine Christians over against Jewish opposition.[2] Mary Magdalene did not see the body of Jesus in his tomb and did not know where it was being kept.

Peter and the other disciple, who is introduced as the disciple loved by Jesus (20:2), came out and went toward the tomb. They ran "together at the same time" (*duo homou* in Greek), but the beloved disciple ran quicker than Peter and came first to the tomb (20:3–4). He bent down and looked inside the tomb. He saw only the linen cloths lying and not Jesus' body. Peter, who followed him, went into the tomb first and found the linen wrappings lying and the face cloth that had been round Jesus' head rolled up by itself (20:5–7). Following Peter, the other disciple also went in and saw everything and *believed* (20:8).

---

1. Kruse 2008: 369.
2. Lincoln 2006: 489.

The Resurrection of Jesus

Some interpret the visit of the two disciples in terms of relationship of the Johannine Christians to the wider church. For them the Johannine community, represented by the beloved disciple, is one with the apostolic church, represented by Peter, and has uniquely contributed to the Johannine Christology. John mentions the beloved disciple as the one who believed first in Jesus' resurrection after seeing its historical evidence,[3] and Peter as a witness to the empty tomb (20:6–7). Both faith and witness are interrelated. Though the author sets the beloved disciple as an example of faith, he does not view the two disciples as competitors to each other. After seeing the empty tomb, both returned home together (20:10). Both the disciples did not understand the scripture that testifies to the necessity of Jesus' resurrection (20:9). The "scripture" may refer to Ps 16:10 (cf. Acts 2:31), but broadly to everything written about Christ in the Law of Moses, the Prophets, and the Psalms (Luke 24:27, 44).[4]

MARY MAGDALENE, AN APOSTLE TO THE APOSTLES (20:11–18)

Mary Magdalene plays a key role in John's resurrection narrative. Obviously soon she came and joined the two disciples at Jesus' tomb. After the two disciples left, she kept standing outside the tomb weeping. While crying, she bent down to look for Jesus' body into the tomb (20:11). She saw two angels in white, one sitting at the head and one at the feet in the place where Jesus had been laid (20:12; cf. Matt 28:3; Mark 16:5; Luke 24:4). They asked Mary, "Woman, why are you weeping?" (20:13a), implying that since Jesus is risen from the dead there is no need to weep. Mary replied from outside the tomb that she is weeping because somebody took away "my Lord" and that she does not know where they have laid him (20:13b; cf. 20:2).

As Mary was speaking, the scene abruptly shifts from a vision of angels to a vision of the risen Lord! She turned around and saw Jesus standing. However, she did not recognize him (20:14). Jesus asked, "Woman, why are you weeping? Whom do you seek?" (20:15a). He knew why she was weeping and whom she sought, but his questions serve as a preparation for his self-revelation. Often the risen Jesus conceals his identity from his disciples at least temporarily (e.g., John 21:4; Luke 24:16).[5] Mistaking him for a gardener, who might have removed Jesus' body and kept it somewhere,

---

3. Quast 1989: 123; Lincoln 2006: 489.
4. Michaels 2010: 993 n. 34.
5. Michaels 2010: 998.

Mary pleaded with him, "Sir, if you have carried him away, tell me where you have placed him, and I shall take him away" (20:15b). Ironically, she asked the living Jesus for his own dead body! At this point Jesus revealed his identity as the risen one by calling her, "Mary." Now she, as his sheep, recognized Jesus by his voice (cf. 10:3, 27). She made a second turning towards him with a sense of wonder and recognition and called him, in Hebrew, "*Rabboni!*" (in Aramaic, *Rabbuni*), meaning, "my Teacher" (20:16). She claimed Jesus earlier as "my Lord" (20:13). Both "Lord" and "Teacher" are complementary titles (13:13–14). The first disciples addressed Jesus as "Rabbi" (1:38). By addressing Jesus with the same title, Mary proves herself to be his female disciple!

Jesus' words "Do not hold on to me," which means, "Stop clinging to me," presuppose that Mary was about to touch Jesus, perhaps his feet, and cling on to him with joy. The reason is that he had not yet ascended to the Father (20:17a). This does not mean that Mary can touch Jesus after his ascension. His invitation to Thomas to touch his wounds (20:27) does not mean that Jesus' ascension took place before he appeared to Thomas. There is no reference that Thomas touched the wounds in Jesus' body. It was an invitation in order to lead Thomas to believe in the risen Jesus, whereas Mary had already believed in Jesus' resurrection. Therefore the particle "for" is to be taken with Jesus' command to Mary to go to "my brothers" and announce the message that he is on the process of ascending "to my Father and your Father, to my God and your God" (20:17b). If so, then Jesus' command not to hold on to him is to hasten her to go to his disciples and convey the message (cf. Matt 28:7–8).

Jesus is now in the process of ascending to the Father after resurrection (cf. 13:1). While there is a distinction between Jesus' relationship with the Father as his only Son and that of his disciples, the phrase, "my Father and your Father, my God and your God," affirms the oneness with which his followers can now approach God through Jesus by virtue of his death and resurrection. Jesus sends Mary to tell them of his ascent to the Father, and of the new filial relationship that is established now by naming them as "my brothers" (cf. 13:33; 16:14–15). This designation confirms that Jesus is risen indeed and that he has created a new family of God, the church (cf. 19:26–27).

Mary Magdalene goes and testifies before the disciples, "I have seen the Lord" (20:18), so that they may believe that Jesus is alive. For the first-century Christians "seeing" the risen Jesus was the primary mark of apostolic witness (20:25; cf. 1 Cor 15:3–9). In this sense, Mary is an apostle who not only saw the risen Lord first, but also announced the message of Jesus' empty tomb to two disciples (20:1–2) and then the message that Jesus is risen to the eleven disciples. Thus, she is "the apostle to the apostles."[6] Mary Magdalene links the "empty tomb" tradition and the appearances of the risen Jesus. The Johannine resurrection narrative shows concern on gender roles and on the relation between faith and sight—the faith of men (20:8) and the prophetic vision of a woman (20:12, 18).[7]

Jesus' appearances to the male disciples (20:19–29)

Appearance and empowerment (20:19–23)

After the risen Jesus revealed himself to his female disciple, he now appears to ten of his male disciples (excluding Judas Iscariot and Thomas), who were behind the shut doors out of fear for "the Jews" (cf. 7:13; 9:22; 19:38). They might have hid themselves out of fear because of rumors that they had stolen the body of Jesus to claim that Jesus was risen from the dead (cf. Matt 28:13).[8] However, on the evening of the day, which was the first day of the week (Sunday), Jesus came through the shut doors, stood among his disciples, and greeted them, "Peace be with you" (20:19). This is a greeting normally used by the Jews, particularly by heavenly beings when they appeared (Judg 6:23; 1 Sam 25:6). In the context of Jesus' appearance to the troubled and fearful disciples, the greeting assured them of peace (cf. 14:27; 16:33).

After this, Jesus showed his hands (i.e., his wounded forearms) and his side (20:20a). Since John alone narrates the piercing of Jesus' side (19:34), he mentions that Jesus showed his side, rather than his feet (Luke 24:39), to assure them that he was the same Jesus who was crucified. Then the disciples could perceive him as Jesus, the risen Lord, and rejoiced on seeing him. Through this appearance Jesus revealed himself as the one who overcame death and who lives forever. It also partly fulfills Jesus' earlier promise that "Your sorrow will turn into joy" (16:20, 22) when they see him again (14:19; 16:16).

---

6. Brown 1979: 190.

7. Michaels 2010: 986.

8. *Gospel of Peter* 26 mentions that the disciples were being sought after as if they were evildoers who wanted to set fire to the temple.

John 20:19-23

The risen Jesus gave them divine peace once again and commissioned them by saying, "As the Father has sent me, even so do I send you" (20:21; cf. 17:18). There is no difference in meaning of the twice-repeated word "sending," though two different Greek words are used. Jesus' death and resurrection built up God's new community, which had taken shape during his earthly ministry. The resurrection is to be followed by Jesus' sending of the Holy Spirit (14:26; 15:26; 16:7-11) who will work as Jesus' presence through the church in this world. Both Jesus' mission and the church's mission originate from the Father and therefore the church's mission is actually God's mission.

The model and ground of the church's mission is what Jesus did and spoke in the world. The purpose of Jesus' appearance to his disciples is not only to show himself alive (cf. Acts 1:3), but to send them into the world to continue the work of building up his community by witnessing to the truth (18:37), by delivering the world from eternal destruction (3:16-17), and by giving divine life in abundance (10:10). Jesus' community is sent to bring "other sheep" into his sheep-old (10:16) so that unity and love may be communicated to the world (13:34-35; 17:21). There is no difference between God sending his Son and the Son sending his newly founded community into the world.

The task of bearing witness to Jesus would be impossible for the church without the power of the Holy Spirit (John 15:26-27; cf. Acts 1:8). Therefore Jesus breathed on the disciples by saying, "Receive the Holy Spirit" (20:22). The use of the verb "to breathe on" is deliberate here. Breathing on them alludes to Gen 2:7, where God creates humanity by breathing into Adam's nostrils the breath of life. In Ezek 37:9 God asks Ezekiel to prophesy to the breath (or "wind") to "breathe on" the slain that they may come back to life. Both the passages describe the breath of God as life-giving source. However, Ezek 37:9-10 refers actually to the resurrection of the dead. In the context of John 20:22, the most acceptable background is Gen 2:7. What Yahweh did in the OT to create humanity, the glorified Jesus does to create a new humanity, which has new life by Jesus' breath.

The empowerment motif, along with the idea of newly created community, is stronger in 20:22. The community that was founded by Jesus is rooted at the cross and is now empowered by the Holy Spirit to accomplish God's mission. The commissioning of Jesus for the work of the Father is naturally followed by empowerment. The Spirit, then, is not any denomination's possession, but is given for the common good, that is, for the growth and function of the whole church (cf. 1 Cor 12:7). The disciples on whom the life of Jesus was breathed represent the universal community of God that will be guided by the Holy Spirit on earth. Is this giving of the Holy Spirit the Johannine Pentecost? Some scholars argue that functionally the Pentecost event in Acts 2 and Jesus' gift of the Spirit in John 20:22 are the same.[9] However, if 20:22 denotes the Pentecostal event, how is it that even after receiving the Spirit the disciples were inactive, keeping themselves behind the shut doors (20:26)?

We should note that the gift of the Spirit is not one-time event, but that it is the continuous manifestation of God's power through the church in its mission, which, against the narrow understanding of proclamation and planting churches, encompasses the complete life and work of the church.[10] The gift of the Spirit in the form of Jesus' breath is a preliminary empowerment of Jesus' disciples to live and serve in the world. Thomas was not present when Jesus breathed on the disciples, and the place of Judas remained vacant. The outpouring of the Spirit will happen only after the circle of the twelve disciples become complete by replacing Judas with Matthias (Acts 1:21–26), to form the new Israel, the church. John's narrative of Jesus' giving of the Spirit, being a symbolic act, anticipates the outpouring of the Holy Spirit on the day of Pentecost (Acts 2), when Jesus' promise of the Holy Spirit (7:38–39; 14:16–17, 26; 15:26; 16:7) will fully be realized.

The main function of God's new community that has received the Holy Spirit is to forgive the sins of others that their sins may be forgiven or to retain the sins of any that their sins may be retained (20:23). This is parallel with Jesus' statement, "Whatever you bind on earth shall be bound in heaven, and whatever you loose on earth shall be loosed in heaven" (Matt 16:19; 18:18). For the Jews, "binding and loosing" expressed the activity of a judge who declared persons innocent or guilty and thus "bound" or "loosed" them from the charges made against them.[11] Similarly, the Spirit-filled community has authority to judge people, a function inherited from Jesus (5:27; cf. Isa 22:22). Retaining sins does not mean that Christ's community should show an unforgiving attitude towards sinners.

20:23 may be interpreted in the light of Johannine dualism, which expresses that the coming of Jesus and his message of salvation divide people into two groups, believers ("insiders") and unbelievers ("outsiders"). The

9. E.g., Brown 1978: 2.1038–9; Beasley-Murray 1999: 381–82.
10. Hoskyns 1961: 547.
11. Köstenberger 2009: 575.

church will receive the same response, both positive and negative, to their life and ministry performed with the authority of the Holy Spirit. The sins of those who accept the church's message and believe in Jesus will be forgiven (cf. 8:34, 36) and the sins of those who do not will be retained (cf. 3:18-21; 9:40-41). In this sense, Jesus' followers will forgive or retain sins. Apart from this, 20:23 does not endorse the sacrament of penance.

Jesus' encounter with Thomas (20:24-29)

20:24-29 discloses that Thomas was not there with the disciples when the risen Jesus appeared to them (20:24). Thomas is first named as "one of the Twelve," the "Twelve" being a fixed term for the twelve disciples even after Judas Iscariot left Jesus. Then as "the Twin," a term that did not necessarily mean literal twins.[12] The "other disciples" mentioned in 20:25 refers to those to whom the risen Jesus appeared earlier. They told Thomas, "We have seen the Lord" (20:25a). John makes them to confess Jesus as "the Lord," the name of Yahweh that was ascribed to Jesus by the early church by virtue of his resurrection. The apostolic characteristic of having seen Jesus as the Lord (cf. 20:18) is exhibited by the disciples. Thomas plainly said that he will not believe unless he sees in Jesus' hands the print of the nails and touches the mark of the nails and his pierced side (20:25b).

Thomas' words cannot be taken negatively as a doubt of Jesus' resurrection, as many interpret today.[13] This interpretation overlooks that even some of the Twelve doubted Jesus' resurrection and that the Twelve at first did not believe, but labeled it "an idle tale" (Matt 28:17; Mark 16:11, 13-14; Luke 24:11). The disciples could believe only after seeing Jesus alive (20:20). Thomas, though lacked faith, wanted to experience the truth personally by seeing the risen Jesus and touching his wounds before he would believe.

The risen Jesus appeared once again when all the disciples, including Thomas, were in the house still behind the shut doors on the eighth day after his resurrection (20:26a). He came through the shut doors once more, stood among them, and declared peace (20:19b, 26b). Now he spoke to Thomas personally, as he had known by divine knowledge what all

---

12. The beginning of the *Gospel of Thomas* identifies Thomas with Judas (not Iscariot), who was regarded as Jesus' brother (Mark 6:3), but there is no evidence that any of Jesus' brothers was among the twelve disciples. In John 14:22 Judas is distinguished from Thomas.

13. Lincoln (2006: 502) comments that Thomas' response involves "an adamant refusal to believe"; Keener (2005 2.1209) thinks that Thomas is skeptical.

Thomas had told the other disciples (cf. 20:25). By using the same words that Thomas had used, Jesus invited him to put his finger "here," implying Jesus' hands and side, and to see by a touch of the wounds in his forearms and also on his pierced side. So saying, Jesus admonished Thomas not to be an unbelieving disciple, but a believing one (20:27). It is not known whether Thomas put out his hand and touched Jesus' wounds. Instead, the sight of Jesus' wounded hands and pierced side and his gentle rebuke touched and convicted Thomas to believe not only in Jesus' resurrection, but also in Jesus' person. He responded with a fresh understanding about Jesus with the emotionally charged words, "My Lord and my God!" (20:28).

"Lord" is God's name (Exod 6:2–3, 6, 7; Isa 42:8), a name above every name that had been given to Jesus during his earthly ministry (17:11–12). Thomas, as representative of the first Christians, could perceive, in Jesus' resurrection the God of the OT who spoke and acted in Jesus. He was transformed by a vision of Jesus to see the one true God, the Lord, in Jesus (14:9–10). Therefore he did not hesitate to confess Jesus as Lord and God for him (cf. Ps 35:23). The twice-repeated possessive pronoun "my" unveils that Jesus is God and Lord not only for Thomas but for any person who believes in Jesus. Therefore the first-century Christians ascribed to Jesus, without hesitation, the honor and worship due to God alone. The invocation "my Lord and my God" may also be a Christian polemic against both the late first-century Eastern cults, which used these titles together, and Emperor Domitian (90–100 CE), who called himself "Lord God." Counteracting to their claim, John contends that Jesus alone is Lord and God.[14]

When Jesus came to his disciples once more for setting Thomas on faith, he put before him the thought-provoking question, "Have you believed because you have seen me?" Then Jesus affirms, by keeping the wider community of future believers in mind (cf. 17:20), "Blessed are those who did not see [me] and yet believe" (20:29). Thomas, without listening to the words of his comrades who had seen the risen Lord, wanted to believe after himself seeing Jesus. Though Thomas is reasonable, his pathway to faith is far less to be appreciated. Jesus pronounces a blessing upon those who would not see the risen Jesus but would still believe. With this beatitude, Jesus foresaw that the new covenant community, which he established and empowered, would grow by the worldwide mission of God done through the eyewitnesses.

---

14. Keener 2005: 2.1211–12.

John's purpose as conclusion (20:30-31)

John, uniquely, gives his purpose of writing the Gospel at its end. The references to what is and what is not written in the book hint that it is drawing to a close.[15] Such conclusions with additional material, perhaps an epilogue, were common in the writings of that time (e.g., Phil 3:1; 4:8-9; 1 John 5:13; cf. 1 Macc 9:22).[16] Bultmann believed that 20:30-31 is the conclusion for the "Book of Signs" (1:19—12:50), since the word "signs" appears only in 20:30 after 12:37.[17] However, all signs recorded in 1:19—12:50 were done not in the presence of the disciples, but before those who did not believe in him.[18] The expression "many other signs" means all the signs recorded and even not recorded in John. Jesus' death on the cross is the supreme sign, because all signs lead to the cross where God's glory was supremely manifested (cf. 2:18-19, 21-22; 3:14). Jesus' death, resurrection, and ascension to the Father, which all constitute one event, are the greatest signs, because in them the symbol (the signs) and reality (the cross) converge.[19] Therefore we may take 20:30-31 as conclusion for the whole Gospel.

Jesus, then, did before his disciples many other signs that are not written in this book (20:30), and if everything were to be written, the universe itself could not contain the books written (21:25). However, what is written is sufficient to instill faith within the readers and hearers. Jesus performed signs publicly "in the presence of the disciples" so that they would see the glory of God in them and testify to him. On their testimony God's new community is built (cf. Eph 2:20).

The purpose of John writing the selected signs is twofold: (i) that the readers may believe that Jesus is the Christ, the Son of God, and (ii) that by believing they may have divine life in his name (20:31). The phrase "that you may believe" can be understood to mean either that the Gospel was written to bring the readers to faith, if the Greek subjunctive is read as aorist tense, or that the Gospel was written to encourage the existing believers to continue in faith, if the Greek subjunctive is understood as present tense (see the Introduction).

15. Cf. Michaels 2010: 1020.
16. Cf. Keener 2005: 2.1213.
17. E.g., Bultmann 1971: 113, 452.
18. Michaels 2010: 1020.
19. Barrett 1978: 78.

John's Purpose as Conclusion

However, John's purpose should be understood in the light of the whole Gospel and in its historical context rather than on the basis of one Greek word used at the end. His overall concern is to bring all human beings to faith and for that purpose Jesus sends his disciples, whom he trained, to bear witness to him in the world. John's primary concern is to lead all humans to accept that Jesus is the Christ and the Son of God, the one who is equal to God and the revelation of God. Those who believe will enjoy divine life, in lieu of eternal condemnation, in the authoritative name of Jesus. It is the believing community, the church, that will bear witness to these. Jesus prepared and empowered this community by the Holy Spirit so that his mission may be accomplished through it. Thus, John's Gospel is meant both for the unbelieving world and for the believing community. John, then, concludes his Gospel at the peak of his Christology and ecclesiology.

JOHN 21
Epilogue

The purpose of John's Gospel in 20:30–31 gives a befitting conclusion to the whole Gospel. Why then should another sign done by the risen Jesus be mentioned in John 21? There are several differences between chapters 1–20 and 21 in language, style, and themes.[1] However, there are thematic links between John 21 and 1–20 (e.g., the complementary relationship between Peter and the beloved disciple, the identification of the beloved disciple as the writer of the Gospel, reference to Nathanael, etc.). There is no textual evidence that John's Gospel was ever published without chapter 21. Weighing the similarities and dissimilarities, we may infer that the final editor from the Johannine community wrote and added John 21 after the death of the Apostle John by using John's written material for the epilogue and to balance the prologue in 1:1–18.[2] If the real author had added it, he would have felt free to move or modify his conclusion in 20:30–31.[3]

This leads us to question: why was it added? Since the Gospel was accepted first in the heretical circles, John 21 might have been added with a final conclusion that is attested by the Johannine community in order to get a wider acceptance of the Gospel (cf. "we know" in 21:24).[4] In the light of the unique pastoral interest and the later church's mission reflected in John 21, we may say that the Gospel looks beyond the horizon of Jesus' resurrection to the life and ministry of his new community.

THE THIRD REVELATION OF THE RISEN JESUS (21:1–14)

After two appearances of the resurrected Jesus to his male disciples, he revealed himself again to them by the Sea of Tiberias, which is the Sea of Galilee (6:1). "And he revealed like this" (21:1) looks forward to the way in

---

1. Cf. von Wahlde 2010: 2.884–88; Kanagaraj 2005: 669–71.
2. Cf. Köstenberger 2009: 583–84; Lincoln 2006: 508–9.
3. Brown 1978: 2.1080.
4. Lindars 1972: 641.

The Third Revelation of the Risen Jesus

which the risen Jesus manifested himself as the Lord. John correctly numbers Jesus' revelation here as the third one after his resurrection (21:14), keeping in mind the two appearances recorded in John 20:19–29. The shift from Jesus' revelation in Jerusalem to the Sea of Galilee is abrupt (cf. Matt 28:10, 16–17; Mark 16:7). Seven of the disciples, some known by their names and some without their names (21:2), saw the risen Jesus. Even the names of the disciples are mentioned with full details as though they are being introduced first time (e.g., "Simon Peter," Thomas called the Twin, Nathanael from Cana of Galilee).

The first and the only reference in the Gospel to "the sons of Zebedee," who, as per the Synoptic Gospels, are James and John the Apostle, the latter being the most likely candidate to be called "the disciple whom Jesus loved" (21:7, 20–24). The expression "two others of his disciples" shows that "the other disciple" need not be taken always as the beloved disciple (e.g., 18:15–16; 21:8). Papias' list of Jesus' disciples follows the order of the disciples shown in 1:35–51 and the list in 21:2, with the only difference that Matthew's name is mentioned, but not Nathanael's. The "other two disciples" are, in the light of Papias' list, Aristion and John the elder who, as the head of Johannine school in Ephesus, could have written John's Gospel.[5] All these disciples gathered together at the Sea of Galilee to go fishing, following Simon Peter, who first said, "I am going fishing." They all got into the boat to catch some fish, but they caught nothing throughout the night (21:3; Luke 5:5).

When it was already early morning, Jesus stood on the shore, but, in spite of his two previous appearances, the disciples did not know that it was Jesus (21:4). Probably in the dim light of dawn, it was not possible for the disciples to recognize the man who was standing there. The risen Jesus appeared not in a supernatural way this time, but as an ordinary man, which recalls his appearance to Mary Magdalene, who also did not perceive him first as Jesus (20:14; cf. Luke 24:15–16). Jesus takes the initiative to speak and says, "Children, you do not have any catch, have you?" They answered, "No," obviously with a sense of disappointment (21:5). The Greek word that denotes a "catch [of fish]" means "a relish eaten with bread" (cf. 6:9, 11; 21: 9, 10, 13 for the same meaning of "fish"). Jesus' instruction to cast their net at the right side and that by so doing they caught a large quantity of fish (21:6) indicate that they were still in the sea. They were not far from the

---

5. *Hist. eccl.* 3.39; Hengel 1989: 16–23; see above the "Introduction".

shore, but were about a two hundred cubits (a hundred yards) away so that they could not miss Jesus' words (21:8).

The reference in Jesus' instruction to the "right side" (cf. Luke 5:4) may have the notion of favorable side, but the point of Jesus' command is that obedience to his words alone will bring success. The disciples cast the net on the right side and got such a large quantity of fish that they could not draw it in (21:6b). Eventually, the other disciples, besides Peter, dragged the net full of fish nearer to the shore. Thus, the man on the shore revealed himself as the risen Jesus who is known by the name of God, "the Lord." The close relationship between the beloved disciple and Peter comes into focus, for the disciple whom Jesus loved identifies Jesus and reveals it to Peter, rather than to any other disciples, that it is the Lord (21:7). The sign reminded him of the same Jesus who was living on earth along with them by bearing God's name (e.g., John 6:16-21; Luke 5:1-11).

On hearing that it was the Lord, Peter wrapped his outer garment around himself, as he was naked, and threw himself into the sea. That Peter was naked does not necessarily mean that he was without any garment. He could have been wearing customarily a small undergarment at the time of fishing. Possibly, Peter could have thrown himself into the water with a guilty conscience that although he himself saw the empty tomb and the risen Jesus, he returned to his job. While we have reference to the other disciples who reached the land with a net full of fish (21:8), there is no reference to the means by which Peter reached the shore; probably by swimming. Later it is Peter who got into the boat and hauled the net full of fish ashore (21:11). It is likely that Peter reached the shore before others and met Jesus.

After the disciples got out on land, they saw a charcoal fire already lit on the beach with grilled fish laid on it and bread beside it (21:9). The risen Lord took the initiative to provide food for his loved ones. There is no hint that Jesus used any of the fish caught, though he told them to bring some of fish caught (21:10). Since they saw the fish and bread awaiting them, they simply left the net full of fish on the shore. Jesus' initiative to give food and his invitation to come and have breakfast (21:12a) are not merely to satisfy his hungry disciples, but to reveal his continuing love and communion with them.

When Jesus asked the disciples to bring some of the fish that they had caught, Simon Peter responded by going up into the boat and drawing the net, full of 153 great fish, ashore. The narrator comments that although there were so many large fish, the net was not torn (21:11). The church fathers gave several symbolic/mystical interpretations to the precise number 153. For Augustine, the total 153 is obtained by adding the numbers from one to seventeen (1 + 2 + 3 + . . . 17 = 153) and the number 17 is made up of 10 plus 7, 10 symbolizing the Ten Commandments and 7 the seven gifts of the Spirit. If so, the 153 fish represents the fulfillment of the Law through the Spirit.[6] However, the exact number of fish simply bears the stamp of an eyewitness and historical accuracy (cf. 21:24), because the caught fish used to be counted to divide them among fishermen.[7]

The intention of the author could be much more than that. Since John 21 follows the commissioning of disciples (20:21–22), the dragging of a large amount of fish, without the net being broken, could be an enacted parable in which the large catch of fish may symbolize the ingathering of many new converts from all nations through the disciples' ministry. The gospel net will never break, no matter how many converts it catches.[8] The miraculous catch of fish, then, looks forward to the success of the mission of God's new community in the world.[9]

Jesus' invitation to the disciples to come and have breakfast (21:12) links with 21:9. This is the breakfast already prepared by Jesus, as Wisdom did (Prov 9:1–6). The love and care of the good shepherd convinced his sheep to recognize the man as the risen Lord! Therefore they did not dare to ask, "Who are you?" (21:12). Jesus, as the host, came and took the bread and gave it to them, and likewise with the fish (John 21:13; cf. 6:11; Luke 24:30). One may quickly find an allusion here to the church's Eucharist.[10] As there is no thanksgiving, it may not be a eucharistic meal, but the resurrection meal in which Jesus serves them (cf. 13:1–20) and unites them as one with him into God's family. The serving of bread and fish may symbolize the source of life that will strengthen Jesus' disciples to continue his mission in the world.[11] John's historical accuracy is reflected in his numbering of Jesus' appearance at the Sea of Tiberias as the third one after his resurrection

---

6. Koester 2003: 312; Kanagaraj 1998a: 19.

7. Cf. Michaels 2010: 1036–37; Keener 2005: 2.1233.

8. Bruce 1992: 401. This interpretation fits well to the context and also to the proposal that 153 is the numerical value of the Hebrew *benê 'elōhîm*, "children of God," whom the fishers would gather in; Keener 2005: 2.1231, by citing Joseph Romeo.

9. Kanagaraj 2005: 677–78.

10. Lincoln 2006: 514.

11. Ridderbos 1997: 664; cf. Lincoln 2006: 514.

John 21:1-14

(21:14; cf. 20:19-23, 26-29). The purpose of this revelation by means of three dimensions of a sign (the miraculous catch of 153 fish, the unbroken net, and the meal kept ready by the risen Jesus) is not merely to reveal Jesus, but also to promote the virtues of love, unity and servanthood within his community.

FINAL REFERENCE TO PETER AND THE BELOVED DISCIPLE (21:15-23)

Prediction on Peter's ministry and destiny (21:15-19)

After breakfast, Jesus turns his attention to Simon Peter and asks him, "Simon, son of John, do you love me more than these?" (21:15a; cf. 1:42). The verb "to love" indicates divine love. "More than these" may be understood either as more than the boat, net, fish, etc., or as more than Peter loves the other disciples, or as more than the other disciples love Jesus. Love for Jesus cannot be compared with one's love for material things. Love for Jesus and love for his followers go together (cf. 1 John 5:1-2) and cannot be compared. Jesus' question may rightly be understood as, "Do you love me more than these other disciples do?" Peter once claimed that he, more than others, would even lay down his life for Jesus (13:37; cf. Matt 26:33; Mark 14:29). But instead of expressing his love, he had denied his Master firmly. Now Jesus deals with his boasting by seeking an assurance from him whether or not he loves Jesus more than other disciples do. By claiming his long association with Jesus, Peter answers in affirmative, saying, "Yes, Lord; you know that I love you."[12] Soon after his assurance, Jesus gives him the charge, "Feed my lambs" (21:15b).

Jesus asks him the same question a second time, but without "more than these." Peter answers in the affirmative. Jesus gives him the same charge, saying, "Shepherd my sheep" (21:16). "Feeding" and "shepherding" imply the two aspects of pastoral ministry: "feeding" means nourishing Jesus' community with the spiritual food, and "shepherding" emphasizes governing the congregation for its overall growth.[13] Thus, Jesus commissions Peter to give pastoral care for the total growth of his people. In spite of Peter's double affirmation of his love for Jesus, surprisingly Jesus asks the

---

12. Both *philein* ("to love"), used by Peter and later by Jesus (21:17), and *agapan* ("to love"), used by Jesus (21:15-16), bear the same sense in this context.

13. Brown 1978: 2.1105.

Final Reference to Peter and the Beloved Disciple

same question a third time. Peter is grieved because Jesus asked him the third time, "Do you love me?" Now Peter responds with grief, "Lord, you know all things; you know that I love you" (21:17).

Jesus' three times repeated question would have reminded Peter of his denial of Jesus three times and of his vain boasting (13:37–38). Peter pledged his loyalty without realizing his human weakness. After he denied Jesus three times, he was grieved realizing that he miserably failed to follow Jesus at any cost. The Synoptic Gospels record that Peter expressed his grief by weeping bitterly (Matt 26:75 par.). In John, Peter's desperate answer, "Lord, you know all things . . . ," acknowledges humbly his past failure. Jesus knows that Peter loves him in spite of his vulnerability. Soon after Peter's acknowledgment of his failure to follow Jesus, Jesus commands him the third time, "Feed my sheep" (21:17b), a combination of "feed" in 21:15 and "sheep" in 21:16. Jesus' three-time injunction confirms his call for Peter to give pastoral care and nourishment to his new community. This charge, however, does not make Peter superior to the beloved disciple or to any other disciples. There is a cost involved in this call. That is, as a shepherd, he has to surrender himself to death (21:18–19).

Jesus discloses to Peter the confirmed heavenly truth regarding his future destiny by using his "truly, truly, I say to you" formula. When Peter was young, he girded himself by a towel or belt and walked around freely wherever he liked to go. However, when he becomes old, he will voluntarily submit his hands, by stretching them out, to be bound and executed.[14] Another will gird him, perhaps by a chain, and carry him to a place where he does not want to go. Peter needs to give up his own will and follow Jesus, the good shepherd, in suffering and death. The narrator rightly comments that Jesus predicted it to show by what death Peter will glorify God (21:19; cf. 12:33; 18:32). As Jesus revealed God's glory in his death on the cross, so also his follower Peter will glorify Jesus through his martyrdom.[15] However, Peter cannot face this destiny unless he depends on Jesus and therefore Jesus exhorts him to keep following him.

---

14. Keener 2005: 2.1237.

15. Later tradition says that Peter was bound to the cross, as someone else girded him (Tertullian in ca. 212 CE), and that Peter requested to be crucified upside down (*Hist. eccl.* 3.1; *Acts of Peter* 37–39).

John 21:20-23

Prediction on the beloved disciple (21:20-23)

At the point of Jesus' prediction of Peter's martyrdom, Peter turned and saw the beloved disciple already following Jesus (21:20). The beloved disciple is reintroduced by citing the Passover meal scene, where he was first introduced as the disciple whom Jesus loved, who, by lying close to Jesus' breast, asked him, at the behest of Peter, to identify the betrayer of Jesus (cf. 13:23-25). When Peter saw his close associate, he asked Jesus, "Lord, but what about this man?" (21:21), which may mean, "How will this man's life and end be?" Obviously he was curious to know of the beloved disciple's future. Jesus discourages such curiosity to know from him of his plan for others. It is the God-given prerogative of Jesus to determine the future of each person, and no one has any business with others' matter. So Jesus said to Peter, "If I wish him to remain until I come, what is that to you? You follow me" (21:22).

Jesus has authority from the Father to give life or to judge in accordance to his will (5:21-22, 27). "To remain" here means "to live." Jesus' reference to "until I come" does not indicate his coming as the Holy Spirit, but his final coming to take his disciples to the Father's house (14:2-3). Jesus has authority to keep anyone whom he chooses to be alive until the endtime. Others, including his own disciples, can hardly intervene in Jesus' will and work. Therefore Jesus admonishes Peter, with an emphatic "you," to follow him by fixing his eyes upon Jesus alone (cf. 21:19).[16] Moreover, Jesus' will is different for each person and others need not be anxious to know it. Jesus' instruction in John ends with "you follow me," signaling that the aim of God's new community should be to constantly look to Jesus in life and work until his final coming (Heb 12:2; cf. Phil 3:13-15). Jesus' saying in 21:22 was misunderstood to spread among the "brothers," the members of Jesus' community, a rumor that the beloved disciple will never die (21:23a).

The editor clarifies Jesus' hypothetical statement concerning the beloved disciple by writing, "Yet Jesus did not say to him that he will not die, but only that if it is his will that he remains until he comes, what is that to you?" (21:23b). In Matthew, the soldiers, on the instigation of the Jewish leaders, spread among the Jews a false message that Jesus' body was stolen by night by his disciples (Matt 28:11-15). John, on the other hand, records a rumor spread among his followers, especially in the Johannine community, that the beloved disciple will not die until Jesus comes (cf. Mark 9:1). John

---

16. Cf. Michaels 2010: 1052.

Final Reference to Peter and the Beloved Disciple

corrects both the rumors in his resurrection and appearance narratives. In fact, both Peter and the beloved disciple had died by the time John's Gospel was published.

CONCLUDING STATEMENTS (21:24–25)

After a preliminary conclusion drawn in 20:30–31 by the real author, the editor affixes the final conclusion in 21:24–25. The expression "this is the disciple" (21:24) looks back to 21:22–23, pointing to the disciple whom Jesus loved as the one who, as an eyewitness (19:35), is bearing witness about these things. "These things" refers to the whole life and work of Jesus recorded in the Gospel, including what is narrated in John 21.

"Bearing witness" in John has a missiological overtone, for it indicates the disciples' proclamation of who Jesus is and what he is doing for human deliverance and welfare (e.g., 1:6–8, 32, 34; 15:26–27). The beloved disciple has borne witness not merely by words, but also by writing the events of Jesus, perhaps in a simple form. His writing was later picked up by one of the leaders in Johannine community to give it the Gospel form with added comments and epilogue by the editor, his fellow member in the community. This explains the plural "we know" (21:24), meaning that the writing and publication of the Gospel was a team effort done in stages by three persons (the implied author, the real author, and the narrator/editor) on behalf of Johannine community, which attests the beloved disciple's written testimony as true. The plural "we," then, is not a rhetorical or editorial "we," but it denotes the eyewitnesses and those who believed through their words (cf. 1:14, 16). By endorsing the content of John's Gospel as "true," the community emphasizes the validity and reliability of the witness borne (cf. 8:14, 16) so that the Gospel may get wider acceptance.

The Fourth Gospel is given a final conclusion: "But there are also many other things which Jesus did, which, if written every one, I presume the world itself would not afford room for the books written" (21:25). This statement is essentially the same as the preliminary conclusion made in 20:30–31. In 20:31, the purpose of the selected signs written in the Gospel is highlighted, whereas 21:25 highlights the fact that the amount of books written on Jesus' words and deeds would be more than what the whole universe could contain (*Post.* 144; 1 Macc 9:22; *Exod Rab.* 30:22).[17] It seems that 21:25 is missing in the first draft of Codex Sinaiticus (א), an earlier

---

17. The "world" (*kosmos*) in 21:25 does not mean the sphere of human affairs or the unbelievers who reject Jesus, but the total universe created by God.

John 21:24-25

Greek manuscript, and that it was added later by the same scribe to end the Gospel.[18] However, the textual evidence for treating 21:25 as a scribal gloss is very slim.[19]

The phrase "I presume" indicates a certain person, probably the editor who added comments, glosses, and the epilogue. He is certainly one among those who endorse the beloved disciple's witness as true. The author begins John's Gospel with the eternal existence of the Logos-Son, who is the Christ (1:1–2), and the editor ends it with the eternal or neverending works of Jesus Christ, the Logos incarnate (21:25). The author refers to the whole creation as made through the Logos in whom there was life (1:3–5). The editor ends with the same note, referring to the whole universe that could not contain the books written on Jesus, the giver of life. Thus, 21:25 does not consider the acts of Jesus being over, but looks forward to many who will bear witness to Jesus verbally and in writing so that the church, God's new community, may grow. To this extent, the Gospel of John is an open-ended Gospel, for it ends not with a period but only with a comma.

---

18. Michaels 2010: 1057.
19. Brown 1978: 2.1125.

Bibliography

Abbott, Edwin A. 1906. *Johannine Grammar*. London: A. & C. Black.
Anderson, Paul N. 2011. *The Riddles of the Fourth Gospel: An Introduction to John*. Minneapolis: Fortress.
Ashton, John. 1991. *Understanding the Fourth Gospel*. Oxford: Clarendon.
Ball, David M. 1996. *"I Am" in John's Gospel: Literary Function, Background and Theological Implications*. Sheffield: Sheffield Academic.
Barclay, William. 1957. *The Gospel of John*. 2 vols. 2nd ed., 2nd impr. Edinburgh: Saint Andrew Press. 1st ed. published 1955.
Barrett, Kingsley C. 1978. *The Gospel According to St. John*. 2nd ed. Philadelphia: Westminster.
———. 1982. *Essays on John*. London: SPCK.
Bauckham, Richard. 1998. "For Whom Were Gospels Written?" In *The Gospels for All Christians: Rethinking the Gospel Audiences*, edited by Richard Bauckham, 9–48. Grand Rapids: Eerdmans.
———. 2006. *Jesus and the Eyewitnesses: The Gospels as Eyewitness Testimony*. Grand Rapids: Eerdmans.
———. 2007. "Historiographical Characteristics of the Gospel of John." *NTS* 53: 17–36.
———. 2008. "The Fourth Gospel as the Testimony of the Beloved Disciple." In *The Gospel of John and Christian Theology*, edited by Richard Bauckham and Carl Mosser, 120–39. Grand Rapids: Eerdmans.
Beasley-Murray, George R. 1991. *Gospel of Life: Theology in the Fourth Gospel*. Peabody, MA: Hendrickson.
———. 1999. *John*. 2nd ed. WBC 36. Nashville: T. Nelson.
Behm, Johannes. 1977. "*Koilia*." In *TDNT*, edited by G. Kittel, translated by G. W. Bromiley, 3:786–89. Grand Rapids: Eerdmans. Originally published 1966.
Bernard, J. H. 1985. *A Critical and Exegetical Commentary on the Gospel According to St. John*. Vol. 2. ICC. Edinburgh: T. & T. Clark. Originally published 1928.
Blomberg, Craig L. 2001. *The Historical Reliability of John's Gospel: Issues & Commentary*. Leicester: Apollos/InterVarsity.
Borgen, Peder, 1968. *Bread from Heaven: An Exegetical Study of the Concept of Manna in the Gospel of John and the Writings of Philo*. NovTSup 10. Leiden: Brill.
Boyd, R. H. S. 1989. *An Introduction to Indian Christian Theology*. Rev. ed. Delhi: ISPCK.
Bratcher, R.G. 1991. "What Does 'Glory' Mean in Relation to Jesus?: Translating *Doxa* and *Doxazo* in John." *BT* 42: 401–8.
Brenton, Lancelot C. L. 1992. *The Septuagint with Apocrypha: Greek and English*. Peabody, MA: Hendrickson. Originally published 1986.
Brodie, Thomas L. 1993. *The Gospel According to John: A Literary and Theological Commentary*. New York: Oxford University Press.
Brown, Raymond E. 1978. *The Gospel According to John*. 2 vols. AB 29, 29A. Reprint. London: G. Chapman. Originally published 1966, 1970 by Doubleday.

Bibliography

———. 1979. *The Community of the Beloved Disciple: The Life, Loves and Hates of an Individual Church in New Testament Times.* London: G. Chapman.

———. 2010. *An Introduction to the Gospel of John.* Edited and updated by Francis J. Moloney. 1st impr. New Haven, CT: Yale University Press. First published, New York: Doubleday, 2003.

Brownlee, William H. 1991. "Whence the Gospel According to John?" In *John and the Dead Sea Scrolls*, edited by James H. Charlesworth, 166–94. New York: Crossroad.

Bruce, Frederick F. 1992. *The Gospel of John: Introduction, Exposition and Notes.* Reprint. Grand Rapids: Eerdmans. Originally published 1983.

Bultmann, Rudolph. 1971. *The Gospel of John: A Commentary.* Translated by G. R. Beasley-Murray. Philadelphia: Westminster. Originally published as *Das Evangelium des Johannes.* Göttingen: Vandenhoeck & Ruprecht, 1964.

Burge, Gary M. 1987. *The Anointed Community: The Holy Spirit in the Johannine Tradition.* Grand Rapids: Eerdmans.

Carson, D. A. 1982. "Understanding Misunderstandings in the Fourth Gospel." *TynBul* 33: 59–91.

———. 1991. *The Gospel According to John.* Grand Rapids: Eerdmans.

Charlesworth, James H., editor. 1983. *The Old Testament Pseudepigrapha.* Vol. 1. Garden City, NY: Doubleday.

———, editor. 1985. *The Old Testament Pseudepigrapha.* Vol. 2. Garden City, NY: Doubleday.

Collins, C. J. 1995. "John 4:23–24, 'In Spirit and Truth': An Idiomatic Proposal." *Presbyterion* 21: 118–21.

Colson, F. H., and G.H. Whitaker, translators. 1979–93. *Philo.* 12 vols. LCL. Reprint. Cambridge, MA: Harvard University Press. Originally published 1927–53.

Cullmann, Oscar. 1976. *The Johannine Circle.* Philadelphia: Westminster.

Culpepper, Alan R. 1989. *Anatomy of the Fourth Gospel: A Study in the Literary Design.* 3rd printing. Philadelphia: Fortress. Originally published 1983.

———. 2000. *John, the Son of Zebedee: The Life of a Legend.* Edinburgh: T. & T. Clark.

Czachesz, István. 2010. "The *Gospel of the Acts of John*: Its Relation to the Fourth Gospel." In *The Legacy of John: Second-Century Reception of the Fourth Gospel*, edited by Tuomas Rasimus, 49–72. NovTSup 132. Leiden: Brill.

Daly-Denton, M. 2000. *David in the Fourth Gospel: The Johannine Reception of the Psalms.* Leiden: Brill.

Danby, Herbert, translator. 1933. *The Mishnah.* Oxford: Clarendon.

Danker, F. W., W. F. Arndt, and F. W. Gingrich. 2000. (BDAG). *A Greek-English Lexicon of the New Testament and Other Early Christian Literature.* 3rd rev. ed. Chicago: University of Chicago Press.

Daube, David. 1950. "Jesus and the Samaritan Woman: The Meaning of *syngkhraomai.*" *JBL* 69: 137–47.

Dodd, C. H. 1957. "The Prologue to the Fourth Gospel and Christian Worship." In *Studies in the Fourth Gospel*, edited by F. L. Cross, 9–22. London: A. R. Mowbray.

———. 1958. *The Interpretation of the Fourth Gospel.* Reprint. Cambridge: Cambridge University Press. Originally published 1954.

———. 1965. *Historical Tradition in the Fourth Gospel.* Reprint. Cambridge: Cambridge University Press. Originally published 1963.

———. 1968. "A Hidden Parable in the Fourth Gospel." In *More New Testament Studies*, by C. H. Dodd, 30–40. Grand Rapids: Eerdmans.

Bibliography

Duke, Paul D. 1985. *Irony in the Fourth Gospel*. Atlanta: John Knox.
Dunn, James D. G. 1970-71. "John V—A Eucharistic Discourse?" *NTS* 17: 328-38.
———. 1983. "Let John Be John: A Gospel for Its Time." In *Das Evangelium und die Evangelien: Vorträge vom Tübinger Symposium 1982*, edited by P. Stuhlmacher, 309-39. WUNT 28. Tübingen: Mohr/Siebeck.
———. 1989. *Christology in the Making: An Inquiry into the Origins of the Doctrine of the Incarnation*. 2nd ed. London: SCM.
———. *Jesus Remembered*. 2003. Christianity in the Making 1. Grand Rapids: Eerdmans.
———. 2011. "John's Gospel and the Oral Gospel Tradition." In *The Fourth Gospel in First-Century Media Culture*, edited by A. le Donne and T. Thatcher, 157-85. LNTS 426. London: T. & T. Clark.
Edwards, Ruth B. 1988. "*Charin anti Charitos* (John 1:16): Grace and the Law in the Johannine Prologue." *JSNT* 32: 3-15.
Elliott, J. K., editor. 1993. *The Apocryphal New Testament: A Collection of Apocryphal Christian Literature in an English Translation based on M. R. James*. Oxford: Clarendon.
Eusebius, Pamphilus. 1927. *The Ecclesiastical History and the Martyrs of Palestine*. Vol. 1. Translated by Hugh Jackson Lawlor and John Ernest Leonard Oulton. London: SPCK.
———. 1992. *Ecclesiastical History*. Translated by Isaac Boyle. Reprint. Grand Rapids: Baker.
Evans, Craig A. 1993. *Word and Glory: On the Exegetical and Theological Background of John's Prologue*. JSNTSup 89. Sheffield: Sheffield Academic.
———. 2000. "Hillel, House of." In *Dictionary of New Testament Background*, edited by Craig A. Evans and Stanley E. Porter, 496-98. Leicester: InterVarsity.
Evans, Stephen C. 2008. "The Historical Reliability of John's Gospel: From What Perspective Should It Be Assessed?" In *The Gospel of John and Christian Theology*, edited by Richard Bauckham and Carl Mosser, 91-119. Grand Rapids: Eerdmans.
Fenton, J. C. 1970. *The Gospel According to John*. Oxford: Clarendon.
Griffith, Terry. 2008. "'The Jews Who Had Believed in Him' (John 8:31) and the Motif of Apostasy in the Gospel of John." In *The Gospel of John and Christian Theology*, edited by Richard Bauckham and Carl Mosser, 183-92. Grand Rapids: Eerdmans.
Gruenler, R. G. 1986. *The Trinity in the Gospel of John: A Thematic Commentary on the Fourth Gospel*. Grand Rapids: Baker.
Guilding, Aileen. 1960. *The Fourth Gospel and Jewish Worship*. Oxford: Clarendon.
Guthrie, Donald. 1985. *New Testament Theology*. Reprint. Leicester: InterVarsity.
Haenchen, Ernest. 1962-63. "Der Vater der mich gesandt hat." *NTS* 9: 208-16.
———. 1984. *A Commentary on the Gospel of John*. Translated and edited by Robert W. Funk. 2 vols. Hermeneia. Philadelphia: Fortress. Originally published as *Das Johannesevangelium*. Edited by U. Busse. Tübingen: Mohr, 1980.
Hakola, Raimo. 2009. "The Burden of Ambiguity: Nicodemus and the Social Identity of the Johannine Christians." *NTS* 55: 438-55.
Harris, Morray J. 1992. *Jesus as God: The New Testament Use of Theos in Reference to Jesus*. Grand Rapids: Baker.
Hengel, Martin. 1989. *The Johannine Question*. Philadelphia: Trinity; London: SCM.
———. 2008. "The Prologue of the Gospel of John as the Gateway to Christological Truth." In *The Gospel of John and Christian Theology*, edited by Richard Bauckham and Carl Mosser, 265-94. Grand Rapids: Eerdmans.

Bibliography

Hoskyns, Edwyn C. 1961. *The Fourth Gospel*, edited by Francis N. Davey. 2nd rev. ed. London: Faber. Originally published 1947.

Hughes, Selwyn. 2007. *Every Day with Jesus: One Year Devotional, A Fresh Vision of God*. Reprint. Hyderabad/Colorado Springs: Authentic Books. Originally published 1986.

Jeremias, Joachim. 1966. *The Eucharistic Words of Jesus*. London: SCM.

———. 1975. *Jerusalem in the Time of Jesus: An Investigation into Economic and Social Conditions during the New Testament Period*. Reprint. Philadelphia: Fortress.

———. 1978. "Poimēn." In *TDNT*, edited by G. Kittel and G. Friedrich, translated by G. W. Bromiley, 6:485–99. 7th printing. Grand Rapids: Eerdmans.

Jonge, de M. 1970–71. "Nicodemus and Jesus: Some Observations on Misunderstanding and Understanding in the Fourth Gospel." *BJRL* 53: 337–59.

———. 1977. *Jesus: Stranger from Heaven and Son of God: Jesus Christ and the Christians in Johannine Perspective*. Missoula, MT: Scholars.

Jones, Larry P. 1997. *The Symbol of Water in the Gospel of John*. JSNTSup 145. Sheffield: Sheffield Academic.

Kanagaraj, Jey J. 1998a. *'Mysticism' in the Gospel of John: An Inquiry into Its Background*. JSNTSup 158. Sheffield: Sheffield Academic.

———. 1998b. "Did the Word Not 'Become' Flesh? A Response to J. C. O'Neill." *ExpTim* 110: 80–81.

———. 2001. "The Implied Ethics in the Fourth Gospel: A Reinterpretation of the Decalogue." *TynBul* 52: 33–60.

———. 2005. *The Gospel of John: A Commentary with Elements of Comparison to Indian Religious Thoughts and Cultural Practices*. Secunderabad, India: OM Books.

Kanagaraj, Jey J., and Ian S. Kemp. 2002. *The Gospel According to John*. Asia Bible Commentary Series. Singapore: Asia Theological Association.

Karris, R. J. 1990. *Jesus and the Marginalized in John's Gospel*. Collegeville, MN: Liturgical.

Käsemann, Ernest. 1968. *The Testament of Jesus: A Study of the Gospel of John in the Light of Chapter 17*. Philadelphia: Fortress.

Keener, Craig S. 2005. *The Gospel of John: A Commentary*. 2 vols. 2nd printing. Peabody, MA: Hendrickson. Originally published 2003.

Koester, Craig R. 2003. *Symbolism in the Fourth Gospel: Meaning, Mystery, Community*. 2nd ed. Minneapolis: Fortress.

Köstenberger, Andreas J. 2007. "John". In *Commentary on the New Testament Use of the Old Testament*, edited by G. K. Beale and D. A. Carson, 415–512. Grand Rapids: Baker Academic.

———. 2009. *John*. BECNT. 4th printing. Grand Rapids: Baker Academic. Originally published 2004.

Kruse, Colin G. 2008. *The Gospel According to John: An Introduction and Commentary*. TNTC 4. Reprint. Downers Grove, IL: InterVarsity. Originally published 2003.

Lightfoot, J. B. 1997. *Colossians and Philemon*. Reprint. Wheaton, IL: Crossway.

Lincoln, Andrew T. 2006. *The Gospel According to Saint John*. BNTC 4. Reprint. Peabody, MA: Henrickson; London: Continuum. Originally published 2005.

Lindars, Barnabas. 1957. "The Fourth Gospel an Act of Contemplation." In *Studies in the Fourth Gospel*, edited by F. L. Cross, 23–35. London: A. R. Mowbray.

———. 1972. *The Gospel of John*. NCB. London: Oliphants.

———. 1992. "Two Parables in John." In *Essays on John*, edited by C. M. Tuckett, 9–20. Leuven: Leuven University Press/Peeters.

Macdonald, J. 1964. *The Theology of the Samaritans*. London: SCM.

Bibliography

Malina, Bruce J., and Richard L. Rohrbaugh. 1998. *Social-Science Commentary on the Gospel of John*. Minneapolis: Fortress.
Martínez, Florentino G. 1994. *The Dead Sea Scrolls Translated: The Qumran Texts in English*. Leiden: Brill. Originally published 1992.
Martyn, J. L. 2003. *History and Theology in the Fourth Gospel*. 3rd ed. Louisville: Westminster John Knox.
McRay, John. 2003. *Archaeology and the New Testament*. 5th printing. Grand Rapids: Baker. Originally published 1991.
Meeks, Wayne A. 1967. *The Prophet-King: Moses Traditions and the Johannine Christology*. Leiden: Brill.
———. 1972. "The Man from Heaven in Johannine Sectarianism." *JBL* 91: 44–72.
Michaels, J. Ramsey. 2010. *The Gospel of John*. NICNT. Grand Rapids: Eerdmans.
Milne, Bruce. 1993. *The Message of John: Here Is Your King!*. The Bible Speaks Today. Downers Grove, IL: InterVarsity.
Morris, Leon. 1995. *The Gospel According to John*. NICNT. Rev. ed. Grand Rapids: Eerdmans.
Motyer, Stephen. 1997. *Your Father the Devil?: A New Approach to John and "the Jews"*. Carlisle: Paternoster.
Moulton, James Hope. 1906. *A Grammar of New Testament Greek: Based on W. F. Winer's Grammar*. Vol. 1. 2nd ed. Edinburgh: T. & T. Clark.
Newbigin, Leslie. 1977. *"The Good Shepherd": Meditations on Christian Ministry in Today's World*. Grand Rapids: Eerdmans.
Neyrey, Jerome H. 2007. *The Gospel of John*. NCBC. New York: Cambridge University Press.
Nicholson, C. G. 1983. *Death as Departure: The Johannine Descent-Ascent Schema*. Chico, CA: Scholars.
Nicol, W. 1972. *The Semeia in the Fourth Gospel: Tradition and Redaction*. NovTSup 32. Leiden: Brill.
Pamment, Margaret. 1983. "The Meaning of *Doxa* in the Fourth Gospel." *ZNW* 74: 12–16.
Perrin, Nicholas. 2010. "The *Diatessaron* and the Second-Century Reception of the Gospel of John." In *The Legacy of John: Second-Century Reception of the Fourth Gospel*, edited by Tuomas Rasimus, 301–18. NovTSup 132. Leiden: Brill.
Phillips, G. L. 1957. "Faith and Vision in the Fourth Gospel." In *Studies in the Fourth Gospel*, edited by F. L. Cross. London: A. R. Mowbray.
Pryor, John. 1992. *John, Evangelist of the Covenant People: The Narrative & Themes of the Fourth Gospel*. Downers Grove, IL: InterVarsity.
Quast, Kevin. 1989. *Peter and the Beloved Disciple: Figures for a Community in Crisis*. JSNTSup 32. Sheffield: JSOT Press.
Ralfs, Alfred. 1979. *Septuaginta: Id est Vetus Testamentum Graece iuxta LXX interpretes*. 2 vols. in 1. Stuttgart: Deutsche Bibelgesellschaft.
Reinhartz, Adele. 2009. "'Rewritten Gospel': The Case of Caiaphas the High Priest." *NTS* 55: 160–78.
Ridderbos, Herman. 1997. *The Gospel of John: A Theological Commentary*. Translated by John Vriend. Grand Rapids: Eerdmans. Originally published as *Het Evangelie naar Johannes: Proeve van een theologische Exegese*. 2 vols. Kampen: Kok, 1987, 1992.
Robinson, John A. T. 1959-60. "The Destination and the Purpose of St. John's Gospel." *NTS* 6: 117–31.
———. 1976. *Redacting the New Testament*. London: SCM.

Bibliography

———. 1985. *The Priority of John*. London: SCM.
Sanders, J. N. "Who Was the Disciple Whom Jesus Loved?" In *Studies in the Fourth Gospel*, edited by F. L. Cross, 72-82. London: A. R. Mowbray.
Sandmel, S. 1979. *Philo of Alexandria: An Introduction*. Oxford: Oxford University Press.
Santram, Pritam. 1975. "The Purpose of St. John's Gospel: The Spread of the Good News." In *India's Search for Reality and the Relevance of the Gospel of John*, edited by Christopher Duraisingh and Cecil Hargreaves, 104-21. Delhi: ISPCK.
Schnackenburg, Rudolph. 1980-84. *The Gospel According to St. John*. Translated by Kevin Smyth. 3 vols. Reprint. London: Burns & Oates. Originally published as *Das Johannesevangelium*. Freiburg: Herder, 1965-84.
Schneiders, S. M. 1993. "Women in the Fourth Gospel and the Role of Women in the Contemporary Church." In *The Gospel of John as Literature: An Anthology of Twentieth-Century Perspectives*, edited by Mark W .G. Stibbe, 123-43. Leiden: Brill.
Simon, U. E. 1957. "Eternal Life in the Fourth Gospel." In *Studies in the Fourth Gospel*, edited by F. L. Cross, 97-109. London: A. R. Mowbray.
Slater, T. E. 1903. *The Higher Hinduism in Relation to Christianity*. London: Elliot Stock.
Smalley, Stephen S. 1984. *1, 2, 3 John*. WBC 51. Waco, TX: Word.
Stibbe, Mark W. G., editor. 1993. *The Gospel of John as Literature: An Anthology of Twentieth-Century Perspectives*. Leiden: Brill.
Strack, H. L. and P. Billerbeck. 1922-61. *Kommentar zum Neuen Testament aus Talmud und Midrash*. 6 vols. Munich: C. H. Beck.
Thomas, J. Christopher. 1991. *Footwashing in John 13 and the Johannine Community*. JSNTSup 61. Sheffield: Sheffield Academic.
Vermes, Geza. 1995. *The Dead Sea Scrolls in English*. 4th ed. Sheffield: Sheffield Academic. Originally published 1962.
Wahlde, von Urban C. 2010. *The Gospel and Letters of John*. 3 vols. ECC. Grand Rapids: Eerdmans.
Whitacre, Rodney A. 1999. *John*. IVPNTCS. Downers Grove, IL: InterVarsity.
Whiston, William, translator. 1981. *The Complete Works of Josephus*. 3rd printing. Grand Rapids: Kregel.
Wijingaards, J. N. M. 1988. *The Spirit in John*. Zacchaeus Studies, New Testament. Wilmington, DE: M. Glazier.
Zerwick, Max, and Mary Grosvenor. 1988. *A Grammatical Analysis of the Greek New Testament*. Unabridged. 3rd rev. ed. in 1 vol. Rome: Editrice Pontificio Istituto Biblico. Originally published 1974.

Author Index

Abbott, Edwin, 66n17
Anderson, Paul N., xxiin11
Ashton, John, 60n14
Ball, David, 92n14
Banerjea, K. M., 193
Barclay, William, 12n28, 17n42
Barrett, C. Kingsley, xxin17, xxiin13, xxiii, xxiiin20, 7n14, 8n18, 15n35, 16n39, 17n40, 27n18, 46n18, 50n22, 59n12, 63n4, 66n16, 69n22, 82n8, 86n19, 101n4, 126n10, 152, 152n1, 155n9, 159n3, 160n4, 175n11, 181n23, 203n19
Bauckham, Richard, xxn5, xxviiin31, xxviiin33
Beasley-Murray, George R., 59n13, 68n19, 74n30, 135n4, 157n11, 159n3, 200n9
Behm, Johannes, 83n11
Bernard, J. H., 62n3
Billerbeck, P., 29n1, 95n20
Blomberg, Craig L., 56n10, 62n1, 74n28, 80n5, 86n16, 86n18, 95n22, 173n4
Borgan, Peder, 68n20
Boyd, R. H. S., 193n33, 193n34
Bratcher, R. G., 7n15
Brodie, Thomas L., 153n6, 184n8
Brown, Raymond E., xixn2, xxn7, xxin8, xxviin30, xxviiin32, xxviiin33, 11n24, 15, 17n41, 20, 20n1, 20n2, 21, 21n3, 22n6, 37n13, 38n15, 43n10, 44n12, 50n23, 51n27, 53n3, 64n7, 65n14, 71n23, 73n26, 77n36, 86n16, 88n3, 135n5, 138n9, 155n9, 163n10, 165n4, 172n2, 178n16, 178n18, 180n21, 184n7, 187n14, 190n24, 198n6, 200n9, 205n3, 209n13, 213n19
Bruce, F. F., 162n8, 208n8
Bultmann, Rudolf, 7n13, 62n3, 65n12, 73n26, 87, 87n1, 94n16, 96n25, 109n8, 203n17
Carson, Don, A., 15n34, 21n5, 26n17, 41n5, 46n16, 64n9, 66n16, 74n30, 94n16, 119n9, 141n19, 144n1, 146n6, 162n8, 175n10
Collins, C. J., 44n11
Cullmann, Oscar, 139n13
Culpepper, Alan, R., xixn1, xxn5, xxn6, xxiin11, xxiiin17, 29n2
Czachesz, István, xxiiin21
Daly-Denton, M., 68n20, 192n32
Daube, David, 40n4
de Jonge, M., 29n2, 46n16, 64n10
Dodd, C. H., xxiii, xxiiin22, 8n18, 37n12, 57n11, 91n10, 159n3, 166n5, 173n4, 183n5
Duke, Paul D., 181n25
Dunn, James D. G., xixn22, xxiv, xxivn25, 1n1, 11n25, 49n21, 73n28, 75n33, 126n11
Edwards, Ruth B., 8n20
Evans, Stephen C., xxviiin31
Fenton, J. C., 53n1, 73n26, 74n31, 128n15
Griffith, Terry, 11n24
Grosvenor, Mary, 80n3
Gruenler, R. G., 38n14, 161n5
Guilding, Aileen, 53, 53n1, 64n7, 66n15
Guthrie, Donald, 150n18
Haenchen, Ernest, 2n4, 59n13, 184n8
Hakola, Raimo, 29n2

Author Index

Hengel, Martin, xxi, xxii, xxiin11, xxiin13, xxiin14, xxiiin21, 1n2, 206n5
Hoskyns, Edwyn C., 26n15, 97n26, 190n26, 200n10
Hughes, Selwyn, 132n22
Jeremias, Joachim, 94n19, 98n27, 108n5, 140n7
Jones, Larry P., 56n8
Kanagaraj, Jey J., xxvin27 6n7, 6n8, 7n17, 8n21, 10n22, 15n33, 26n16, 26n17, 45n14, 48n20, 54n6, 71n24, 74n32, 94n17, 102n7, 104n10, 114n1, 121n3, 124n8, 125n9, 128n14, 130n18, 131n20, 138n12, 140n16, 140n8, 146n5, 147n8, 150n17, 152n2, 180n22, 184n6, 187n15, 190n27, 193n35, 205n1, 208n6, 208n9
Karris, R. J., 50n25
Käsemann, Ernest, 6n9, 165n2
Keener, Craig, xix, xixn3, xxivn26, 6n11, 7n12, 17n40, 21n4, 24n12, 25n14, 34n6, 43n9, 48n20, 83n10, 84n13, 88n4, 95n21, 95n23, 96n24, 106n1, 110n11, 112n14, 120n11, 121n14, 132n21, 136n6, 139n13, 140n14, 140n15, 154n8, 165n1, 168n9, 175n11, 183n2, 184n7, 184n8, 185n10, 186n12, 187n17, 187n18, 189n23, 201n13, 202n14, 203n16, 208n7, 208n8, 210n14
Koester, Craig R., 124n5, 142n21, 188n19, 190n29, 208n6
Köstenberger, Andreas J., xxiin15, 39n3, 41n6, 51n28, 53n3, 64n8, 64n9, 67n18, 71n23, 82n9, 84n12, 85n14, 86n18, 87n2, 90n8, 91n9, 91n13, 94n16, 94n18, 100n2, 108n5, 117n5, 119n9, 118n6, 119n8, 124n4, 124n5, 127n13, 131n19, 135n1, 141n19, 145n4, 146n7, 148n10, 152n3, 159n1, 163n9, 164n12, 167n6, 167n7, 173n5, 174n6, 177n14, 180n20, 180n21, 182n1, 183n3, 184n8, 185n11, 187n14, 189n23, 200n11, 205n2
Kruse, Colin G., 23n9, 23n10, 24n11, 31n3, 36n8, 37n11, 50n24, 64n6, 69n22, 65n11, 84n12, 91n11, 99n1, 103n9, 123n1, 123n3, 145n2, 147n9, 149n14, 149n15, 159n2, 163n11, 176n13, 186n13, 190n24, 191n30, 195n1
Lightfoot, J. B., 8n19
Lincoln, Andrew, T., 50n24, 53n4, 54n5, 60n15, 61n17, 64n6, 64n9, 66n13, 73, 73n27, 80n5, 86n15, 93n15, 94n16, 95n23, 96n25, 99n1, 102n6, 106n1, 111n12, 120n11, 121n15, 128n15, 135n1, 145n3, 145n4, 148n11, 150n16, 153n4, 154n7, 159n1, 162n6, 168n10, 169n11, 173n3, 179n19, 185n9, 187n18, 188n22, 190n25, 195n2, 196n3, 201n13, 205n2, 208n10, 208n11
Lindars, Barnabas, 8n21, 37n10, 116n3, 124n7, 127n13, 205n4
Macdonald, J., 43n8, 45n13
Malina, Bruce J., xixn1, 78n1, 140n14
Martyn, J. L., xixn2, 101, 102n5
McRay, John, 65n11
Meeks, Wayne A., 184n8
Michaels, Ramsey, J., 13n30, 107n3, 108n6, 110n6, 111n13, 116n3, 118n7, 119n8, 123n2, 139n13, 141n19, 142n22, 165n3, 167n8, 175n11, 175n12, 177n15, 178n17, 180n20, 183n4, 188n21, 196n4, 196n15, 198n7, 203n15, 203n18, 208n7, 211n16, 213n18

Author Index

Milne, Bruce, 6n10
Morris, Leon, 91n13
Motyer, Stephen, 89n6, 89n7
Moulton, James H., 46n15
Newbigin, Leslie, 113n15, 153n5
Neyrey, Jerome H., xixn1, 4n5,
    14n32, 17n41, 29n2, 46n16,
    53n1, 61n17, 72n25, 89n5,
    103n8, 108n7
Nicholson, C. G., 135n2
Nicol, W., 63n5
Pamment, Margaret, 7n16
Perrin, Nicholas, xxiiin18
Phillips, G. L., 33n5
Pryor, John, xixn4, xxviiin33
Quast, Kevin, xxn5, xxivn24, 174n9,
    175n11, 196n3
Ridderbos, Herman, 13n29, 20n1,
    31n3, 37n12, 56n9, 62n2,
    76n34, 74n29, 86n17, 116n4,
    136n8, 144n1, 162n6, 208n11
Robinson, John A. T., xxiii, xxiiin23,
    126n12

Rohrbaugh, Richard L., xixn1, 78n1,
    140n14
Sanders, J. N., 175n10
Sandmel, S., 10n22
Santram, Pritam, xxviin29
Schnackenburg, Rudolf, xxn7, 2n3,
    22n7, 43n7, 44n12, 61n16,
    62n3, 66n16, 129n16, 136n7,
    178n18
Schneiders, S. M., 21n3
Slater, T. E., 193n33, 193n34
Smalley, Stephen S., 190n28
Stibbe, Mark W. G., xixn1
Strack, H. L., 29n1, 95n20
Thomas, Christopher J., 138n11
Wahlde, von Urban C., xxiiin19,
    107n2, 110n9, 205n1
Weiss, B., 65, 66
Whitacre, Rodney A., 48n19
Wijingaards, J. N. M., 149n13
Zerwick, Max, 80n3

Subject Index

abiding in, 93, 153–55
Abraham (the patriarch), 94, 95, 97, 98, 131
ascending/to ascend, 18, 32, 43, 197
ascension, Jesus', 33, 44, 82, 142, 151, 158, 179, 197, 203
believing, xxv, 5, 15, 17, 32, 33, 50, 51, 68, 72, 74, 86, 91n12, 93, 110, 130, 131, 144, 146, 166, 167, 190
bread from heaven, the, 68, 69, 73
bread of life, the, 69, 74, 90
Christ, (the), xxiv, xxv, xxvi, xxvii, xxviii, 6, 10, 11–16, 16n38, 18, 31, 27, 32, 36, 37, 41, 45, 46, 64, 77, 79, 80–82, 84–86, 102, 105, 110, 112, 116, 117, 125, 129, 187, 190, 192, 196, 198, 203, 204, 213
Christ, Jesus, xxv, xxviii, 8, 10
Christ, pre-existence of, 1, 10
Christ, pre-existent, 4, 13, 59
church, the, 16, 21, 44, 134, 156, 161, 168, 187, 190, 191, 197, 199, 200, 201, 204, 213
community (the), 2, 3
    a/the new, xxviii, 10, 16, 20, 23, 30, 47, 84, 127, 129, 134, 135, 152, 199
    Christ's, 16, 200
    God's chosen, 153
    God's (new), xix, xxviii, 10, 16, 18, 20, 34, 35, 43, 44, 47, 52, 102, 104, 109, 113, 117, 122, 134, 136, 141, 147–49, 155, 157, 160, 163, 169, 170, 187, 188n20, 198, 200, 203, 208, 211, 213
    Jesus', 16, 26, 29, 30, 32, 51, 52, 136, 145, 147, 148, 150, 156–58, 199, 209, 211
    Jesus' disciples', 18, 21, 157
    Jesus' new, 14, 21, 49, 153, 188, 205
    multiethnic, 52
    new covenant (the), 5, 8, 9, 11, 14, 19, 31, 49, 72, 134, 161, 202
    the believing, 4, 44, 165, 167, 168, 204
    the Johannine, xxii, xxiii, xxv, xxviii, 7, 8, 12n26, 190, 211
condemnation (eternal), 34, 35, 47, 89, 120, 131, 160, 204
covenant, 37
    a/the new, xix, 5, 9, 71, 72, 109
    God's, 5, 7–9, 35, 44, 84, 113, 126, 155, 180
    the blood of the, 8
    the Book of the, 8
cross (the), xxviii, 13, 26, 28, 33, 34, 43, 46, 73–75, 77, 81, 82, 93, 96, 98, 112, 115, 119, 124, 127–30, 135, 136, 138, 139, 141, 147, 148, 151, 158, 160–62, 163n10, 164, 166, 179, 182, 185–88, 190–93, 199, 203, 210, 210n15
darkness, 3, 29, 35, 115, 128, 130, 131, 141, 156, 180
death
    eternal, 57, 92, 193
    Jesus', 12, 13, 21, 22, 25, 33, 44, 77, 120, 122, 136, 137, 145, 151, 161–64, 174, 187, 189, 191, 197, 199, 203, 210
departure, Jesus', 99, 115, 124, 130, 134, 144, 159, 160, 167, 170
disciple, the other, 174–75, 195
disciple whom Jesus loved/ beloved disciple, the, xix, xx, xx–xxin7, xxii, xxiii, xxv, 139,

Subject Index

175, 187, 195–98, 201, 206, 207, 211–13
devil, the, 95, 96, 128–129, 135, 138
dualism/dualistic, 3, 32, 34, 37, 38, 67, 92, 130, 156, 200
end-time, the, 7, 41, 44, 47, 57, 70, 90, 107, 127, 132, 149, 150, 211
equality with God, Jesus', 56, 58, 117, 131, 150
Eucharist/eucharistic, the, 64, 73, 74, 208
faith, xxvii, xxviii, 5, 7, 16, 17, 22, 26, 27, 30, 46, 48, 68, 69, 72, 74, 76, 81, 84, 97, 116, 117, 119, 131, 134, 147, 153, 158, 163, 169
Father, the/my, xxvii, 2, 3, 9, 14, 14n31, 21, 37, 38, 44, 56, 68, 70, 120, 128
flesh, xxvi, xxvii, 3, 5, 5n6, 6, 7, 9, 10, 31, 75, 76, 90, 91
feast of Tabernacles, the, 78, 79, 83, 89, 90
feast of the Dedication, 110
foot washing, 135–38
foreknowledge, Jesus', 16, 17, 42, 45, 63, 76, 78, 82, 115, 136, 142–43, 172–73
from heaven/from above, 30, 32n4, 36–38, 48, 57, 92, 93, 96, 144, 183, 193
  Jesus came down, 68, 69, 70, 71, 72, 75
  life-giving bread, 69
  the bread that comes down, 72, 74
glory, xxv, 4, 27
  divine, 6, 7
  God's/ the Father's, xxv, 6, 7, 9, 10, 18, 19, 27, 32, 33, 38, 80, 115, 116, 119, 137, 156, 165–67, 169, 180, 203, 210
  Jesus'/the Son's, 7, 20, 22, 23, 27, 67, 68, 96, 97, 131, 161, 165, 166, 169, 183
glorification, Jesus', 32, 33, 74, 115n2, 141, 163n10, 165, 190

God
  the one (true), 2, 6, 9, 10, 38, 57, 202
  the only, 8, 45, 60
  the only true, xxvi, 165, 166
  the pre-existent, 9, 166
  heavenly origin (of Jesus), 37, 69, 70, 72, 75, 80, 95, 105, 169, 170, 183
  holistic healing/wholeness, 55–56, 81n6, 99, 100, 104
Holy One of God, the, 76–77, 117
Holy Spirit, the, xxviii, 14, 15, 30, 31, 31n3, 37, 38, 41, 42, 44, 74, 88, 126, 148, 149, 160–63, 199–201, 204
hour, an, 43, 44, 158, 163, 163n10, 164
hour, the/my/his (Jesus'), 21, 43, 44, 91, 127, 128, 135, 140, 141, 151, 158, 162–64, 166, 173, 179
hour of the Father, the, 55, 58, 122, 159
"I am"/"I, I am," 45, 66, 69, 72, 89, 92, 93, 97, 108, 117, 138, 152, 166, 173
"I am he," 45, 45n14, 173
"I am he who sent me," 91
I am that I am, 5, 45, 89, 107, 173
incarnation/ incarnate, the, 6, 7, 32, 44, 75
indwelling, the, xxv
  mutual, 2, 169
  reciprocal, 2
judgment, 22, 47, 61, 104, 104n11, 105, 159, 160 God's, 35, 70, 88, 128, 130, 153, 156, 184
  the Son's, 57, 58
  the Son of Man's, 129
King/king (the), 179–80, 182, 184–86, 192
  the/messianic, 11, 65, 81, 124, 125, 130, 183
King (of Israel), 17, 30, 41, 117, 124, 125, 185

225

Subject Index

King of the Jews, 112, 125, 126, 179–82, 184–86, 192
Kingdom
　eternal, 130
　God's, 18, 23, 29, 30, 32, 185, 192
　Jesus', 173
　Messiah's, 17, 183
kingship, Jesus', 65, 126, 179, 180
Lamb of God, the (Passover), 13, 186, 188, 189, 191
last day, the, 70, 73, 74, 131, 156
Law, the (Mosaic), xxiv, 8, 9, 15–17, 24, 29, 31, 54, 55, 58, 61, 71, 73, 75, 80, 85, 86, 87, 88, 90, 91, 111, 112, 129, 141, 145, 146, 157, 196, 208
leadership, 113, 136
life (the), 31, 33, 34, 38, 145, 213
　divine, xxviii, 2, 7, 14, 30, 32, 41, 55, 57, 58, 67–69, 73, 76, 90, 120, 146, 149, 188, 189, 199, 203, 204
　(the) eternal, xxvi, 4, 31, 33, 34, 38, 41–43, 57, 60, 67–70, 72, 74–76, 86, 110, 127, 132, 165, 190
　God's, 2, 33, 38, 96
　heavenly, 30, 34, 38, 41, 47, 67, 72, 92, 107, 108, 166, 191
　Jesus', 9, 18, 19, 33, 153
　Jesus the giver of, 34
　new, 31, 34, 190
　the Holy Spirit's, 41
　the eschatological, 41
　the light of, 90
　true, 146
life of the age to come, 111, 165
Light (the), xxvii, 2–5, 9, 29, 35, 87, 90, 116, 130, 131, 156, 180
　the true, 4
Light of the world, the, 83, 89, 90, 100, 115, 141, 180
living bread, the, 69, 72
living water(s), 41, 42, 83, 84
Logos (the), 1–10, 190, 213
Logos incarnate, the, 7, 35, 213

Lord (the/my), 39, 69, 72, 76, 105, 117, 137, 159, 166, 195–98, 201, 202, 206–8
love/to love, xxvi, 7, 20, 35, 141, 142, 154, 155, 169, 170, 209, 209n12, 210
　divine, 154, 155, 179
　God's, 7, 8, 19, 27, 34, 38, 93, 104, 111, 120, 124, 138, 141, 169, 170, 180, 186
　Jesus', 27, 110, 115, 135, 138, 139, 142, 147, 152, 154, 155, 158, 161, 179, 187, 207
　the Father's, 57, 128, 154, 163
　the disciples', 187, 209
Messiah, the, xxv, 5, 11, 13–17, 16n38, 19, 45, 48, 56, 64, 65, 69, 81, 82, 85, 86, 97, 101, 105n12, 108, 117, 124, 125, 129, 136, 148, 149, 160–61, 183, 185, 191
messianic secret, the, 65, 110
ministry
　Jesus', 11, 16–20, 23, 29, 35, 36, 40, 50, 78, 82, 126, 128, 166, 169, 202
　the church's, 52, 201
　the disciples', 47, 208
mission
　God's, 9, 36, 46, 47, 77, 93, 199, 202
　Jesus', xxviii, 9, 21, 32, 34, 47, 63, 95, 108, 138, 150, 151, 155, 161, 163, 179, 180, 199, 204, 208
　Jesus' disciples', 45, 47, 168
　the Baptist's, 3, 11, 12, 35 37
　the church's, 47, 199, 200, 205, 208
misunderstanding, 42, 136
mutual indwelling, 111, 112, 146, 149
mutual union, 74, 153
mysticism, Jewish, xxi
mysticism, Merkabah, xxiv
non-understanding, 22, 26, 30, 41, 46, 55, 103, 145, 146, 161
oneness of God (the Father)

Subject Index

and Jesus (the Son), 7, 8, 111, 112, 131, 132, 146, 150, 156, 157, 161, 167
oneness between the believers/ Jesus' disciples, 1, 109, 167, 169, 197
oneness with the Father, Jesus', xxvii, 6, 27, 54, 71, 90, 91, 93, 98, 109, 138
oneness with the Son, God's, 71, 109
one/he who is coming, the, 64, 65, 117, 124, 125
Paraklētos (helper, advocate), 148, 148n12, 157
Passover, the, 23, 24, 26, 63, 66, 73, 122, 123–25, 127, 134–35, 178, 180, 189, 192
Prajāpati, 193
pre-existence with God
 the Logos', 9
 Jesus', 7, 10, 67, 71, 72, 98
 Christ's, 80, 81, 131
prophet, a/the, 6, 12, 43, 64, 65, 84, 86n16, 101
punishment, eternal, 58, 72, 184
regeneration/rebirth, 9, 31, 32
resurrection
 eschatological, the, 120
 final, 58
 Jesus', xix, 12, 13, 21, 22, 26, 33, 44, 120, 122, 128, 129, 130, 136, 137, 144, 145, 148, 149, 151, 161–63, 170, 172, 177, 189, 195–97, 199, 201–3
 Lazarus', 7, 114, 119
resurrection of all humans, 21
resurrection of the believers, 33
revelation of/ to reveal, God, 5, 7, 9, 10, 15, 18, 19, 32, 60, 66, 72, 204
revelation of Jesus'/God's glory, 20, 65
revelation of the Father, 144
righteousness, 159, 160, 169
ruler/prince of this world, the, 128–29, 151, 160, 168, 188
salvation, xxvi, xxviii, 3, 12, 13, 34, 44, 46–48, 55, 58, 92, 93, 97, 104n11, 121, 125, 130, 142, 147, 150, 153, 187, 188n20
end-time/final, 3, 82, 84
Savior of the world, 48, 49
Scripture(s), the, xxiv, 12, 15, 16, 25, 26, 83, 84, 111, 112, 126, 138, 139, 167, 173, 186, 191, 196
second coming, Jesus', xxv, 145, 150, 151, 162, 211, 212
seeing, 15, 27, 30, 33, 50, 91n12, 162
self-revelation, Jesus', 40, 66, 89, 105, 149, 196, 198, 205–6, 207
self-revelation of God, the, 2, 69, 70, 107, 147, 156, 166
sign(s), 20–23, 22, 25–28, 30, 50, 51, 64–66, 68, 70, 81, 99, 114, 115, 119–22, 126, 130, 131, 146, 156, 203, 207, 209, 212
sign, the greatest, 28, 59
sin(s), 9, 13, 25, 33, 34, 92, 94, 99, 105, 140, 147, 156, 159, 160, 168, 185, 186, 188, 191, 193, 201
society, God's new, 46, 55
Son, the, 34, 35, 37, 38, 46, 58, 70, 120, 128, 131
Son, the only, 7, 8, 14, 34, 94, 197
Son of God, the, xxvii, xxviii, 1, 8, 12–14, 17, 21, 27, 37, 55–58, 64, 76, 86, 111, 112, 115, 115n2, 117, 125, 183, 190, 203, 204
Son of Man, the, 18, 18n43, 19, 27, 32, 32n4, 33–35, 58, 64, 67, 73–75, 93, 99, 104, 105, 105n12, 127, 129, 130, 141, 141n20
Spirit, God's, 14, 30, 67
Spirit, Jesus', 148, 189
Spirit, the, 5, 13, 14, 26, 31, 38, 42, 74, 75, 83, 84, 148, 149, 157, 159–61, 163, 190, 199, 200, 208
Spirit of truth, the, 134, 148, 148n11, 157, 159, 160
subordination/submission to the Father, Jesus', 57, 91, 93, 132, 150

Subject Index

supernatural knowledge, Jesus', 26, 40, 48, 54, 75, 135, 161
testimony, 27, 31, 32, 36, 46, 190, 212
  Jesus', 29, 38, 79, 90
  the church's, 32
testimony of the Baptist, 11, 15, 35
"the Jews", xxiv, xxv, 11, 11n24, 13, 25, 36, 54, 56, 57, 59, 70–72, 78, 79, 91–93, 95–98, 101–3, 108n4, 110, 111, 172, 178–86, 188, 191, 192, 198
to abide in Jesus, 74
to abide in the Father, 74
to accomplish/fulfill, 46, 47, 54, 70, 99, 108, 166, 188, 191, 198
to bear fruit, 74, 152–55
to bear witness, 3, 10, 14, 27, 38, 58–61, 90, 91, 126, 139, 149, 157, 157n10, 180, 190, 191, 193, 199, 204, 212, 213
to be exalted, 32, 33
to be glorified, 32, 33, 115, 126–30, 141, 141n20, 155, 167
to be lifted up, 32, 33, 129, 130, 138
to be sent, 14, 36, 38, 57, 166
to believe, xxvii, xxviii, 8, 13, 14, 23, 26–28, 30, 32–35, 38, 41, 43, 45, 46, 47, 60, 61, 67–70, 79, 83, 85, 90, 94, 104, 105, 109, 110, 112, 115, 116, 120–22, 125, 126, 129–31, 138, 151, 158, 160, 164, 167–69, 186, 189, 190, 194–97, 201–3, 212
to breathe on, 199, 200
to dwell/indwelling, 6–8, 36,
to dwell within one another, 74
to glorify (God/Jesus), 81, 96, 97, 115, 128, 152, 154, 161, 164, 166, 210
to judge/to be judged, 34, 38, 58, 61, 89–91, 93, 132, 153, 200, 211
to know/knowing, xxvi, 4, 15, 33, 43, 44, 59, 91, 91n12, 97, 102, 103, 108, 109, 111, 128, 146, 158, 165–67, 166n5, 169, 191, 210, 212
to love one another, 154, 155

to remain/remaining, 13–15, 38, 93, 152–54, 211
to reveal, 18, 19, 22, 27, 38, 44, 45, 59, 90, 113, 128, 130, 146, 154, 156, 165, 166, 170, 180, 186, 197, 207, 209, 210
to save, 34, 46, 48, 65, 132, 173
to see/seeing, 15, 17, 18, 27, 30, 33, 38, 45, 50, 63, 67, 68, 70, 91n12, 104, 105, 116, 119, 120, 127, 128, 131, 146, 148, 161, 167, 186, 197, 201, 202
to send/sending, 33–35, 46, 47 55, 57, 58–60, 91, 94, 99, 120, 131, 137, 156, 157, 159, 166, 168, 169, 189, 197, 199, 204
to testify (to Jesus), 26, 32, 37, 38, 55, 56, 59, 60, 79, 90, 139, 180, 193, 196, 197, 203
to witness (about Jesus), 20, 100
to worship (God), 21, 24, 43–45, 57, 104, 126–27
to worship (Jesus), 105
truth (the), 7, 8, 18, 22, 23, 25, 26, 35, 44–46, 93, 95, 96, 105, 139, 145, 146, 160, 168, 179, 180, 190, 193, 199, 201
truth, heavenly, 29, 32, 68, 159, 168, 210
union
  between Jesus and the Father, 14n31
  between Jesus and his followers, 14n31, 152, 153
unity of the Father and the Son, 57, 146
vine and branches, 152–54
vision of Jesus/Jesus' glory, 14, 18, 20, 26
witness(es), 3, 8, 11–13, 36, 58, 59, 90, 91, 110, 139, 176, 187, 190, 191, 196, 213
Word, the, xxvii, 1, 3, 5, 6
Word incarnate, the, 90
word(s), God's, 38, 50, 80, 108, 130–32, 146, 147, 153, 160, 161, 167–69, 173

Subject Index

word(s), Jesus', 17, 38, 47, 48, 75, 76, 80, 85, 86, 50, 109, 110, 112, 131, 132, 136, 146, 149, 151–53, 156, 161, 173, 176, 197, 207, 212, 213
work(s), God's, 67, 68, 90, 99, 130, 146, 168
work(s) of Jesus, the, 23, 47, 59, 81, 86, 110, 112, 146, 156, 189
work(s) of the Father, 46, 57, 90, 112
work(s) of the Holy Spirit, 31, 147

world (the), xxviii, 4, 11, 13, 14, 20, 34, 35, 38, 46, 72, 73, 78, 79, 113, 126, 148, 149, 155–56, 159–61, 164, 167–70, 179, 180, 185, 199, 204, 208, 212, 212n17
worship, xxv, 24, 25, 43–45, 128
   spiritual, 26
   the eschatological, 44
   true, 26, 43, 44

Scripture Index

OLD TESTAMENT

Genesis

1	9, 50
1:1	1
1:1—2:3	20
1:3–8	89
1:19-2:1	20
1:21	2
1:24–25	2
1:26–27	2
1:28–30	3
1-2	2
2:2–3	56
2:7	2, 75, 199
3	109
4:8	96
12:1–4	97
12:7	97
15:1	66
15:4–6	97
17:6–8	97
17:10–14	80
17:17	97
18:1–9	95
18:17	154
21:4	80
22	13
22:2	34
22:8	13
22:9–10	34
22:16	34
26:24	66
28:12–27	18
28:17	107
29:7	40
32:27–30	5
33:18–20	39
33:19	39
48:22	39

Exodus

3:13–14	5, 45, 89, 166
6:2–3	5, 202
6:6, 7	202
12	13, 24
12:3–6	13
12:18	135
12:21–22	188
12:46	13, 189, 191
13:21–22	90
14:19–25	90
15:24	70
16:2, 7–12	70
16:4, 14–15	68
16:4, 15	68
17:3	70
19:5	5
19:5–6	167
20:5	99
20:19, 22	59
22:28	177
24:7–8	8
24:15–17	7
25:8	7
25:8–9	6
29:45–46	6
31:14–15	55

Scripture Index

31:18	88
32:16	88
33:11	103, 154
33:18–19	7, 166
34:5–6	166
34:6–7	7, 9
40:35	7
40:38	90

Leviticus

1	24
1–15	11
3	24
11:32–38	22
11:44	167
11:44–45	168
12:1–3	80
17:10–12	73, 74
18:5	55
19:18	141
20:10–12	88
20:14	88
21:6–8	77
21:15	77
21:9	88
22:9	77
23:5–6	135
23:33–43	78
23:34	82
23:36a	82
23:36	83
23:41, 42	82
24:11–16	98
24:16	111, 183

Numbers

3:14–15	129
9:6–13	122
9:12	13, 189, 191
11:1	70
12:8	103
14:2, 27	70
15:33–36	55
21:5–9	33
21:9	129
25:7–13	158
27:17	107
35:25	174n8
35:30	90

Deuteronomy

1:16–17	86
4:7	91
4:15, 33, 36	59
5:1–21	8
5:9	99
5:15	54
5:24–26	59
6:4	95, 166
6:5	141
7:6	155
7:7–8	155
8:3	46
8:19	88
9:10	88
11:29	43
12:4–7	43
12:5, 11	166
12:21	43
14:2	155
14:22–26	43
15:11	124
17:4	86
18:5	155
18:15	12
18:15, 18	84
18:15–19	64
18:18	12
18:20	60
19:8	86
19:15	58, 90
21:22–23	189
22:2–24	88
27:12–13	43
27:26	85
28:15	85

231

Scripture Index

Deuteronomy (*continued*)
28:25	82
30:4	82
30:18–19	34
32:18	5
32:39	97
34:10–11	103

Joshua
8:2	185
24:32	39

Judges
6:22–23	66
6:23	198

Ruth
2:14	64

1 Samuel
2:6	97
8:7	185
9:17 LXX	183
25:6	198

2 Samuel
5:2	108
7:1	129
7:12–16	84
7:14	14, 17
13:23	122
14:4	125
18:28, 31	138n10
20:21	138n10

1 Kings
8:1–8	78
8:10	7
8:10–11	166
8:11	7
8:13	7, 166
8:17–20	166
8:29	7, 166
9:3	7, 166
14:21	43
16:24	39n2
17:1	86
21:9, 10, 13	98
22:19	18

2 Kings
4:42–44	63
5:7	97
14:6	99
14:25	86
17:24–34	40
17:41	40
19:30	127

1 Chronicles
16:28–29	102

2 Chronicles
6:20	7, 166
12:13	43
13:19	122
16:14	192
20:7	154
23:6	77
30:15–19	122
35:3	77

Nehemiah
3:1, 32	53
9:15	68
12:39	53
13:15–22	55

Esther
8:8	38
8:10	38

Job

9:8	66
38:16	66

Job

2:8	116
2:13	116

Psalms

1:3	42
2:7	5, 14, 17, 89
7:9	27
16:10	196
18:50	84
22:15	188
22:16	186, 189
22:18	186
23	107
23:2	107
25:1 LXX	110n10
27:1	3
29:11	150
33:6, 9	9
33:15	27
34:20	191
35:19	157
35:23	202
36:9	3, 89
39:9 LXX	83n11
40:8	83n11
41:9	138, 167
42:2	188
51:10	31
55:12–13	138
63:1	188
69	25
69:4	157
69:9	24
69:21	188
69:25	167
75:8	174
76:1	44
77:19	66
78:1–8	72
78:23–24	68
78:23	107
78:24	68
78:70–72	108
80:1	107
80:4	18n43
80:8–19	152
80:17	18
86:4 LXX	110n10
86:11	145
89:3–4	84
89:35–37	85
89:36	129
89:51	129
104:29–30	75
105:40	68
107:20	9
109:3	157
109:8	167
110:4	129
111:9	167
118:10–12	110
118:19, 20	107
118:25–27	125
119:21	85
119:30	145
119:161	157
121:1–2	120, 165
121:4, 7–8	56
122	24
123:1–4	165
132:17b	59
139:1–24	27
143:10	160
147:2	82

Proverbs

3:19–20	1, 9
8:22–31	2, 9
8:23	1
9:1–6	69, 208
9:5	83
15:24	145

Scripture Index

Ecclesiastes

11:5	31

Isaiah

2:3	44
2:11	70
2:17	70
2:20	70
5:1–7	152
6	xxiv–xxv
6:3	167
6:1–7	131
6:9–10	131
6:10	130
8:16–18	25
8:18 LXX	27
9:8–9	9
11:1–2 LXX	14
11:1–5	17
11:1	81, 85
11:10	85
22:22	200
26:16–19	162
27:2–6	152
30:20–21	145, 160
34:13	182
35:4	17, 125
35:5–6	82
40:3	12
40:6	6
41:4	45, 66
41:8	154
41:8–9	155
41:10	66
41:22–23	161
42:6, 8	66
42:8	5, 45, 202
43	92
43:1	66
43:10	45, 66, 92, 98, 155
43:11, 13	45
43:14	76
43:15	45
43:16	66
43:25	45, 66, 92
44:1	155
44:3	31, 84n13
44:3–4	42
44:6–8	125
45:4	155
45:18	66
46:4	66
47:4	76
49:3	155
49:6	82
49:7	76
49:10	42
50:6	182
51:6–16	66
51:10–15	66
51:12 LXX	66
51:17, 22	174
52:7	150
52:13	32, 129
52:13—53:12	32–33
53	190
53:1	130
53:4–10	168
53:4–7	13, 186
53:4–6	13
53:7	13
53:9	192
53:10	13, 108n4, 168
53:12	13, 108, 168, 172, 186
54:5	76
54:7	72
54:13 (MT, LXX)	71, 72
55:1–2	69
55:11	9
56:6–8	109, 127
56:7	24
57:19	150
58:11	84
61:1	82, 99
62:5b	37

66:7–14	162	3:1	18n43
66:18–19	27	4:1	18n43
66:18–21	109	4:1–3	25
		4:3	27
Jeremiah		6:1	9
1:4	9	8:14	116
2:2	37	11:19–20	31
2:13	41	15:1–8	152
2:21	152	16:8–14	37
3:15	108	17:1–10	152
6:9	152	19:10–14	152
7:11	24	20:11, 13	57
8:13	152	22:27	108
12:10	152	23:31–34	174
17:10	27	34	107
17:13	41	34:1–10	106
17:21–22	55	34:11–16	108
21:8	145	34:23–24	108
22:10	161	36:22–32	9
23:1–4	108	36:23	84
23:5	81, 85	36:25–27	31, 84
23:24	56	36:26–27	31
23:25	60	37:1–14	75
25:15–17	174	37:9	199
29:9, 25, 31	60	37:9–10	199
31:3	71	37:14	84
31:12	23	37:15–24	109
31:31–34	9, 84	37:24	108
31:33–34	4, 72	37:26	150
34:5	192	37:26–27	149
38:3 LXX	71	47:1–12	84
48:24	77n36	47:9	31
		47:9–12	42
Lamentations			
2:6	118	**Daniel**	
		4:34	165
Ezekiel		5:5–9	88
		5:24–28	88
1	xxiv	7	xxv, 18, 18n43
1:1	18	7:9–27	18, 58
1:3	9	7:13	18
1:4	9	7:13–14	12n27, 18n43, 130
1:26–28	19	12:2	33, 58, 69
2:1	18n43		

Scripture Index

Hosea

2:16	37
6:1–3	166n5
10:1	152
10:12 LXX	3

Joel

1:2	95
2:4–5 LXX	95
2:28	84n13
2:28–29	31
3:18	23, 84

Amos

2:2	77n36
3:1	9
3:2	4
3:8	9
5:18–20	70
9:13–14	23

Micah

4:2–4	127
5:2	81, 85, 86, 108

Nahum

1:1	86
1:10	182

Habakkuk

2:16	174

Zephaniah

3:14–17	17, 125
3:15	125

Zechariah

2:10–11	6, 7
6:12	183
9:9	125
9:9–10	17
12:10	108, 189, 191
13:1	191
13:7–9	108, 108n4
14:8	84
14:8–9	41
14:9	109
14:16	109
14:16–17	24
14:16–19	127

Malachi

3:1	11, 84
4:5	84
4:5–6	11

APOCRYPHA

Baruch

3:9—4:4	9

1 Esdras

8:11, 13, 26	154

1 Maccabees

1:54	110
2:18	184
3:38	184
6:14	184
9:22	203, 212
13:51	125

2 Maccabees

1:27	82
1:29	121
5:19	121
10:1–9	110
10:7	125
14:36	167

Sirach

1:1–10	2, 9
7:26, 27	3
15:1	9
17:11	3
19:20	9
24:3	9
24:5–6	66
24:8, 10	6
24:12	69
24:19–21	83
24:23	9
25:24	96
34:8	9
39:1	9
51:23–34	83

Wisdom of Solomon

1:6	27
2:24	96
7:22 LXX	7
7:25	166
7:26, 27	3
9:1–2	9
9:10–11	166
16:7	33

New Testament

Matthew

2:23	173
3:1–12	11
3:3 par.	12
3:10	153
3:11	125
3:11 par.	4, 12
3:16 par.	14
4:19–22	16
4:49, 50	50
5:16	35
7:7–11	162
7:13, 14	107
7:19	153
8:5	16
8:5–13	50
8:14	16
8:22	16
9:9	16
9:36–38	47
10:24 par.	137
10:40 par.	138
11:2–5	82
11:3	64, 117, 125
11:28	15
12:22–23	82
12:28	82, 88
12:38–39	27
12:39–40	25
13:24–30	47
13:36–43	47
13:40	153
13:41–42	153
13:42	153
13:50	153
15:55–57a par.	71
13:57 par.	49
14:9	50
14:15 par.	63
14:21 par.	64
14:23	65
14:26–27	66
14:34	62
15:21–28 par.	50
16:1	27
16:4	27
16:4 par.	50
16:16	17, 117
16:17	5n6
16:19	200
16:20	17
18:3	30
18:16	58
18:18	200
19:16	68

Scripture Index

Matthew (*continued*)

20:22–23	174
21:8	125
21:12–17 par.	23
21:13 par.	24
21:14	26
21:17	123
21:46	101
22:35–40	141
23:39	125
24:3	27
24:24	27
24:30	27
25:1	37
25:10	107
25:31–46	58
26:6–13	123
26:8–9	124
26:14–16	135, 140
26:15–16	124
26:20–24 par.	139
26:20	xx
26:27 par.	64
26:30	172
26:31	164
26:33	209
26:34	177
26:35 par.	142
26:36 par.	172
26:38	128
26:42 par.	174
26:48–50 par.	173
26:52a	174
26:55 par.	172
26:56b	164
26:58 par.	174, 175
26:61	25
26:64	18
26:75 par.	210
27:11 par.	179
27:15	181
27:19	184
27:30 par.	182
27:33 par.	185
27:34	25
27:38	186
27:40	26
27:48	25, 188
27:50	188–89
27:55–56 par.	187n15
27:57	192
27:60	192
28:1	195
28:3	196
28:7–8	197
28:10	206
28:11–15	211
28:13	198
28:16–17	206
28:17	201

Mark

1:1–5	3
1:1–8	11
1:10	18
1:11	128
1:14	36
1:17	16
1:20	16
1:21	16
1:29	16
2:2	10
2:5	99
2:14	16
2:19	37
3:21–22	109
3:22–30	88
4:4–5	124
4:14	10
4:26–29	47
6:3	201n12
6:14–22	50
6:15	101
6:16	149
6:34	63
6:39	63

6:45	62	15:36	188
6:46	65	15:43	192
6:47	65, 66	16:1	195
6:53	62	16:5	195
8:11	82	16:7	206
8:11–12	27	16:11	201
9:1	211	16:13–14	201
9:2	139		
9:7	128		
9:11–12	11		
9:43, 45, 47	107		
11:2	192		
11:8	125		
11:10	192		
11:12	123		
11:17	24		
13:4	27		
13:7–8	164		
13:19	164		
13:21–22	82		
13:22	27		
13:24–25	164		
14:3–9	123		
14:10–11	140		
14:12	134		
14:17–18	xx		
14:19 par.	63, 64		
14:27–31	158		
14:27	164		
14:29	209		
14:33	139		
14:34	128		
14:50	164		
14:54	176		
14:58	25		
14:61–64	110		
14:62	18		
14:71	177		
15:6	181		
15:7	181		
15:14	178		
15:23	188		
15:27	186		
15:29	25		

Luke

1:1–17	11
1:12–13	66
1:47	48
2:9–10	66
2:11	48
2:49	25
3:15	4
4:31	16
4:38	16
5:1–11	207
5:1	62
5:4	207
5:5	206
6:16	140
7:1–10	50
7:2–5	127
7:9	117
7:36–50	87, 123
7:39	101
9:10–17	62
10:2	47
10:25–28	141
11:9–13	162
11:16	27, 82
11:19	27
11:26	88
13:24, 25	107
19:30, 38	192
19:47	87
20:1	87
21:7	27
21:11	27
21:25	27
21:37–38	87

Scripture Index

Luke (*continued*)

22:11	xx
22:14	xx
22:15	134
22:37	186
23:8	27
23:17	181
23:19	181
23:27	161
23:33	186
23:36	25
23:46	189
23:50	191, 192
24:1	195
24:2	193
24:4	196
24:11	201
24:15–16	206
24:16	196
24:19	6, 101
24:25–27	15
24:27	196
24:30	208
24:32	15
24:39	198
24:44	196

John

1:1–18	1, 5, 205
1:1–5	1
1:1–3	1
1:1b	1
1:1b-2	2
1:1c	2, 150
1:1	5, 111, 131
1:1–2	166, 213
1:2	2
1:3	2, 57
1:3–5	1, 213
1:4a	2
1:4b	2
1:4	3, 33, 90
1:4–5	130
1:5	xxviii, 3, 35, 90
1:6–8	1, 3, 180, 212
1:7–8	59, 126
1:8	xxvii, 3
1:9	35, 90, 117, 149, 152, 163
1:9–10	4
1:9–11	xxviii, 35
1:9–12	130, 131
1:9–13	4
1:10	4, 11, 92, 97, 148, 155, 169
1:10–11	1
1:11b	5
1:11	179
1:12	5, 33, 35, 91n12, 94
1:12–13	1, 30, 90, 96, 122
1:13	5, 30
1:14–16	1
1:14a	3, 5
1:14b	6
1:14c	7, 146
1:14	xxv, xxvii, 4, 5, 6–8, 23, 38, 44, 73, 93, 111, 141, 148, 150, 165, 166, 169, 180, 212
1:15	1, 3, 4, 12, 13, 59, 83, 98, 126, 131
1:16–18	4
1:16	8, 148, 212
1:17	8, 12, 61, 93, 146
1:18	xxv, 7–9, 59, 72, 111, 149, 166
1:19—12:50	203
1:19	11, 88
1:19–20	11
1:19–28	11, 36, 59
1:19-2:1	20
1:20	xxvii, 36

Scripture Index

1:20–21	84	1:50	17, 27, 51
1:21	11	1:50–51	26, 32
1:23	36	1:50b–51	xxv, 20
1:24	11, 88	1:51	17, 19, 20, 32, 66, 145
1:26	14		
1:26–27	4, 12, 31	2	20, 26
1:27	13, 98	2:1–11	24, 27
1:28	11, 75	2:1–12	20
1:29–36	59	2:2	21
1:29–34	12, 36	2:3	21
1:29	12–14, 34, 94, 185, 186, 188	2:4a	21
		2:4	22, 43, 58, 79, 81
1:29–30	4	2:5	22
1:30	36	2:6	22
1:31	13	2:7	22, 63
1:32	14, 212	2:7–8	22
1:33	31	2:9	22
1:32–33	14, 38	2:10	23
1:33	13, 14	2:11a	22
1:34	12, 14, 212	2:11	23, 27, 120, 128, 166, 169
1:35–51	14, 206		
1:35–40	139n13	2:12	21, 23, 35, 177, 187
1:36	14, 34, 94, 186	2:13	23, 63, 78
		2:13–22	24, 122
1:37–41	175	2:14	24
1:38	15, 16n38, 137, 197	2:15	24
1:39b	15	2:16	24, 56, 144
1:39	17	2:17	24
1:40	14	2:17–22	25
1:41–48	157n10	2:17	26
1:41–45	65	2:18–22	28
1:41	15, 16, 16n38, 111, 117	2:18	25, 27, 68
		2:18–19	203
1:42	16, 27, 209	2:19–22	187
1:43	16	2:19	25
1:44	16, 62, 127	2:19–20	26
1:45	15, 16, 26, 65, 111, 117	2:20	25n13
		2:20–22	26
1:45–46	84	2:21	26
1:46	17, 48	2:21–22	203
1:47	17	2:22	26, 126, 136, 150
1:47–48	27, 40	2:23–25	17, 26, 40
1:48	16, 17	2:23a	26
1:49	17, 65, 117, 125	2:23b	26

241

Scripture Index

John (*continued*)

2:23	30, 81
2:24	27
2:24–25	16
2:25	27
3	85
3–4	29
3:1	29
3:1–12	29, 32
3:1–21	35, 37, 86
3:1–30	37
3:2	15n37, 29, 30, 37, 137, 192
3:3	5, 29, 30, 31, 33, 36, 41, 92
3:4	31
3:5	29, 30, 33, 41
3:5–6	42
3:6	31, 37, 90
3:7	31, 58
3:8	5, 31, 41
3:9	31, 48
3:10	29, 31
3:12	32
3:13	xxv, 18n43, 19, 32, 103, 104, 135n3
3:13–15	34, 35
3:13–16	68
3:13–21	32
3:14	32, 34, 74, 93, 129, 141, 203
3:14–15	28, 47, 67, 191
3:14–16	58
3:15	33, 34
3:15–16	33–35, 38
3:16	7, 13, 34, 92, 109, 141, 149
3:16–17	70, 120, 155, 188, 199
3:16–18	35
3:16–21	xxviii, 34, 57
3:17	34, 46, 68, 89, 95, 104n11, 132
3:18	7, 34, 35, 92, 104n11, 160
3:18–21	128, 201
3:18–19	131
3:19	34, 35, 128, 148, 163
3:19–20	79, 115
3:19–21	xxviii, 3, 29, 35, 130, 156
3:20	35, 90, 130, 159
3:20–21	115
3:21	35, 37, 90
3:22	35, 35n7
3:22–30	35
3:22–36	37
3:23	36
3:24	36
3:25	36
3:26a	36
3:26b	36n9
3:26	36, 74
3:26–30	59
3:27	36
3:28	11, 36
3:29	36
3:30	37
3:31c	37
3:31	30, 32, 37, 98, 135n3
3:31–36	35, 37
3:31–32	90
3:32a	38
3:32	38, 72, 80
3:32–33	180
3:33	38, 67, 80, 166
3:34	38, 46, 111, 80, 146, 149, 150, 156, 160, 167
3:35	38, 135, 154
3:36	31, 38
4	62
4:1–3	49
4:1, 3	78

Reference	Pages
4:1–6	39
4:1b	42
4:1	36, 36n9, 39, 40, 88
4:2	35, 39
4:3	39
4:4–42	175
4:4	39
4:5–6	39
4:6	15n37, 40
4:6–7	188
4:7	40
4:8	40
4:9	39, 40, 40n4, 96
4:10	41
4:11	137
4:11–12	41
4:12	80, 97
4:13–14	42
4:14b	83
4:14	14, 40, 41, 75, 83, 188
4:14–15	31
4:15	42, 50, 69, 137
4:16–18	16, 40
4:17	42
4:18	42
4:19	30, 43, 50, 64, 101, 137
4:20b	43
4:20	43
4:21a	43
4:21b	43
4:21	22
4:23	21, 44
4:23–24	25, 44
4:24	44
4:25	45
4:25–26	64, 111, 161
4:26	45, 66, 69, 105
4:27–38	45
4:27	45
4:28	45
4:29	45, 46, 81n7
4:30, 31, 32,	46
4:33	46, 48
4:33–34	126
4:34	21, 46, 59, 68, 70, 99, 146, 188
4:35a	46, 136
4:35b	47
4:35	46
4:36, 37, 38	47
4:39	46, 48, 169
4:39–42	48
4:40, 41	48
4:42	46, 48, 169
4:43–54	49
4:43, 44, 45	49
4:46–54	20, 50
4:46	49
4:47	50
4:48	50
4:49	137
4:51, 52	50
4:52–53	51
4:53	28, 51
4:54	20, 50, 51
5	78, 81n6
5:1	78
5:1–18	53
5:1	23, 53
5:2	53
5:3, 4, 5, 6b	54
5:7, 8, 9, 9b	54
5:7	137
5:9	111
5:10	54
5:11–13	100
5:11, 12	55
5:13a, 13b	55
5:14a, 14b	55
5:14	99
5:15	100
5:16	28, 54, 111
5:16, 17	56
5:17–18	56

Scripture Index

John (*continued*)

5:17	57, 70, 99, 111, 120, 146, 150, 164
5:18	xxiv, xxv, xxvii, 14, 28, 54, 58, 79, 80, 91, 117, 121, 183
5:19–21	70
5:19–23	xxvii
5:19–30	56
5:19–47	56
5:19	55, 56, 81, 132, 146, 150
5:19–20	90
5:20	57, 154
5:21	33, 55, 58, 67, 71, 74, 111, 165
5:21–29	57
5:21–24	57
5:21–22	57, 211
5:22	38, 57, 89, 91, 111, 184
5:22–23	57
5:23a	57
5:23	60, 96, 102, 141
5:24	xxv, 33, 35, 38, 57, 67, 74, 92, 94
5:24–25	117, 132
5:24–26	68
5:25–29	57
5:25	21, 22, 33, 57, 58, 128,
5:26	33, 38, 57, 74, 111
5:26–27	34
5:27–29	67, 91, 128
5:27	38, 58, 67, 89, 104, 111, 184, 200, 211
5:28	58
5:28–29	22, 58, 70, 117, 120
5:29	33, 68, 74, 165
5:30a, 30b	58
5:30	57, 58, 70, 88, 150
5:31–47	58, 90
5:31–38	180
5:31–37	126
5:31–32	91
5:31	58
5:32	58, 59
5:33, 34	59
5:35	xxvii, 3, 59
5:36	46, 59, 99, 110, 146, 156, 188
5:37	58, 59
5:37–38	68
5:38	59, 60, 93, 158
5:39	26, 60, 61, 112, 157
5:39–40	79
5:39, 46	72
5:40	60
5:41	60, 80, 96
5:42	27
5:42–43a	60
5:43b	61
5:43	110, 147
5:44	60, 80, 166
5:45	61, 103
5:45–47	79
5:46–47	60
5:46	60, 61, 72, 80, 103, 131
5:47	61
6	62
6:1–15	62
6:1	53, 62, 78, 205
6:2	63
6:3	63
6:4–71	122
6:4	53, 63, 66, 78
6:5a, 5b	63
6:5	62, 165
6:6b	63
6:7	63, 64
6:8–9	62, 63
6:9	64, 175, 206
6:10	63
6:11	64, 120, 147, 170, 206, 208

244

Scripture Index

6:12	64	6:37	15, 38, 70, 76, 104, 108, 129, 149
6:13	64	6:38	18n43, 32, 46, 70, 103, 135n3, 144, 163
6:14	12n26, 64		
6:14–15	65, 121		
6:15	27, 65, 179		
6:16–17	65	6:39	70, 71, 173
6:16–21	65, 207	6:39–40	108
6:17	62, 65	6:40	xxv, 33, 70, 71, 72, 117
6:18	65		
6:19a	65	6:41	69, 70, 103, 135n3
6:19b	65	6:41–42	18n43
6:20b	66	6:42	32, 70, 71, 81, 103
6:20	69	6:43	71
6:21	66	6:44	70, 71, 76, 117, 129
6:22	67	6:45	71, 76
6:22–25a	67	6:46	1, 32, 38, 59, 72, 81, 90, 92, 111, 144, 169
6:22–59	67		
6:23	67, 120, 137		
6:24	62, 67	6:47	33, 72, 74
6:25a	67	6:48	69, 72
6:25b	67	6:49	72
6:25b-34	67	6:50	72, 73
6:25–34	69	6:50–51	18n43, 32
6:26	27, 67	6:51	33, 69, 72, 73, 103, 144, 149
6:26–27	27		
6:27a	67	6:51–56	xxvii
6:27b	67	6:52	70, 73
6:27	34, 68, 69, 72	6:52–59	72, 190
6:28	68	6:53	73, 74
6:29	67, 68	6:53–54	33
6:30	68	6:53–58	73, 74
6:31	68, 71, 72, 74	6:54	33, 73, 74, 74n29, 117
6:32–58	64		
6:32	32, 68, 152	6:55	74
6:32–33	68	6:56	74, 149, 153
6:33	33, 68, 72, 144	6:57	33, 74
6:34	42, 68, 69, 137	6:58	32, 74, 117
6:35	68, 69, 72, 74, 83	6:59	75
6:35–37	33	6:60	76
6:35–51	69	6:60–61	75
6:35–59	69	6:60–71	75
6:36	67, 70	6:61	27, 75
6:36–51	72	6:62	32, 75, 104, 135n3, 166

245

Scripture Index

John (*continued*)

6:63	6, 74, 75, 90, 177
6:64	27, 76
6:65	70, 71, 76
6:66	76
6:67	64, 76, 76n35
6:68	76, 132, 137
6:69	28, 76, 79, 117, 137
6:69–70	76
6:70	64, 76n35, 77, 128, 167, 168
6:70–71	76, 136, 138, 151
6:71	64, 76n35, 77
7	78, 89
7:1–13	78
7:1	39, 53, 78, 95, 102, 121
7:2	53, 78
7:3–5	79
7:3–9	65
7:5	187
7:6	79
7:7	11, 79, 92
7:8–9	79
7:10	23, 79
7:11–12	79
7:12	85
7:13	79, 88, 192, 198
7:14–36	79
7:14	23, 79
7:15	79
7:16	42, 80
7:17b	80n3
7:17	80, 81, 160
7:18a	80n3
7:18	46, 80, 81, 96
7:19	80, 81, 95, 102
7:20	41, 80, 109
7:21	80
7:22	80
7:23	81
7:24	81, 90
7:25	80, 81, 95, 102
7:25–27	84
7:26b	81
7:26	81
7:27a	81
7:27b	81
7:27	81
7:28	80, 81, 83, 95, 97, 131, 152, 166
7:29	59, 81, 103
7:30	81, 85, 102, 121
7:31	81, 84
7:32	82, 88, 95, 102, 121
7:33–36	91
7:33–34	141, 142
7:33	82, 92, 99, 130, 142, 148, 159
7:34	82
7:35–36	92
7:35	82
7:36	82
7:37	83, 131
7:37b–38	83
7:37–38	83, 191
7:37–39	14, 31, 41
7:37–52	82
7:37–38a	84
7:38a	83
7:38b	84
7:38	84, 84n13
7:38–39	84, 190, 200
7:39	83, 126, 190
7:40	12n26, 64, 84
7:40–43	64
7:40–44	84
7:41b	81
7:41	84
7:41–42	48
7:42	81, 85, 86
7:43	85, 109
7:44	85
7:45	85, 102
7:45–52	30, 32, 88
7:46	85

7:47	85	8:20	75, 81, 91, 94, 95, 102, 121
7:48	85	8:21–30	91
7:49	85	8:21	91, 92, 99
7:50	85	8:22	82, 89, 92
7:50–51	29	8:23	11, 18n43, 30, 32, 36, 37, 92, 93, 103, 135n5, 144, 163
7:51	86		
7:52	64, 84, 86, 86n16		
7:53-8:11	87		
7:53	78, 87	8:24	92, 93, 97, 138, 160
7:56	18	8:25a	92
7:59	147	8:25b	93
8	78	8:26b	38
8:1–11	78, 87	8:26	90, 93, 111, 132, 154, 156, 160, 166
8:1	87		
8:2	87	8:26–27	93
8:3–4	87	8:26–28	80
8:3	88	8:28a	93
8:4	88	8:28b	93, 146, 149, 154
8:5	87, 88	8:28	xxv, 78, 93, 97, 129, 132, 138, 150, 153, 156, 160, 167, 191
8:6a	88		
8:6b	88		
8:6	88	8:28–29	xxvii
8:7	89	8:29	xxv, 93, 164
8:8	88, 89	8:30	93
8:11	87, 89, 137	8:31–47	93
8:12a	90	8:31	89, 93, 153
8:12b	90	8:31–32	94
8:12	3, 35, 83, 89, 93, 100, 115, 127, 131	8:32	34, 93
		8:33–47	94
8:12–20	89	8:33	94
8:13–18	180	8:34	93, 94, 201
8:13	58, 89, 90	8:35	94, 136
8:14a	90	8:36	93, 94, 201
8:14b	90	8:37	95
8:14	92, 93, 164, 212	8:38	95
8:15	90, 97	8:39	80, 95
8:16b	92	8:39–40	95
8:16	xxvii, 57, 58, 91, 93, 164, 212	8:40	102
		8:41–43	95
8:17–18	91	8:41	91, 95
8:17	90, 112, 157	8:42	92, 95
8:18	58, 90, 93	8:43	95
8:19	91, 97, 158, 169	8:44	95, 102, 128, 129
		8:45	95, 96

Scripture Index

John (*continued*)

8:46	96, 159, 177
8:47	96
8:48	41, 80, 89, 96, 109
8:49	96
8:50	80, 96, 97
8:51	31, 38, 97
8:52	38, 80, 89, 96, 97
8:53	31, 42, 97, 98
8:54	80, 97, 141
8:54–55	97
8:56	95, 97, 131
8:57	89, 97
8:58	13, 42, 97, 131, 138
8:59	81, 93, 94, 98, 102, 111, 121
9	99, 106
9:2	99, 137
9:3	99
9:4	99, 100
9:1	99
9:1–5	99
9:1–12	99
9:4	46, 115
9:4–5	29, 130
9:5	35, 100, 115, 131
9:6–7	99, 100
9:7	100
9:8	99, 100
9:8–12	99
9:9	100
9:10	100
9:11	100, 105
9:12	100
9:13	100, 108
9:13–34	100
9:13–17	99
9:14	54, 100, 111
9:15	100
9:16	101, 109
9:17	12n26, 101, 105
9:18	101
9:18–23	99
9:19	101
9:20–21	101
9:22	xxiv, 79, 88, 108, 131, 158, 192, 198
9:24	102
9:24–27	55
9:24–34	99
9:25	102
9:26	103
9:27	103
9:28a	103
9:28b	103
9:29	103
9:30	103
9:30–32	30
9:31	104
9:32	104, 109
9:33	32, 104, 105
9:34	104, 106, 108
9:35	104
9:35–37	111
9:35–39	99
9:35–38	28, 64, 169
9:35–41	104
9:36	30, 105, 137
9:36–38	120
9:37	105
9:38	27, 105, 137
9:39	104
9:40	105
9:40–41	99, 201
9:41	56, 105, 107, 156
10	78
10:1	106, 107, 174
10:1–6	107
10:1–18	xxv, 106
10:1–21	106
10:2	106
10:3	107, 180, 197
10:3–4	111
10:4	135
10:5	106, 107
10:6	106

10:7	106, 107	10:30–33	183
10:7–16	122	10:31	111, 115, 121
10:7–18	107	10:32	111
10:8	106, 107	10:33	xxiv, 111
10:9	106, 107	10:34	91, 157
10:10	108, 108n4, 111, 188, 199	10:36	xxiv, 168
		10:38	27, 131, 146, 169
10:10b	69	10:39	81, 121
10:10–14	167	10:39–40	118
10:11	106, 108, 142, 154, 168	10:40	114
		10:42	79
10:11–15	173	11	114, 123
10:12	106, 108	11:1	114
10:12–15	111	11:1–44	114
10:14	106, 107, 108, 111, 135	11:1–16	114
		11:2	114, 136
10:14–15	9	11:3	114
10:15	xxv, 59, 97, 109, 142, 154, 168, 169	11:4	7, 27, 115n2, 116, 119, 128, 141
10:16	109, 169, 174, 180, 199	11:4–42	150
		11:5–6	115
10:17	109, 154	11:6	114
10:17–18	109, 154, 168	11:7	115
10:18b	109	11:8	114, 115, 121
10:18	109, 189	11:9a	115
10:19	109	11:9b-10	115
10:20	80, 109	11:9–10	114, 130
10:21	109	11:10	29
10:22	53, 110	11:11	115, 116
10:22–31	110	11:11–16	126
10:22–42	110	11:12–13	116
10:23	110	11:13a	116
10:24	110	11:14	115, 116
10:24–25	65	11:15	115, 116
10:25a	110	11:16	116
10:25b	110	11:17	116
10:25	147	11:17–27	116
10:26	111	11:18	116
10:26–29	110	11:19	116, 118
10:27	111, 180, 197	11:20	116
10:28	111, 167, 173	11:21	114, 116, 118
10:29	70, 111, 135	11:22	117, 119
10:30	xxv, xxvii, 14, 111, 131, 150	11:23	117
		11:24	117

Scripture Index

John (*continued*)

11:25a	117
11:25b	117
11:25b–26a	41
11:25	34
11:25–26	114
11:25–27	27
11:26b	117
11:26	33, 117
11:27	64, 117, 125, 137
11:28	117, 137
11:28–37	117
11:29	118
11:30	116, 118
11:31	118, 161, 195
11:32	114, 118
11:33	118, 119, 139, 161
11:34	118
11:35	119
11:36	119
11:37	114, 119
11:38	118
11:38–44	119
11:39	48, 119
11:40	7, 27, 115, 119, 128, 166
11:41	63, 120, 165
11:41–42	147, 170
11:42a	120
11:42b	120
11:42	115
11:43	120
11:44	120
11:45	11n24, 28, 82, 115, 120, 121
11:45–57	121
11:46	121
11:46–53	114, 115
11:46–57	28
11:48	36n29, 115, 121, 126
11:49	121, 174
11:49–50	174
11:50	121
11:51	168, 174
11:51–52	122
11:53	122
11:54	122, 177
11:55	78, 122
11:56	122
11:57	102, 114, 122, 126
12	123
12:1	63, 123
12:1–11	123
12:1–8	118
12:2	123
12:2–3a	123
12:3	136, 192
12:4–5	124
12:5	123
12:6	124, 140
12:7	124, 192
12:8	124
12:9	23, 125, 177
12:9–11	28
12:10	125
12:11	125
12:12	23, 63
12:12–19	114, 125
12:13	64, 65, 125, 147, 185
12:13–22	23
12:14	125
12:14–15	192
12:15	65, 125
12:16	126, 136, 150
12:17	126
12:18	126
12:19	36n9, 126
12:20	126
12:20–36	126
12:20–26	82, 126
12:20–22	177
12:21	127
12:21–22	16
12:22	127

Scripture Index

12:23	21, 74, 96, 127, 129, 128, 135, 141, 159, 165, 166	12:46a	131
		12:46b	131
		12:46	29, 35, 90, 130
12:23–24	33	12:47	35, 104n11
12:24	127	12:47–48	132
12:25	127	12:48b	128
12:25–26	82	12:48	70, 128, 132
12:26a	127	12:49	xxvii, 38, 80, 132, 146, 149, 150, 153, 154, 156, 160, 167
12:26b	127		
12:27	21, 128, 135, 139, 165, 166		
		12:50a	132
12:27–36	128	12:50b	132
12:27–28	120	13	134
12:28a	128	13:1a	135
12:28	166	13:1b	135
12:29	128	13:1	21, 63, 124, 139, 140, 154, 155, 163, 165, 197
12:30	128		
12:31	77, 128, 151, 160, 164, 168, 188		
		13:1—17:26	134
12:32	71, 96, 129, 192	13:1–20	xxv, 134, 208
12:32–34	74	13:1–17	124
12:32–33	178	13:1–11	137
12:33	96, 128, 129, 210	13:1–2	xx
12:34	19, 111, 129	13:1–3	134
12:35	29, 82, 90, 130, 148	13:2	xx, 76, 77, 128, 129, 134, 135, 136, 138, 140, 151, 168
12:35–36	33, 35, 100, 116, 131		
		13:3	82, 164
12:36	29, 90, 124, 130	13:4	134
12:37	17, 28, 130, 131, 203	13:4–5	135
		13:6	xx, 136
12:37–50	130	13:7	136
12:38	130	13:8a	136
12:39–40	130	13:8b	136
12:40	130n18, 131	13:9	136
12:41	xxv, 97, 131, 166	13:10a	136
12:42	xxiv, 28, 85, 88, 131, 158, 192	13:10b	136
		13:10	136
12:43	131	13:11	136
12:44	83, 91n12, 111, 131, 144	13:12–20	137
		13:12	137
12:44–45	xxv, xxvii, 33, 60, 131, 146	13:13	137
		13:13–15	xx
12:45	91n12, 111	13:13–14	137, 197

Scripture Index

John (*continued*)

13:14	137
13:14–15	147, 155
13:15	137
15:16a	155
13:16	136, 137, 156
13:17a	137
13:17b	137
13:18a	138
13:18	136, 151, 167, 187
13:19	138, 158
13:20	138
13:21	139, 144
13:21–38	139
13:21–30	76, 139
13:22	139
13:23–25	211
13:23	xx, 114, 139
13:23–24	33
13:24	xx, 51n28, 139, 140
13:25	140
13:26	140
13:27	xx, 77, 129, 140, 151, 168
13:27–29	140
13:28	140
13:29	124, 140
13:30	29, 140
13:31	141, 166
13:31—16:33	xx
13:31—14:31	159
13:31–38	141
13:31–35	141
13:31–34	97
13:31–32	33, 96, 111, 115, 128, 165
13:32	141, 166
13:32–33	33
13:33	82, 141, 142, 144, 145, 164, 197
13:34	147
13:34–35	141, 199
13:35	142
13:36a	142
13:36	xx, 82, 142, 144, 145, 159
13:36–38	141n19, 142
13:36–37	163
13:37	xx, 142, 177, 209
13:37–38	210
13:38	16, 142, 144, 177
14–16	141
14:1a	144, 150
14:1b	144
14:1—16:33	144
14:1–31	141n19
14:1–14	144
14:1–3	162
14:2	127, 144
14:2–7	159, 164
14:2–3	94, 142, 145, 150, 169, 211
14:3	127, 144, 145, 149, 150
14:4	145
14:5	xx, 116, 142, 145, 159, 163
14:6	34, 145, 148, 160, 193
14:7	146
14:8	146, 163
14:8–11	xxv, 146
14:8–11	147, 166
14:8–9	xx, 16
14:9	91n12, 111, 146
14:9–11	xxv, xxvii, 14
14:9–10	202
14:10a	146
14:10	146, 149, 156, 160
14:10–11	9, 74, 111, 131, 146, 169
14:12	147
14:13–14	147, 153, 170
14:14	162n7
14:15	147, 149, 154, 187
14:15–31	147
14:16	148, 157

252

Scripture Index

14:16–17	200	15:9	153, 154, 170, 171
14:17a	148	15:10	150, 154
14:17b	148	15:11	154, 162, 168
14:17	92, 148, 149, 160	15:12	147, 154, 155
14:18	148, 150	15:12–13	142
14:19	82, 148, 198	15:13	154, 168
14:21	149, 154, 187	15:14	154
14:22	xx, 149, 201n12	15:15a	155
14:23b	149	15:15	154, 155
14:23	149, 150, 169	15:16b	155
14:23–24	147, 154, 187	15:16c	155
14:24	80, 149, 153	15:16	138, 147, 155, 170
14:25	149	15:17	141, 155
14:26a	157	15:18	11, 79, 156, 158
14:26b	157	15:18–27	155, 158
14:26	26, 126, 148, 150, 160, 199, 200	15:18–25	128, 148, 155
		15:18–19	4, 92
14:27a	150	15:19a	156
14:27b	150	15:19b	155
14:27	92, 198	15:20	156
14:28a	150	15:21	156, 158
14:28b	150	15:22	156, 160
14:28	xxvii, 2, 144, 159	15:23	79, 156
14:29	151, 158	15:24	156
14:30	77, 128, 151, 168, 188	15:25a	157
		15:25b	157
14:31a	151	15:25	91
14:31b	151	15:26	148, 189, 199, 200
14:31	150	15:26–27	xxviii, 157, 199, 212
15	151, 152		
15:1a	152	15:27	158
15:1b	152	15:34	141
15:1—16:33	159	16	151
15:1–17	152	16:1	158
15:1–11	74, 156	16:1–4	158
15:1–10	154	16:2	xxiv, 22, 102, 158
15:2	152	16:3	158
15:3	136, 153	16:4a	158
15:4a	153	16:4b	158, 159
15:4	xxv, 149	16:5	159, 161, 162, 164
15:5	99, 153	16:5–15	159
15:6	153	16:6	159
15:7	93, 153, 155, 170	16:7a	150
15:8	154, 155		

Scripture Index

John (continued)

16:7	126, 147, 159, 189, 200
16:7–11	147, 199
16:8	159, 169
16:8–11	159
16:9	35, 92, 160
16:10	160, 161, 169
16:11	77, 128, 160, 168, 188
16:12	160
16:13b	160
16:13	148
16:13–14	160
16:14a	161
16:14b	160
16:14	26
16:14–15	197
16:15b	160
16:15	161
16:16	82, 161, 198
16:16–33	161
16:16–24	163
16:16–19	148
16:17	161
16:18	161
16:19	27, 161, 162
16:20	161, 198
16:21	162
16:22	162, 198
16:23a	162
16:23	147, 162n7, 163
16:23b–24	162
16:23–24	162, 170
16:24	162, 163, 168
16:25a	163
16:25b	163
16:25	22, 162, 163
16:25–28	164
16:26b	162
16:26	163
16:27	163
16:28	163
16:29	163
16:30	27, 162, 164
16:31	164
16:31–32	173
16:32b	164
16:32	21, 164
16:33a	164
16:33b	164
16:33	198
17	144, 151, 162, 165
17:1	21, 63, 96, 120, 128, 165, 166
17:1–26	xxviii, 147
17:1–5	165
17:2	38, 70, 165, 166
17:3	xxvi, 58, 152, 165, 166
17:4	46, 59, 96, 99, 146, 166, 188
17:4–5	128
17:5	7, 75, 96, 120, 141, 165, 166, 169
17:6	5, 38, 66, 70, 111, 135, 147, 166, 167, 169, 170
17:6–19	108, 166
17:6–8	166
17:7	167
17:8	33, 163, 167–169
17:9	135, 166, 167
17:10	5, 135, 161, 167
17:11a	167
17:11b	167
17:11	111, 120, 165, 166, 202
17:11–12	7, 38, 147, 166, 168
17:12a, 12b	167
17:12	173
17:13a	167
17:13b	168
17:13	154
17:14	4, 168
17:14–16	128, 148
17:15	168

254

17:17	136, 153, 160, 168	18:14	121, 174
17:18	47, 137, 155, 168, 199	18:15	174
		18:15–16	175, 175n11
17:19	168	18:16	175
17:20	xxviii, 169, 202	18:17	175, 176
17:20–26	169	18:17–18	177
17:20–21	xxviii	18:18	176, 177
17:21	120, 149, 165, 169, 199	18:19	176
		18:19–24	174
17:21–23	xxv, xxvi, xxvii	18:19–20	80
17:22	7, 38, 165–67, 169	18:20	176
17:23	xxviii, 169, 170	18:21	176
17:23b–24	38	18:22	176
17:24a	169	18:24	177
17:24b	7, 169	18:25	176, 177
17:24	7, 57, 120, 127, 141, 145, 149, 154, 161, 166	18:25–27	177
		18:26	177
		18:27	177
17:24–25	165	18:28a	178
17:25a	169	18:28	15n37, 122, 135, 188
17:25b	169		
17:26a–b	170	18:28–40	178
17:26	5, 7, 147, 166, 171	18:28b–29	178
18:1	151, 172	18:28b–40	178
18:1—20:31	172	18:29	178
18:1—19:42	172	18:29–32	178
18:1–11	172	18:30	178
18:2	172	18:31	178
18:3	172	18:32	173, 178, 210
18:4	173	18:33	48, 179
18:5a	173	18:33–38a	178
18:5b	173	18:34	179
18:6	173	18:35	179
18:7	175	18:36	65, 174, 179
18:8	173	18:37a	179
18:9	70, 173	18:37b	180
18:10	173	18:37c	180
18:10–11	179	18:37	194, 199
18:11a	174	18:38a	180
18:11b	174	18:38b	180
18:11	188	18:40	181
18:12	174	19:1	182
18:12–27	174	19:1–6	182
18:13	174, 176, 177	19:1–3	178, 182

Scripture Index

John (*continued*)

19:2–3	182
19:3	176
19:4	180, 182
19:4–8	178
19:5	19, 182
19:6a	183
19:6b	183
19:6	180
19:7	56, 98, 117, 183
19:8	183
19:9	183
19:9–11	178
19:10	183
19:11b	183
19:11	30, 36, 183
19:12a	184
19:12b	184
19:12–16	178
19:13	184
19:14a	184
19:14b	184
19:14	135, 183
19:14–15	181
19:15b	185
19:15c	185
19:15	183, 184
19:17	185
19:17–30	185
19:18a	186
19:18b	186
19:18	185
19:19	186
19:19–22	181
19:20	186
19:21	186
19:22	186
19:23	30, 185, 186
19:24a	186
19:24b	187
19:24	187, 191
19:25	187
19:26a	187
19:26b	187
19:26	21, 43
19:26–27	xx, 197
19:27	139, 187
19:28	40, 46, 187, 188, 191
19:30a	188
19:30b	188
19:30	25, 46, 166
19:30–42	30
19:31	135, 189
19:31–42	189
19:31–37	189
19:32	189
19:33	189
19:34b	190
19:34	41, 189, 198
19:34–35	190
19:35	xix, 139, 190, 212
19:36	13, 135, 188, 191
19:36–37	187
19:37	189, 191
19:38	191, 198
19:38–42	32, 191
19:39	15n37, 29, 85, 192
19:40	192
19:41	192
19:42	15n37, 135
20:1	15n37, 192, 193, 195
20:1–10	xx, 139, 195
20:1–2	198
20:2	175, 195, 196
20:2–5	xx
20:3–4	195
20:5–7	195
20:6–7	120, 192, 196
20:7	192
20:8	xx, 195, 198
20:9	196
20:10	196
20:11	161, 196
20:11–18	196
20:12	196, 198

20:13a, b	196	21:4	66, 196, 206
20:13	195	21:5	206
20:13–29	144	21:6	16, 206
20:14	196, 206	21:6b	207
20:15a	196	21:7	xx, 137, 195, 207
20:15b	197	21:8	207
20:15	137	21:9	206–208
20:16	137, 197	21:10	206, 207
20:17a, b	197	21:11	207, 208
20:17	75	21:12a	207
20:18	195, 198, 201	21:12	137, 195, 208
20:19b	201	21:13	206, 208
20:19	15n37, 192, 198	21:14	206, 209
20:19–29	198, 206	21:15a	209
20:19–23	102, 198, 209	21:15b	209
20:20a	198	21:15	210
20:20	137, 201	21:15–23	209
20:21	46, 47, 137, 138, 155, 199	21:15–19	209
		21:15–16	209n12
20:21–23	xxviii, 14, 189	21:16	209, 210
20:21–22	208	21:17b	210
20:22	20, 41, 75, 162, 199	21:17	209n12, 210
20:23	147, 200, 201	21:18–19	142, 210
20:24	201	21:19	210, 211
20:24–29	201	21:20	211
20:25a, b	201	21:20–24	xx, 139
20:25	16, 195, 198, 201, 202	21:20–23	211
		21:21	211
20:26a, b	201	21:22	211
20:26	200	21:22–23	212
20:26–29	206	21:23a	211
20:27	16, 197, 202	21:23b	211
20:28	xxvii, 137, 195, 202	21:23	xxv
20:29	17, 51, 202	21:24	xx, xxii, 205, 208, 212
20:30	121, 203		
20:30–31	xxii, 27, 203, 205, 212	21:24–25	xxii, 212
		21:25	xxii, 121, 155, 190, 203, 212n17, 213
20:31	xxv, xxvii, 33, 111, 190		
21	xxii, 205, 208, 212	**Acts**	
21:1	66, 205	1:3	199
21:1–14	205	1:8	199
21:2	xxii, 175, 206	1:13	xx, 149
21:3	206		

Scripture Index

Acts (continued)

1:20	167
1:21–26	200
1:22	3, 157
2	200
2:31	131, 196
3:1	xx
3:3, 4	xx
3:11	xx, 110
4:13	xx
4:19	xx
5:12	110
5:31	48
6:14	121
7:58–60	158
8:14	xx
8:27–28	127
10:1–2	126
10:37	3
11:20–21	82
12:1–3	158
12:2	139
13:16	126
13:23	48
13:23–25	3
14:25	10
17:4	126
19:1–7	xxv
20:29–30	108
21:28	121
22:24	182
23:5	177
23:33–36	178

Romans

1:20–21	156
2:6–11	58, 70
2:15–16	156
2:17	91
2:29	60
3:23–26	185
3:25	174
5:12–14	96
5:12–21	109
6:1–14	132
6:2–11	186
6:16–23	94
7	55
8:3	6
8:3–4	55
8:19–22	3
8:24–25	51
9:4–5	44
10:16	130
11:9–10	25
12:15	119
13:8–10	141

1 Corinthians

1:23	10
2:2	10
5:7	13, 135
8:6b	2
8:6	166
11:23	172
11:24–25	64
12:7	200
14:24	159
15:3–9	198
15:6	116
15:50	5n6

2 Corinthians

1:22	67
4:5–6	10
4:10–12	127, 132
5:7	51
8:9	6
10:18	60
11:2	37

Galatians

1:11–12	59
2:20	186
3:1	10

3:6–7	94
3:8	97
3:13	189
3:16	97, 129
3:19b	8
5:17	31
5:19–21	31
5:22–23	31

Ephesians

1:13	67
2:20	203
3:3–6	52
4:1–7	170
4:3	171
4:9–10	32
5:23–27	37
5:31–32	37

Philippians

2:6	150
2:7	6, 135
3:1	203
3:13–15	211
3:20	48
4:8–9	203

Colossians

1:16–17	2

1 Thessalonians

2:4	60
4:14–16	116
4:16–17	145

1 Timothy

1:1	48
2:3	48
4:10	48
5:10	137
6:16	6

2 Timothy

1:10	48

Titus

2:10, 13	48

Hebrews

1:2	2
2:17–18	6
9:11–14	25
9:12	145
9:24	145
11:1	51
11:13	97
11:17–19	13, 34
12:2	211
13:13	186

James

2:9	159
2:14–26	147
2:23	154
3:15–16	92

1 John

2:1	148
2:13–14	128, 164
2:19	xxvi, 76
2:22	76
3:2	169
3:8	96
3:9, 10	96
3:11–15	155
3:12	96, 128
3:16	142
3:17–18	142
3:23	149
4:2	73
4:2–3	76
4:4	96, 164
4:6	96
4:7–12	142

Scripture Index

1 John (continued)

4:8	154
4:9–10	34
4:16	154
5:1–2	209
5:3	154, 187
5:4–5	164
5:6	190
5:6–10	190
5:8	190
5:13	203
5:18	128
5:18–19	96
5:19	128
5:20	58

2 John

1	xxii
6	187
7	76

3 John

1	xxii
8	6

Jude

15	159

Revelation

1:17	66
3:7	58
3:14	2
4:1	18, 107
5:6	13
5:8	13
5:12	13
5:13	13
6:16	13
7:9	125
7:9–10	13
7:14	13
7:15	7
7:17	13
10:5	66
11:9	18
12:1	18
12:9	129
15:1	18
20:10	129
21:2	37
21:3	7, 149
22:1	13
22:3	13
22:12	47
22:17	37

Ancient Sources Index

JEWISH SOURCES

Dead Sea Scrolls

CD - A (*Damascus Document*ᵃ)
1.13	145

1QH (*Thanksgiving Hymns*)
5.11–12	81
8.4–36	81
9.23	159

1QM (*War Scroll*)
1.1, 5	129
1.11–16	130n17
1.13	129
4.2	129
11.8	129
13.5–6, 14–15	3

1QS (*Rule of the Community*)
1.9–10	130n17
1.18, 24	129
2.5, 19	129
3.1-4.6	35
3.7	90
3.13–26	130n17
3.18–19	148n11
3.19–22	3
4.21	41
4.23	148n11
5.11	60
8.14–15	145
9.11	12, 64
9.16–17	160
9.17–18	145
10.1–2	3
10.21	145

1QSa (*Messianic Rule*)
2.11–12	14

4QFlor (*Florilegium*)
1.1–19	14

4QTest (*Testimonia*)
5–8	12, 64

Josephus

Jewish Antiquities
6.12.4–5	121n15
8.4.1	78
12.7.7	110
15.11.3	110
17.8.3	192
18.4.1	43
20.9.1	158
20.9.7	110

Jewish War
2.12.6	174n8
3.8.5	92
3:10.7	62, 65
5.5.1	110

Philo of Alexandria

On Agriculture
10.44	108n5
12.49	108n5
12.50–52	108n5

Ancient Sources Index

On the Cherubim
36 — 9
87–90 — 56

The Worse Attacks the Better
146 — 160

Who Is the Heir?
2–5 — 9

Allegorical Interpretation
1.5–6 — 56

On the Life of Moses
2.127 — 10

On the Creation of the World
4, 16 — 10

On the Posterity of Cain
122 — 10
144 — 212

Questions and Answers on Genesis
2.62 — 9

Questions and Answers on Exodus
68 — 10

On the Sacrifices of Cain and Abel
8 — 9

On Dreams
1.229–230 — 9

On the Special Laws
3.57 — 63

Pseudepigrapha

Ascension of Isaiah
1:3 — 129
2:4 — 129
10:9 — 129

1 Enoch (Ethiopic Apocalypse)
37–71 — 18, 58
38:2–3 — 81
45:3–6 — 70
45:3 — 129
48:6 — 129
49 — 129
51:3 — 129
55:4 — 129
61:8 — 129
62:7 — 12n27

4 Ezra
11–13 — 58
12–13 — 18
12:32 — 81
13:2–4 — 12n27
13:52 — 12n27

Jubilees
14:21 — 97
15:17 — 97
16:19 — 97

3 Maccabees
2:2 — 167
5:3 — 184
5:19 — 154, 184
5: 26, 29 — 154, 184
5:34, 44 — 154, 184

4 Maccabees
1:16–17 — 9

Psalms of Solomon
7:1 — 157
8:34 — 82
17:40–42 — 108

Testament of Abraham
11–13 — 58

Testament of Dan
5:10 — 44

Ancient Sources Index

Testament of Gad
8:1   44

Testament of Judah
20:1–5   148n11

Testament of Naphtali
5:4   125
8:2   44

∽

RABBINIC LITERATURE

Mekilta

Exodus 21:2	135n4
Leviticus 25:9	135n4

Mishnah

ʾAbot 1:12	71
Bekorot 8:7	24
Berakot 5:5	131
Beṣah 2:3	22
Kelim 5:11	22
Ketubbot 2:9	90
Middot 2:7	82
Nedarim 3:11	80
Niddah 4:1	40n4, 45
Pesaḥim 8:6	180
Roš Haššanah 3:1	90
Šabbat 7:2	55, 101
Šabbat 10:1–5	55
Šabbat 11:1–2	55
Šabbat 18:3	80
Šabbat 19:1–2	80
Sukkah 4:1	83
Sukkah 4:5	91
Sukkah 4:8	82
Sukkah 4:9	78, 82–83
Sukkah 4:9–10	83
Sukkah 5:1–4	78
Sukkah 5:2–4	89

Sanhedrin 6:2	176n13
Sanhedrin 6:5	191

Tosefta

Šabbat 15:16	80

Babylonian Talmud

Baba Batra 126b	100
ʿErubin 54a	17
Yoma 85b	80

Midrash Rabbah

Genesis Rabbah 1:19	60
Exodus Rabbah 30:22	212

Targumim

Targum Onqelos on Genesis 3:8	9
Targum on Isaiah 6:1	131
Targum on Isaiah 48:13	9

∽

NEW TESTAMENT APOCRYPHA

Gospel of Peter
26   198n8
50   195

Gospel of Thomas   201n12

Acts of Peter
37–39   210n15

Ancient Sources Index

OTHER CHRISTIAN WRITINGS

Iranaeus
Against Heresies
3.3.4	xxv
3.11.1	xxv

Eusebius, Pamphilus
Ecclesiastical History
3.1	210n15
3.11	187, 187n16
3.23.3–4	xxi
3.23.6	xxi
3.31.3	xxi, xxiin13
3.39	87, 206n5
3.39.4	xxi, xxii
3.39.6	xxi
5.8.4	xxi
5.20.4	xxi
5.24.3	xxi, xxiin13
6.15.5–7	xxviin28
7.25.16	xxi

HELLENISTIC WRITING

Corpus Hermeticum
13:6–7	9
13:7–8	9